Essentials
for Working with Young Children

COUNCIL
— *for* —
PROFESSIONAL
RECOGNITION

Child Development Associate®
CDA
National Credentialing Program

The Council for Professional Recognition

2460 16th Street, NW Washington, DC 20009-3547

Local: 202-265-9090   Toll Free: 800-424-4310

Visit the Council's Website at **www.cdacouncil.org**.

Essentials for Working with Young Children

First Printing, Printed and bound in the United States of America

October 2013

ISBN: 978-0-9889650-6-5

Acknowledgements

The Council for Professional Recognition would like to acknowledge
the following people who contributed to the creation of this textbook:

Laura Colker, for her wise words throughout

Angie Sanders and Susan Werner, for their writing and editing

Theresa Crockett, for the beautiful design and layout of the book

Myra Crouch, Mike Leone, Jill Seibert, Eric Strobel and Myra Haileselassie –
the Council's executive team

Vivienne Oxford, Brocklin Qualls and Vilma Williams – the Council's program staff

Richard Cohen, for his early childhood expertise and editing skills

The children, families and staff of School for Friends, St. Columba's Nursery School and the
Thurgood Marshall Child Development Center for appearing in the many images throughout

Table of Contents

Biography: Valora Washington, Ph.D. 1

Introduction: Edward Zigler, Ph.D. 2

Purpose 4

    Figure 1. CDA Competency Standards At-A-Glance 6

Competency Standard I

Functional Area 1: Safe

.... 9

Maintaining a Safe Physical Setting 10

  Keeping Indoor/Outdoor Settings Safe 10

    Figure 2. Daily Safety Indoor/Outdoor Checklist 12-14

    Figure 3. Suggested First-Aid Kit Contents 15

    Figure 4. Indoor and Outdoor Plants That May Be Harmful to Children 16

    Ensuring Children's Supervision 16

    Securing Furniture and Equipment 17

    Maintaining a Lead-Free Setting 17

    Figure 5. Protecting Children from Lead 18

    Preparing and Serving Food 18

    Using Technology 20

    Ensuring Sleep Safety 20

    Diapering and Bathroom Safety 21

    Protecting Children From Sun Exposure 21

    Enjoying Field Trips Safely 21

Teaching Children About Safety 22

  Making and Reviewing Safety Rules 22

    Figure 6. Tips for Establishing Safety Rules With Young Children 22

    Figure 7. Discussing Safety Rules in Everyday Conversations 23

  Pacing Your Safety Instruction 23

Teaching Pedestrian Safety 24

Teaching Safety on Riding Toys 25

Teaching Car/School Bus Safety 26

Teaching Fire/Burn Safety 26

Teaching Water Safety 28

Teaching Stranger Danger 28

Modeling Safe Practices 29

Implementing Emergency Plans 31

Figure 8. Administering First-Aid Treatment 32

Devising Fire Emergency Plans 34

Other Emergency Plans 34

Involving Parents in Classroom Safety 35

Functional Area 2: Healthy 38

Promoting Wellness 39

Keeping the Setting Healthy 39

Figure 9. Checklist for Healthy Indoor Settings 40-41

Figure 10. Preparing/Using Bleach Solution for Disinfecting Surfaces 42

Figure 11. Prohibited Animals... 43

Monitoring Children's Health Records... 43

Communicating Children's Allergies.. 44

Performing Daily Health Checks 44

Figure 12. Example of Daily Health Check...................................... 45

Responding to Illness 45

Meeting the Needs of Children With Chronic Illness 47

Administering Medication 50

Enabling Children With Special Needs... 50

Providing Nutritious Snacks and Meals 52

Feeding Choices... 52

Storing Breast Milk 52

Figure 13. Storing Breast Milk for Healthy Full-Term Infants 53

Thawing Breast Milk Safely..53

Preparing and Storing Infant Formula...54

Feeding Infants 54

Introducing Solid Foods to Infants and Weaning 54

Feeding Toddlers and Preschoolers 55

Figure 14. Tips on Starting a Nutritional Program in Your Setting 56

Dining Family Style..57

Figure 15. Tips for Family-Style Dining 58

Snacking 58

Learning Good Health Practices..59

Handwashing..60

Figure 16. The Steps of Proper Handwashing..61

Coughing, Sneezing, and Nose-Blowing 62

Care for Infants 62

Assisting Toddlers and Preschoolers When They Cough, Sneeze,
and Blow Their Noses..62

Figure 17. Coughing and Sneezing Healthily 62

Enforcing Proper Dental and Oral Care...63

Toileting 64

Diapering Infants 64

Learning about Toileting 67

Toileting Preschoolers 67

Learning About Their Bodies 68

Nap Time 68

Partnering With Families 69

Figure 18. Troubleshooting as a Team..70

Identifying/Reporting Child Abuse and Neglect 71

Identifying Abuse 71

Reporting Abuse..73

Functional Area 3: Learning Environment.........75

Designing the Indoor Setting 76

Indoor Settings for Infants and Toddlers 76

Planning Preschool Indoor Settings for Play 78

Figure 19. Sample Infant Setting.........81

Figure 20. Sample Toddler Setting.........82

Figure 21. Sample Preschool Setting 83

Configuring the Preschool Setting.........84

Figure 22. Learning Center Configuration Tips 84-85

Figure 23. Configuring Outdoor Settings 87

Selecting Appropriate Materials 88

Figure 24. Eight Quick Ways to Analyze Children's Books for Biases 90

Stocking Your Setting.........91

Organizing Materials 95

Defining Quality Curriculum for Young Children 95

Developing the Daily Schedule.........97

Infant and Toddler Schedules.........97

Figure 25. Sample Daily Schedule for Infants 98

Figure 26. Sample Daily Schedule for Toddlers.........98

Preschool Schedules.........99

Figure 27. Sample Program Guide for Preschoolers.........100-102

Implementing the Daily Schedule 103

Infants and Toddlers.........103

Preschool 104

Daily Schedule Components: Choice Time 104

Daily Schedule Components: Group Meetings and Small Group Times.........105

Daily Schedule Components: Routines 106

Daily Schedule Components: Transitions 106

Weekly and Lesson Planning 107

Figure 28. Sample Weekly Planning Grid 107

Figure 29. Lesson Plan Form 108-109

Competency Standard II

Functional Area 4: Physical 113

Understanding Physical Development of Infants, Toddlers, and Preschoolers 114

Promoting Children's Gross Motor Development 115

    Figure 30. Gross Motor Skills for Young Children 117

    Promoting Gross Motor Skills 118

        Young Infants (birth–8 months) 118

        Mobile Infants (9–17 months) 118

        Toddlers (18–36 months) 118

        Preschoolers (3–5 year olds) 119

        Figure 31. Mastering Baseline Skills at the Preschool Level 126

    Promoting Physical Health 127

Promoting Children's Fine Motor Development 127

    Figure 32. Fine Motor Skill Development: Birth to 5 Years Old 128

    Strategies for Developing Fine Motor Skills 129

        Young Infants (birth–8 months) 129

        Mobile Infants (9–17 months) 129

        Toddlers (18–36 months) 129

        Preschoolers (3–5 year olds) 129

    Figure 33. Materials for Promoting Fine Motor Development in Preschoolers 132

Connecting Children's Physical Development to the Development of the Whole Child 133

Functional Area 5: Cognitive 135

What is Early Childhood Cognitive Development? 136

Major Learning Theories. 137

Jean Piaget 137

Lev Vygotsky 139

Urie Bronfenbrenner 140

Erik Erikson 141

Abraham Maslow 141

Howard Gardner 142

Figure 34. Brain Research on Cognitive Development 143

Executive Function and School Readiness 144

Learning Through Play 146

Figure 35. How Preschool Learning Centers Impact Cognitive Growth 146-148

Learning Throughout the Day 149

Identifying and Building Children's Skills and Abilities 151

Children As Scientists: Content Learning 154

Mathematics 154

Counting 155

Measurement 157

Geometry, Patterning, and Representing Data 157

Science and Social Studies 158

Technology 160

Functional Area 6: Communication 161

Creating an Environment That Supports Language and Literacy 162

Displaying Labels and Print 163

Young and Mobile Infants 163

Toddlers 163

Preschoolers 164

Dual Language Learners 164

Selecting Books 165

Young and Mobile Infants 165

Toddlers 166

Preschoolers 166

Figure 36. Evaluating Books for Preschoolers 167

Figure 37. Categorizing Books 167

Setting Up the Preschool Literacy Center.. 168

Book Area 168

Writing Area... 169

Listening Area 169

Technology Area 170

Publishing Area 171

Figure 38. Creating Literacy-Rich Learning Centers 172

Supporting Children's Oral Language Development 173

Conversations.. 173

Using Everyday Experiences to Strengthen Language Skills 174

Young Infants 175

Mobile Infants.. 175

Toddlers.. 176

Strategies to Enhance Preschool Conversations.. 177

Model Conversations 177

Scaffold Children's Language 178

Support Children With Special Needs 179

Vocabulary Development... 180

Developing Phonological Awareness 181

Supporting Dual Language Learners 183

Language and Literacy Learning.. 184

Fostering Children's Reading Development 186

Young Infants 186

Mobile Infants.. 186

Toddlers.. 187

Reading With Preschoolers 188

Shared Reading... 190

Figure 39. How Reading Aloud Benefits Children 191

Alphabet Knowledge 191

Fostering Children's Writing Development 192

Supporting Children's Writing 193

Figure 40. Supporting Reading and Writing Skills for

Children With Special Needs 195

Partnering With Families 196

Functional Area 7: Creative 198

Environments That Promote Creativity 200

Creativity in Infant and Toddler Settings 200

Figure 41. Fostering Creativity in Preschool Settings 201-202

Creativity Through Daily Interactions and Experiences 203

Figure 42. Supporting Creative Thought 204

Promoting the Visual Arts 204

Drawing and Painting 205

Figure 43. Other Art Activities 205

Supporting Children's Exploration 206

Creativity Through Music, Movement, and Dance 208

Singing 208

Sparking Musical Creativity 209

Music, Movement, and Culture 211

Figure 44. Questions That Promote Music and Movement Creativity 211

Creativity Through Dramatic Play and Story Retelling 212

Competency Standard III

Functional Area 8: Self 217

Appreciating Each Child 218

Infants 219

Toddlers 220

Preschoolers 220

Gender 221

Temperament 221

Approaches to Learning 222

Strengths and Challenges 223

Family Circumstances 224

Promoting Children's Sense of Self 228

Valuing Children's Families 230

Developing a Sense of Racial Identity 231

Guiding Children in Expressing Their Feelings 232

Figure 45. Emotion Words to Teach Young Children 234

Helping Each Child Flourish 234

Optimism 234

Resilience 236

Functional Area 9: Social 238

Encouraging Successful Social Interaction 239

Supporting Children's Play 241

Configuring the environment for play 242

Infants and Toddlers in Play 243

Preschool Children in Dramatic Play 244

Children's Group Interaction 245

Forming Friendships 247

Figure 46. Encouraging Friendships 249

Helping Children Resolve Conflict 249

Building Prosocial Skills 251

Functional Area 10: Guidance 253

Setting Effective Rules 254

Addressing Challenging Behaviors Positively..257

    Figure 47. Positive Guidance Versus Punishment................................259

Employing Positive Guidance Techniques...260

Understanding Time-Out and Effective Alternatives 264

Addressing Ongoing Challenging Behavior 268

Stopping Bullying 269

Partnering with Families 271

Competency Standard IV

Functional Area 11: Families...274

Defining Family 275

  Types of Family Structures...276

  How Culture Impacts Family Dynamics 278

Establishing Partnerships With Families...279

  Initiating Partnerships..281

  Handling Personality Conflicts With Families....................................284

Encouraging Family Participation 285

    Figure 48. Reading Aloud 286

  Preparing Families for Visits to the Setting 287

    Figure 49. Sample Questions/Comments for Infants and Toddlers......288

    Figure 50. Sample Questions/Comments for Preschoolers 289-290

Communicating With Families 291

    Figure 51. Resources to Help You Create Setting Websites and Blogs 294

Meeting Formally With Families...294

  Home Visits...294

  Parent–Educator Conferences 296

  Parent Meetings and Workshops 299

    Figure 52. Topic Ideas for Parent Meetings................................300

Supporting Families in Their Child's Development..............................300

Figure 53. Topic Ideas for Parent Workshops..301

Supporting Children With Special Needs 301

Figure 54. Organizations That Support Families With Children

Who Have Special Needs 302

Maintaining Confidentiality...302

Competency Standard V

Functional Area 12: Program Management.....................303

Observing Children Within the Setting 304

Observing With Purpose 305

Observation and Assessment..306

Observing Consistently and Effectively..307

Objective and Subjective Observation..308

Figure 55. Words to Avoid While Recording Observations 309

Figure 56. Recording Your Observations 310-311

Figure 57. Sample Learning Story 312

Summarizing Observational Information 313

Documenting Children's Learning...313

Portfolios...314

Documenting the Group's Learning..315

Planning and Evaluating 316

Figure 58. The Cycle of Curriculum Planning 316

Planning for Individual Children 317

Figure 59. Individual Planning Form...319-320

Planning for Children on an IFSP or IEP 321

Planning for Groups of Children 321

Working With Colleagues and the Community 322

Colleagues and Supervisors..322

Handling Disagreements and/or Criticism..322

Substitute Early Educators 323

External Community 323

Figure 60. Community Resources 324

Competency Standard VI

Functional Area 13: Professionalism 325

Educating With Intentionality and Reflection 326

Intentional Early Educators 326

Figure 61. Characteristics of Intentional Education 328

Reflection 329

Making Ethical Decisions 332

Figure 62. Reflective Questions 333

Articulating Values, Vision, and Passion 337

Continuing Your Professional Development 338

Connecting With Professional Groups 339

Figure 63. Early Childhood Education Professional Groups 340-342

Advocating for Children and Families 342

Figure 64. Advocacy Organizations 343-344

Figure 65. Ways to Advocate for Children 345

References 346

Index 357

Biography

Valora Washington, Ph.D.

Dr. Valora Washington is the president and CEO of the Council for Professional Recognition since January 2011.

Throughout her career, Dr. Washington has co-founded several organizations, including Voices for Michigan's Children, a statewide advocacy group; the Early Childhood Funders Collaborative; and The CAYL Institute. Frequently tapped for senior-level service, she has been co-chair of the Massachusetts Governor's School Readiness Commission; board chair of Voices for America's Children; secretary of the National Association for the Education of Young Children (NAEYC); chair of the Black Caucus of the Society for Research in Child Development; and co-chair of the National Head Start Association Commission on 2010. She has been a member of numerous task forces and boards including for the Boston Children's Museum and Wheelock College.

Prior to founding The CAYL Institute in 2003, Dr. Washington was CEO of the Unitarian Universalist Service Committee and vice president of the W. K. Kellogg Foundation. She has held executive and tenured teaching positions at institutions including Antioch College and the University of North Carolina at Chapel Hill. Since 2001, she has been a certified association executive with the American Society of Association Executives™.

Committed to action, research, and policy change, Dr. Washington has co-authored or co-edited over 50 publications, including *Children of 2010; Children of 2020; Ready or Not: Leadership Choices in Early Care and Education;* and *Role, Relevance, Reinvention: Higher Education in the Field of Early Care and Education.* Her advocacy work includes working to change the voucher system in Massachusetts, which gave 52,000 children opportunities for a 1-year certification period. Through the Families for Kids initiative, Dr. Washington designed and coordinated efforts to change the child welfare system in 13 states. This initiative is regarded as a precursor to important legislative changes enacted by President Clinton.

Among many honors, Dr. Washington holds honorary doctorate degrees from Bennett College and Meadville Lombard Theological School, and in 2009 she was selected for the prestigious Barr Fellowship. Dr. Washington has received professional recognition from Boston AEYC; NAEYC Black Caucus; Cambridge Resource and Referral Agency; Center for Adoption Research, University of Massachusetts; National Association of Black Social Workers; United Way of Massachusetts Bay; and others. She was named one of "25 Most Influential Working Mothers" by *Working Mother* magazine in February 1997, and in 1980 she was chosen as one of "Ten Outstanding Young Women of America" from among 62,000 nominations. Dr. Washington was educated at both Indiana State University and Michigan State University

Introduction

An Interview with "the Father of the CDA," Edward Zigler, Ph.D.

Why do you think the field of child care and early education is important?

Preschool education, in the years since we invented Head Start in 1965, has just grown by leaps and bounds.

The research has now made very clear to us that the single most important determinant of a child's educational performance, whether it be in preschool or fifth grade, or high school for that matter, is how good the teacher is. So, it's absolutely imperative that we make sure that our children are taught by teachers who have demonstrated their competency. It's really at the heart of our whole educational issue in the United States.

There are four systems that determine children's healthy growth and development where we should be concentrating. The first is the family, particularly the parents. The second, which we still have work to do on, is health. Children are not going to develop properly, and they are not going to learn properly, if they are ill. The third is education and the fourth is child care where so many children spend those first five formative years of life before they ever go to school. These systems are not independent, they're synergistic – each one affects the other. If you're not healthy you're not going to do well anywhere. If you have five lousy years of child care before you go to school, you're not optimally ready for school.

What were the origins of the Child Development Associate (CDA) Credential®?

I don't think it's too much hubris for me to say that I am the father of the CDA. There was no such thing; there wasn't anything like that in anyone's mind until I invented the concept.

In 1971 I revamped Head Start: we started home-based services, resource centers and a number of programs that were new. I was also deeply immersed in the drafting the Child Development Act of 1971. That bill was going to put into place a huge national child care system in America that any parent could access. But, the primary question was 'Who's going to staff all these child care centers?' That was my primary motivation for inventing the Child Development Associate Credential®.

What was revolutionary about it was the performance-based or competency idea behind the CDA Credential®. I didn't care if you knew who Piaget was but I did want to know if you could effectively interact with children and teach them. The fact is a paper and pencil test alone, is really not valid to the degree that an observation of a person actually functioning is in determining that person's qualifications.

But we needed a template for how to evaluate them. I mean, you go in and look at a teacher and anybody that knows early childhood education can tell you in fifteen minutes whether the teacher is competent or not but it had to be more than that.

But what exactly should we look at that? The emotional warmth between the teacher and the child, the independence that the teacher gives the child to lead, to discover what 'Teachable Moments' are – these are the things you look at. But I handed that specific task to my colleagues at the National Association for the Education of Young Children and they really did the 'heavy lifting'. I can't thank NAEYC enough. They really made it whole. Bank Street College then led the group to develop what became the thirteen Functional Areas that they now look at. So it evolved from a kind of look-see into a much more formal, evaluation process.

What do you think about the way the CDA Credentialing process is evolving?

The CDA is a good, solid certificate for new caregivers. The changes to the credentialing process sound like a very good move. Everything should evolve. Nobody should ever stand pat on anything, I don't care who invented it. We need to be always trying to upgrade and improve what we're doing.

I also think the reflection aspect of the new CDA process is very solid and very worthwhile. People should become conscious and reflect on what it is that they're doing and putting that into the credentialing process is a very good step.

Any final thoughts about the CDA?

The Council overshot my goal by 50%. When I started this, my goal was 200,000 credentialed caregivers and, given the needs in child care at that time, that wasn't too many. Now there are over 300,000 – I think that's great!

Dr. Edward F. Zigler is the Sterling Professor Emeritus of Psychology; Emeritus Faculty; Director, Emeritus, The Edward Zigler Center in Child Development & Social Policy, Yale University. Dr. Zigler was interviewed by Richard Cohen, former Associate Chief Officer of the Council for Professional Recognition, on May 23, 2012.

Purpose of This Book

Welcome to *Essentials*!

This textbook is a practical manual for parents, teachers and providers who work with children from birth to age 5, either in homes, centers or school settings. It is also an essential companion and study guide for candidates working towards the Child Development Associate Credential®. It has been designed to provide the comprehensive breadth of information needed to effectively care for and educate young children, for those who are either new to the field, or are new to formally studying child development and early childhood best practices. *Essentials* is a practical guide yet it is deeply rooted in current childhood development research and theory.

The Child Development Associate (CDA) Credential™ is the most widely recognized credential in early childhood education (ECE) and is a key stepping stone on the path of career advancement in ECE. The CDA Credential is based on a core set of Competency Standards, which guide early care and learning professionals as they work toward becoming qualified teachers of young children. These professionals have the knowledge of how to put the CDA Competency Standards into practice and the understanding of how the Standards help children move with success from one developmental stage to another.

The Child Development Associate (CDA) Credential™ is the "best first step" because: The CDA National Credentialing Program® is based on the knowledge of the nation's leading scholars in early care and learning. Utilizing multiple sources of evidence, the Program is the only comprehensive system of its kind that recognizes the essential competencies needed by entry-level and all early childhood professionals. The CDA credentialing process is now a powerful cohesive professional development experience, infused with meaningful activities that facilitate the reflective practice of working professionals.

For more information about obtaining a CDA, please visit www.cdacouncil.org

In particular, this *Essentials* textbook is the perfect companion for anyone preparing to earn a Child Development Associate (CDA) Credential because:

- The ideas and examples contained throughout were specifically written to correlate with many of the questions asked in the required CDA Exam taken by every CDA Candidate as part of the credentialing process.

- Each Competency Standards section of this book is followed by the specific reflective activities required of CDA Candidates as they create their Professional Portfolios.

By reading the thirteen *Essentials* chapters in order and then following the "Reflections" section after each Competency Standard, you will be well prepared to both take the CDA Exam and create a valuable Professional Portfolio that meets the credentialing requirements.

Structure

Essentials has been structured around the CDA Competency Standards and Functional Areas (please see Figure 1. for the full Competency Standards chart).

Candidates seeking to earn the CDA Credential are assessed based upon the CDA Competency Standards. These national standards are the criteria used to evaluate an early care and learning professional's performance with children, families, colleagues and their community.

There are six *Competency Standards* - statements that set the standard of competency for professional behavior. The first four Standards relate directly to the experiences of young children and are therefore presented within a *Developmental Context*. Each Developmental Context presents a brief overview of relevant child development principles related to the Functional Areas within that Standard. The last two standards relate to program management and professionalism.

The six Standards are then defined in more detail in 13 *Functional Areas*, which describe the major tasks or functions that an early care and learning professional must complete in order to meet each Competency Standard.

Figure 1. CDA Competency Standards At-A-Glance

Competency Standard	Functional Area	Definitions
I. To establish and maintain a safe, healthy learning environment	**1. Safe**	Candidate provides a safe environment and teaches children safe practices to prevent and reduce injuries.
	2. Healthy	Candidate provides an environment that promotes health and prevents illness, and teaches children about good nutrition and practices that promote wellness.
	3. Learning Environment	Candidate organizes and uses relationships, the physical space, materials, daily schedule, and routines to create a secure, interesting, and enjoyable environment that promotes engagement, play, exploration, and learning of all children including children with special needs.
II. To advance physical and intellectual competence	**4. Physical**	Candidate uses a variety of developmentally appropriate equipment, learning experiences and teaching strategies to promote the physical development (fine motor and gross motor) of all children.
	5. Cognitive	Candidate uses a variety of developmentally appropriate learning experiences and teaching strategies to promote curiosity, reasoning, and problem solving and to lay the foundation for all later learning. Candidate implements curriculum that promotes children's learning of important mathematics, science, technology, social studies and other content goals.
	6. Communication	Candidate uses a variety of developmentally appropriate learning experiences and teaching strategies to promote children's language and early literacy learning, and help them communicate their thoughts and feelings verbally and nonverbally. Candidate helps dual-language learners make progress in understanding and speaking both English and their home language.
	7. Creative	Candidate uses a variety of developmentally appropriate learning experiences and teaching strategies for children to explore music, movement, and the visual arts, and to develop and express their individual creative abilities.
III. To support social and emotional development and to provide positive guidance	**8. Self**	Candidate develops a warm, positive, supportive, and responsive relationship with each child, and helps each child learn about and take pride in his or her individual and cultural identity.
	9. Social	Candidate helps each child function effectively in the group, learn to express feelings, acquire social skills, and make friends, and promotes mutual respect among children and adults.
	10. Guidance	Candidate provides a supportive environment and uses effective strategies to promote children's self-regulation and support acceptable behaviors, and effectively intervenes for children with persistent challenging behaviors.
IV. To establish positive and productive relationships with families	**11. Families**	Candidate establishes a positive, responsive, and cooperative relationship with each child's family, engages in two-way communication with families, encourages their involvement in the program, and supports the child's relationship with his or her family.
V. To ensure a well-run, purposeful program that is responsive to participant needs	**12. Program Management**	Candidate is a manager who uses observation, documentation, and planning to support children's development and learning and to ensure effective operation of the classroom or group. The Candidate is a competent organizer, planner, record keeper, communicator, and a cooperative co-worker.
VI. To maintain a commitment to professionalism	**13. Professionalism**	Candidate makes decisions based on knowledge of research-based early childhood practices, promotes high-quality in child care services, and takes advantage of opportunities to improve knowledge and competence, both for personal and professional growth and for the benefit of children and families.

Competency Standard I:

To establish and maintain a safe, healthy learning environment

Developmental Contexts

Functional Area 1: Safe

Young and mobile infants *(birth–17 months)* need affectionate and competent physical care geared to their individual needs and rhythms. Adults support infants by establishing routines that regulate their eating, sleeping, and other activities gradually, while continuing to balance the infant's and the group's needs.

Toddlers *(18–36 months)* imitate and learn from the activities of those around them. Safety awareness can be established through modeling, encouraging, and discussions about safe behaviors. Toddlers are increasingly curious about their world. They stretch boundaries and test everything in their surroundings. Adults must be attentive to their activities and ensure their safety while giving them simple explanations for safety precautions.

Preschoolers *(3-5 years old)* are gradually able to understand the relative danger or safety of situations. In a safe setting, children will gradually learn to protect themselves and look out for others.

Functional Area 2: Healthy

Young and mobile infants *(birth–17 months)* need affectionate and competent physical care geared to their individual health, physical growth, and nutrition. Adults *individualize* infants' eating, sleeping, and other daily routines, while continuing to balance the infant's and the group's needs.

Toddlers *(18–36 months)* imitate and learn from those around them. Good health habits can be established through modeling and encouraging hand-washing, nutritious eating, etc.

Preschoolers *(3-5 years old)* are ready to learn the reasons and take responsibility for good health practices including hygiene, hand-washing, and good nutrition. They are fascinated by their own bodily functions and can gradually learn about them.

Functional Area 3: Learning Environment

Young infants *(birth–8 months)* are learning from their immediate surroundings and daily experiences with a few important people. The sense of well-being and emotional security conveyed by a loving and skilled provider create a readiness for other experiences. Before infants can creep and crawl, adults should provide a variety of sensory experiences and encourage movement and playfulness.

Competency Standard I (continued)

Mobile infants *(9–17 months)* are active, independent, and curious. They are increasingly persistent and purposeful in doing things. They need many opportunities to practice new skills and explore the setting within safe boundaries. Adults can share children's delight in themselves, their skills, and discoveries and gradually add variety to the learning setting that will continue to foster relationships and exploration.

Toddlers *(18–36 months)* are developing new language skills, physical control, and awareness of themselves and others each day. They enjoy participating in planned and group activities, but they are not yet ready to sit still or work in a group for a very long time. Adults can support their learning in all areas by maintaining a setting that is dependable but flexible enough to provide opportunities for them to extend their skills, understanding, and judgment in individualized ways.

Preschoolers *(3-5 years old)* continue to develop new language skills, physical control, and awareness of themselves and others each day. They enjoy participation in planned and group activities. They learn by doing. Adults can support their learning in all areas by maintaining a setting that has a wide range of exploratory and adaptive materials; provides opportunities for them to extend their vocabulary, mathematical, and scientific skills; and promotes social and emotional growth. Adults can observe children's play; give them time and space to repeat familiar activities; and expand the learning setting in response to their developing skills, interests, and concerns about themselves and their world.

Chapter 1
Safe

CDA Functional Area 1: Candidate provides a safe environment and teaches children safe practices to prevent and reduce injuries.

Safe

Introduction

The National Association for the Education of Young Children's *Code of Ethical Conduct* states that early educators "shall place the welfare and safety of children above other obligations" (NAEYC, 2011). Children's safety is your first priority. When children feel secure in a safe, stable, and trusting setting, they are better prepared to learn.

In this chapter, we will examine the following ways to keep children safe:

- **Maintaining a Safe Physical Setting.**
- **Teaching Children About Safety.**
- **Modeling Safe Practices.**
- **Implementing Emergency Plans.**
- **Involving Parents in Classroom Safety.**

Maintaining a Safe Physical Setting

Quality early childhood education begins with a safe environment. Your first and most important obligation to families is to keep their children free from harm. Know the local/state requirements for keeping children safe in your setting. These requirements cover such topics as early educator to child ratios and plants prohibited in both the indoor and outdoor settings. Your setting should comply with or exceed these requirements to maintain licensure.

Keeping Indoor/Outdoor Settings Safe

Take a proactive approach to safeguarding your indoor and outdoor settings for children. Your setting's safety requirements should match or exceed local/state requirements. Know these requirements and remove possible dangers to prevent accidents.

Get down on the floor—at the children's level—and look around the room. From a child's perspective, you can pinpoint where many dangers lie. Ask yourself questions like the following:

- Is this space used wisely to protect young infants' play from toddlers' play?
- Are all the toys and materials nontoxic, nonflammable, and/or water-based?

- Is all equipment and furniture appropriate for the children's size and developmental level who will use them?

- Are all of the furnishings secure to the ground or wall to prevent them from falling on a child?

- Are materials stored so that children can safely use them on their own?

- Are computer cords tied to prevent tripping accidents?

- Is our setting free of lead paint and exposed asbestos?

- Are all choking hazards removed?

- Are all electrical sockets covered?

- Is our setting lead-free?

Outside, keep play areas free of debris, structural hazards, matches, chipping paint, toxic plants, small objects that could be choking hazards, balloons, and plastic bags. Avoid exposing infants from birth to 6 months to the sun and work to protect older infants', toddlers', and preschoolers' skin from sunburn.

Use Figure 2. to conduct safety checks of your indoor/outdoor settings daily before children arrive.

All equipment and furniture should be appropriate for the children's sizes and developmental levels.

Figure 2. Daily Safety Indoor/Outdoor Checklist

 INDOOR (Infant/Toddler Settings)

❑ Never leave infants unattended—even for a second—on a changing table, in a bath, or in a wading pool.

❑ Cribs are intact; slats are no more than a soda can's width apart to prevent head entrapment.

❑ Mattresses are firm to the touch and fit snugly in place, with no more than two fingers' width between mattress and crib frame to prevent suffocation.

❑ Position evacuation cribs near exits.

❑ Toys and balls are too large to swallow.

❑ Do not hang toys across the cribs of infants who can sit up on their own.

❑ Do not hang rattles, pacifiers, or teething toys around children's necks.

❑ Remove safety pins, coins, toys an infant's hand can totally enclose, small buttons, and other choking hazards from the setting.

❑ High chairs, strollers, and swings are in good condition.

❑ Do not use infant walkers, because they may move children too quickly.

❑ Use safety gates to block access to stairs and other areas. Ensure that gates are closed and used properly.

❑ Post current emergency numbers for each child, the police, fire station, poison control, and other first responders nearby. Also post phone numbers for medical staff, ambulances, and hospitals.

❑ Keep two, well-stocked first-aid kits in a locked cabinet available to staff and out of children's reach.

❑ Ensure that functioning smoke alarms are located in the setting in accordance with fire codes.

❑ Fire extinguishers are easy to reach, visible, and charged for use. Post operating instructions in staff members' home languages.

❑ Toys and equipment are developmentally appropriate, in good condition, and contain no splinters, sharp edges, chipped paint, lead paint, or loose nuts and bolts.

❑ Adapt furnishings, toys, and equipment to meet the needs of children with special needs.

❑ Cover electrical outlets with safety plugs.

❑ Tie cords and wires and remove them from high-traffic areas.

❑ Inspect electrical and heating/cooling systems monthly.

❑ Cover radiators, fans, and space heaters, and keep them out of children's reach.

❑ Store cleaning products, medicines, plastic bags, Styrofoam™, knives, blenders, and other equipment with sharp edges in locked cabinets, in their original containers, and out of children's reach.

❑ Steps, inclines, and platforms are padded and have protective railings.

❑ Bookshelves, furniture, wall hangings, furnishings, and blinds are secure and cannot tip over or fall on children.

❑ Monitor temperature and air quality to ensure health and safety.

Figure 2. Daily Safety Indoor/Outdoor Checklist (continued)

 ## INDOOR (Toddler and Preschool Settings)

- ❑ Adult-to-child ratios meet local or state standards and are appropriate for children's ages.
- ❑ Do not leave children unsupervised, including during nap and bathroom time, mealtimes, outdoor activities, or field trips.
- ❑ Furniture is child-sized, in good condition, and contains no sharp edges.
- ❑ Arrange furniture to avoid "runways" and to allow children to use the space without crowding each other.
- ❑ Secure carpeting and ensure that it lies flat and has no frayed edges.
- ❑ Flooring is clean, dry, and has nonskid surfaces.
- ❑ Toys and equipment are developmentally appropriate, in good condition, and contain no splinters, sharp edges, chipped paint, lead paint, or loose nuts and bolts.
- ❑ Adapt furnishings, toys, and equipment to meet the needs of children with special needs.
- ❑ Cover electrical outlets with safety plugs.
- ❑ Tie cords and wires and remove them from high-traffic areas.
- ❑ Inspect electrical and heating/cooling systems monthly.
- ❑ Cover radiators, fans, and space heaters, and keep them out of children's reach.
- ❑ Store cleaning products, medicines, plastic bags, Styrofoam™, knives, blenders, and other equipment with sharp edges in locked cabinets, in their original containers, and out of children's reach.
- ❑ Steps, inclines, and platforms are padded and have protective railings.
- ❑ Install scald-guard features on faucets, or set water temperature manually to prevent scalding.
- ❑ Exit signs are lit. Exit doors are free of barriers.
- ❑ Closet and bathroom doors have release hardware and can be opened from the inside.
- ❑ Window shades/blinds have plastic rods and cords that are short or fastened out of children's reach.
- ❑ All plants in the room are nontoxic. (See Figure 4. in your *Essentials* textbook for a list of toxic plants.)
- ❑ Current emergency numbers for each child are posted nearby, as are emergency numbers for the police, fire station, poison control, and other emergency first responders. Phone numbers for medical staff, ambulances, and hospitals are also updated and posted.
- ❑ Post current emergency numbers for each child, the police, fire station, poison control, and other first responders nearby. Also post phone numbers for medical staff, ambulances, and hospitals.
- ❑ Keep two, well-stocked first-aid kits in a locked cabinet available to staff and out of children's reach.
- ❑ Ensure that functioning smoke alarms are located in the setting in accordance with fire codes.
- ❑ Fire extinguishers are easy to reach, visible, and charged for use. Post operating instructions in staff members' home languages.
- ❑ Post emergency plans in children's home languages and practice regularly.
- ❑ Bookshelves, furniture, wall hangings, furnishings, and blinds are secure and cannot tip over or fall on children
- ❑ Monitor temperature and air quality to ensure health and safety.

Figure 2. Daily Safety Indoor/Outdoor Checklist (continued)

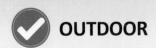 **OUTDOOR**

- ❑ A fence or natural barrier encloses the play area.

- ❑ Create a separate play area for children 2 years old and under.

- ❑ Playground gates can only be opened by adults.

- ❑ The outdoor play area is free of trash, standing water, ice, or any potentially poisonous plants.

- ❑ Equipment is sturdily anchored and in good condition.

- ❑ Do not use trampolines.

- ❑ Shock-absorbing materials—such as wood mulch, pea gravel, or rubber surfacing—surround all climbers, swings, and slides.

- ❑ Play equipment and play surfaces are designed to accommodate children with special needs. All walking and riding surfaces are free of holes and have a nonslip finish.

- ❑ Sandboxes are constructed to permit drainage and are covered when not in use to prevent animals from entering.

- ❑ Riding toys are age-appropriate, have a low center of gravity, and are in good or excellent condition.

- ❑ Children wear helmets when using riding toys.

- ❑ There is shade protection outdoors to minimize sun exposure and sunburn.

- ❑ Drinking water is available for children to access.

(AAP, APHA, & HRA, 2011)

Riding toys should be age-appropriate and in good or excellent condition. These toys should also have a low centers of gravity.

First aid kits should be easily available to staff and out of children's reach.

Figure 3. Suggested First-Aid Kit Contents

- **Disposable, nonporous gloves** (protect hands from blood or body fluids)

- **Sealed antiseptic packages** (clean wounds)

- **Scissors** (cut tape or dressings)

- **Tweezers** (remove splinters)

- **Nonglass thermometer** (take children's temperature)

- **Bandage tape** (hold gauze pads or splint in place)

- **Sterile gauze pads** (clean injuries/cover cuts and scrapes)

- **Flexible roller gauze** (hold gauze pad, eye pad, or splint in place)

- **Triangular bandage** (support injured arm or hold a splint in place)

- **Safety pins** (pin triangular bandages)

- **Eye dressings** (cover injured eye)

- **Small plastic metal splint** (immobilize injured fingers)

- **Pen/pencil and notepad** (write information and/or instructions)

- **Cold pack** (ice bumps and bruises)

- **Current American Academy of Pediatrics or American Red Cross infant/child first-aid resource or equivalent guide** (treatment instructions)

- **Syrup of ipecac** (induce vomiting of poisonous substances, if recommended)

- **Water** (clean injured areas and wash hands)

- **Liquid soap** (wash hands)

- **Emergency medication needed for children** (e.g., auto-injector in case of bee stings) **and written instructions for how to use the medication in all staff members' home languages.**

- **List of emergency first-responder phone numbers and all parents' home, work, and mobile phone numbers**

(AAP, APHA, & HRA, 2011)

Sample pictures of poinsettia, split leaf philodendron, and hydrangea.

Figure 4. Indoor and Outdoor Plants that May Be Harmful to Children

- Amaryllis
- Arrowhead Plant
- Asparagus Fern
- Avocado
- Azalea
- Bird-of-Paradise
- Bittersweet
- Boston Ivy
- Caladium
- Chenille Plant
- Christmas Rose

- Chrysanthemum
- Creeping Charlie, Ground Ivy
- Creeping Fig
- Croton
- Crown of Thorns
- Cyclamen
- Dieffenbachia
- English Ivy
- Gold Toothed Aloe
- Heartleaf Philodendron

- Hydrangea
- Jerusalem Cherry
- Lantana
- Lily-of-the-Valley
- Marble Queen
- Majesty
- Narcissus
- Needlepoint Ivy
- Oleander
- Poinsettia
- Pothos

- Primula (Primrose)
- Red Princess
- Rhubarb
- Ripple Ivy
- Saddle Leaf
- Split Leaf Philodendron
- Umbrella Plant
- Weeping Fig

(University of Nebraska Cooperative Extension [UNCE], n.d.)

Ensuring Children's Supervision

Know your state regulations concerning adult–child ratios in your setting and adhere to this requirement at all times. **While children are in your care, ensure that you can see them at all times and that you are aware of their well-being.** Take special care to monitor infants, as they learn to roll on their sides. Be aware and attentive. If you need to step away to take a phone call from a parent or respond to an emergency, make sure that either one of your colleagues can see the children or take the children with you, if possible. During diaper changes, place infants on the floor and make sure a colleague can see them.

Ensure that children leave your setting at the end of the day with their parents or adults whom parents have authorized to pick up their children.

Securing Furniture and Equipment

Secure all blinds; wall hangings; and tall, heavy furniture and furnishings to a wall using angle braces or anchors to ensure these things never fall on a child. Place toys, games, and other items that children can access and use on shelves and tables that children can reach. Prevent children from climbing on furniture by locking items that they should not use in a closest or storage room.

Secure all heavy furniture and structures to the wall.

Maintaining a Lead-Free Setting

The Centers for Disease Control (CDC) says that 6% of all children 1–2 years old have blood lead levels in the toxic range (American Academy of Child & Adolescent Psychiatry [AACAP], 2012). This figure jumps to 11% of African-American (non-Hispanic) children 1–5 years old. (AACAP, 2012). Lead poisoning is the leading setting-induced illness in children. Because they are undergoing rapid neurological and physical development, children under 6 years old are at greatest risk.

When exposed to only small amounts of lead, children may appear inattentive, hyperactive, and irritable. Children exposed to greater lead levels may also experience problems reading and learning, delayed growth, and hearing loss. At its highest levels, lead can cause permanent brain damage and even death (AACAP, 2012). Early identification and treatment of lead poisoning reduces the risk that children will suffer permanent damage.

Dust and chips from deteriorating lead paint on interior surfaces is the source of most lead poisoning detected in children today. Contaminated soil and water may also have lead. Most buildings built before 1978 have lead-based paint (CDC, 2012). Children who live, or spend a lot of time, in buildings built before 1978 are at the highest risk for lead poisoning. If your setting was built before 1978, have it tested for lead hazards by an EPA-certified firm. Contact your local health department for a list of these firms.

Even if your setting was built after 1978, have your soil tested for lead and other contaminants.

Safe

Figure 5. Protecting Children from Lead

The State of New York Department of Health (SNYDOH, n.d.) devised the following tips to help early educators keep children safe from lead:

Fix peeling lead paint and make building repairs safely.

- Remove all peeling paint and paint chips.

- Regulations for child care providers state that peeling or damaged paint or plaster must be repaired promptly. Before making repairs on a building built before 1978, call your local health department to learn how to keep dust levels down during the repair.

- Children should not be permitted near repairs that disturb old paint, such as sanding or scraping. Children should be kept away until the area is cleaned using wet cleaning methods and a HEPA vacuum (not dry sweeping).

Wash dust off hands, toys, bottles, windows, and floors.

- Wash children's hands and faces after play, before meals, and before bed.

- Wash toys, stuffed animals, pacifiers, and bottles with soap and water often.

- Mop floors often, and use damp paper towels to clean window wells and sills.

Be careful about contact with lead from toys, jewelry, old furniture, and outside play areas.

- Remove any recalled toys from your setting.

- Test your soil for lead and other toxins. Cover bare soil that might be contaminated with grass or woodchips. Never allow children to play in bare soil. Lead might be present especially in urban settings and on sites that previously housed factories.

- Old painted toys, high chairs, and furniture can contain lead paint and varnish. Regulations for early educators ban the use of toxic paints or finishes on anything that children use or is within their reach.

- Never allow children to chew on metal, brass, lead, or pewter objects such as keys or figurines, fishing weights, blinds, old furniture, or windowsills.

Keep lead out of your food and tap water.

- Let tap water run for 1 min before using it, if it has not run for a few hours. Both town and well water could contain lead from old plumbing.

- Only use cold tap water for drinking, cooking, and making baby formula. Boiling water does not get rid of lead.

- Use lead-free dishes.

Preparing and Serving Food

Choking, foodborne illness, and food allergies pose significant safety risks for the children in your care. Follow these guidelines to keep children safe during mealtimes:

- Serve food that is fresh, nutritious, properly stored, and safe to eat. Use utensils, plates, and cups that are clean, dried, and safe.

- Keep the food preparation areas separate from eating, playing, laundry, and toileting areas.

- Keep all pets and their food out of the children's food preparation area.

- When children are brushing their teeth after a meal, ensure that they only use a pea size or smaller amount of toothpaste to avoid choking.

- Never serve honey to infants younger than 12 months old. This includes honey used in cooking and baking. Honey can contain spores that cause botulism in infants.

- Avoid microwaving breast milk or formula for infants. Microwave ovens can heat milk unevenly and burn infants' mouths and throats. If infants in your care consume foods stored in containers (e.g., commercially prepared baby food), serve the food in a bowl or dish. After feeding, place the food container in the refrigerator promptly. Discard uneaten food left in the dish.

- Avoid foods with pits (e.g., olives and cherries), hard candies, nuts, grapes, peanut butter not served on bread or crackers, and hot dogs that are not minced or finely sliced when feeding children under 4 years old. Hot dogs are the number one cause of choking in children under 3 years old (Pesheva, 2010). Cut fruit, such as pears, into fine cubes for children under 4 years old

- Make it a rule that children who can sit on their own sit at the table while eating. Children who eat while walking or moving around are more likely to choke on their food.

Hold infants in your lap with a bottle.

- Hold infants in your lap with a bottle. When they can sit up with minimal support and eat solid foods, allow them to sit in high chairs and child-sized chairs. Never put infants in their cribs with bottles or let mobile infants walk around with bottles or while eating.

- Keep the refrigerator clean and maintain an internal temperature of 35–40°F. Foods should be cold to the touch, but not frozen.

- Store canned goods and other shelf-stable items in a cool, dry place; rotate foods so you use older supplies first. Store your dry foods including flour, cereals, cornmeal, and dry beans in tightly covered containers on shelves to protect from rodents.

- When cooking or preparing food with young children, ensure that you keep children far away from hot surfaces and flames.

- Ensure that children wash their hands before and after preparing and cooking foods. Ensure that you or another early educator is always present while children are preparing, cooking, or eating food.

Using Technology

Children's learning experiences are enhanced when they actively explore, engage, and manipulate various materials and resources. By introducing technology—like computers and software, tablets, and digital cameras— in the setting, children can engage and extend their learning independently. For example, an early educator may display photos of a toddler's family members on a tablet. Toddlers may touch the screen when they see each photo and the early educator describes it. Interactions with technology should be playful and engaging and should support creativity, exploration, and pretend play.

Prohibit passive screen time for children under 2 years old. Similarly, discourage passive and noninteractive screen (television, videos, and DVDs) time for 2–5-year-olds. Instead, use these technologies with the children—either individually or as a group—to support your interactions with each other. Also, make assistive technology available to support your interactions with children with special needs.

As you work with older children to use the Internet, model and ensure safe use. Never post images of the children in your care online without written consent from their parents.

Ensuring Sleep Safety

The Centers for Disease Control estimate that "more than 4,500 infants die suddenly of no immediately, obvious cause" each year in the United States. Sudden Infant Death Syndrome (SIDS) causes half these deaths and is the leading cause of death among infants aged 1–2 months. CDC defines SIDS as "the sudden death of an infant less than 1 year of age that cannot be explained after a thorough investigation is conducted, including a complete autopsy, examination of the death scene, and review of the clinical history" (CDC, 2013).

Infants are at greater risk of SIDS if they are exposed to secondhand smoke and/or overheat during naps. Work to keep the children in your care safe while sleeping. Ensure that cribs, beds, and cots are set up and secured properly to prevent infants and young children from falling. Place all infants aged 0–12 months on their backs when sleeping. If infants roll over, allow them to sleep in the position they have chosen.

Cover crib mattresses with fitted sheets. Do not place any other soft materials—including pillows or soft toys—inside cribs. Keep soft or loose bedding away from sleeping infants and out of safe sleep environments.

Place all sleeping equipment—including cribs, cots, and mats—away from windows, electrical sockets, and hanging decorations. Do not string toys across cribs for infants or toddlers to use.

Do not allow infants to sleep in a car safety seat, beanbag chair, bouncy seat, infant seat, swing, jumping chair, playpen or play yard, highchair, chair, futon, or any other type of furniture/equipment that is not a safety-approved crib.

Diapering and Bathroom Safety

To prevent accidental drowning and falls from changing tables, ensure that children are always supervised during diaper changes or while using the toilet. A toddler can drown in a toilet in 2 min. Always keep at least one hand on an infant or toddler on the changing table at all times. Know if the infants and toddlers in your care have allergies to specific types of diapers. If some of these children wear cloth diapers, dress them in a waterproof diaper covering and fresh clothes. Use clean, hands-free diaper disposal containers. When cleaning this container daily, pour the used water into the toilet and not the sink. See Chapter 2 for more on healthy diapering and toileting practices.

Protecting Children From Sun Exposure

Infants' skin is especially sensitive; do not expose infants aged 0–6 months to the sun or apply sunblock to their skin. Children aged 6 months and older can wear sunblock safely. Apply it to their hands and other uncovered areas. There are multiple brands of sunblock that are SPF 15+ and have water resistant, tear-free formulas that will not sting children's eyes. Also, set up sun shades in your outdoor setting to help protect children from the sun (Skin Cancer Foundation [SCF], 2013).

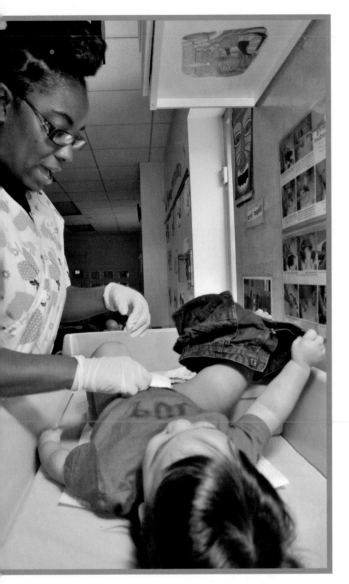

Always keep at least one hand on an infant or toddler on the changing table at all times.

Enjoying Field Trips Safely

Plan and organize field trips well in advance to ensure children's safety and maximum enjoyment. Also, let parents know about the upcoming trip so that you can obtain permission for their children to attend, address their health and safety concerns, and recruit parent volunteers for the trip. Secure safe modes of transportation, adequate supervision for children, first-aid kits, any necessary medications, food and water for the children, and emergency phone numbers and other contact information.

Teaching Children about Safety

While you can prevent many accidents and injuries by simply securing your indoor and outdoor settings, teach toddlers and preschoolers to take responsibility for their own safety.

Making and Reviewing Safety Rules

Think about the rules that you have in your setting, such as the following:

- We need to walk indoors. If we want to run, it must be outdoors.

- We need to be kind to one another. Biting, pushing, and hitting are not allowed.

- If we want to use sharp tools like knives or paper cutters, we need to be with adults who can help us and can use them properly and safely.

Are you surprised at how many of these rules target children's physical safety? In Chapter 10, we will examine more closely how to use rules to guide young children's behavior. In this section, however, we will focus on using rules to keep young children safe. See Figure 6. for tips on making your safety rules most effective.

Figure 6. Tips for Establishing Safety Rules With Young Children

- Begin with just a few short, clear rules that children can repeat easily. Add more rules once the children master these.

- Relate rules to ideas children already know.

- Help children to understand the "why" behind a rule.

- Give children the opportunity to participate in creating rules.

- State rules positively. Tell them what they can do rather than what they cannot (e.g. , instead of "Do not run inside," try "Be safe, walk inside").

- Illustrate rules with pictures for children who are not yet readers or are learning English as a second language.

- Repeat the rules in all the children's home languages.

- Let children practice using the rules.

- Apply rules consistently over time.

- Remind children of rules gently when they forget.

- Help children notice when they are following a rule and acknowledge their efforts.

Figure 7. Discussing Safety Rules in Everyday Conversations

Weave safety discussions gradually and naturally into your conversations with all children about new and existing toys, equipment, and materials. Explain the actions that you are taking and the safety reasons behind those actions. For example, when introducing a waterwheel into play at the water table, say, "We need to make sure that there are towels and a mop nearby to wipe up spills. It's easy to splash water on the floor when we're having fun. It's also easy to slip and fall on wet floors. That's why we need to have towels and a mop handy."

Here are more examples of safety conversations you might have with the children in your setting:

- "Antonio, thank you for telling me that the wheel on the ride-on car is broken. We'll put it in the cupboard until one of the maintenance staff can fix it. We wouldn't want anyone to get hurt riding a broken car."

- "Sammi, thank you for washing your plate after lunch. Let's double-check together to make sure no water splashed on the floor to prevent any of your friends from slipping. Could you please get a paper towel to dry the floor? Thank you."

- "I know that everyone's excited about baking bread today. Before we begin, let's go over the safety rules for using the oven."

- "Aarika, I'm sorry that you got kicked by Eduardo when you were going down the slide. I think that we need to review our safety rules for playing on the slide so that this doesn't happen again."

Talk about safety when you first introduce children to the learning centers in your setting:

- "We need to wipe up any paint or glue spills so that no one slides and falls." *(art center)*

- "Remember that we should build constructions no higher than our shoulders so that the blocks won't fall on anyone." *(blocks center)*

- "To keep our eyes safe, we need to always put on goggles before doing any woodworking projects." *(woodworking center)*

Pacing Your Safety Instruction

With all there is to know about staying safe, children can become overwhelmed quickly and easily. Do not bombard them with too much information at once. Instead, start with what you think they can understand, and build on this information over time. Then add details as children's skills and reasoning grow.

Infants, for example, are just learning to feel secure and trust that adults will keep them safe. Have a plan to support an infant who is crying and seems inconsolable. Never shake a child.

Use these "teachable moments" to introduce safety messages in a natural way. Toddlers can begin to understand the need for safety rules—that rules are needed to keep both themselves and others safe. Older toddlers can understand simple safety guidelines like taking turns at the slide so that children don't kick one another, biting is not kind behavior, and blocks are for building not throwing. When crossing a street, teach toddlers how to look and listen for approaching cars. Toddlers can also learn that matches are tools used only by adults, not toys for children's play. By the time children are preschoolers, they can cognitively understand that their actions lead to consequences and that there are specific steps they can follow to stay safe.

As you introduce children to new safety messages, give them lots of opportunities to test and practice them with you. Be realistic about the children's ability to grasp and retain these messages successfully.

Selecting Aids for Teaching Safety

Various commercial materials and curricula exist that are designed to help you teach children about safety—particularly fire and water safety or how to deal with strangers. Some of these aids are designed by educators who understand how young children learn and may include excellent activities to try in your setting. Others are not developmentally appropriate and often rely on coloring activities and stickers. Before using any of these materials, read through them carefully and approach them cautiously. Review them ahead of time and select only those that are developmentally appropriate for the children in your setting.

Teaching Pedestrian Safety

When children chase a rolling ball or a beloved pet into the street, safe pedestrian practices are not the first things on their minds. Help guard children against pedestrian accidents by teaching them a few necessary safety behaviors:

- Hold on to an adult's hand when crossing the street.

- Walk on sidewalks. If there is no sidewalk, walk on the left, facing traffic.

- When crossing a street, look for the pedestrian crosswalk. Before crossing a street, look left, right, and left again.

As you walk with children, point out the safe walking behaviors you are both performing. Narrate your actions: "Before we cross the street we need to make sure no cars are coming. Let's stand on the curb and look to the left. Now let's look to the right. Now let's check to the left again. I don't see any cars coming. Do you? I don't hear any car motors either. Do you?

It looks like it's safe to walk across the street now. Let's keep checking both sides as we cross to make sure no cars are coming." Many accidents are caused by children surrendering the responsibility for their safety to adults. Be sure that children are active participants in the pedestrian safety process.

When adult–child ratios make it impossible for each child to have an adult's hand to hold, consider using knotted travel ropes during neighborhood or nature walks. Each child holds onto a knot while adults lead and follow the rope "train." Multiseat strollers work for younger children who are not yet stable walkers.

Get into the habit of following these safety precautions while walking with a group:

- Make sure that each child is wearing a tag with the name of your setting and phone number on it. (Do not include the child's name.)

- Carry a list of the names of all the children you are supervising and their emergency contacts.

- Maintain required adult–child ratios.

- Bring a cell phone and a first-aid kit.

- Practice traffic safety rules with children ahead of time. Games such as "red light, green light" help young children become aware of traffic lights and safety measures.

Teaching Safety on Riding Toys

Riding toys may be popular among the children in your setting. Before taking their first ride, teach children these rules:

- Children younger than 3 years old cannot safely use riding toys. Children's feet should reach the foot pedals.

- Children can use only riding toys in good repair.

- Children may ride only on flat, hard surfaces, such as designated tracks or blacktops, and obey any traffic safety signs.

- Children must put on helmets before riding.

Children should use only riding toys that are in good repair.

- Children must ride alone.

- Bumping other drivers is not permitted.

Teaching Car/School Bus Safety

More young children are killed getting on and off school buses than riding on them (Savage, Kawanabe, Mejeur, Goehring, & Reed, 2002). Teach children to look at the driver and make eye contact before stepping onto the bus or crossing in front of it. Children should wait for the driver to wave them on before crossing.

Infants, toddlers, and preschoolers should sit in the backseat of vehicles. Airbags in the front dash, if released during an accident, could crush children's bodies. Allowing a child to sit in an adult's lap is risky. If there is a sudden stop, the child could fly out of the adult's arms and into a window, windshield, or another passenger.

Secure children under 2 years old in a rear-facing car seat. Secure toddlers into forward-facing car seats if these toddlers meet height and weight requirements. Fasten infants' and toddlers' seat belts securely, with no more than an inch of "give." Preschoolers must ride in booster seats that you secure with the car's lap and shoulder belts. Help children make fastening their seat belts or strapping into a booster seat second nature to them.

Teaching Fire/Burn Safety

Children under the age of 5 years old are more than twice as likely to die in a fire than older children and adults (U.S. Fire Administration [USFA], 2003). There are four important things you can do to prevent fires:

- Ensure that smoke alarms and fire extinguishers are accessible and in working condition.

- Devise and practice fire emergency plans. Fire experts recommend having both a primary and a back-up plan. If the proposed fire exit is blocked or engulfed in flames, you will know to take your back-up route out of the building.

- Designate a meeting place outdoors where everyone can reunite should the group separate during evacuation.

- Hold fire drills monthly so that escape procedures become second nature for everyone in your setting.

Making Traffic Safety Fun

Children can practice both pedestrian and traffic safety using road signs when they play with blocks or on the play-ground when they use ride-on toys. Use children's books like the following to teach traffic safety messages:

- *The ABC's of Traffic Safety* by Whitney M. Hemstock.

- *Safety on the School Bus* by Sarah Florence.

- *Road Safety* by Sue Barraclough.

Teach children what to do in case of a fire emergency:

- Each time a smoke detector or fire alarm sounds, children should follow the plan you have taught and practiced with them.

- **Exiting the building with a responsible adult is the most important action children can take to ensure their safety.** Children need to practice leaving immediately—without stopping for coats or other personal items. If you care for infants or toddlers, you and your colleagues are fully responsible for getting these children to safety. Place evacuation cribs— wheeled cribs that can hold multiple children—near designated emergency exits.

- Make children understand that they cannot hide from a fire. Taking shelter in a closet or waiting under furniture until the worst is over places children at high risk. Evacuation is the only plan that works.

- Inhaling smoke is dangerous. If children encounter smoke while trying to leave the building, have them get down on their knees and crawl low to the ground. Practice this skill. Set up a ceiling of bed sheets and have children crawl below the sheets to safety.

- After evacuating, children need to know to stay out of the building. No one—child or adult—should ever go back into a burning building for any reason.

- Prepare children for fire emergencies. For example, teach them what to do if their clothing catches fire. Children should "stop, drop, and roll" immediately —meaning that they stop whatever they are doing, fall to the ground, and roll their bodies. As they roll, they should cover their eyes with their arms until the fire is smothered. Again, practice this skill often. Let children know that you will be practicing fire safety that day. When children are indoors or outdoors, yell, "Stop, drop, and roll!" Have everyone— including you—act it out.

Playing with matches is the leading cause of home fires (USFA, 2003). Children are naturally curious about fire and attracted to flames. Toddlers as young as 2 years old have started home fires. Teach children that matches or lighters are tools for adults only—even though these tools may not be allowed at your setting. Children should learn to never pick up matches or lighters and to tell an adult if they find these items.

Making Fire Safety Fun

Your local fire station can help you teach the children in your setting about fire safety. For children, a trip to the fire station is not only an opportunity to learn about what to do in a fire emergency, but a chance to see where the firefighters eat and sleep—and to try on a firefighter's helmet.

Also, read picture books about fire safety aloud to the children. Relate the stories to what children already know about fire safety. Here are a few titles to consider:

- *Firehouse Fun!* by Abby Klein.

- *Sparkles the Fire Safety Dog* by Dayna Hilton.

- *Fire Drill* by Paul DuBois Jacobs and Jennifer Swender.

Teaching Water Safety

Accidents can occur any time children use or play near water. In the art center, at the water table, or even in the bathroom, water can spill on the floor and cause children to slip and fall. Wipe or mop any floor spills immediately.

On the other hand, young children can drown in as little as 1 in. of water. Within 4-6 min underwater, children can suffer irreversible brain damage (National Safe Kids Campaign [NSKC], 2004). While residential swimming pools and open water sites pose the greatest danger to young children, many places in your setting can be deadly, like wading pools, sinks, baby bathtubs, water tables, buckets of water, or even toilets. A toddler can drown in a toilet in 2 mins. Supervise children while they are using the toilet. Guard against leaving standing water anywhere other than in the toilet. Empty your setting's water table every day, both to prevent accidental drowning and to guard against growing bacteria.

Teaching Stranger Danger

Though children must learn about the danger that strangers may pose, children should not adopt a blanketed fear of every person they do not know. Help them to recognize that real dangers do exist without instilling fear.

Children's families—who may be strangers to the other children—are welcome in your setting. So, too, are program visitors, such as the fire marshal or the dentist. More often than not, strangers will be helpful to children. Because of this, avoid giving children a broad safety rule like, "Don't talk to strangers." Tell children that it is often okay to speak to people who are strangers. However, be sure that all children are supervised at all times—meaning that you and/or your colleagues can see and hear the children at all times. Properly interview visitors before they enter your setting. Ensure that you or one of your colleagues is always present and within reach when visitors are present.

Incorporate safety messages into your daily conversations and interactions with children. For example, remind children about the rules of walking together as a group during nature walks. If a stranger offers assistance during this walk, explain to the stranger that only authorized adults may assist. Give children a sense of confidence about their safety while teaching them some simple strategies that they can use if they get lost during a field trip or a neighborhood walk:

- Ask an adult for help—preferably someone with a badge, such as a police officer or security guard.

Reading About Stranger Danger

Here are some books you can read aloud to children to teach them to be safe around strangers:

- *Are You a Good Stranger?* by Susan Nicholas.

- *The Berenstain Bears Learn about Strangers* by Stan and Jan Berenstain.

- *Helping Hand Books: Ashley Learns About Strangers* by Sarah, Duchess of York.

- Stay put and do not go in search of the group. In other words, wait to be found and reunited.

- Do not get in a car with, or accept a ride from, a stranger.

- Do not accept candy, treats, or gifts from a stranger.

- Do not talk to strangers who ask you if you want to pet their puppy, say your parents have been injured or in an accident, or ask you for directions.

- Teach children that if a stranger grabs them, kick hard, yell "NO!," and run away.

- Many children can tell instinctually if a stranger means them harm. Teach children that if they get a bad feeling about a person or situation, they should leave immediately.

Modeling Safe Practices

Children will understand the importance of safety when they see you respecting safety rules and doing everything you can to keep everyone around you safe. Think about the many things you do that model safe practices:

- Supervising children carefully and always maintaining required adult–child ratios.

- Working safety topics into your daily conversations with children.

- Practicing and enforcing safety rules. For example, every time you drive or ride in a car, you use a seatbelt.

- Teaching and practicing emergency routines with the children, such as fire drills.

- Talking calmly and with authority in an emergency. You offer reassurance and address children's fears, whether real or imagined.

- Completing a pediatric first-aid course so that you can treat injuries and respond to emergencies.

- Staying abreast of current safety practices and the latest safety regulations for children's toys, equipment, and furnishings.

- Knowing the signs of abuse and providing a setting that encourages children to share their feelings.

Always be on the lookout for ways to make settings safer for children and explain to children how you do it. Let them see and understand how you solve safety issues. Not only will you model safety practices, but you will illustrate the vital skill of problem-solving.

Teaching Safety and Problem-Solving

Darnell: "Teacher, I hurt my hand on the tray."

Teacher: "I've noticed lately that a lot of us have been burning our hands when we take something out of the oven. Let's figure out what's happening and see if we can do something to prevent it."

Sharmaine: "Maybe Darnell had the oven on too hot."

Teacher: "That's a good thought, Sharmaine. But I remember helping Darnell adjust the oven temperature. We had it at 350 degrees, which is the same temperature we usually use for baking. So I don't think the oven was hotter than usual."

Louis: "Maybe Darnell forgot to use potholders."

Darnell: "I did not forget! You can ask Miss Washington. She was helping me take the tray out."

Sharmaine: "I saw him. He used potholders."

Teacher: "Well, let's take a look at these potholders. Darnell, would you please bring me the potholders you used?"

Darnell: "Here you go."

Teacher: "Oh, these are the beautiful ones you made for us in the art center, Suzanna. They're very pretty, but they're also very thin. See, if we hold them up to the window, light goes through them. That means heat can go through them, too. I think these are a little too thin for using in our kitchen. However, they'd be great in the dramatic play center. Suzanna, would you please move these potholders to the play kitchen area?"

Darnell: "Well what do we use in the real kitchen?"

Teacher: "That's an excellent question, Darnell. For safety reasons, we won't be able to use the oven until I get us some new oven mitts. As soon as I can, I'm going to get us some made out of silicone. Silicone allows you to touch things as hot as 500 degrees.

Sharmaine: "Wow! That's hot!"

Teacher: "It sure is. Silicone mitts should protect everyone's hands when we take something out of the oven. I think our problem is solved."

Implementing Emergency Plans

Teaching children about safety and knowing what to do during emergencies are critical components of the CDA Functional Area 1. Share your safety knowledge with supervisors, colleagues, and parents so that everyone can work together to send children unified, accurate messages.

As a CDA candidate, the pediatric first-aid course you will complete teaches you how to handle emergencies such as the following:

- Choking.
- Insect, animal, or human bites.
- Falls.
- Cuts or scrapes.
- Injuries that result in heavy bleeding.
- Accidental poisonings.
- Allergic reactions.
- Head injuries.
- Dental emergencies.
- Eye injuries.
- Sprains and fractures.
- Accidental drowning.

Keep two, well-stocked first-aid kits in your setting.

Knowing how to handle these emergencies will help prevent additional injury and even death. **Report all injuries and falls to parents the day they occur.** See Figure 8. for examples of how you would use your first-aid knowledge in your setting:

Safe

Figure 8. Administering First-Aid Treatment

INCIDENT	FIRST-AID RESPONSE
Keisha burns herself when touching a hot pot on the stove.	• Since this is a minor burn, hold Keisha's affected hand under cold, running tap water. • Dry and bandage the affected area. • Fill out an incident report and notify Keisha's parents.
Timothy breaks a glass when trying to pour juice, and cuts his hand. It is bleeding.	• Because there is only light bleeding involved, hold Timothy's cut thumb under cold, running tap water. • Clean the wound with soap and paper towels. • Dress the wound with clean gauze. • Fill out an incident report and notify Timothy's parents.
Tonio trips and falls on a rock while playing outdoors. His knee is scraped and bleeding lightly.	• Treat the wound as above in Timothy's example. • Clean the scrape thoroughly to prevent infection. • Fill out an incident report and notify Tonio's parents.
Emilia begins choking while eating lunch.	• Perform the Heimlich maneuver on Emilia. • Once she is breathing well, comfort her and explain what has happened. There is no need to call 911 if she is conscious and breathing. • Fill out an incident report and notify Emilia's parents.
Mary Lou is stung by a bee while gardening.	• Remove the stinger from Mary Lou's arm. • Check to see that the child is not having a reaction to the bee venom (e.g., shortness of breath or hives). • Apply ice if there is redness and swelling at the site of the sting. • Fill out an incident report and notify Mary Lou's parents.
Anna bites Pedro in a fight over a coveted toy.	• Comfort Pedro. Involve Anna in comforting him. • State the rule about being kind to our friends calmly and firmly. Tell Anna that if she still has an urge to bite, she can bite an apple. • Fill out an incident report and notify Pedro's parents. • Notify and discuss the situation with Anna's parents.

Council for Professional Recognition • 800-424-4310

Treat children's injuries calmly but straightforwardly. They will take comfort in knowing that you are in charge and know what to do in this situation. They receive the message that their safety is important to you and that you will ensure it. Likewise, when you tell parents immediately what has happened, they realize that their child's safety is a high priority for you.

However, know when you should reach out for assistance in an escalated emergency situation. Call 911 and get children to the hospital if they experience any of the following symptoms:

- Loss of consciousness.

- Breathing difficulties.

- Severe bleeding.

- Unequal pupils.

- Seizure or convulsions.

- Neck, back, or head injuries.

- Continuous clear drainage from nose/ ears after a blow to the head.

- Severe headache.

- Stiff neck or neck pain when head is moved.

- Hives that appear quickly.

- Repeated forceful vomiting or vomiting blood.

- Severe abdominal pain that causes a child to double-over.

- Possible broken bones.

- Shock.

(AAP, APHA, & HRA, 2011)

Treat children's injuries calmly but straightforwardly.

Notify children's parents of the emergency and ask them to meet either you or the person assigned to accompany their children at the hospital. If you accompany a child to the hospital, bring any medical records and emergency authorization forms that your setting has on file for the child.

Devising Fire Emergency Plans

Include explicit instructions in your fire emergency plan for determining whether staff should attempt to put out a fire with an extinguisher or call 911.

Evacuate the children before attempting to extinguish the fire. Ensure that they are outside of the building with a colleague or other responsible adult to supervise. If you think that the fire is small and contained, such as a kitchen or wastebasket fire, use an extinguisher to put it out. Standing approximately 8 ft from the fire, aim the extinguisher at the fire's base—not the flames. **Do not underestimate the power of a fire.** If it appears out of control, it is. **If you have any doubts, evacuate.**

Your evacuation plan should also answer these questions:

- What route and back-up route will we use to evacuate? Have a back-up route in case you are unable to evacuate according to your first chosen route.

- Where is our outdoor designated meeting place in case our group separates during the evacuation?

- What are each adult's responsibilities (e.g., accounting for all children, assuring that no one is left behind, administering any necessary first aid, carrying cell phones, and calling 911)?

Practice fire emergency plans monthly to make sure that children know what to do. Regular fire drills ensure that children will be able to evacuate without thinking about it. Have children practice crawling on the floor to get outside in the event that smoke fills the play area.

Test smoke alarms monthly and replace batteries annually. Check extinguishers monthly to ensure the following:

- They are in their designated places.
- There are no obstructions to accessing them.
- Safety seals are intact.
- Operating instructions are clearly legible (and in all staff members' home languages).
- Fullness is confirmed by lifting.

Other Emergency Plans

Beyond administering first aid and responding to individual emergencies, know how to respond to emergencies that threaten the entire group of children and adults in your setting. Devise emergency plans to properly respond in the following situations:

- Weather-related disasters, such as tornadoes, flash floods, earthquakes, and hurricanes.

- Interruptions in water or electricity service.

- Criminal incidents, such as kidnappings, robberies, bomb threats, or acts of terrorism.

- Evacuations in response to military actions (if your setting is located in a war zone).

Include in your natural disaster plans instructions for evacuating the building and designated meeting places outdoors to ensure everyone's safety. Designate who will call 911, administer first aid, take roll, and monitor the children. Keep all related emergency phone numbers readily accessible. Share all evacuation plans with the children's families in their home languages. Add diagrams, sketches, or photos to these plans if you think they will help reinforce the messages. Children's families should be familiar with these plans so they can discuss them with their children and participate in drills when they are in your setting.

Involving Parents in Classroom Safety

Children's safety is a top priority for parents and for you. Ease parent's minds by sharing with them the many ways you make work to keep your setting safe:

- Releasing their children only to authorized persons who must sign children in and out of the setting.

- Supervising children at all times.

- Developing emergency plans in the families' home languages and posting them.

- Regularly practicing emergency procedures with children.

- Being certified in pediatric first-aid.

- Performing safety checks on indoor and outdoor settings daily.

- Developing and enforcing safety rules with children.

- Teaching children how to prevent accidents and injuries from fire, water, riding toys, and strangers.

Reassure parents that their children will be safe at your setting.

- Helping children learn how to walk safely in traffic and ride safely in cars and buses.

- Filling out an incident report and informing parents every time their child is injured or involved in an accident.

Actively involve families in your setting's safety program. Obtain the following information from them:

- Emergency phone contacts (both cell and landline).

- A list of persons to whom children are permitted to be released and the names of any individuals to whom their children are **specifically not allowed** to be released.

- Permission to photograph their child (or instructions not to).

- Special needs that their child may have that could impact safety and evacuation procedures.

- Languages that their child understands.

- Specific circumstances that could impact safety and evacuation procedures.

Make sure that families are aware of how you deal with injuries and accidents. Provide families copies of your emergency procedures and encourage them to familiarize themselves with the procedures.

Parents should understand that you will inform them if there is an accident or injury involving their child. When you use incident reports and share them with parents, you ensure that they are aware of every safety concern that has involved their child during the day. Reassure parents that you will call 911 and have their child transported to the hospital during an emergency and that you will notify them. Staff will consult them before making any decisions regarding their child's treatment.

Keep parents informed of any changes in your safety program. If, for example, you encounter a new safety challenge, involve families in solving the problem. For example, if Doug is hurting other children—either by biting or throwing things—confer with his parents. Ask: Have these behaviors happened before? Are they occurring at home? Are there any stresses in Doug's life? Brainstorm ideas to rectify the situation with the family. Then decide on an approach that both you and the family can implement to end the behavior.

If you encounter a new safety challenge, involve families in solving the problem.

The same safety measures children are learning in your setting will help keep them safe at home. Invite families into your classroom to be a part of your safety program. If parents speak a home language other than English, make sure that there is safety information available in their home languages. Hold parent workshops during the year to share safety information with families. Here are some example parent workshop topics:

Two thirds of home fires in which children die occur in homes without working smoke detectors (USFA, 2003). Invite a firefighter to speak to families about keeping smoke detectors in working order. Similarly, work with parents in teaching preschoolers to dial 911 if there is a home fire or other emergency.

Share with families how you store household cleaning products, medicines, and other potentially harmful substances in their original containers, in locked cabinets, out of reach. Families will likely also be interested in knowing what plants are potentially toxic and how to recognize them. Tell parents that, in case of an emergency, they can always contact the National Capital Poison Center from anywhere in the United States at 1-800-222-1222. Parents can get immediate information in their own language when they call.

Help parents understand safety procedures thoroughly so that they can be your active partners in safety. By working together, you give children a clear, consistent message on the importance of safety in your setting and at home. ■

Chapter 2
Healthy

CDA Functional Area 2: Candidate provides an environment that promotes health and prevents illness, and teaches children about good nutrition and practices that promote wellness.

Healthy

Introduction

Early educators' fundamental responsibilities are to provide children with healthy environments and skills to foster wellness. When you work daily to keep children safe, nourished, and healthy, you enhance their learning significantly.

In this chapter, we will explore a number of important aspects involved in keeping children healthy:

- **Promoting Wellness.**
- **Responding to Illness.**
- **Providing Nutritious Snacks and Meals.**
- **Learning Good Health Practices.**
- **Identifying/Reporting Child Abuse and Neglect.**

Promoting Wellness

Your first responsibility in supporting children's health is to promote their wellness. Be proactive. Look for ways to prevent illness and health problems instead of reacting to them once a child is sick. Ensure that children have the recommended immunizations and monitor their health daily. Provide a clean and sanitized setting to reduce the likelihood of harmful germs breeding and illnesses spreading. Positive actions like these go a long way toward creating settings that keep children healthy and ready to learn.

Keeping the Setting Healthy

To ensure that indoor settings are as healthy as possible, familiarize yourself with both your setting and state/federal health requirements. State/federal requirements serve as a baseline for quality. Your setting requirements should match or exceed them. The more rigorous your requirements, the healthier the setting will be for children. It is important that you know what these measures are. Ask your supervisor for help if you have trouble locating either of these documents.

Use Figure 9. to double-check the health requirements of your indoor setting, learn the new guidelines for preparing bleach solution to sanitize setting surfaces and objects, and view a list of prohibited animals in settings with children.

Figure 9. Checklist for Healthy Indoor Settings

❑ Keep rooms ventilated. Clean air conditioners regularly (if used) to remove dust and prevent mold. Do not use chemical air fresheners and scented products. (These products can trigger asthma attacks or nauseate children.)

❑ Keep rooms well lit.

❑ Maintain comfortable and healthy heat and humidity levels. Keep room temperature 70°F or slightly lower to prevent colds. If your setting climate is dry during the winter months, use a cool mist humidifier. Clean and disinfect this humidifier daily.

❑ Meet all local and state requirements for food preparation and storage. Wash, rinse, and sanitize food preparation surfaces, tabletops, counters, high chairs (if used), eating utensils, and dishes before and after each use.

❑ Provide children with their own cubbies for storing personal items. The child's name and photo should be visible on the cubby.

❑ Store children's clean personal care items (e.g., combs or change of clothing) in individually labeled containers or cubbies. Do not allow children to share these items. Older children can access their own personal care items without assistance.

❑ Keep children clean and dry. Change their clothing as needed after outdoor play, food spills, or toileting accidents.

❑ Keep drinking water available at all times at child-sized water fountains or in pitchers children can pour themselves. Discard single-serve drinking cups after each use. Sanitize nondisposable cups by hand or in a dishwasher. Clean and disinfect drinking fountains (if used) daily.

❑ Empty trash cans with plastic liners daily. If children eat in the room, empty trash after lunch and at the end of the day. If you care for infants and toddlers, discard disposable diapers in a covered trash with a foot pedal. Change the liner daily.

❑ Keep tissues, liquid soap, and paper towels accessible to children and always in bathrooms. If you have a diaper changing area, use either a plastic cover you can sanitize after each diaper change or a paper cover that you can discard after every diaper change. Control odors through exhaust system ventilation.

❑ Prepare fresh bleach solution daily to sanitize surfaces and disinfect toys and play props. (See Figure 10. in your *Essentials* textbook to learn the new guidelines for preparing bleach solution.)

❑ Wash, rinse, and sanitize bathrooms—including sinks, faucets, countertops, and toilets—diaper pails, and potty chairs (if used) daily with bleach solution prepared that day. Remove bathroom odors through exhaust system ventilation.

❑ Wash, rinse, and sanitize doors and cabinet handles daily.

❑ Mop floors daily. Sweep floors throughout the day, especially after meals or snacks. Broom sweeping is the best method for removing food scraps on the floor/carpet area when children are present.

❑ Vacuum carpets and large area rugs only when children are not present. Spot clean as needed. Fully clean twice yearly.

❑ Wash, rinse, and sanitize tables at the start of each day, in between activities, and before any food is served. Allow bleach solution to sit for at least 2 min before a child sits at the table.

Figure 9. Checklist for Healthy Indoor Settings (continued)

❑ Shake small rugs outside or vacuum daily. Launder as needed.

❑ Clean and sanitize computer keyboards after each use.

❑ Sanitize water tables with bleach solution daily.

❑ Cover outdoor sand tables to prevent animals from entering. Spray sand in tables with bleach solution weekly. Replace sand regularly.

❑ Keep cribs (without Plexiglas® partitions) 3 ft apart and cleaned weekly as long as the same child uses it. Clean and sanitize cribs after each child. Disinfect daily any crib parts (such as railings) that children can mouth.

❑ Place toddler and preschooler cots or mats at least 3 ft apart. These mats should be at least 2 in. thick, waterproof, washable, and appropriate for the size and weight of the children. Position children head to toe on mats for nap time. They should have their own cots or mats. Clean and sanitize cots and mats after each child.

❑ Do not share children's bedding, including crib bedding. Wash bedding weekly or when soiled. Store bedding between use in a labeled bag or in the child's cubby. Do not allow children's bedding to touch.

❑ Wear disposable gloves while cleaning bodily fluids (e.g., blood, urine, vomit, feces, mucus, and saliva). Immediately clean with bleach solution any surfaces exposed to bodily fluids.

❑ Wash dress-up clothes and accessories weekly.

❑ Choose classroom pets according to setting and local and state regulations. Allow only animals that do not pose a health or safety risk to children. Permissible pets include dogs, cats, hamsters, rabbits, gerbils, guinea pigs, and fish—unless a child or staff member has an allergy or a compromised immune system. Maintain animals' health, immunize if applicable, and have a veterinarian certify these animals to meet regulations. Keep animals away from food preparation and eating areas. Only early educators should clean animal habitats, and they should clean and sanitize all areas affected by animal droppings immediately. Children should not clean animal habitats or animal droppings, even if supervised. (See Figure 11. in your *Essentials* textbook for a list of prohibited animals.)

❑ Keep pet food and litter boxes out of children's reach. You can teach children to feed the animals, but supervise children during these feedings. Children should never pick up animal droppings, even with adult supervision.

❑ Allow children to play and exercise outside daily unless the weather poses a health risk (e.g., a windchill factor below 15 °F and a heat index above 90 °F). Children should wear appropriate protective clothing. Provide appropriate shelter from heat or wind.

Allow only animals that do not pose a health or safety risk to children.

Healthy

Figure 10. Preparing/Using Bleach Solution for Disinfecting Surfaces

In March 2013, the National Resource Center for Health and Safety in Child Care and Early Education (NRC, 2013) released the following guidelines about preparing bleach solution for sanitizing and disinfecting:

Wash surfaces with soap before applying bleach solution.

"The concentration of bleach solutions sold in stores has changed in many areas of the country. The new bleach solution available in many stores is now 8.25% sodium hypochlorite solution (higher than the formerly available bleach solution of 5.25%-6%). Several companies have communicated to us that they have discontinued manufacturing the 5.25%-6% sodium hypochlorite bleach solution and it will no longer be available at many stores. The 8.25% solution is being produced by both brand name companies as well as companies that produce generic products. Many of these products are now EPA-registered products as well.

"The NRC has been working with national experts and has determined that because of the variety of products available, it is no longer possible to provide a generic bleach recipe for sanitizing and disinfecting in early care and education programs. In addition, if you are using an EPA-registered product you should not be using a generic recipe, but should be following label instructions for use …

"The NRC recommendation is:

• Use EPA-registered products for sanitizing and disinfecting.

• Follow the manufacturer's instructions for diluting the EPA-registered product for sanitizing or disinfecting, as well as for the contact time.

• If you are not using an EPA-registered bleach product at this time, we recommend you contact your state and/or local health department for assistance in creating the safe dilutions for the bleach products you are using to sanitize and/or disinfect surfaces in your early care and education environment."

Visit the NRC website (cfoc.nrckids.org/Bleach/FindingEPARegInfo.cfm) for information on how to locate EPA registration information.

Figure 11. Prohibited Animals (LIST)

- **Wild animals** caught or found in the wild often have diseases.

- **Ferrets** are likely to bite if startled.

- **Hermit crabs** pinch repeatedly.

- **Bats** can carry rabies, parasites, and viruses.

- **Chickens and ducks** carry disease-causing bacteria.

- **Reptiles** can transmit salmonella to humans.

- **Parakeets, parrots, macaws, and cockatiels** frequently carry bacteria that cause disease. (Finches and canaries are acceptable for your setting.)

(AAP, APHA, & HRA, 2011)

Monitoring Children's Health Records

You are required to monitor children's health, growth, and development using their health records . Be sure that children are current in their immunizations. The Centers for Disease Control and Prevention (CDC), the American Academy of Pediatrics (AAP), and the American Academy of Family Physicians jointly publish a schedule each year of what immunizations children under the age of 6 years old should receive and when. Visit the CDC website (http://www.cdc.gov/vaccines/schedules/index.html) to access the most recent schedule.

In addition to checking immunization records, check annually that each child complies with your setting and state/federal health standards. These requirements will likely include annual dental and physical exams (with identification of any allergies or other health concerns); entry vision and hearing exams; and developmental screening for developmental delays.

Like all confidential records, keep health records in a locked file cabinet and available to staff only as needed.

Immunizations

For years, concerned parents and other individuals have questioned whether thimerosal—a preservative found in many childhood vaccines—and autism are linked. Thimerosal was "removed or reduced to trace amounts in all childhood vaccines" (except one flu vaccine) in 2001. A 2004 Institute of Medicine (IOM) study concluded, "The evidence favors rejection of a causal relationship between thimerosal-containing vaccines and autism." The CDC supports this conclusion (CDC, 2012a).

Communicating Children's Allergies

If Sam has a wheat allergy, then everyone who encounters him—including early educators, parents, volunteers, and setting staff—should know this information. It is important to keep a record of all known allergies for each child in your setting. Prominently display this information both in your setting and in the food preparation area. Get parental permission beforehand to post this information in your setting, and keep all adults informed. Be sure to review your state/federal standards on handling and communicating children's allergies.

Performing Daily Health Checks

When you conduct a daily health check with each child in your setting, your goal is to determine whether any child is sick and should not attend the setting that day. Sick children may need medical attention and their illnesses could be contagious. Another reason to conduct health checks is to add to your observational data about each child. With your daily records, you can chart children's behavior and physical symptoms over time. If you note changes, talk with the children's parents or health professionals about your concerns. Parents can then determine if their children need treatment.

Though important, these checks take less than a minute to perform properly. Observe children when they arrive at your setting. Ask the children and their parents a few questions. If children usually arrive to the setting alone, set up a system for communicating with their parents about their children's health each morning. You may communicate via e-mail, notes that the child brings to the setting daily, or daily checklists parents fill out and send with their children. Perform the daily health check when you greet children and parents. Remember, the daily health check is not a physical exam. Respect the children, their feelings, and their cultures.

Observe each child when he/she arrives to the setting.

Figure 12. Example of Daily Health Check

1. If children can talk, ask them questions like "How are you today?" and "How are you feeling?"

2. Ask parents questions like: "How is LeShawn today?," "Did he sleep well?," "Are there any changes in his behavior?," and "Is there anything new that I should know about?"

3. Hold children or kneel down to their height to observe them.

- Do they seem different somehow? Listless or clingy? Unusually irritable?

- Check their breathing.

- Listen for coughs.

- Are there any rashes or swelling on their skin?

- Are they scratching their scalps?

- Does their skin look yellowish or pale?

- Are their eyes watering, swollen, or crusty?

- Are they pulling at their ears?

- Does their breath smell fruity or odorous?

- Gently touch children's foreheads or cheeks with the back of your hand. Do they feel feverish or clammy?

Even if children appear fine physically when you greet them in the morning, continue to observe them throughout the day for such things as frequent visits to the bathroom, loss of appetite, scratching, listlessness, or irritability.

Health experts recommend that you keep a record of these daily health checks for a month at a time. You can use a checklist or record notes on paper or electronically. Check your setting requirements to ensure that you are performing and recording daily health checks properly.

Maintaining a healthy setting, monitoring children's health records, and conducting daily health checks are necessary steps for promoting children's health. Your positive actions send children and families the message that you value good health and are dedicated to preserving it.

Responding to Illness

Just because children show symptoms of illness does not mean you should automatically send them home. For example, a fever of 101°F or less could mean the child is overheating or overdressed. The group of pediatricians who wrote Caring for Our Children (AAP, APHA, & HRA, 2011), said that there are only three reasons to exclude a sick child from your setting:

1. The illness prevents the child from participating comfortably in activities.

2. The illness results in a need for care that is greater than the staff can provide without compromising the health and safety of other children.

3. The illness poses a risk of spreading harmful diseases to others.

On the other hand, the following symptoms are serious enough that a child should be sent home (AAP, APHA, & HRA, 2011):

• Fever above 101°F (if taken orally).

• Diarrhea.

• Blood or mucus in stools.

• Vomiting.

• Abdominal pain.

• Mouth sores with drooling.

• Rash with fever or behavioral change.

• Suspected of having contagious conditions such as impetigo, strep throat, head lice, and chickenpox which are easily spread in close and crowded conditions.

Have compassion for sick children. They may be frightened of their symptoms. Find a quiet place away from others where sick children can rest until their parents pick them up. Offer them clear fluids to drink. If you think the illness may be contagious, keep the number of staff exposed to the child to a minimum.

If the staff decides that a child should go home, then contact the child's parents or emergency contact. This is one reason why it is important to have current emergency phone numbers for each child's parents, nearest relative, and the child's medical providers. Please review state/federal standards concerning sick children in your setting. Just as your setting will have specific policies in

Some sick children can remain in the setting and participate in activities.

place concerning when to send sick children home, your setting has also developed policies concerning when these children are allowed to return. The following guidelines are typical (AAP, APHA, & HRA, 2011; Colker, 2009):

- Fever: children may return to the setting after they have been free of fever for 24 hr without the use of fever-reducing medications.

- Uncontrollable diarrhea: children should remain home until diarrhea symptoms are not present for 24 hr.

- Strep throat: children are on antibiotics for 24 hr before returning to the setting.

- Chickenpox: Children's lesions are dry, crusted, fading, and/or disappearing before returning to the setting. This is usually 6 days after the onset of the rash.

- Impetigo: Children are free of weeping lesions. The lesions are covered and medical treatment initiated before returning to the setting.

- Head lice: keep children out of the setting until after the first treatment.

Meeting the Needs of Children With Chronic Illness

There may be children at your setting who are chronically ill. The University of Michigan Health System (UMHS, 2012) defines a chronic illness as a health problem that lasts more than 3 months, affects a child's normal activities, and requires extensive medical care. Based on this definition, UMHS estimates that 15–18% of children living in the United States have chronic illnesses. The following chronic illnesses are most common (UMHS, 2012):

- Asthma.

- Diabetes.

- Cerebral palsy.

- Sickle cell anemia.

- Cystic fibrosis.

- Cancer.

- HIV/AIDS.

- Epilepsy.

- Spina bifida.

- Congenital heart problems.

Healthy

Become knowledgeable about the chronic illnesses of children in your care. Find out what triggers their symptoms. For example, scents from air fresheners or other products in your setting may trigger a child's asthma attack. Although these children need special care, be careful not to limit their activities unnecessarily to keep them from harm. You may undermine the children's self-confidence—and fun. Children with long-term illnesses, like all children, benefit from participating in your full curriculum. If the children receive special services, you will have explicit instructions on how to support their health specialists.

Teaching Safety and Problem-Solving

Four-year-old Samantha has epilepsy, a seizure disorder. It is free-play time, and Samantha is in the dramatic play area, washing a baby doll. Suddenly her body stiffens and she falls to the floor. Her teeth clench and her arms and legs jerk rapidly and rhythmically.

Eduardo rushes toward you. "Samantha needs help," he shouts. Remaining calm, you reassure Eduardo and the other children that Samantha will be okay. You ease Samantha to the floor, ensuring that the area around her is clear. You place a folded blanket from the doll's crib under Samantha's head. Then you turn Samantha gently onto her side to keep her airway clear. Samantha's parents have instructed you not to force her mouth open, hold her tongue, put anything in her mouth, or restrain Samantha's movements.

After a minute, the seizure stops, and Samantha returns to consciousness. You tell her calmly what has happened and that she is okay. You encourage her to rest for a few minutes before she returns to play with the dolls. You fill out an incident report to be shared with Samantha's parents detailing the seizure's time, severity, length, and type.

Whether children have epilepsy, asthma, or other chronic illnesses, remember that they are children first. Their parents will provide you with detailed information that clearly outlines illness triggers (e.g., asthma or a seizure), medications and how to administer them, symptoms that indicate that the illness is worsening or out of control, and what to do in an emergency. Keep this information on an action card in a place you can access easily.

Though their conditions are part of chronically ill infants' or toddlers' daily lives, they understand very little about their illnesses. These children are just beginning to develop a sense of trust and security. Be accessible to them at all times and work to make their days as safe and predictable as possible.

Because of their illnesses, they may feel that they do not fit in with other children. The ongoing need for medical attention can be unsettling and make children feel different from their healthier peers. The unpredictable nature of chronic illness can be frightening to children who yearn for predictability. If a child receives special education services, this too can add to the feeling of being different.

Preschoolers, who are learning to be independent, may find that being sick and having to visit doctors interfere with their desire to be in control. As a result, some chronically ill children may act out and test limits. Try some of the following tactics to help children deal with their frustration, stress, and anger:

Helpful Tips

Some children will resist taking their medicine. Here are some tips to make administering medications easier on you and them:

- Allow children to suck on ice to numb their taste buds.

- Pour liquid medicine along the side of their mouths. Medicine poured down the center of children's palates triggers their gag reflexes.

- Place tablets on the backs of children's tongues to prevent the child from spitting out the medication.

- If the child's pediatrician agrees, combine liquid medicine with strongly flavored food, like pudding, or dilute the medicine in strong-tasting liquid, like cranberry juice.

- Never refer to medicine as "candy." Children should never confuse medication with M&M's® or other treats.

- Do not bargain with children. Although you should be warm and supportive, the bottom line is that children must take their medicine.

(Dixon & Rosas, n.d,)

- Give children some sense of control by offering them choices: "Emily, which medicine would you prefer to take first—the blue pills or the syrup?"

- Provide children play opportunities to calm their emotions (e.g., water or sand play) or act out their fears (e.g., puppets or dramatic play). Dramatic play can be an especially helpful vehicle for helping children deal with negative emotions. Giving sick children an opportunity to play a doctor or nurse puts them in control. For once, they can administer shots and care for a sick doll.

- Teach children stress-reducing techniques such as deep breathing exercises, yoga, meditation, or visualization.

- Read aloud and discuss children's books about dealing with chronic illnesses. The following titles can get you started:

  - *Little Tree: A Story for Children With Serious Medical Problems* by Joyce C. Mills.

  - *Lara Takes Charge (For Kids With Diabetes, their Friends, and Siblings)* by Rocky Lang.

  - *I Have Asthma* by Jennifer Moore-Mallinos.

- Help children understand that they are not the cause of their illnesses and that "being good" will not make them better.

Administering Medication

You are required to take a course in medication administration—taught by a licensed health professional—before you can give children medicine. During this course, you will learn your state and local regulations concerning dispensing medication. Know the side effects of each medication you administer and monitor children closely for these reactions.

Inform parents that any medication their children bring to the setting should be in its original bottle/packaging so that there are no misunderstandings about dosage. This bottle/packaging should be childproof. Confirm that the label includes the following:

- First and last name of the child.

- Name and phone number of the health professional who prescribed the medication.

- Date the prescription was filled.

- Expiration date.

- Specific instructions for administering, storing, and disposing medication.

Health experts recommend that you **check and double-check** that you are giving the child the correct medication and dosage before proceeding. Document the time and amount of medicine you give and any side effects you have witnessed in the child. Fill out a daily medication form and share it with the child's parents. Store the medicine in a locked cabinet, out of children's reach, away from food (especially if stored in the refrigerator), and at the appropriate temperature.

For over-the-counter medications, make sure that a parent has had the child's health provider write down dosage and how often you should administer it. Do not interpret parents' vague instructions, like "Give Sam some medicine if he starts coughing."

Remember to bring emergency medications along when you and the children leave the setting for field trips or other outings. For example, you may care for a child who is highly allergic to bee stings. Ensure that you have the child's auto-injector on your person if you both will be outdoors or on a field trip.

Enabling Children With Special Needs

Enabling all children to participate actively and independently within your setting is one of your daily goals. Adapt your setting's policies, equipment, practices, and routines for children with special needs to ensure their active participation. Ask: How do I need to adapt the setting to ensure successful participation? How do I support each child's feeling of competence? How do I promote peer acceptance? How do I avoid overprotection? (Aronson, 2012).

Under the Individuals with Disabilities Education Act (IDEA), children with the following special needs are often eligible for support services:

- Autism.

- Deaf-blindness.

- Deafness.

- Emotional disturbance.

- Hearing impairment.

- Intellectual disability.

- Multiple disabilities.

- Orthopedic impairment.

- Other health impairment.

- Specific learning disability.

- Speech or language impairment.

- Traumatic brain injury.

- Visual impairment (including blindness).

Some children are eligible for two types of services:

1. Early intervention services. The early intervention program, known as Part C of IDEA, is available in every state, the District of Columbia, and U.S. territories for children under 3 years old. It involves designing and delivering an Individualized Family Service Plan (IFSP) to address the child's unique needs.

2. Special education and related services. These services, available for children 3 years old and older, include specially designed instruction and a wide range of support to address the children's individual needs resulting from a disability. An Individualized Education Program (IEP) will specify the goals and objectives for each child.

If you suspect a child could benefit from any of these services, let the child's parents know that these services are available. Advise parents that assessment and screening may be required and to follow up with their child's physician.

Providing Nutritious Snacks and Meals

As an early educator, you will plan age-appropriate, nutritious meals and snacks for the children in your care. Collaborate with parents and frequently share with them information concerning nutrition, including appropriate ages for weaning and introducing solid foods. Respect each family's practices and values. Also, teach children healthy attitudes about food and eating. Let them know that it is important to eat a variety of nutritious foods in moderation, food helps our bodies grow strong and healthy, and food is not a reward or punishment.

Use food to nourish children's bodies, not to reward or punish them.

Feeding Choices

The American Academy of Pediatrics (AAP) and the American Medical Association (AMA) recommend breast milk for infants from birth to 12 months. Although breast milk defends young infants against allergies, infections, and numerous chronic illnesses, breastfeeding may not be possible for all women. Some women are unable physically to breastfeed or choose not to because of medical considerations or lifestyle. These mothers feed their infants formula. Before these infants' first days in your setting, discuss their feeding patterns and routines with their parents. When you follow these schedules and routines closely in your setting each day, you will ease infants' transitions into your setting and strengthen your relationship with their families. Be attentive and follow infants' cues. For example, infants may make sucking sounds to indicate that they are hungry 20 min before their usual feeding times. Meet infants' needs on demand. Record daily the amount of breast milk, formula, or solids infants consume and the time of each feeding. Share this information with infants' parents.

Storing Breast Milk

Parents should label each breast milk container with their child's name and the date the milk was expressed. Store these containers in the refrigerator or freezer. See Figure 13. for proper guidelines. Do not mix recently expressed breast milk with frozen breast milk. Do not save milk from a used bottle for another feeding.

Figure 13. Storing Breast Milk for Healthy Full-Term Infants

Location	Temperature	Duration	Comments
Countertop, table	Room temperature (up to 77 °F or 25 °C)	6–8 hr	Keep containers covered and cool. (Covering the container with a cool towel may keep milk cooler.)
Insulated cooler bag	5-39 °F or -15-4 °C	24 hr	Keep ice packs in contact with milk containers at all times. Limit opening cooler bag.
Refrigerator	39 °F or 4 °C	5 days	Store milk in the back of the refrigerator.
Freezer			
Freezer compartment of a refrigerator	5 °F or -15 °C	2 weeks	Store milk toward the back of the freezer, where temperature is most constant. Though milk stored for longer durations in the ranges listed is safe, some of the milk lipids will degrade, resulting in lower quality.
Freezer compartment of a refrigerator with separate doors	0 °F or -18 °C	3–6 months	
Chest or upright deep freezer	-4°F or -20°C	6–12 months	

(CDC, 2010)

Thawing Breast Milk Safely

To thaw frozen breast milk, the Centers for Disease Control recommend keeping milk containers in the refrigerator or submerging them in warm water. Do not thaw or heat containers or bottles of breast milk in a microwave oven. These ovens heat the milk unevenly, destroy the milk's nutrients, and cause the container to explode. The hot liquid could scald an infant.

Do not refreeze breast milk once it has thawed (CDC, 2010).

Healthy

Preparing and Storing Infant Formula

Follow the directions on the infant formula container to prepare infants' bottles properly. Room-temperature tap water is safe to use to mix the formula, if your local/state health departments have deemed the tap water in your area safe to drink.

Formula is ready for the infant to consume immediately after you prepare it, without additional refrigeration or warming. The infant should consume the prepared formula—or you should store the prepared, **unused** formula in the refrigerator—within 1 hr. Discard any prepared formula that has remained at room temperature for over 1 hr. If an infant does not consume all the formula in the bottle, discard the unused portion. **Never save used, prepared formula.**

You can prepare formula up to 24 hr ahead, and store it in the refrigerator, preventing the formation of bacteria. Open containers of ready-made formula, concentrated formula, and formula prepared from concentrate can be stored safely in the refrigerator for up to 48 hr (Nemours Foundation, 2013).

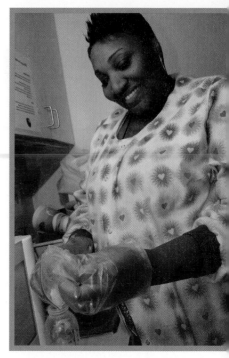

When preparing infant formula, follow the directions written on the formula packaging.

Feeding Infants

Feeding times strengthen your bond with each infant in your care. Wash your hands properly and wear a clean pair of disposable gloves before and after handling breast milk and feeding each infant. To learn infants' unique feeding cues, early educators should feed the same infants each day. For infants who are too young to sit up on their own, hold them in your lap during feedings. Discard the bottle's contents once the infant has finished eating. **Do not save used milk or formula.** Also, discard the contents of any bottle left out of the refrigerator for over 1 hr.

Infants should consume only the breast milk or formula their parents have provided. If an infant drinks from another infant's bottle, notify both sets of parents immediately. Consult your local health department's guidelines concerning HIV exposure in the event that infants consume breast milk from a source other than their families.

Introducing Solid Foods to Infants and Weaning

Experts recommend introducing solid foods to infants who are between 4 and 6 months old. Parents will often decide when to introduce solid foods based on their pediatrician's recommendations. Introducing solid foods or juices to infants too early may cause digestive issues or allergies.

Meal Planning

- Offer children different foods daily.

- Encourage children to choose from a variety of fresh fruits and vegetables.

- Serve low- or no-sugar foods and foods rich in vitamin C, like berries, oranges, cantaloupe, broccoli, and spinach. These foods promote dental health.

- Avoid all processed foods and foods containing artificial additives, coloring, and flavorings.

- Serve foods in small portions. Allow children to have seconds.

- Do not insist that children finish all the food on their plates.

- Reward children with your attention, not food. Using food as a reward (or punishment) forms unhealthy attitudes toward food.

- Involve children in preparing the food they eat.

- Make mealtimes a social affair. Ask questions, lead conversations, and set a pleasant tone.

- Set a good example by trying new foods and making healthy choices children can model.

- Ensure that all young children get 6–8 servings of water daily. Water accounts for a higher percentage of body weight in young children than in adults, so children can quickly dehydrate. Offer water several times a day, even when water fountains or bottled water are visibly available.

Infants' first solid food is usually a semisolid, iron-fortified infant cereal. You can introduce infants between 6 and 8 months to vegetables and fruits. Infants at this age may also be ready for you to wean them from a bottle to a cup. By 8 or 9 months, you can introduce infants to food in one-quarter cubes or lumps that infants can easily mash, chew, or swallow whole. By 12 months, infants are ready to eat most table foods and drink whole (recommended) cow's milk.

Some parents may choose to wait longer to introduce solid foods to their children or wean them from their bottles. Communicate closely with parents to ensure you understand their goals and expectations.

Feeding Toddlers and Preschoolers

In gaining their independence, toddlers are learning and eager to feed themselves. Early educators can reinforce this new independence by providing toddlers with healthy, nutritious meals and snacks and empowering them to adopt positive attitudes toward eating. Establish regular meal and snack times. Offer toddlers smaller amounts of food so that they are not overwhelmed. Offer them seconds when they finish or request more food. Set up a safe, pleasant, and relaxed eating environment to further reinforce toddlers' positive attitudes toward eating.

Toddlers and preschoolers probably receive one or more meals or snacks a day in your setting. Although a trained nutritionist may plan these meals and snacks, know what makes a meal or snack healthy. Ensure that all meals and snacks that you serve contribute to children's nutritional needs. *Dietary Guidelines for Americans* (USDA & HHS, 2010), published by the U.S. Department of Agriculture (USDA) and Health and Human Services (HHS), can help you plan these meals. The guidelines emphasize three major goals:

Healthy

1. Balance calories with physical activity to manage weight.

2. Consume more of certain foods and nutrients, such as fruits, vegetables, whole grains, seafood, and fat-free and low-fat dairy products.

3. Eat fewer foods with sodium (salt), saturated fats, trans fats, cholesterol, added sugars, and refined grains.

Visit www.choosemyplate.gov to explore USDA dietary information and food plans for young children. Use this interactive website as a tool for planning menu items and portion size for children.

Cut food into small pieces before serving it to young children. The younger the child, the smaller the pieces should be to prevent choking. For example, slice hotdogs lengthwise and then into smaller pieces. Cut sandwiches into fourths so that children may help themselves to manageable portions. Finely cube fruit, such as pears and apples.

Figure 14. Tips on Starting a Nutritional Program in Your Setting

❑ Meet all state, local, and setting guidelines for food selection and preparation.

❑ Post a list of children's food allergies—in all staff and children's home languages—in both the food preparation area and in the setting.

❑ Maintain excellent communication with families.

❑ Be aware of the general health of infants and toddlers in your care and be attentive to their needs.

❑ Plan menus in advance and share them with children's families in their home languages.

❑ Serve foods that represent a variety of cultural preferences, especially family favorites.

❑ Respect dietary restrictions and family preferences.

❑ Scale plates, cups, utensils, and serving pieces to children's size. Provide children with physical disabilities access to adaptive plates, cups, and utensils to help them eat independently.

❑ Encourage parents to pack healthy foods for their child daily. These foods should be low in sugar and salt and should not contain unnecessary chemical additives, artificial coloring, and flavoring. For celebrations or cooking experiences, encourage parents to bring these same kinds of foods.

❑ Establish a relaxed mealtime and feeding routine that makes eating or drinking a bottle a pleasant experience for each child.

Children with special needs typically have the same nutritional needs as other children. Modify the texture and consistency of certain foods for children who have difficulty chewing, swallowing, or feeding themselves. Also, check children's health records and be aware of conditions, such as food allergies and digestive or metabolic problems, when planning meals. A qualified nutritionist can help you plan for meeting these needs.

See Figure 14. for a checklist with tips on starting a nutritional program.

Dining Family Style

Mealtimes are opportunities to promote toddlers' and preschoolers' physical, social-emotional, cognitive, and language development. During meals, children make decisions and share. They also learn good manners, responsibility, how to communicate with others, and how food nourishes their bodies. Their participation during mealtimes—whether they are eating or setting the table—helps develop their eye–hand coordination, muscle control, and overall independence. Family-style dining reinforces these skills in children.

When children dine family style, they eat in their classroom, enjoy all the same foods, and participate in conversation. Children serve themselves (if able) and decide their portions, which makes them more likely to try new foods. Staff sits at the tables with the children, and parents who are present are invited to join.

Plan food-related activities around these meals to increase children's knowledge of food and nutrition and establish sound, long-term, and positive food habits and attitudes. For example, you and the children may shop for food and prepare it together. Help them set the table or make place mats or centerpieces. Children can also learn from other activities, like field trips, tasting parties, preparing their own food, planting and growing food, reading aloud books about food, dramatic play, making scrapbooks and exhibits, feeding classroom pets, and planning menus to share with parents. Use food-related activities to teach language arts, color, texture, math, science, social skills, and hygiene.

While dining family style, encourage conversation on topics that will interest the children.

Figure 15. Tips for Family-Style Dining

- Plan to seat four to six children and one adult at each table.

- Leave tables in the learning centers instead of moving them to a central location.

- Wash, rinse, and sanitize all tables properly before and after eating.

- Encourage all adults who join a table group—whether staff, parents, or volunteers—to model appropriate manners, promote self-help skills, and engage children in conversation.

- Assign children responsibility for setting the table, bringing food to the table, and cleaning the table.

- Serve food in child-sized bowls and platters with child-sized serving utensils.

- Serve drinks, including milk, from small pitchers (not cartons) so children can serve themselves.

- Avoid serving salt and sugar.

- Seat all of the children before allowing anyone to begin eating. Table groups, however, need only wait for everyone at their table to be seated.

- Invite children to begin passing the food clockwise.

- Encourage children to serve themselves only as much as they can eat. However, if they take too much food, don't force them to finish.

- Ask children who do not want to eat a certain food to take one bite to try. Do not push them to eat more.

- Maintain a leisurely dining pace so children do not feel hurried.

- Encourage conversation about the foods served, the day's events, or other topics of interest to the children.

- Have children clean up their own spills.

- Allow children to leave the table when finished. They can clear their dishes, wash their hands, brush their teeth, and get ready for nap time. Allow slower eaters to take their time.

- Ask the children to help clean up and wipe down the tables using a wet cloth and soapy water. Children should not use the bleach solution.

- Spray the tables with the bleach solution once the tables have been wiped.

Support children's fine-motor-skill development by teaching them to open food containers. Allow older toddlers and preschoolers to open their lunch bags or lunch boxes on their own and remove the contents. Provide water and milk in small pitchers and cups so that older children can serve themselves.

Snacking

Keep snacks available to children throughout the day. These snacks should contribute to the children's total daily nutritional needs according to USDA guidelines. Choose snack foods that contribute not only to the children's nutrient needs but also to good dental health. Serve high-fat snacks (under a nutritionist's recommendation) to children struggling to maintain weight. Serve low-cholesterol snacks to children with documented high cholesterol levels. Avoid sweets.

Display dated menus (in families' home languages) in the classroom. Identify specific food items—for example, specify "orange juice" rather than "fruit juice." Any substitutions should be indicated on the menus.

Research shows that children who participate in preparing their own foods are more motivated to eat them than are children who do not help with preparation. To help older toddlers and preschoolers prepare their own snacks, provide recipe cards with pictorial instructions. Children can also consult a posted picture menu and sign a snack sheet to record that they have had a snack.

Learning Good Health Practices

When children are infants, they need adults to feed them, put them down for naps, and attend to their personal hygiene. As they grow, adults begin to transfer these self-help responsibilities to the child. Empowering children to learn about and do these things on their own helps them become independent and teaches them problem-solving and decision-making skills. It also builds children's competence and confidence.

As an early educator, model and teach children healthy habits that will last a lifetime. There are a number of skills you can work on with children, such as handwashing, eating, drinking, toothbrushing, sneezing and coughing, toileting, and napping.

For the very youngest children, like Michael for example, start talking about these routines as you perform them. Explain to him, "I'm going to put you in your crib now, Michael, since you're starting to fall asleep. Getting rest is very important for both your body and your mind." As he grows, begin involving him in helping you with the task. "Michael, can you hold the other end of the blanket and help me put it on your mat, please? Why don't you get your stuffed bear, Mr. B, out of your cubby and bring him to your mat for nap time?" By the time he is a preschooler, Michael will be able to follow your step-by-step directions and get his mat out on his own to ready himself for nap time.

One excellent way to help children master self-help skills is through dramatic play. Children can feed their baby doll, put her to bed, brush her teeth, and comb her hair—doing for the doll all the tasks they need to learn to do for themselves. They also learn by mimicking you and your colleagues as you model washing your hands and sneezing into your elbow. In just a few short years, children will move from being totally dependent on adults to feeding themselves when they are hungry, putting themselves down to nap when they are tired, and using the bathroom.

Healthy

Handwashing

There is no other health practice more important than handwashing. Consider these facts:

- Handwashing can reduce the risk of respiratory infections by 16%.

- Washing hands with soap and water could reduce diarrheal disease-associated deaths by up to 50%.

- Researchers estimate that if all individuals routinely washed their hands, 1 million deaths could be prevented each year (CDC, 2011b).

Give children lots of practice handwashing.

Caring for Our Children (AAP, APHA, & HRA, 2011) recommends that children and staff wash their hands at these times during the day:

- Upon arrival for the day or when moving from one group setting to another.

- Whenever hands look dirty.

- Before and after

    - handling food,

    - feeding a child,

    - eating,

    - providing medication or first aid,

    - diapering an infant or toddler, and

    - playing in water used by more than one child.

- After

    - helping a child use the toilet or a potty seat;

    - using the toilet;

    - wiping children's noses or mouths;

    - handling bodily fluids (e.g., mucus, blood, urine, vomit, feces, saliva) or clothes soiled by bodily fluids;

    - assisting a sick child;

    - sneezing;

    - coughing;

- blowing your nose or assisting a child in doing so;

- handling pets, pet waste, pet toys, and cages;

- playing in the sandbox;

- cleaning and sanitizing surfaces;

- handling garbage and changing the trash can liner; and

- playing outdoors.

You can best teach children to wash their hands by modeling the procedure. Help them try out the task, narrating the steps as you go. Have children sing the "Happy Birthday" song twice to time their handwashing. Supervise them when they try doing the task by themselves. Ensure that the water temperature is warm—not cold—to get children to rinse their hands thoroughly.

Praise children when they can do the task on their own. Give them lots of practice, reminding them that it's time to wash their hands after they come in from outside or before they eat a snack. Offer children opportunities to wash their dolls' hands in water play or pretend to wash a stuffed animal's hands during a make-believe picnic. Read aloud and discuss such books as *Why Do I Wash My Hands?* by Angela Royston.

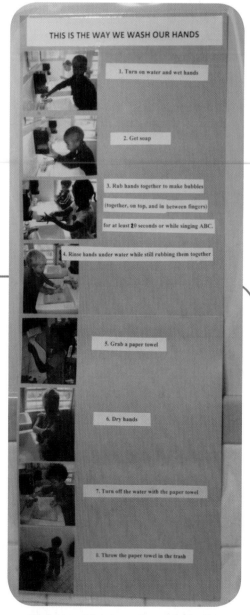

Figure 16. The Steps of Proper Handwashing

1. Adjust faucet so that water is at a warm, comfortable temperature and moisten hands.

2. Apply liquid soap from a dispenser to hands.

3. Vigorously rub hands to form soapy lather. Wash the backs of hands, wrists, between fingers, and under nails. Rub for at least 20 seconds—the time it takes to sing the "Happy Birthday" song twice.

4. Rinse.

5. Dry hands with a paper towel.

6. Use paper towel to turn off faucet. Discard paper towel.

Use visuals to reinforce the steps for proper handwashing.

Coughing, Sneezing and Nose Blowing

Prevent colds in your setting by keeping the room temperature at 70 °F or slightly lower. If your setting climate is dry during the winter months, use a cool mist humidifier. Clean and disinfect this humidifier daily. However, coughing, sneezing, and nose-blowing can occur even when children display no signs of illness or infection.

Care for Infants

Keep infants with stuffy noses upright so that mucus will drain away from their ears. Infants may not be able to blow their noses. You can use a soft, rubber bulb with a soft, narrow tip to suck out (aspirate) mucus for them. Ask parents to bring in an individual aspirator for their infant, and use it only for that child. Wash your hands before and after using the aspirator. To clean inside the aspirator, submerge the tip in warm, soapy water and squeeze the bulb. Shake the soapy water inside the bulb before squeezing. Rinse well by repeating the process several times with clear, warm water. Suspend the syringe, tip side down, in a glass to dry. Do not allow multiple aspirators to touch. Label and store aspirators properly.

Assisting Toddlers and Preschoolers When They Cough, Sneeze, and Blow Their Noses

By about 2 years old, most children can blow their noses successfully and are coughing/sneezing into either a tissue or their elbow. Remind them when they lapse and acknowledge their healthy behaviors when they remember. However, some older children still may have trouble blowing their noses. Teach them how by holding one of their nostrils shut and getting them to breathe through the other. Help toddlers who have just learned how to blow their own nose by holding the tissue for them. Most children delight in copying their early educator and parents. When they see you doing this for them, they will learn to do it on their own.

Figure 17. Coughing and Sneezing Healthily

- Cover your nose and mouth with a tissue. Afterward, discard the tissue and wash your hands.
- Cough or sneeze into your inner elbow. Wash your hands afterward.

Model these practices and gently remind children of them. With practice, this will become part of your routine and theirs.

Enforcing Proper Dental and Oral Care

Dental decay is the number one chronic disease of children. This disease is painful, can lead to other illnesses, and can even affect learning. Almost half (48%) of 4-year-olds in Massachusetts suffer from tooth decay. As a result, the state passed a law in 2010 requiring that children who eat meals at state-licensed child care centers have their teeth brushed (Santos, 2010).

Children learn about toothbrushing even before they have teeth. When you wash your hands then wipe infants' gums with a soft cloth, you are not only maintaining infants' oral health, but you are teaching them that it is important to keep their mouths clean. When their first teeth appear and you brush them with a soft toothbrush and a tiny dab of toothpaste, these children see this process two or three times daily. By the time these children are toddlers, you can narrate the process, describing how you brush both sides of their teeth to make sure they are clean. Explain to them the relationship between food and dental health and that sweets cause tooth decay.

Preschoolers can learn to brush their own teeth with supervision. Show them how, step by step:

1. Moisten the child-sized toothbrush.

2. Apply a pea-sized dab of fluoride toothpaste to the bristles.

3. Start with the upper left back teeth. Clean all of the front teeth in a circular motion, moving clockwise.

4. Repeat the same procedure with the bottom teeth, starting with the lower left teeth.

5. Brush the backside of all teeth.

6. Brush the tongue.

7. Have children rinse their teeth with water and spit.

The entire process should last 2–3 min. Bring in a timer to let them see that this is probably a longer process than they realize. After watching you go through the steps, gradually transfer responsibility for the task to them. Let children narrate the steps for you, explaining how they position the toothbrush to clean their teeth and gums.

In time, children will know to retrieve their toothbrushes and brush their teeth after snacks and meals. Instead of using the sink, give each child a paper cup of water. They can use it to wet their toothbrushes, rinse their teeth, and spit before discarding. When children consume meals or snacks outside the setting, give them cups of water to rinse and spit with before discarding.

Although children should already be seeing a dentist regularly, having one as a guest in the setting may make these visits a lot less frightening. Incorporate dental care into your setting activities. Allow children to practice their brushing technique on a model tooth. Help them use puppets to brush other puppets' teeth or set up a dental office in the dramatic play area. Make charts that track which children in the setting have lost teeth. Read books aloud, like *Riley's Lost Tooth* by Diane Cantrell, and ask children to compare their experiences to those of the little girl in the story.

Early educators should also keep their teeth and gums healthy with regular toothbrushing. Bacteria from active tooth decay can be transmitted to infants in your care.

Toileting

Diapering Infants

Change infants' diapers soon after they are wet to prevent diaper dermatitis (diaper rash). Diaper changes give early educators the chance to begin familiarizing children with diapering. Talk to infants about what you are doing throughout the process. Set a gentle, calm, and unhurried tone for them. When you are gentle, nurturing, and relaxed, infants learn that their early educator respects their body and that body waste is a natural part of life. During this one-on-one time, early educators can strengthen their bond with each child.

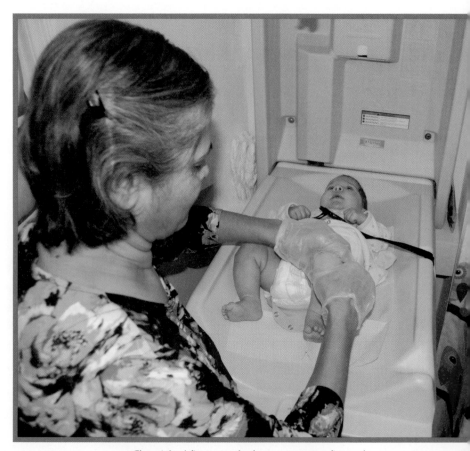

However, diapering and toileting carry distinct health risks for children and adults. Diligence in frequent, proper handwashing; sanitizing the changing area; and good personal hygiene habits are the first line of defense against the spread of infectious diseases caused by fecal contamination. Use the following diaper-changing steps as a daily safety reminder:

1. Get organized.

* Before you bring children to the diaper-changing area, wash your hands.

Change infants' diapers soon after they are wet to prevent diaper rash.

- Gather your materials:
  - nonabsorbent paper liner (large enough to cover the sanitized changing surface from the child's shoulders to below the child's feet);
  - fresh diaper;
  - clean clothes (if needed);
  - wipes (removed from the container);
  - plastic bag (for soiled clothes);
  - disposable gloves (optional); and
  - diaper cream (if the child uses it).
- Place a dab of diaper cream on a corner of the disposable paper.
- Put on the disposable gloves (optional).

2. Carry children to the changing table, keeping soiled clothing away from you.

- If children's feet and clothing cannot be kept out of diapers during the changing process, completely remove their shoes, socks, and other clothing items so that they do not contaminate them.
- Place any soiled clothes in the plastic bag, and tie it securely so that parents can transport it home safely.

3. Clean children's diaper areas.

- Place children on the diaper-changing surface, and unfasten the diapers. Leave soiled diaper under children.
- Always keep one hand on children while they are on the changing table.
- Use disposable wipes to clean children's bottoms. Remove stool and urine from front to back. Use as many wipes as needed, ensuring that you always wipe from front to back to prevent spreading bacteria.
- Place soiled wipes into the soiled diaper or directly into a plastic-lined, hands-free, covered can. (This covered can should have a step pedal.)

4. Remove the soiled diaper. Avoid contaminating other surfaces.

- Fold the soiled diaper inward.
- Place the soiled diaper into the plastic-lined step can.
- If children are wearing reusable cloth diapers, place soiled cloth diapers and their covers in plastic bags to give to children's parents or a laundry service. Do not rinse or wash the contents. Emptying and rinsing soiled diapers poses the greatest health risk for early educators and children.

Healthy

- Check for spills under children. If there are any, fold over the disposable paper under the children's feet so that a fresh unsoiled paper surface is now under their clean bottoms.
- If you wore disposable gloves, remove them and place them into the plastic-lined step can. Do not perform other tasks while wearing these gloves, as it poses a health and safety risk to you and the children.
- Clean your hands and the children's. Use separate disposable wipes for these tasks. Place the wipes into the plastic-lined step can.

5. Put clean diapers on the children and dress them.

- Apply any necessary ointments or creams to children's diaper areas.
- Note and report any skin problems, such as redness.
- Slide fresh diapers under the children and adjust and fasten the diapers. For cloth diapers, place your hand between the children and the diapers when inserting the pin.

6. Wash children's hands and return them to a supervised area.

- Use soap and water at a sink to wash the children's hands, if possible. If not, use the following method:
    - Wipe the children's hands with a damp paper towel or a clean disposable wipe.
    - Discard the towel or the wipe into the plastic-lined step can.

7. Clean and sanitize the diaper changing surface.

- Place the paper liner you used on the diaper changing surface in the plastic-lined step can.
- Clean any visible soil from the changing surface with water and soap or detergent.
- Spray a bleach solution to wet the entire changing surface. (See Figure 10. of your *Essentials* textbook to learn the new guidelines for preparing bleach solution.)
- Store the bleach solution properly.
- Leave the bleach sanitizer on the diaper changing surface for at least 2 min. Wipe the surface dry or air dry.

8. Wash your hands. Record diaper changes children's daily logs.

- Wash your hands using soap and warm water.
- Use a paper towel to turn off the faucet.
- Use hand lotion to keep your hands moisturized.
- Describe the contents of diapers and any problems such as diarrhea, an unusual odor, blood in the stool, or any skin irritations in children's daily logs.

Learning about Toileting

Children are ready for toilet training when they reach the ages of 2–3 years old. Toilet training is one of children's major developmental milestones that will test and enhance their cognitive, social, emotional, and physical skills. Work with the child's parents to determine the best method of toileting for their child.

Toddlers should feel good about themselves, their bodies, and their accomplishments— particularly during toilet training. Parents' and early educators' encouragement and patience are crucial for children to develop successful skills and attitudes concerning toileting.

NEVER rush, shame, tease, or punish children while you are toilet training them. Instead, encourage toilet learning when children are mature enough. Help them feel good about their bodies and growing up. Remember that children will have accidents while learning this new skill. **However, praise and encouragement are much more effective than ridicule.**

What words should you use when you talk about toileting? Some experts suggest you use only terms such as urinate and bowel movement. On the other hand, some parents and children are more comfortable with terms like pee-pee, tinkle, go potty, or poop. Respect parents' wishes for what they want to call toileting functions. Try to be flexible and accept terms that are not offensive. Children in a group will generally all start using the same word—especially one that is fun to say.

When children use offensive terms in your setting, speak with them privately and calmly. For example, explain, "We don't use words like that here. Those words offend some people." Usually, children will use such language less often if you ignore it.

Toileting Preschoolers

Preschoolers in your care will most likely be fully toilet trained and ready to use the bathroom independently. Make them feel comfortable about going to the bathroom whenever they need to. Girls and boys can share the facilities; closed stalls provide them privacy.

Again, accidents happen. However, you can help children recover from these accidents calmly and respectfully. Explain to children that these accidents are common, but they will happen less and less frequently as the children grow. Tell them not to be ashamed. Help them get clean, change their clothes, and wash their hands.

Bathroom stalls provide children privacy.

Healthy

Encouraging children to reenact bathroom habits with dolls and puppets may be helpful. Read books like *Who's in the Bathroom?* by Jeanne Willis and *Everyone Poops* by Taro Gomi that will make children feel more confident about their need to use the toilet.

Learning About Their Bodies

Bathroom time is an opportunity for preschoolers to see how their bodies work and learn the names of body parts. Children are naturally curious, so let them know that this curiosity is normal. Speak to them in a matter-of-fact tone to help them learn more about their bodies. Answer their questions with factual information that they can understand developmentally. Do not panic when children begin noticing the bodily differences between boys and girls. Again, keep the conversation factual, at the child's level, and wholly unemotional.

Discovering Gender Differences

Ms. Duncan is in the bathroom with 3-year-old Keisha. "Larry's a boy," Keisha tells Ms. Duncan after 3-year-old Larry walks out of a stall, washes his hands, and leaves the bathroom.

"Yes, Larry's a boy," Ms. Duncan says, wary of the conversation's direction.

"Do you know how I know Larry's a boy?" Keisha asks.

"No, Keisha, how do you know Larry's a boy?" Ms. Duncan asks cautiously.

"Because Larry's a boy's name!" Keisha says proudly.

Nap Time

Nap time is a key component of a child's day in your setting. Sleep directly impacts children's cognitive and physical development.

Plan this time just as you would plan the curriculum. Create a calming transition, such as a particular song or rhyme, to let the children know that it is now time to prepare for nap time. Children must have their own cribs, mats, or cots to rest on. Infants will have unique sleeping and feeding schedules, so follow their individual rhythms. Toddlers and preschoolers who choose not to sleep should perform quiet activities like reading and assembling puzzles.

Keep cribs 3 ft apart. If a child uses the same crib daily, clean this crib weekly. Cribs should be free of Plexiglas® partitions. Clean and sanitize each crib before a different child uses it. Clean and disinfect any crib parts, such as railings, that children can mouth.

Place toddlers' and preschoolers' cots/mats at least 3 ft apart. Mats should be at least 2 in. thick, waterproof, washable, and appropriate for the size and weight of the children. Position children head to toe on these mats during nap time. If different children use the same cots/mats, clean and sanitize each of them after each use.

Children should not share bedding. Wash bedding weekly or whenever soiled. Between uses, store bedding in a labeled bag or the child's cubby. Children's bedding should not touch.

Partnering With Families

Collaborate with parents to ensure that their children receive similar, consistent health messages in your setting and at home. For example, if parents do not enforce proper handwashing practices at home, then children will question the value of taking personal responsibility for this habit. It's vital, therefore, that you and the children's parents agree on an approach to keeping their children healthy.

Help to forge a bond with families by sharing all of your policies with them in their home languages, including the following:

- Expectations for health visits and immunizations.
- Daily health checks.
- Sick child policy (when children are sent home/when they can return).
- Incident reports.
- Caring for children who are chronically ill.
- Medication policy.
- Food and nutrition practices.
- Handwashing policy.
- Personal hygiene practices (sneezing, coughing, blowing nose, tooth brushing, toileting).
- Child abuse reporting policies.
- Maintenance of health records and safeguards for privacy.

Some families need help locating appropriate health resources, such as a community health clinic or a pediatrician who speaks their home language. Check to see if you have this information on file to share with parents. If not, consult the health staff in your setting or ask your supervisor for assistance in finding appropriate referrals.

Keep phone numbers on file for the following people and places:

- Family members authorized to pick up each child, in the order staff should contact them in case of an emergency. Keep both landline and cell numbers for these individuals.

- Each child's medical health providers, including specialists.

- Each child's dentist.

- The preferred hospital each child should be taken to in an emergency.

Parents need to know that they will be called as soon as staff determines that their child is too sick or contagious to remain in your setting's care. Tell them that you will call 911 and have their child transported to the hospital in a medical emergency. Reassure them that staff will never make any decisions regarding their child's treatment without first consulting them. Although you are parents' partners in caring for their children, they are the ones who are ultimately responsible for their children's well-being.

Figure 18. Troubleshooting as a Team

Mackenzie, a 3-year-old, has been toilet trained since she was 2 years old. However, she is suddenly having frequent toileting accidents. She does not know why this is happening. Your setting has remained consistent, and Mackenzie's behavior offers no clues. However, when you speak to her parents, you learn that they are adopting a baby and Mackenzie is not excited. She may feel that her parents are spending too much time and energy on preparing to welcome the new baby into their lives and not enough time with Mackenzie.

Could her accidents be her way of gaining more attention? Share your theory with her parents and work together to rectify the situation.

Consider planning parent workshops during the year to address relevant, health-related issues, like a workshop that advises parents on how to choose healthy meals and snacks. During this workshop, share with families your nutritional goals for their children and how you plan menus. Help parents understand what foods are healthy to bring to the setting or send for their child to eat.

Here are some additional topic ideas for parent workshops:

- Explain why family-style dining is an effective tool for teaching toddlers and preschoolers self-help skills and good food habits.

- Help parents understand that involving children in food preparation makes them motivated to want to eat the food. Show them how to make picture-based recipe cards that they can use in cooking with their children. Stress that cooking teaches literacy, math, fine-motor, and science skills.

- Involve families in creating a classroom cookbook featuring family favorites.

- Discuss head lice outbreaks—especially after they occur. Ask a nurse or other health care worker to be present. Make sure everyone gets the message that head lice, hygiene, and wealth are unrelated. Let parents know what you are doing in the setting to eliminate head lice and what they should do at home. Organize a group clean-up day to launder linens and vacuum stuffed animals.

- Brainstorm hygiene and sanitation practices to prevent or curb the spread of flu in the setting. Get parents' approval to have a pediatrician or nurse administer flu shots to children and staff.

Teaming with parents makes your job easier. Working together keeps their children healthy.

Identifying/Reporting Child Abuse and Neglect

According to the Children's Defense Fund, 750,000 children are abused or neglected each year in the United States. That is one child every 42 seconds. Children who suffer abuse and neglect suffer side effects beyond the abuse—including behavioral problems, learning difficulties, low self-esteem, and abusiveness toward others (Karageorge & Kendall, 2008).

Identifying and reporting child abuse is never easy, but your actions can save a child's life. Prepare for this challenge by doing the following:

- Learn the signs of abuse and neglect and be keen to them.

- Make sure children feel comfortable talking to adults and expressing their feelings in your setting.

- Share with children's parents clear policies on handling abuse. Write them in the families' home languages.

- Know how to report any suspicions in accordance with your setting's policies and state law.

- Be an advocate for children.

Identifying Abuse

Karageorge and Kendall (2008) explain four types of maltreatment:

- **Physical abuse** includes any nonaccidental physical injury, including burning, beating, biting, kicking, hitting, or punching a child. Children under 5 years old are at the greatest risk of injury or death from physical abuse.

- **Sexual abuse** includes any sexual behavior with a child. It also includes commercial exploitation of a child through pornographic photos and films.

- **Psychological maltreatment,** sometimes called emotional abuse, involves belittling, rejecting, isolating, and terrorizing children. It also includes passive-aggressive behaviors toward a child, in which the adult expresses his or her anger at the child indirectly.

- **Neglect** involves omissions of care that result in harm to the child. There are at least seven types of neglect:

  - **physical neglect:** abandonment or failure to meet children's basic nutritional, clothing, or hygiene needs;

  - **medical neglect:** failure to meet children's medical and dental needs when resources are available;

  - **inadequate supervision:** exposing children to hazards or leaving children in the care of someone who does not or cannot appropriately care for them;

  - **environmental neglect:** exposing children to unsanitary or hazardous living conditions;

  - **emotional neglect:** failure to meet children's needs for affection and attention;

  - **educational neglect:** failure to meet children's needs for education and schooling; and

  - **newborns' addiction/exposure to drugs:** exposing unborn children to drugs, causing them to be born with addiction or the side effects of drugs.

Abuse and neglect may involve one incident or a pattern of ongoing behavior. Some signs of abuse and neglect are obvious, such as unexplained bruises, burns, or broken bones. Look for these physical signs that might indicate a child is being abused:

- **Signs of physical abuse:** extensive and frequent bruises, especially in areas of the body that wouldn't be hurt in an accidental fall, such as the abdomen, head, neck, backs of legs, and genitals. Other signs can include burns, bite marks, bald spots on the scalp, or dental injuries.

- **Signs of sexual abuse:** pain when walking, running, or sitting; problems with urination; pain/itching or discharge in the genital area.

- **Signs of psychological maltreatment:** eating problems, sleeping problems, bed-wetting, self-abusive behaviors such as head banging and hair pulling.

- **Signs of neglect:** height and weight significantly below normal expectations, poor hygiene, wearing inappropriate clothing for the weather, fatigue and sleepiness.

Other kinds of abuse, such as psychological maltreatment and neglect, may have no outward signs. Behavioral changes may be your only clue. Children may seem overly afraid of upsetting their parents or have sudden crying jags. Perhaps a lively girl may suddenly withdraw from everyone around her. A boy who is always happy to greet his mother at the end of the day may freeze and cry suddenly when his aunt arrives at the setting. Children may act out their feelings during play. A child may involve two dolls in sexual gestures. Or during a puppet show, the "father" puppet may start vigorously beating the "little boy" puppet.

Communicating Abuse

Tomas, a 5-year-old, is a quiet, shy child. He never spends much time in the art center, but today he paints a picture entirely in black and brown.

Ms. Turner: "Tomas, can you tell me about your painting, please?"

Tomas: "The daddy had to spank the little boy with his belt."

Ms. Turner: "I don't understand why he had to do that."

Tomas: "Because the little boy wouldn't listen."

Ms. Turner: "I hope the little boy wasn't hurt."

Tomas: "He has to learn to be good."

Ms. Turner: "Does the little boy know that he can talk to his mother or his teacher about this problem? No one should be hurting him this way."

Tomas does not answer Ms. Turner's question and walks toward the block area.

Ms. Turner knows to monitor Tomas's behavior carefully for other signs that Tomas may be a victim of abuse. She will speak with her supervisor about the situation and follow state law requirements.

Reporting Abuse

Early educators residing and practicing in the United States and all U.S. territories are legally required to report suspected abuse. Proof of abuse is not required legally; suspicion is all you need to file a report. Waiting for proof leaves a child at risk for further abuse or neglect. However, because not all suspicions will be confirmed as actual abuse, the law protects people who report abuse in good faith. Legally, early educators cannot be sued or prosecuted. **Do not let fear stop you from reporting abuse.**

You also have an ethical responsibility to report your suspicions. The National Association for the Education of Young Children (NAEYC, 2011) states the following in Principle 1.8 of its *Code of Ethical Conduct and Statement of Commitment*:

> We shall be familiar with the risk factors for and symptoms of child abuse and neglect, including physical, sexual, verbal, and emotional abuse and physical, emotional, educational, and medical neglect. We shall know and follow state laws and community procedures that protect children against abuse and neglect.

Check your setting's policy regarding how and to whom you should report abuse. This policy should be explicit. Share the policy with parents in their home languages at the start of the year.

Identifying and reporting abuse is only the beginning. No matter what the situation's outcome may be, you are obligated to inform the family that you and the rest of the setting's staff are there to support, not condemn, them. Your objective is to keep the children in your setting safe and healthy. Be patient and support these families once treatment plans are established. Reassure parents that everything regarding their child and their family will remain confidential. ■

Chapter 3

Learning Environment

CDA Functional Area 3: Candidate organizes and uses relationships, the physical space, materials, daily schedule, and routines to create a secure, interesting, and enjoyable environment that promotes engagement, play, exploration, and learning of all children including children with special needs.

Learning Environment

Introduction

The learning environment you create within your setting is the foundation for children's growth and development. This environment comprises the setting itself (indoors, outdoors, and all materials and equipment); the people within the setting (early educators, children, parents, volunteers, administrators and visitors); and any routines and schedules you establish within the setting. How this environment is configured directly impacts children's mastery of social, emotional, cognitive, and physical and language skills.

In this chapter, you will learn how the following critical elements work together to create an effective learning environment:

- Designing the Indoor Setting.
- Selecting Appropriate Materials.
- Planning Curricula for Children.
- Developing the Daily Schedule.
- Implementing the Daily Schedule

Designing the Indoor Setting

The configuration of your indoor setting influences what and how children learn and offers them rich and meaningful early learning experiences. When you begin thinking about this configuration, ask: How do children think and behave at various ages and stages of development? How can my setting support children's learning and developmental needs? Questions like these will help you translate what you know about the children who use your setting into a working design plan.

Indoor Settings for Infants and Toddlers

A well-planned indoor setting for infants and toddlers uses color and design effectively to create a calm, playful, and home-like space that makes the children and their families feel welcome. The ideal indoor setting is stimulating (not overwhelming) and designates areas for play and routines, like diapering, toileting, feeding, napping, and dressing. The indoor space should also incorporate elements of children's home cultures effortlessly. The following tips will help you design your indoor setting according to how children will use it:

- Arrange the indoor setting so that all children are visible at all times.

Include comfortable seating throughout the space, like soft chairs, sofas, and gliders.

- Choose floor surfaces, such as carpeting or vinyl, according to how children will use the area.

- Identify areas for routines and experiences and think strategically about their placement. For example, choose the quietest areas to arrange cribs for nap time.

- Define areas that need protection, like areas where infants will play on the floor.

- Create a variety of areas for mobile infants and toddlers to explore.

For young infants in particular, the Early Head Start National Resource Center (2010) suggests creating a "YES" indoor setting. In other words, ensure that everything infants can reach is safe and acceptable for them to use. These infants require soft, comfortable areas throughout the setting and a variety of views. They need several protected areas where they can see setting activity from the floor. Place soft toys within infants' reach, and hang photos at their eye level on the wall or near their cribs. Design areas for infants to explore, be creative, engage in parallel play, or have quiet time. Include comfortable seating throughout the space, like soft chairs and gliders, for adults to sit on while holding the infants.

Mobile infants, on the other hand, need "YES"-protected areas where they can crawl, climb, pull themselves up, and walk. Their areas should include sturdy furniture with rounded edges; low, secure railings for them to pull up on as they attempt to stand; and low dividers so that adults and infants can see each other as the infants move around and explore freely. Mobile infants' areas should also include appropriate seating and spaces for eating and other routines. They also need areas designed for exploration, parallel play, creativity, language, and quiet time.

Toddlers have some of the same needs of an indoor setting as mobile infants. However, you may need to adjust the design to keep toddlers challenged and engaged. Define toddler areas for creating art, pretend and parallel play, music experiences, sand and water, books and stories, puzzles, blocks, and toys.

Your setting should be large enough to accommodate the wider range of activities in which children will engage.

Learning Environment

Planning Preschool Indoor Settings for Play

Ensure that the play area for preschoolers is stimulating (not overwhelming) by dividing it into learning centers (defined areas where specific learning activities occur). Learning centers are designed specifically to support learning through play and help children progress to more challenging tasks. These centers allow children to choose interesting activities and concentrate on them for extended periods of time. Learning centers provide room for children to play in pairs, small groups, or alone.

While creating these centers, consider the children's interests. Make a list of possible learning centers and think about the learning opportunities these centers will provide. How will these centers—and the stimulating, varied materials that accompany them—help to develop the children's social, emotional, cognitive, and physical development? Will the centers support the children's content learning in areas like language, literacy, mathematics, science, technology, social studies, and art?

Remember, there is no standardized list of learning centers or stringent requirements for what to call them. However, to help you begin thinking about the best learning centers for your indoor setting, here is a suggested list from the National Association for the Education of Young Children (NAEYC) used in its publication for preschool teachers, Teaching Young Children:

- Blocks
- Art
- Literacy
- Dramatic Play
- Music & Movement
- Science
- Math & Manipulatives
- Sand Play/Water Play
- Cooking
- Outdoors (See Figure 23. for tips on setting up your outdoor setting.)

When you have finalized the list of learning centers your setting will include, use chart paper to make a plan for your room. This blueprint will help you visualize where you will place each learning center and its furnishings and equipment. Though you may realize during planning that your indoor space is less than ideal, discover how you can make the most out of the space. For example, you may be

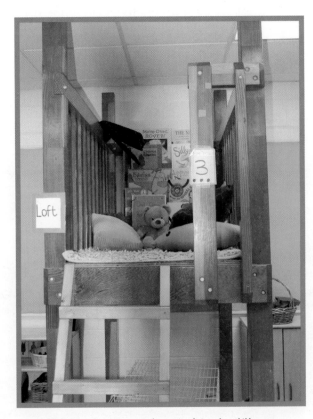

Work cozy places into your indoor-setting design where children can work or relax alone or in small groups.

Assign messy activities, like art, to areas with washable flooring.

able to convert an odd-shaped corner to a nook where one or two children can sit and read together. Or turn a loft into a library with two levels or a dramatic play area that doubles as a pretend townhouse or department store. Is there a chalkboard affixed to one wall? Use this wall for the writing area of your literacy center. Or use the area as your art center. The children can create chalk drawings or draw on butcher paper you attach to the board.

Do any of the children in your setting have special needs? Consider these needs as you draw your blueprint. For example, the passageways in the setting should be wide enough (usually 3.5 ft) to accommodate any children who use wheelchairs or walkers. Review your state/federal requirements for additional information about setting configurations.

Here are a few other factors to consider when drawing the blueprint for your indoor setting to foster engaging play:

Size. If the children who use your setting vary in age, then the setting should be large enough to accommodate the wider range of activities in which these children will engage. Also, ensure that there is a meeting area that allows for children to sit spaciously and undistracted and does not require setting staff to move furniture. Also, consider the size of your learning centers. You will be configuring nine centers into your indoor setting. This presents a challenge for small spaces. However, you have options, like conducting music activities indoors and movement activities outdoors. Some areas, like the block center, need as much space as possible to accommodate children's creativity.

Electricity. Match your learning centers to the resources they require. For example, electrical outlet locations determine where you will place computers, CD/DVD players, light tables, kitchen appliances, or other equipment.

Water. Determine where the water sources are and which learning centers—including art, sand and water play, and cooking—should be located near these sources.

Lamps create incandescent pools of light that warm the room and define areas subtly.

Lighting. Art, science, and literacy centers may require natural light. Can you place floor or table lamps near these centers? Lamps create incandescent pools of light that warm the room and define areas subtly.

Flooring. Ideally, your indoor setting would feature both carpet and washable flooring, like linoleum. Assign messy activities, such as cooking, art, and sand and water play, to areas with washable flooring. Reserve carpeted areas for the literacy and music & movement centers.

Placements. Are there any centers that should be adjoined? Perhaps the block center should be near the dramatic play center to encourage pretend play while children build block towers, bridges, or cities. The centers that yield the most noise should be close in proximity. Group the quietest centers together so that children can work undisturbed.

Cubbies. Are there any centers that should be adjoined? Perhaps the block center should be near the dramatic play center to encourage pretend play while children build block towers, bridges, or cities. The centers that yield the most noise should be close in proximity. Group the quietest centers together so that children can work undisturbed.

Nooks. Work cozy places into your indoor setting design where children can work or relax alone or in small groups, such as a rocking chair in a corner or an area filled with pillows under a loft.

See Figures 19., 20., and 21. for sample infant, toddler and preschool indoor-setting floor plans. These floor plans are examples, not standards. Remember that you floor plan is a working document. Once children begin using your indoor setting, you will begin to see the changes you should make to ensure the space is safely and fully utilized.

Determine how to best incorporate cubbies into your room design.

Nooks provide children opportunities to be alone or engage in very small groups.

Figure 19. Sample Infant Setting

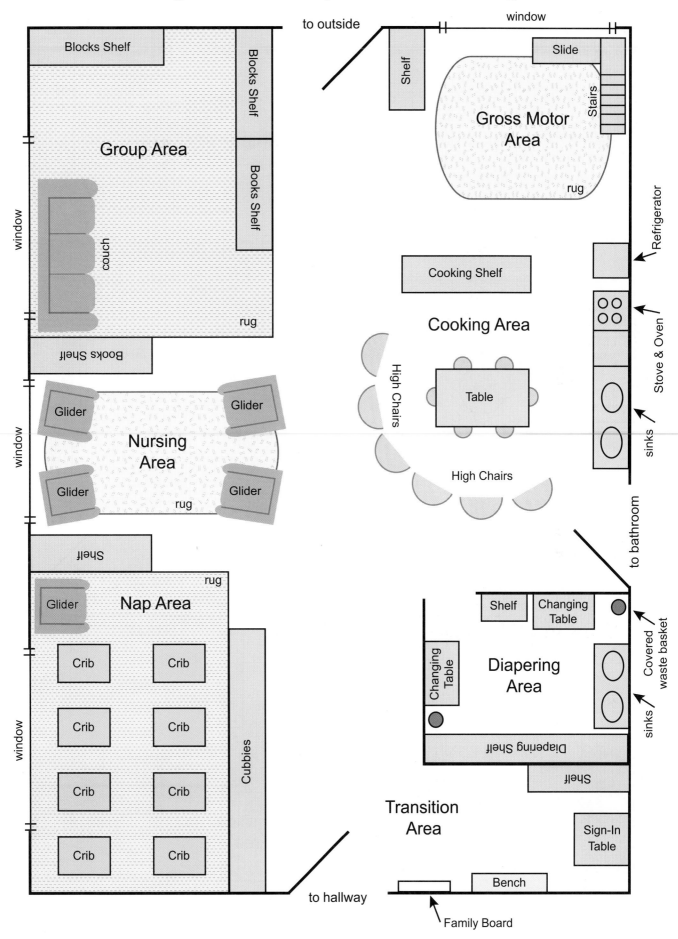

Figure 20. Sample Toddler Setting

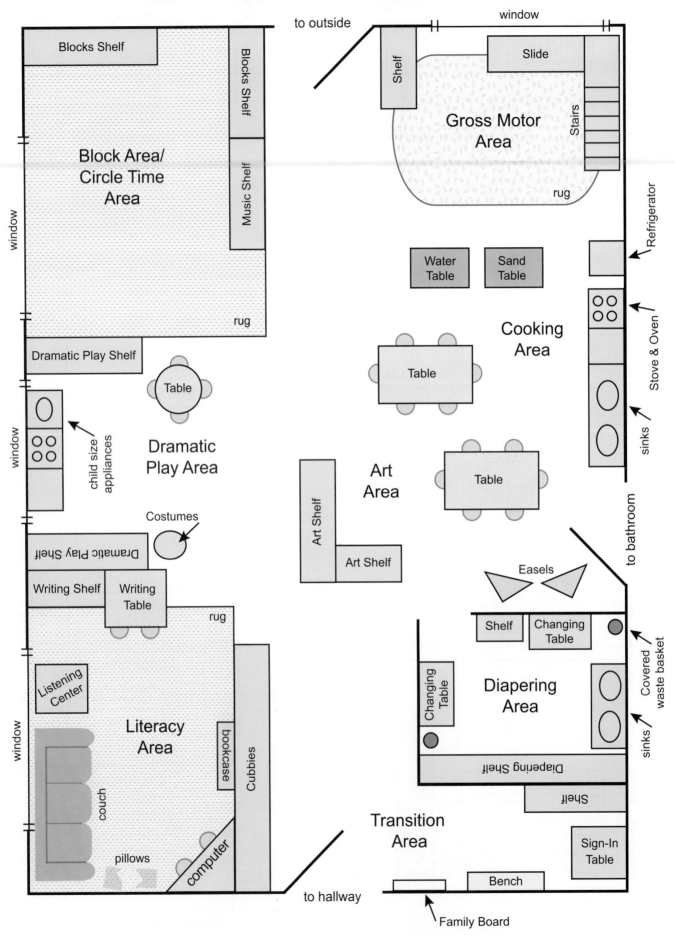

Figure 21. Sample Preschool Setting

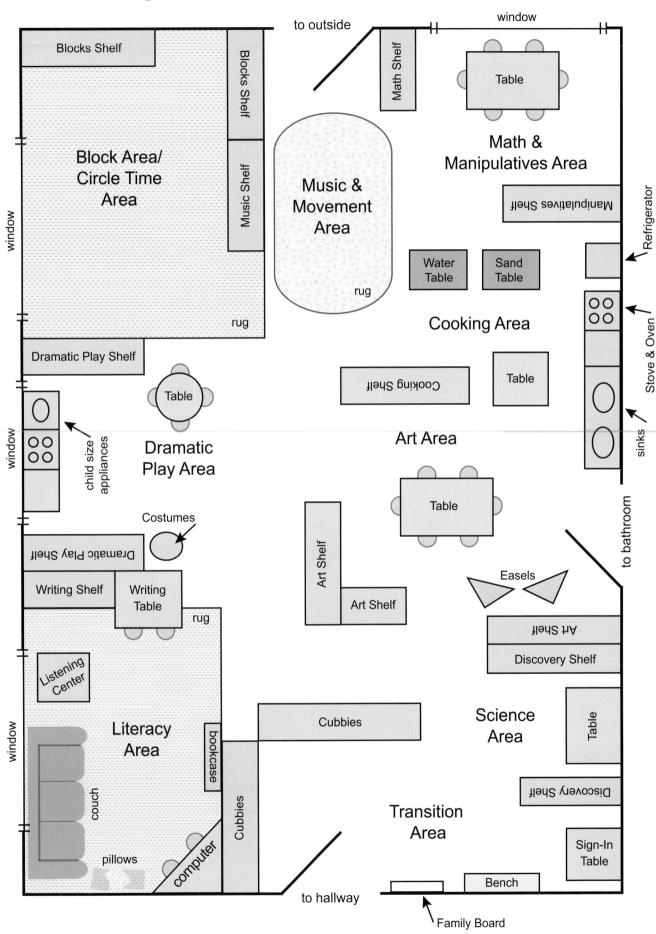

Learning Environment

Configuring the Preschool Setting

After drawing your working indoor-setting blueprint, get down on the floor—at the children's level—and look around the room. Keeping a child's perspective in mind, ask: What will greet the children when they first enter the setting? Is it clear where they go to place their belongings and play? Have I weaved all the centers into my plan so that children can easily access them, out of the way of foot traffic? Have I placed quieter learning centers closer together? Have I positioned noisier centers next to each other? Now stand and ask: Am I, the early educator, able to see everywhere, so that I can supervise all the children effectively? Correct long corridors or large open areas in your design that invite children to run. Create clear pathways around every learning center.

Low room dividers or shelves (no more than 36 in. high) that are anchored securely will help you enclose and separate learning centers and allow you to supervise the children. The dividers also help children access materials in each learning center easily. Also, use furniture, equipment, or room accents—including couches, easels, or rugs—to define learning centers.

See Figure 22. for tips on configuring the learning centers in your setting.

Figure 22. Learning Center Configuration Tips

Learning Center	How Children Use This Center	Configuration Tips
Blocks	Children learn math skills, such as proportion, shape and size, seriation, numbers, patterns, and measurement. As children recreate the world around them in constructions, block play becomes a stepping-stone to abstract thinking.	Use walls and divider shelves to enclose the block center on three sides; locate it near the dramatic play center, if possible.
Art	Children are encouraged to use open-ended materials creatively—performing activities that are safe and that fulfill their desire to express themselves and create beauty. They also develop fine motor skills, solve problems, and learn about cause and effect when they paint, draw, mold clay, create collages and mobiles, and weave potholders.	Locate the art center near a water source, on washable flooring (or use oilcloth, a small tarp, or newspapers to protect carpet). Use two-sided easels to enclose the center. Include a table that seats 4–6 children for drawing, molding clay, weaving, or making collages. Use double-sided easels and a drying rack for paintings.
Literacy	Children learn the fundamental skills needed to read, write, and operate a computer. They learn to recognize and write letters, recreate stories, and create their own books.	This center needs ample space for using computers, writing, and reading books. Computer and listening activities (using devices, like CD or DVD players) require electrical outlets. Use a book stand to section off this center. Include a table that seats 2–4 children for writing and a computer table with two chairs. Use a couch, rocker, or large pillows for a quiet reading area.

Figure 22. Learning Center Configuration Tips (continued)

Learning Center	How Children Use This Center	Configuration Tips
Dramatic Play	Children recreate familiar roles and confront scary situations. They negotiate roles and learn how to regulate their own behavior. Pretending and imagining sets the stage for abstract thinking.	Toy appliances—including stoves, refrigerators, and sinks—and child-sized furnishings can be used to define the area. This center should be located next to the block center so that pretend play can influence block construction.
Music & Movement	Playing instruments and singing are creative outlets. Children express themselves and find comfort through music, dance, and movement. They learn patterning and create a foundation for math when they chant and keep time with music.	Designate a carpeted area for floor exercises, like yoga and meditation. Marching and dancing activities require a large area and electrical outlets for playing music. Use a rack or shelf to hold musical instruments and to section off the center.
Science	Children observe natural collections, insects and worms, and weather and other natural phenomena. They predict, experiment, and graph results.	This center requires sunlight so that children can view natural objects and conduct experiments. House aquariums and pet cages in this center.
Math & Manipulatives	Children learn counting, patterning, seriation, and geometry by playing with puzzles and games. They also learn to follow directions for games and practice fine motor skills.	Designate an area for children to assemble puzzles and play games while seated on the floor, at a table, or while standing. Include a table that seats 4–6 children for playing lotto, working on parquetry blocks, assembling puzzles, and stringing beads.
Sand/Water	Children express feelings and calm themselves through sand and water play. They experiment with math skills such as patterning, volume, and shape as they make sand constructions or pour water.	This center is located near a water source and on washable flooring. Tables define the area. Keep mops and cleaning supplies nearby.
Cooking	Children express creativity through cooking projects. They learn math (measuring), science (watching bread dough rise), and literacy skills (using recipe cards). Children also develop fine motor skills through cutting, kneading, and mixing.	Kitchen appliances require electrical outlets. This center should also be located near a water source. Use the back of a shelf or a wall to hang enlarged recipes for children to see. Use a table that seats 4–6 children to present self-serve snacks or seat children for cooking experiences.

As you configure your indoor setting according to your working blueprint, ensure that you are creating an inviting and organized space that accommodates the needs of every child. Incorporate a variety of fabrics and textures. Learning centers should be well-equipped but not overcrowded. Designate an area for children to move and use their large muscles (if possible), when weather conditions keep them indoors. Ensure that all furnishings are sturdy, safe, and appropriately sized for the children in your setting. Furnish the setting with tables and chairs that vary in size so that all children can sit comfortably. Also include just enough tables and chairs for each child. Additional tables and chairs may clutter the room. Other furnishings to include are area rugs; open-shelf room dividers to enclose learning centers and hold materials; and pegboards for displaying props, utensils, and tools.

Again, your indoor-setting blueprint is a working document. There is no one correct way to configure a setting. What works well for your setting today may not work as well next year or with a different group of children. For example, your current group of children may enjoy using building blocks and require a larger area for this activity than last year's group did. Or this year's group has discovered a path for running that previous groups never knew existed. Monitor how children move and operate within your setting's design and adjust accordingly.

Low room dividers that are anchored securely will help you enclose and separate learning centers.

Figure 23. Configuring Outdoor Settings

Your outdoor setting can support the same types of learning activities that occur indoors and engage children in all areas of development and learning. Designate separate outdoor learning settings for mobile infants/toddlers and preschoolers. Outdoor settings should be fenced and include areas of level ground to keep children safe. Also ensure that outdoor learning settings are away from areas with heavy traffic, high air pollution levels, or gas/oil storage tanks. The outdoor setting should include places for children to engage in the following activities:

- Use outdoor play equipment, such as swings, slides, sandboxes or sand tables, and climbers.

- Act out pretend play scenarios in a playhouse, fort, tent, or old boat.

- Read a book alone under a tree.

- Listen to an early educator read a story to the group.

- Garden and plant herbs and vegetables.

- Build constructions out of weather-resistant large blocks.

- Create art using finger paint or sidewalk chalk.

- Paint the side of a building with water.

- Weave ribbons/yarn through a chain-link fence.

- Dance and sing to music.

- Jump rope.

- Play with sand, mud, and digging tools.

- Play games like "tag," "Simon says," or "duck, duck, goose."

- Play with water at a water table or with a sprinkler or hose (in warm weather).

- Hammer nails into a tree stump or pieces of wood.

- Conduct science experiments, like collecting and comparing leaves, looking at a ladybug through a magnifying glass, washing stones, or tracing shadows.

- Ride tricycles and scooters.

- Write or draw while sitting at a picnic table.

- Blow bubbles using homemade frames, like a plastic six-pack holder, a mesh net, or plastic hangers.

- Prepare and eat a picnic snack or lunch.

Though outdoor "learning centers" do not require boundaries, consider using landscaping to designate play areas. For example, use stones or a planter box to frame a garden, or designate a paved track for riding toys. Also consider filling your outdoor setting with natural decor like flowers, plants, herbs, boulders, a willow tunnel or shaded walkway, sun catchers, and wind chimes.

Selecting Appropriate Materials

The materials in your setting should be age, individually, and culturally appropriate for each child (Copple & Bredekamp, 2009). These materials should be safe and engaging. Instead of toys that encourage passive observation, opt for learning toys that support children's social, cognitive, physical, and language development. For older children, include materials appropriate for children 6 months younger than the youngest child through 6 months older than the oldest child in your setting. For example, if the youngest child in your setting is 18 months old and the oldest child is 4 years old, make sure materials are available for children from 1 year old to 4 and one-half years old. This range of materials offers children a choice between activities that they may have mastered and others that are more challenging.

Be sure to use materials that are safe and engaging.

The children in your setting all have different interests and skills. Tameka can count more than 20 objects accurately, but struggles to write her name. Malcolm is interested in postal workers and the process of sending and receiving mail. Rochelle loves cars, and can identify makes and models effortlessly. When you include materials in your setting that are recognizable, interesting, and challenging, children are more likely to engage with these items. Think about how you can incorporate the interests of children like Tameka, Malcolm, and Rochelle into a few of the learning centers in your setting.

For children in your setting who have special circumstances—including developmental, speech, and language delays—consider the types of adaptive materials and resources you can include so that these children can work independently. For example, include larger materials and toys that a child can grasp more easily. Some children may benefit from reading books with larger print and enlarging the windows on computer screens so that illustrations and print are more visible. Perhaps you can modify materials so that they are easier for children to use. For example, attach a rubber gripper to flatware so that children with cerebral palsy can eat independently. Talk with children's parents and intervention teams to determine what other adaptations would be helpful.

Using the materials and print in your setting, expose dual language learners to both their home languages and the languages they are learning. Display multiple children's books in both sets of languages in each of the learning centers. For your music & movement center, choose music and audio recordings that are sung or spoken in the children's home languages. Invite family members into your setting to interact with children, record songs and books, and help hang signage and labels in the language spoken in the classroom and in children's home languages.

The materials you choose for your setting should not only meet children's developmental needs, but should also reflect their individual cultures. *Culture* refers to the way we eat, sleep, talk, pray, play, and value things and concepts (Derman-Sparks & Edwards, 2010). Help children identify with race, ethnicity, and customs daily through the music, books, and other materials you provide as well as the foods you prepare and serve. This sends children the vital message that their cultures are an important part of your learning community every day—not just during holidays and special occasions. In addition, introduce children to the reality of our world's diversity with books like, *What If All the Kids Are White?: Anti-Bias Multicultural Education with Young Children and Families* by Louise Derman-Sparks, Patricia G. Ramsey, and Julie Olsen Edwards or *Anti-Bias Curriculum: Tools for Empowering Young Children* by Louise Derman-Sparks and the A.B.C. Task Force.

Provide weather-resistant large blocks in your outdoor setting.

Though well-intentioned, books and illustrations sometimes reinforce stereotypes, like mothers who stay at home while fathers work outside the home and athletic-looking White male heroes. A stereotype is a generalization about a particular group, race, or gender. When searching for books and other materials that celebrate the cultures of the children in your setting and introduce them to new ones, examine these materials individually and think about the messages they convey. Although exposing children to classic fairy tales and other literature is fine, also choose materials that defy stereotypes, for example stories featuring a female construction worker, an overweight child who is popular, or a child of color who stands up to a bully. Find characters in illustrations who have distinct, but not exaggerated, features and who wear clothing that represents their everyday appearances.

See Figure 24. for a checklist that will help you evaluate how cultures are represented in your materials.

Figure 24. Eight Quick Ways to Analyze Children's Books (and Other Materials) for Biases

Preview books and other materials before including them in your setting. Some children's books or materials may unintentionally promote biases—including racism, sexism, ageism, ableism, and homophobia. In your review, consider the following:

☐ **Check the illustrations and text for stereotypes of various ethnic/racial groups.** Do characters of a particular ethnic or racial group have overly exaggerated features? Also, be wary of "token" illustrations in which all African Americans and Hispanics appear as dark-skinned people with Caucasian facial features.

☐ **Check the plot.** Examine the roles of the women and men in the story. Are men active and women passive? Do the White characters help resolve the non-White characters' problems? Do seniors need to be cared for? Do people with special needs appear helpless? Was the book written to promote a particular religion or belief system? (This would be appropriate, however, in faith-based programs.)

☐ **Look at the characters' lifestyles.** Do people of color only live in ghettos, barrios, or migrant camps? Are some people always wearing traditional clothing? Are elderly people only in nursing homes? Are families only headed by both a mother and a father?

☐ **Consider the relationships among the characters.** Do only the White characters possess power and show leadership? Do only men take charge and solve family problems?

☐ **Note the heroes and heroines.** Do non-White heroes exhibit the same positive qualities as White heroes? Are they admired for the same attributes? Do only boys perform brave and important deeds? Are heroes all young, handsome, and strong men? Are there powerful female heroes?

☐ **Consider the effects on a child's self-image.** Are there positive characters with whom minorities, seniors, girls, children with nontraditional families, and people with special needs can identify?

☐ **Watch for loaded words.** These are words or phrases with insulting or historically negative overtones, like *savage, primitive, conniving, superstitious, treacherous, wily, crafty, lazy, Indian giver, sit Indian-style,* and *oriental* (when used to describe a human being). In addition, a word may assume a different meaning when used with a different audience. *Ambitious,* for example, is a complimentary term to describe a man, but is often less than complimentary when used to describe a woman.

☐ **Check the copyright date.** Recent books, maps, or posters are more likely to mirror our diverse world and the lives of the children and families in your setting. Do not disregard classic books and fairy tales, but know that some materials with earlier copyright dates do not reflect today's diversity.

(Derman-Sparks & Edwards, 2010)

Stocking Your Setting

Be intentional about the materials you choose for your setting. Your goal is not to amass all the materials you can. Rather, choose wisely those items that will contribute to children's learning. Again, consider the children in your setting and how they think, learn, and behave. This information will guide you in your material selection. Also, the materials you choose should, as a whole, offer children a balance of the following attributes:

- Small muscle/large muscle activity.

- Quiet/active activity.

- Short interest/extended play.

- Cause-and-effect scenarios.

- Creativity.

- Unlimited possibility (open-ended)/forced choice (closed-ended) activity.

- Messy/neat activity.

- Pretend/real activity.

Display materials for children so that they can retrieve and return these items independently.

Young infants (birth–8 months). Infants at this age are not moving around much independently, so they look, listen, and rely on you to change their scenery. Their materials should possess some of the following qualities:

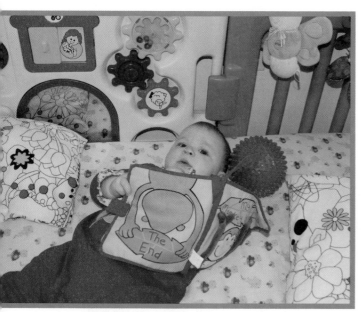

Provide infants materials with bright or contrasting colors and interesting shapes and designs.

- Bright or contrasting colors (e.g., board books and pictures).

- Interesting shapes and designs (e.g., mobiles, pictures, books, and blankets).

- Items with movable parts (e.g., mobiles and balls).

- Shiny, reflective surfaces (e.g., unbreakable mirrors mounted on the wall at children's eye level and small mirrors children can hold).

- Noisy parts (e.g., rattles, balls, pots and pans, and squeaky toys).

- Tactile surfaces (e.g., spoons, texture balls, and cloth/rubber dolls or animals).

- Large "chewable" materials that children cannot swallow (e.g., teething rings).

Early educators can also participate personally in infants' activities:

- Talk, sing, recite poems, play "peek-a-boo" and "this little piggy," move infants from place to place for different views, and hold and cuddle them.

- Hold infants in your lap while reading.

Provide materials that help children balance, rock, and climb.

Mobile infants (8–17 months). These infants' language skills are growing rapidly, and they can increasingly use their hands to make things happen. Materials should allow mobile infants to do the following:

- Crawl over, under, and through (e.g., obstacle course of large cushions and empty boxes).

- Hold on while walking (e.g., low table and cushions).

- Balance, rock, and climb (e.g., rocking chairs, climbers, steps/slide combination, carpeted climbing areas and rocking horses).

- Hold and manipulate (e.g., cars, trucks, planes, boats, cardboard books with round edges, dolls, large cardboard blocks, unit blocks, and puzzles with 2–4 pieces).

- Achieve a result, like make noise (e.g., knobs to turn, buttons to push, squeaky toys, telephones, balls, maracas, bells, piano, pounding benches, and stacking toys).

- Begin to scribble (e.g., watercolor markers and large pieces of paper).

- Mimic familiar behaviors (e.g., purses, dolls with ethnic features and skin colors, cradles, dishes and pitchers, and steering wheels).

- Push or ride (e.g., steerable, low-riding vehicles without pedals; toy lawn mowers; and pretend baby strollers).

- Solve problems (e.g., nesting baskets).

Provide these materials in multiples to encourage parallel play.

Younger Toddlers (18– 24 months). Toddlers at this age are active, becoming independent, and can do many things with their fingers and hands. Younger toddlers are becoming more familiar with their communities. They are aware of others and like to imitate them. Their materials should allow them to do the following:

- Separate and reattach (e.g., puzzles with 4–6 pieces, sorting toys, large plastic building sets, and stacking boxes or dolls).

- Dump and refill (e.g., buckets of spools or beads, different sizes of containers, and pieces that can be placed inside).

- Cooperate with others (e.g., balls and wagons).

- Refine fine motor skills (e.g., spools or beads to string, blunt-end scissors, clay, tempera paints—including brown and black—with wide brushes at easels, watercolor markers, sturdy crayons, large sheets of paper, and finger plays).

- Jump, throw, climb, and kick (e.g., climbers and balls).

- Push, pull, ride (e.g., steerable, low-riding vehicles without pedals; pull toys; shopping carts; and large trucks).

- Pretend (e.g., dress-up clothing and accessories, medical props, baby care items, play food and appliances, dolls, small realistic vehicles, and rubber animals).

Provide these toys in multiples to encourage parallel play.

Provide opportunities for children to cooperate with others.

Older Toddlers (24–36 months). Toddlers at this age typically play alone or with one or two other children and sometimes take turns. They are curious, learning more about language, and very active. Materials and activities for older toddlers allow them to:

- Try out and practice new skills (e.g., dress-up clothing, watercolor markers and large sheets of paper, tempera paints, blunt-end scissors, clay dough, finger paints, paste, and glue).

- Use numbers and letters in real situations (e.g., distributing napkins and plates for snack, following simple recipes with assistance, viewing lists and labels, and reading picture books with simple plots).

- Play alone or with one or two children (e.g., small tables so children can work side by side, pegboards, beads, art, table blocks, more dramatic play props, and zoo and farm animals).

- Run, jump, push, pull, gallop, or ride (e.g., balls, tricycles, large cardboard blocks, obstacle courses, and climbers).

- Explore cause and effect (e.g., unit blocks; sand and water with scoops, funnels, and cups; toys that come apart, latch, open, and/or close; rhythm sticks, drums, tambourines; and construction sets with fairly large pieces).

Preschoolers (3–5 years old). Children at this is the age will demonstrate initiative. Their play is more sophisticated, complex, and social. Materials for preschoolers should help them do the following:

- Be independent (e.g., materials and games that they can use and play with alone, such as assembling puzzles, feeding fish, setting the table for snack time, or serving a pretend meal in the dramatic play area).

- Devise and implement plans (e.g., blocks with blueprints for building towers, bridges, airports and cities; using recipes, kitchen utensils, and gadgets to prepare snacks and meals; puppets for creating puppet shows; and books that they can reenact).

- Play together (e.g., board games, lotto, and LEGO® building bricks they can use together; musical instruments for a marching band; balls to throw and catch; and toy food items to prepare a pretend meal in the dramatic play area).

- Share (e.g., multiples of favorite toys that encourage children to take turns).

- Learn literacy and math content (e.g., books, magazines, writing materials, reading and writing software, recipe cards, flannel board letters, magnetic letters, paintings and drawings, parquetry boards, counting puzzles, dominoes, and Magna-Tiles®).

- Experiment with science (e.g., materials for making volcanoes and tornadoes in a bottle; magnifying glasses, prisms, and collections of natural objects; graph-making materials; and an ant farm to observe).

Incorporating Children and Families in Setting Décor

Here are a few tips to consider when choosing wall hangings and other décor for your indoor setting:

- Hang all pictures, posters, signs, and accessories intended for children at their eye level. Hang information for parents at their eye level.

- All pictures, posters, signs, and accessories should reflect and celebrate diversity.

- Hang the children's work and documentations of their learning, like photographs taken during a recent field trip or children's charts documenting the growth of plants in the outdoor garden. These should be items the children have chosen for display. Use these items to facilitate meaningful and rich conversations about the children's experiences in your setting. Avoid commercial art.

- Display photos in the setting of the children and their families. Place photos of the children in their cubbies, and family photo albums in the literacy center. Post photos of the children playing in each center on the centers' dividers.

- Incorporate homey accessories, like curtains, fresh flowers, plants, a welcome mat at the front door, and magnets on the toy refrigerator in the dramatic play area.

- Setting décor should be uncluttered, aesthetically pleasing, and support children's learning and development.

- Learn about other countries and cultures (e.g., books like *Bread, Bread, Bread (Around the World Series)* by Ann Morris; music like *Multicultural Children's Songs* by Ella Jenkins; instruments from around the world, like a Russian balalaika or a djembe drum from Africa; and ingredients and appliances for cooking Jewish latkes or Greek tzatziki).

- Engage in complex dramatic play roles and scenarios (e.g., prop boxes to create additional dramatic play scenes, such as a doctor/vet office, beach, school, or store).

- Realize their gender, race, and culture (e.g., dress-up clothing representing genders, occupations, and cultures).

- Refine gross motor skills (e.g., balls, tricycles, swings, slides, climbers, parachutes, and tunnels).

- Refine fine motor skills (e.g., beads for stringing, writing tools, safety scissors and collage materials, drawing tools, painting tools, musical instruments to play, and puzzles).

- Change interests (e.g., materials that meet a broad range of interests and can be rotated over time).

Organizing Materials

Present infants with appropriate materials during floor time. Display materials for mobile infants, toddlers, and preschoolers so that they can retrieve and return these items independently. Group the materials by function. For example, store all plastic and rubber figurines in a clear, plastic container on a shelf in the block center. Store larger items, like puppets and stuffed animals, in baskets placed on the floor or on a shelf. Store toys with small parts in plastic containers. Group hardwood blocks by size and shape and store them on low, open shelves. Placing solid-colored contact paper the same shape as the block directly on the shelf where the block pieces are stored enables children to retrieve and return blocks independently. Label all storage containers with a written label and a photo of the items inside. This helps children begin to associate words with pictures. Write labels in the language spoken in your setting and the home languages of each child. Assign each language a different color to help children differentiate them (Nemeth, 2012). For example, designate the color blue for Spanish. Display all Spanish language signs, song lyrics, labels, and greetings in blue. Place a blue sticker on Spanish CDs, books, puzzles, games, and menus/food containers in the dramatic play area. Do not label every object and piece of furniture.

Defining Quality Curriculum for Young Children

In this chapter, you have discovered that children learn best through play. Your setting is a learning environment that lays the foundation for children's growth and development. A more structured approach to laying that foundation—beyond your indoor and outdoor settings, the people in them, and the materials—involves planning and delivering a curriculum. Copple and Bredenkamp

(2009, p.20) say that "the curriculum consists of the knowledge, skills, abilities, and understandings children are to acquire and the plans for the learning experiences through which those gains will occur."

You may choose to deliver one of the well-known established curricula in your setting, such as Montessori, Reggio Emilia, HighScope, Tools of the Mind, The Creative Curriculum, and Program for Infant and Toddler Care (PITC). Many of these approaches are founded upon the work of theorists like Jean Piaget—whom you will learn more about in Chapter 5—and the concept of engaging children in hands-on play and learning. The curriculum you deliver in your setting should match your settings' philosophy and mission.

Be wholly familiar with your setting's chosen curriculum and ensure that you are fully capable of delivering it. This curriculum provides the framework for your teaching, so you will need to deliver it seamlessly. If you have not been trained to deliver this curriculum, ask your supervisor to help you learn and deliver it successfully. Also ensure that the curriculum clearly aligns with domains of learning and your state's specific early learning standards. In determining how to deliver the methods, approaches, and/or strategies to help young children learn, consider the following:

- Select a curriculum that describes realistic goals for children's learning and development, as well as, the materials, experiences, and teaching strategies that you can use to help children to achieve their goals.

- Plan a curriculum that helps recognize children, their families, their cultures, and languages. Appreciate and plan for individual differences.

- Choose learning experiences and teaching strategies that help children reach those goals. Listen to children when they express their interests and monitor them as they refine their skills.

- Ask: What are children learning by engaging in these activities?

- Encourage children to ask questions, experiment, and discover information independently.

- Ask lots of open-ended questions (What would happen if…? or Why did this…?) rather than questions that have one correct answer.

- Encourage children's creativity and provide many open-ended opportunities. Avoid models, coloring books, worksheets, and patterns. Allow children to create original artwork.

- Provide real, hands-on experiences.

- Ensure that children are spending more time doing and learning versus watching, e.g., child-directed.

- Help children learn to appreciate beauty and diversity in the world around them (art, nature, music, and literature) through daily, culturally authentic activities.

- If something more interesting diverts children's attention from a current activity, offer them the opportunity to learn more about a new activity versus the routine of an existing activity.

- Present activities with enthusiasm to build children's interest and curiosity. Exhibit a playful, cheerful attitude. Demonstrate respect for all people.

- Treat children and their work with respect and interest. Instead of asking, "What is it?," engage children in conversation about their work and play.

- View every minute of the day as a learning opportunity.

Developing the Daily Schedule

When you develop daily schedules, you provide structure for children's learning. The schedule sets a daily routine for the children, designating times for them to engage in individual, small group, and large group activities. The daily schedule you develop should be developmentally appropriate for the children in your setting and support their growth and development.

Again, observing and learning each child's interests, skills, knowledge, and attitudes is paramount to creating daily schedules that meet their specific needs. Also, reflect on the children's experiences in your setting—including the time they spend in the learning centers, outdoors, or engaging in small and large group activities. Ask: Were these experiences successful? How long did the children choose to remain engaged? What did the children learn? Were they interested? What will I do next based on these experiences? What did I learn from these experiences? Answering these specific questions will help you increase the effectiveness of the learning experiences you plan.

The following sections include sample infant/toddler and preschool daily schedules. Use these sample schedules as your starting point, not a standard. You may need to plan for special activities (such as visits from specialists) or your setting may operate for fewer or more hours each day. Adjust your schedules accordingly. For example, your setting may be open to children for half a business day. Therefore, you would condense your schedule, omitting lunch, nap, and afternoon activities, and end your day with the closing meeting and departure time.

Infant and Toddler Schedules

Infant schedules should be flexible. Consider their personal rhythms for eating and sleeping, tendency to play alone or alongside another child, and the length of time they are able to maintain interest in activities.

Structure your daily schedule for toddlers so that they are engaged and moving during the day. Give these children your individual attention. Have lots of conversations with all children, and include their home languages. Greet each child personally, talk throughout the day about what the child is doing, thinking, and feeling, and say goodbye at the end of the day. Small group times provide opportunities for interactions that address developmental skills at the child's individual level.

Figure 25. Sample Daily Schedule for Infants*

Time	Activity
8:00–9:00	Arrival
8:00–9:15	Play/lap book reading
8:00–10:00	Diapering/bottles
8:30–11:00	Naps/individual play/diapering
10:30–12:00	Outdoor walk/play
11:30–1:00	Diapering/lunch/mid-day bottles
12:30–2:30	Naps/individual play/diapering
2:00–4:00	Bottles/outdoor play/diapering
3:00–5:00	Naps/songs/lap book reading/play/diapering
4:30–6:00	Play/bottles/leave

*Notice the extended time from 8:00 a.m.–11:00 a.m. allotted for infants' diapering, feeding, napping, and individual play. Infants have unique needs, so follow their individual schedules. Also infants should spend most of their day at play. They want to move, vary their scenery, and get involved with what is happening around them. Push younger infants in their strollers outside. Allow mobile infants plenty of time and space to crawl and walk.

Figure 26. Sample Daily Schedule for Toddlers*

Time	Activity
7:30–8:30	Arrival
8:30–9:15	Diapering and toileting
7:30–10:15	Individual and group activities
10:15–11:00	Outdoor play
10:45–11:00	Diapering and toileting
11:00–11:30	Lunch
11:30–12:00	Diapering, washing up, tooth brushing, singing
12:00–2:30	Nap time
1:30–2:30	Individual and group activities
2:30–3:00	Self-initiated snack
2:00–3:00	Diapering and toileting
3:00–4:00	Outdoor play
4:00–5:30	Individual activities, story reading, departure
4:00–4:30	Diapering and toileting

*Group activities hold a toddler's attention for no more than 5 min. They need to be active, so do not expect them to spend extensive time in one place or on one activity. Rather, rotate the children through daily activities. For example, one group of children may wash their hands while another group brushes their teeth. Rigid time restrictions may frustrate toddlers. Plan how you can help them transition from one activity to another in your schedule. For example, it is helpful to give a child a signal (like singing a particular song) that it is nap time.

Preschool Schedules

A well-planned daily schedule for preschoolers reflects the children's ages and developmental needs. Consider the children's needs, interests, and skills when allocating time to each activity. For example, children require 40–45 min to become fully involved in an activity, so allot at least 1 hr for self-selected activities in learning centers. Include outdoor activities (lasting 45 min to 1 hr) in the daily schedule during both morning and afternoon, following periods where children have engaged in less active indoor activity. Keep large group activities (such as the morning meeting) to 15–20 min. Begin the year with shorter meetings (10 min), and then lengthen the meeting gradually during the year.

Work to achieve a balance in your daily schedule. Plan for both child-initiated and teacher-directed learning; alternate quiet times with active times; sequence outdoor play to follow indoor play; and plan for individual, small group, and full group activities.

Because preschool children are aware of the daily sequence, post a picture-based schedule at their eye level. Also, post a written schedule for all adults—including staff, visitors, parents, and volunteers. Note periods of the day, from the setting's opening in the morning to the children's departure in the evening, on this schedule.

Group meetings assemble the entire group to start the day, recap the day's learning, or participate in an activity.

Figure 27. Sample Program Guide for Preschoolers*

Time	Children's Activities	How You Support the Children
8:00–8:30 (30 min)	**Planning**	• Staff meet to review day's plans before the children arrive. • Conduct daily health and safety checks. (See Figure 2. in Chapter 1 of your Essentials textbook for a daily safety indoor/outdoor checklist.) • Ensure all necessary materials are available to children.
8:30–9:00 (30 min)	**Arrival:** Parents and children arrive at the setting. Healthy breakfast foods are available so that children can serve themselves. Quiet centers, such as the math & manipulatives and literacy centers, are available to children as they enter.	• Greet parents and children individually. • Share information with parents. • Help children store belongings and select an activity, such as "writing" in their journals or reading books.
9:00–9:15 (15 min)	**Group Meeting:** Discuss what the children did the night before or over the weekend. Take attendance (ask children to count who is present and absent). Assign children helper duties for the day. Read a story aloud or introduce songs and finger plays. Review the daily schedule with the children and ask them to predict what activity comes next. Complete a shared reading, choral reading, song, or group writing activity related to current concepts and project studies.	• Lead circle time. Conduct educator-directed instruction. • Lead counting and word-sound activities. • Other staff engage individual children who are not yet ready for large group activities.
9:15–10:15 (1 hr)	**Indoor Choice Time:** Children choose to participate in centers and/or a small group activity. Children may explore materials or concepts introduced at morning meeting. At end of choice time, all children clean up and put on jackets, if needed, for going outdoors.	• Observe and interact with individual children in ways that extend play and learning. • Staff and parent volunteers lead a small-group activity that builds on children's skills and interests and/or is related to the current project study. • Encourage children to clean up after themselves.
10:15–10:30 (15 min)	**Small group time:** Children can work in small groups with early educators on specific activities, like literacy, science, or math activities, that are engaging and interesting to children and will support development of skills and learning.	• Select developmentally appropriate activities that you and other early educators in your setting can work on with small groups, like cooking experiences or math games.

Figure 27. Sample Program Guide for Preschoolers (continued)*

Time	Children's Activities	How You Support the Children
10:15–11:00 (45 min)	**Outdoor Choice Time:** Children choose their outdoor activity, like playing on swings, climbers, and slides; riding tricycles; or participating in ball games. Some children may prefer quiet activities such as reading a book, playing with sidewalk chalk, or tending a garden. NOTE: Incorporate morning snack into either indoor or outdoor choice time.	• Supervise play on equipment. Interact individually with children, asking open-ended questions. • Staff and parent volunteers lead small group gardening activity, woodworking project, or bubble-blowing session.
11:15–11:30 (15 min)	**Story/Lunch Preparation:** Children store their jackets. Early educator reads story aloud to the children, while selected helpers work with staff and parent volunteers to set tables for lunch. Children use toilet and wash hands in small groups.	• Read a story using props. • Staff and parent volunteers oversee children setting placemats, dishes, glasses, flatware, and napkins. • Adults fill serving dishes and place bowls of food on tables. Staff supervise children as they use the bathroom and wash hands.
11:30–12:15 (45 min)	**Lunch:** Children and adults enjoy a family-style meal together. Children clean up after themselves, wash hands, and get cots/mats for nap time as they finish eating. Slower eaters are allowed to finish.	• Staff help children settle in for lunch. • Adults sitting at tables with children encourage conversations about nutrition and topics of interest to the children. • Early educators and other staff guide children in eating, cleaning up, washing hands, brushing teeth, and preparing for nap time. • Adults help children set out cots/mats.
12:15–1:45 (1½ hr)	**Nap Time:** Children sleep or rest quietly on cots/mats. Nonsleepers are given a book or puzzles to play with quietly.	• Staff help children relax, if needed, by rubbing backs and singing lullabies so that children can fall asleep. • Once children are asleep or resting, early educators and staff use this time for breaks and planning.
1:45-2:45 (1 hr)	**Indoor Child Choice:** Children wake up, put away mats, use the bathroom, and wash their hands. Afternoon snack is available to all children. Children choose their own activities or conduct small-group investigations as part of project work. At the end of indoor choice time, all children clean up and put on jackets, if needed, for going outdoors.	• This is the second opportunity for children to have a snack. • Interact with children individually. • Staff and parent volunteers help children with investigations.

Figure 27. Sample Program Guide for Preschoolers (continued)*

Time	Children's Activities	How You Support the Children
2:45-3:45 (1 hr)	**Outdoor Choice Time:** Children choose their outdoor activity, like playing on swings, climbers, and slides; riding tricycles; or participating in ball games. Early educators may organize a special project such as planting a garden or taking a nature walk.	• Interact with children individually or as part of a group if conducting a special activity.
3:45-4:00 (15 min)	**Afternoon Meeting:** Children store jackets, wash hands, and sit in a circle. Early educators and children review the day's activities and apply content studied to children's lives. Discuss plans for next day.	• Lead circle time discussion.
4:00–4:30 (30 min)	**Departure:** Children clean up and prepare to leave. Families pick up children.	• Help children clean up and prepare to leave the setting. • Staff greet parents and provide information about what children did during the day. • Staff say goodbye to individual children and their families, making sure that children take home artwork, projects, and parent information from their cubbies.
4:30–5:00 (30 min)	**Planning Period**	• Staff discuss day's events—what worked, what needs improvement. Staff discuss activities and progress of individual children—skills, needs, interests. • Staff plan for the next day, week, and month and prep learning centers for the next day. • Staff hang children's artwork. Early educators complete paperwork as needed.

*Build morning and afternoon snacks into choice times. When snack time is a separate schedule component, valuable learning time is lost. Give children control over eating when they are hungry, which helps them develop healthy eating habits. Build activities like cleanup, going to the bathroom, brushing teeth, and putting on coats into choice time activities. Incorporate these activities into play.

(Colker, 2009)

Implementing the Daily Schedule

As you implement your setting's daily schedule, you are facilitating children's learning and engaging them in activities that foster their growth and development. Your relationships with each child are fortified as you continue to observe their actions, document their learning, discuss what you see happening, and ask probing questions.

Your daily schedule should be flexible enough to adjust for field trips, guest presenters, and other preplanned activities. This flexibility provides opportunities for you to extend children's learning and interests. For example, if children demonstrate a particular interest in certain books or other materials, your schedule should be fluid enough to incorporate this interest into the day's activities.

A flexible schedule also helps you to accommodate teachable moments that may interrupt your plans for the day. Owocki (1999) describes *teachable moments* as "knowledgeably observing children and seeking out relevant opportunities to help them extend their understandings." For example, snowstorms or rainbows are opportunities to forgo the scheduled activity at that time and discuss these natural occurrences. Bring a handful of snow to the water table so that children can touch and experience it. Read a book aloud about the colors of the rainbow and ask the children to look for these colors in the real rainbow. Other teachable moments stem from children's home lives, like the pending arrival of a new sibling, or questions like, "How did the worms get under the swing set?"

As always, be aware of the children's interests, feelings, and questions. They may be worth taking an unplanned turn in your day to follow the children's lead.

Infants and Toddlers

Document children's learning on bulletin boards or posters.

We recommend the primary caregiving model for early educators working with infants and toddlers. Employing this model involves assigning early educators responsibility for the same small group of infants or toddlers from the moment these children arrive until the moment they leave the setting each day. The primary caregiving model ensures that infants and toddlers create secure attachments with the same early educators daily and maintains continuity in the children's care. However, early educators must communicate clearly and frequently throughout the day regardless of what model your setting employs.

To reinforce continuity in children's care, we also recommend that the same early educator(s) works with the same small group of children from birth until 3 years old. Though this standard is not possible in all settings, early educators must communicate clearly and frequently throughout the day and help children develop secure attachments and close, trusting relationships with their early educators.

As an early educator working with infants and toddlers, follow their individual rhythms, needs, and interests. Throughout the day, early educators working with infants and toddlers will follow individual rhythms, needs, and interests as much as possible. This flexibility promotes the children's interest in and engagement with different materials and develops their independence, positive self-concept, and strong bonds with you and other early educators. Facilitate small group activities that toddlers can choose to participate in—including cooking experiences, working with specific open-ended art media, and engaging in musical experiences.

Again, reflecting on specific experiences in your setting and your role as an early educator will help you grow professionally, develop deeper relationships with the children, and refine your teaching strategies. Ask questions like: Why did that child react that way to the situation? What could I have done differently? What will I do next time with the specific child or with other children in a similar situation?

Preschool

A major component in planning for effective early childhood programs is a consistent daily schedule. Dodge and Colker (1992) note the importance of consistency in the daily routine:

> Young children feel more secure when they can predict the sequence of events and have some control over their environment. They delight in reminding the teacher that 'snack time comes next' or telling a visitor that 'now we go outside.' In addition, predictability provides children with a rudimentary sense of time, as they begin to learn what comes first in the day, second, next, and last. A consistent schedule also helps build trust in the environment. (p. 37)

Children should have ongoing opportunities to learn important skills, knowledge, and dispositions. As an early educator, you are incorporating a daily schedule into your setting that is busy with conversations, projects, experiments, reading, and building activities. These materials and activities are individualized and challenge children's intellectual development.

Use these opportunities to reflect on specific learning experiences to improve your teaching practices and support children's learning and development. Evaluate and improve your schedule often.

Daily Schedule Components: Choice Time

During indoor and outdoor choice times, allow children to engage in activities that most interest them. Observe their play, discuss with them what you observe (when appropriate), and ask

Supporting Learning During Choice Time

Ms. Bennett is observing Yan in the block center. Yan has built his block tower several times, but it keeps collapsing. After several tries, he says, "I don't like these blocks."

Ms. Bennett: "What is it that you don't like about the blocks, Yan?"

Yan: "They don't work. They keep falling."

Ms. Bennett: "Let's take a look at the blocks and see if we can understand why they fall. Will you make another tower, so we can watch what happens together?"

Yan and **Ms. Bennett** count blocks as Yan stacks four of them. When he adds the fifth block, the tower falls.

Yan: "I can only make a tower of four blocks."

Ms. Bennett: "True. We know that four blocks makes a sturdy tower. But what if you wanted a higher tower?"

Yan: "I can't do that, Ms. Bennett. It'll fall. The blocks are too skinny to stand."

Ms. Bennett: "I think you're on to something, Yan. What could you do to make a fatter base? A fatter base might just hold a fifth block."

Yan: "Um…I could put two blocks at the bottom."

Ms. Bennett: "That's a smart idea. Let's try that now!"

open-ended questions that will expand their thinking. Interact with all children individually and get better acquainted with them. Be nurturing, enthusiastic, playful, and respectful. Children should be able to express themselves to you openly while viewing you as an authority and a role-model.

Daily Schedule Components: Group Meetings and Small Group Times

These sessions—also referred to as "circle time"—assemble the entire group to start the day, recap the day's learning, or participate in an activity, such as a finger play or introducing new equipment. However, not every child can or will participate in a group meeting. Do not force children who are upset, ill, or unable to sit to remain with the group. If children wander regularly during this particular session, evaluate whether the activity or information you are presenting is engaging and developmentally appropriate.

On the other hand, small group times allow you and other early educators to engage deeper with a few children at a time, working on specific skills or knowledge. This may occur during choice time. For example, a group of children in your setting may have difficulty using scissors. Invite these children to work with you in the art area. Guide them in using scissors as a group or individually.

Daily Schedule Components: Routines

Routines—including arrival/departure, dressing/undressing, mealtimes, handwashing, toileting, and napping—are opportunities for children to learn self-help and academic skills. Show them how to zip their coats, button their sweaters, or tie their shoelaces. Allow them to practice washing their hands and setting the table for meals. When Delia places one placemat on the table in front of each chair, she is learning one-to-one correspondence. Or when you lead a discussion during the meal about how eating carrots helps our eyesight, children learn life science. Routines are not "downtime." Rather, they provide chances for children to learn life skills, increase content knowledge, and build self-esteem.

Daily Schedule Components: Transitions

Convert the transition into a game.

Transitions should keep children engaged while they shift from one activity to the next. To achieve this goal, incorporate transitions into your routines and activities. For example, if the children still have a few minutes of inside choice time and need to use the bathroom before outside choice time, take a few children at a time to the bathroom while the rest continue to play. This strategy keeps children occupied while they wait to use the bathroom. Or appoint a few children to work with a staff member or parent volunteer to prepare for lunch while you read a board book aloud to the rest of the children. Another staff member can take a few children at a time to wash their hands. Again, these strategies keep the children occupied until they sit down for lunch.

Here are five tips for incorporating smooth transitions into your daily routines:

- **Give children a 5-min warning before a transition occurs.** For example, a warning lets children know when it is time to return their toys and materials to the shelves and prepare for another activity. Give additional, whispered time-warnings to children who have difficulty with transitions.

- **Convert the transition into a learning activity.** For example, announce, "All children whose names begin with an S sound may go put on their coats to go outside," or "Everyone who has VELCRO® straps on their shoes may go wash their hands now."

- **Convert the transition into a game.** For example, announce, "Let's all go outside hopping like kangaroos," or "Let's do the Electric Slide to our cubbies to put away our jackets." Other ideas include singing cleanup songs or counting the steps it takes to put on their coats.

- **Allow children to leave out their work for future play.** If Hector is in the middle of building an elaborate block construction or creating an art project, let him leave out the work so that he can finish it at a later time. Help him make a *Building in Progress* or *Please Do Not Touch* sign to protect the work from others

- **Avoid completing transitions as a full group.** Small group transitions ensure that children remain occupied while they wait.

Weekly and Lesson Planning

Weekly planning allows you to view the activities you have scheduled each day over the course of one week. Use a grid, like Figure 28., to record the time and duration of daily and weekly routines and activities. This grid may also detail staff responsibilities, necessary preparations, target objectives, and learning standards, ideas for involving families and the community, planned field trips, and the arrival of special invited guests. Post the completed grid to keep early educators and children's parents informed of setting activities. Your setting may also require early educators to develop daily lesson plans, using forms like Figure 29., that detail specific activities and the materials you will use. The purpose of these plans is to explain how an activity will be performed and match the activity to specific learning outcomes or objectives. ■

Figure 28. Sample Weekly Planning Grid

	Monday	Tuesday	Wednesday	Thursday	Friday
Group meeting					
Learning centers (changes to centers including materials added or removed)					
Small group					
Outdoor time					
Transitions					

Figure 29. Lesson Plan Form

Lesson plan title: _____ Date of lesson: _____

Concept / topic to teach: _____

_____

_____

_____

_____

❑ Small group ❑ Full group ❑ Individual activity

Early Learning Standards addressed: _____

_____

_____

_____

_____

Specific learning outcomes/objectives (domains of learning)**:** _____

_____

_____

Required materials and preparation needed: _____

_____

_____

_____

_____

_____

_____

How I will introduce the activity: _____

_____

_____

Council for Professional Recognition • 800-424-4310

Figure 29. Lesson Plan Form (continued)

Step-by-step procedures: _____

_____

_____

_____

_____

_____

_____

_____

_____

_____

_____

_____

Follow-up (for example, related materials I may put in a learning center after this lesson)**:** _____

_____

_____

How I will evaluate the activity: _____

_____

_____

Adaptations (for children with special needs) **if needed:** _____

_____

_____

Adaptations (for dual language learners) **if needed:** _____

_____

_____

Possible connections to other topics: _____

_____

_____

Competency Standard II:

To advance physical and intellectual competence

Developmental Contexts

Functional Area 4: Physical

Young infants *(birth–8 months)* use physical movement, taste, touch, smell, sight, and sound to explore and learn about their world. By moving their arms, hands, legs, and other body parts, by touching and being touched, infants develop an awareness of their bodies and their ability to move and interact with the environment. By using their mouths to explore, hands to reach and grasp, whole bodies to roll over and sit up, they master the necessary strength and skills needed for the developmental stages that follow.

Mobile infants *(9–17 months)* delight in practicing and achieving new physical skills—crawling, standing, sitting down, and walking. They interact with their environment in a practical way, using all senses to examine and manipulate objects and begin to understand cause and effect, space, and distance in this way.

Toddlers *(18–36 months)* continue to master physical skills at their own individual rates. Their learning and interaction with the environment continues to be active. Although they are gaining greater control and satisfaction through use of their small muscles (for example, painting, drawing, or working with puzzles), they need opportunities to exercise their large muscles often each day.

Preschoolers *(3-5 years old)* are gradually refining new skills: skipping, drawing, threading, throwing, and catching. They are interested in learning subtle differences through their senses: sweet and sour, rough and smooth, high and low, loud and soft. They can attend and persist for longer periods of time when they are absorbed in using their small muscles on a puzzle or an art project. They also need daily opportunities to exercise their large muscles in free play and organized activities. Daily physical activities can promote children's cognitive, creative, and language growth as well as their physical development.

Functional Area 5: Cognitive

Young infants *(birth–8 months)* learn best within the context of their relationships with caring adults in a secure environment. Some of their early cognitive (intellectual) development includes becoming familiar with distance and space, sounds, similarity and differences among things, and visual perspectives from various positions—front, back, under, and over.

Competency Standard II (continued)

Mobile infants *(9–17 months)* actively learn through trying things out; using objects as tools; comparing, imitating, looking for lost objects; and naming familiar objects, places, and people. By giving them opportunities to explore their environment, objects, and people and by sharing children's pleasure in discovery, adults can build children's confidence in their ability to learn and understand.

Toddlers *(18–36 months)* enter into a new and expansive phase of mental activity. They are beginning to think in words and symbols, remember, and imagine. Their curiosity leads them to try out materials in many ways and adults can encourage this natural interest by providing a variety of new materials for experimentation. Adults need to create a supportive social environment that contributes to learning by showing enthusiasm for children's individual discoveries and by helping children use words to describe and understand their experiences. Children's cognitive and social development are deeply connected.

Preschoolers *(3-5 years old)* continue their cognitive development by actively exploring their world and manipulating objects, thinking and solving problems, talking and engaging with adults and other children in a variety of roles, and repeating and practicing their learning. Their increasing ability to describe objects and experiences with words reinforces their understanding of abstract concepts. Adults can expand learning through play, introduce a variety of new opportunities for learning, and ensure that preschoolers experience a balance of challenge and success.

Functional Area 6: Communication

Young infants *(birth–8 months)* need adults who are attentive to their nonverbal and pre-verbal communication. Adults can provide better care when they respond sensitively to the individual signals of each infant. Infants' early cries, babblings, and coos are early forms of communication. An infants' speech development is facilitated by an encouraging partner who responds to their beginning communications and who sings and talks with them about themselves and their world.

Mobile infants *(9–17 months)* begin to babble expressively, name familiar objects and people, and understand many words and phrases. Adults can build on this communication by showing an active interest in children's expressions, interpreting their first attempts at words, repeating and expanding on what they say, talking to them clearly, singing songs, and telling stories.

Toddlers *(18–36 months)* increase their vocabularies and use of sentences daily. Although there is a wide range of typical language development during this time, it can also be an opportunity for early intervention if there are language delays or difficulties. Adults should communicate actively with all toddlers—model good speech, listen carefully, and provide a wide range of vocabulary. Language should be used in a variety of pleasurable ways each day, including songs, stories, instructions, comfort, conversations, information, and play.

Competency Standard II (continued)

Preschoolers *(3-5 years old)* develop a wide range of abilities to communicate both verbally and nonverbally. Adults should communicate actively with each child—modeling good speech, listening carefully, responding actively to their expressions, engaging in conversations with them, and building on their verbal and nonverbal understanding and vocabulary. During the preschool years, early literacy experiences provide the foundation for later success in learning to read and write.

Functional Area 7: Creative

Young and mobile infants *(birth–17 months)* are creative in their individual styles of interacting with the world. Adults can support their creativity by respecting and enjoying the variety of ways very young children express themselves and act on their environment.

Toddlers *(18–36 months)* are interested in using materials to create their own product—sometimes to destroy and create it again or to move on. For example, they become absorbed in dipping a brush in paint and watching their stroke of color on paper. They use their voices and bodies creatively— swaying, chanting, and singing. They enjoy making up their own words and rhythms, as well as learning traditional songs and rhymes. Adults can provide water, sand, blocks, and other open-ended and raw materials and opportunities for toddlers' creativity and can show respect for what they do. Make-believe and pretend play appear gradually and are signs of emerging cognitive capacity to understand symbols. Adults can join in imaginative play, while helping toddlers distinguish between what is real and what is not.

Preschoolers *(3-5 years old)* can express their creativity in increasingly symbolic ways through the use of their bodies, words, and materials (building blocks, music, dance, art) and through make-believe. Adults can promote creativity by providing space, time, and materials for children to create and recreate their individual works, their own dramas, and their unique solutions to problems and by respecting the process of creativity as much as the product.

Chapter 4
Physical

CDA Functional Area 4: Candidate uses a variety of developmentally appropriate equipment, learning experiences, and teaching strategies to promote the physical development (fine motor and gross motor) of all children.

Physical

Introduction

Children's physical development is not just a matter of biology; it is a process fueled by experience and opportunity (Bredekamp, 2011). As an early educator, you promote physical development by giving children chances to use their large and small muscles and build their coordination.

In this chapter, we will discuss the following ways you can support children's physical development:

- Understanding Physical Development of Infants, Toddlers, and Preschoolers.

- Promoting Children's Gross Motor Development.

- Promoting Children's Fine Motor Development.

- Connecting Children's Physical Development to the Development of the Whole Child.

Understanding Physical Development of Infants, Toddlers, and Preschoolers

The most rapid human physical development occurs between birth and 35 months. Because children acquire physical skills at an individual pace, their progress may vary. However, physical development of young children typically follows predictable developmental patterns. Infants' and toddlers' bodies develop from the top down and from the center out:

1) **From the head to the foot** (the cephalocaudal trend). Because brain growth is rapid during the first 3 years of a child's life, infants' heads grow faster than the rest of their bodies initially, and then growth slows in proportion to body growth.

Head control is the first movement that babies gain. Their neck muscles are developing, which is necessary for achieving additional movement such as sitting, crawling, and walking. For example, infants at about the age of 2 months old will learn to hold their heads up to see the world around them. Before this age, their neck muscles are too weak to support their heads. As they notice light and sounds, curious infants will look from side to side, developing strength and coordination in their necks and upper back muscles. At 3 to 4 months old, infants will often roll over for the first time while trying to reach for a favorite toy. Around 6 months old, when placed in a sitting position, infants will prop themselves up with both arms to stay balanced.

Within a month or two, they are able to get into and out of sitting position without help and use both hands to explore a toy. They can scoot across the floor on their tummies and use their hands and knees to crawl. Generally, infants begin to stand at around 10–12 months, walk at around 12–16 months, and walk up stairs at around 18–20 months.

2) From the center of the body to the extremities (periphery of the body; the proxomodistal trend). Infants are capable of moving their shoulders before they develop the fine motor skills in their hands to cut paper with scissors. Typically, children can hold objects with the whole hand at around 5–6 months; pick up objects using the thumb and forefinger at around 12 months; hold a spoon at around 16 months; scribble with a fat crayon at around 18 months; and eat with a fork at around 24 months. The skeletal system also grows rapidly in infancy, slows, and then returns to rapid growth during adolescence.

Physical Development milestones are divided into two major components: gross motor and fine motor development. *Gross motor development* refers to the large muscles of the legs, arms, and torso. *Fine motor development* refers to the smaller muscles of the body including the muscles of the hands, feet, and eyes.

Promoting Children's Gross Motor Development

Gross motor development involves large muscle movements of the limbs and torso—including rolling, crawling, running, jumping, twisting, dancing, and skipping to name a few skills. These skills can be grouped into three areas (Gallahue & Ozmun, 2011):

Children's bodies crave movement.

- **Moving from one place to another (or "locomotion"):** crawling, running, leaping, jumping, galloping, and hopping.

- **Giving or receiving objects with force:** throwing, catching, and kicking. This type of movement is sometimes called "gross motor manipulative movement" because in addition to body movements, it involves handling objects, like balls.

- **Stability movements:** balancing, stopping and starting, and riding a tricycle or bicycle.

Gross motor skills are learned, evolve in an orderly fashion, and develop predictably based on experience and practice. These skills move from simple to complex. For example, before children can run, they must first be able to walk independently. Before they can gallop, they must be able to run. Typically, each skill is sequential and dependent on the one before it.

Developmental milestone charts will give you a general idea of typical childhood development at any age. **However, each child is unique; do not rely on these charts as a standard.** For example, some infants may begin walking at 10 months whereas other infants may not begin walking until 15 months. Joshua, a 3-year-old in your setting, might be able to balance himself well enough to use roller skates, but Xavier, a 5-year-old, might fall each time he tries to skate. Both Joshua and Xavier may be developing typically—according to their own biological clocks.

Throwing and catching are gross motor manipulative movements.

The Figure 30. located on page 117 describes some of the gross motor skills that children are typically developing at this age.

Children's bodies change dramatically from birth to 5 years old, and they develop new skills at a rapid pace. However, maintain realistic expectations for children's growth. Infants, toddlers, and preschoolers need a great number of opportunities to help them develop physical skills (Shonkoff & Phillips, 2000; Albrecht & Miller, 2000). Configure your indoor and outdoor settings to ensure that children receive numerous stimulating and challenging opportunities daily.

Figure 30. Gross Motor Skills for Young Children

Age	Developing Gross Motor Skills
Young Infants birth–8 months	• Turns head from side to side. • Rolls from back to stomach. • Holds head and chest up when lying on stomach. • Uses arms and legs to move forward when on stomach and back. • Begins to sit without assistance.
Mobile Infants 9–17 months	• Sits without assistance and maintains balance while playing with a toy. • Scoots on stomach. • Crawls after a toy. • Pulls self up from sitting to standing positions or lowers self from standing to sitting positions. • Walks while holding onto furniture or people and later walks without assistance.
Toddlers 18–36 months	• Throws large ball. • Carries large objects. • Walks easily or runs from place to place without assistance. • Propels riding toys with feet. • Walks up stairs alternating feet. • Runs. • Builds with blocks. • Jumps on two feet. • Balances on one foot.
Preschoolers 3–4 years old	• Stands on tiptoes with hands overhead for more than 3 seconds. • Hops on one foot forward 1–3 times. • Walks down stairs by placing one foot on each step (alternating gait). • Able to walk on 2 in. line for 10 ft without stepping off once. • Throws tennis ball underhand 10 ft using upper trunk rotation, arms, and legs moving in opposition. Initiates throw by moving arm down and back. • Pedals tricycle for long distances, turns corners, and makes U-turns. • Gallops 5 ft.
Preschoolers 4–5 years old	• Completes somersaults with chin tucked and without turning to side. • Gallops 10 ft with weight transferred smoothly and evenly; arms move freely in opposition to legs. • Jumps and turns so feet land in opposite direction from starting position (180-degree turn in the air). • Hops eight consecutive times on one foot followed by eight hops on other foot. • Skips eight steps using opposing arm and leg movements and using alternating feet while maintaining balance. • Hits a target 12 ft away with tennis ball using overhead throw. • Catches tennis ball from 5 ft away with hands outstretched. • Runs while pumping arms.

(Centers for Disease Control and Prevention [CDC], 2012)

Physical

Promoting Gross Motor Skills

Young Infants (birth–8 months)

During this time, infants are growing and developing rapidly. They are beginning to roll over, sit up independently, and grab and hold objects. Configure your setting so that infants can experience open spaces in ways such as lying on their backs on a blanket on the floor in a safe area. Place materials—including mobiles, squeaky toys, rattles, bells, balls, hand puppets, plastic measuring spoons, teething rings, and hollow building blocks—in the setting that will stimulate infants and promote their gross motor skills. When infants are ready to roll over onto their stomachs, allow them to spend time in this position to help them develop the use of their legs, neck, arms, and hands. Place toys or safe items within infants' reach to encourage them to roll over when they are able to do so. When infants begin crawling, place toys nearby that they can choose to investigate.

Mobile Infants (9–17 months)

Provide safe and interesting places for infants to move around and explore, and ensure that there is ample space for crawling and walking around the setting. Place materials around the room that mobile infants can access—including books, large hollow blocks, balls, and manipulatives—that are interesting and stimulating. Provide push toys, such as toy strollers and shopping carts. Provide materials and equipment that are safe for infants to use to pull themselves up to standing position, such as a low bookshelf containing age-appropriate toys that is anchored to the wall. If infants pull themselves up then fall to a sitting position, observe their reactions and encourage them to stand again. As you observe mobile infants, you will know when they require your support and when they can

Children can practice gross motor skills while playing alone or with peers.

maneuver independently. For example, 12-month-old Ruby climbs up a climber. By observing her, you know that she is unable to climb down on her own. Step in to help Ruby down from the climber.

Toddlers (18–36 months)

Create safe spaces and opportunities—both indoors and outdoors—for toddlers to walk, run, jump, and climb. Allow them to explore your setting and to use independently the motor skills they have acquired recently. Observe their developing skills, along with their newfound balance and coordination, and provide toddlers with interesting materials and equipment that will test these skills. Provide riding toys and climbing structures with steps, swings, and slides. These toys promote toddlers' developing pedaling, balancing, climbing, jumping, traveling, running, and hopping skills. Provide balls, beanbags, and rings that children can roll, toss, and catch. When children are excited by rolling a new toy across the floor, think of other materials you have in your setting that the child can roll safely.

Preschoolers (3–5 year olds)

Engage preschoolers daily in enjoyable gross motor activities that require them to use their entire bodies. Apply some of the following strategies to encourage children to practice their skills:

Provide morning and afternoon periods of unstructured play. In Chapter 3, you learned that scheduling for infants and toddlers should follow the children's own rhythms and patterns. You also learned that preschoolers need alternate periods of active and quiet time throughout the day as well as 45 min to 1 hour of scheduled outdoor play both in the morning and the afternoon. These scheduled play times provide children with ample time for gross motor activities. According to the National Association for Sport and Physical Education (NASPE, 2012), preschool children should not be at rest or sitting for more than 60 min at a time unless they are sleeping. Children crave movement. Early educators support this need by ensuring that there is plenty of time for children to move and explore. For example, if you see children climbing on a book shelf or other structure in your setting, work with your colleagues to figure out how to promote the development of the children's climbing skills in a safe manner.

Discover ways to ensure that children have opportunities to explore and develop gross motor skills indoors on days when you are unable to go outdoors. Do you have a space inside where children can climb, skip, and crawl? If there is no gym or "gross motor room" available to you, then find or create a space in your setting that children can use for movement activities. If your music and movement center has space, children can march, dance, or exercise. Or use the space in the

Allow children to create games that will get their bodies moving.

Physical

block center for movement activities. Be sure to provide equipment like balance boards, tunnels, hula hoops, and tumbling mats if they are available.

Stock your program with equipment and toys that will support gross motor development.
Outdoor equipment includes swings, slides, climbing structures, tricycles, wagons, and hollow blocks. Smaller equipment, like roller boards and scooters, will provide exciting experiences for older preschoolers who are adept at balancing themselves. Indoor equipment includes balance boards, large blocks, large foam wedges, ramps, and crawl-through tunnels. Materials that will encourage large muscle movement include jump ropes (7-ft ropes are recommended for young children), balls, beanbags, hula hoops, balance beams, tumbling mats, large blocks, foam or plastic bats, paddles, parachutes, and streamers.

While choosing equipment and materials, consult the children's parents to see if there are any materials that represent their home cultures. Make children feel more at home by incorporating these playthings into your setting. Ask parents to suggest games, activities, music, and dances to incorporate into your gross motor program.

Provide space and equipment for aiming activities. Provide children with bats, tennis balls, beanbags, targets, plastic bowling balls, bowling pins, and other safe materials to play aiming games.

Schedule daily opportunities for movement experiences. Include opportunities for movement—including forming a marching band, performing tumbling routines, dancing to music, running an obstacle course, or making an outdoor parachute billow into a temporary "tent"—in both indoor and outdoor free play times.

Introduce children to games that will require them to use their large muscles. Games, like "duck, duck, goose", get children moving and stopping on demand. Other games, like "Simon says", "follow the leader", "tag", and "hide and seek", get children practicing advanced motor skills. You will use these games as gross motor opportunities. Children will play them to have fun.

Finally, include short (1–2 min) activities in circle time or during routines, such as after nap time, that will get children's blood flowing. For example, stretching after an activity clears children's minds and exercises their muscles.

Schedule outdoor play for 45 min to an hour both in the morning and afternoon.

Make gross motor activities exciting and interesting. Consider ways to challenge children and motivate them into action, like running obstacle courses, wandering through simple mazes, and crawling through pretend tunnels. Try changing the rules to a familiar game. For example, instead of playing Simon Says, have children play Reverse Simon Says. In this version of the game, if you say, "Simon says touch your head," children should touch their toes.

Allow children to enjoy the process of learning gross motor skills. Let them focus more on the activity itself than the final result or product. For example, Ms. King demonstrates how to saw wood safely. Ms. King's goal is for her 4-year-old children to enjoy the process of sawing the wood, not to produce a heaping pile of it.

Plan movement experiences that allow children to participate according to their skills and interests. These activities, like dancing, moving like wheat blowing in the wind, or pretending to be snakes crawling through the rainforest, should be open-ended rather than competitive. The goal is for everyone to participate, not to see who performs the activity best.

Children with physical disabilities who can walk can most likely participate in any of the motor activities the other children do (Gould & Sullivan, 2004). Children with physical disabilities go through the same sequence of development you learned about earlier in the chapter. Although the timing of milestones is likely to be different, the order in which skills develop is typically similar. Let children show you what they can do, rather than setting your expectations prematurely. Follow their lead, and you will learn how best to adapt your program to meet their individual needs.

Adapting Gross Motor Play to Meet Children's Needs

The children in Ms. Priscilla's class are running relay races. Julian, a 4-year-old, can walk, but not run. Ms. Priscilla wants Julian to join in the children's gross motor play, but worries that he will fall and become frustrated. She does not want Julian to "fail" in front of his peers. She considers appointing him score-keeper so that he can still be involved in the activity and avoid "failure." However, this would deprive him of the chance to really experience gross motor activity. Ms. Priscilla decides to schedule a scavenger hunt in the afternoon, during which the children will work in teams and walk around the playground in search of clues. This activity successfully meets Julian's skills where they are and allows him to fully participate with his peers.

Challenge children to expand their skills. Provide individual children with new personal challenges. For example, if Marta has learned to kick a ball but gives no thought to where it goes, give her some targets to practice her aim. Likewise, if Louis can walk a straight line on the ground, challenge him to walk along the edge of the sandbox. Give children group challenges, such as

"Hop on your right foot as many times as I clap." Or, as you slowly lift a jump rope off the ground, ask the children to, "One at a time, jump forward, backward, and sideways over the rope." Children will enjoy honing and mastering these skills.

Children with special needs may have a more difficult time participating in certain gross motor activities. For example, if you have a child diagnosed with cerebral palsy or dyspraxia (a motor-skills disorder that affects how well the brain sends signals to muscles), they may have delays in their motor development. Children with visual impairments are also likely to have poor physical fitness because of their anxiety about moving where they cannot see (Gould & Sullivan, 2004).

As an early educator, identify gross motor activities in which all the children in your setting can participate. See what children can do and tailor activities to build on these strengths. Children who are wheelchair-bound, for example, can steer around obstacles and objects. They can also practice throwing and catching beanbags. If you have access to equipment specially designed for wheelchair-bound children, such as scooter boards, platform swings, or prone standers, help children out of their wheelchairs and let them experience these gross motor activities. If you work with the children's therapists and parents, help to plan a gross motor program that will address children's needs more specifically.

All children in your setting need and deserve your support in promoting their gross motor development. Observe them all to see if children who are not receiving special education services might be in need of such assistance. Are there any children who are not running, jumping, hopping, or balancing themselves? While all children have their individual time clocks for development, there is an expectation they should reach certain milestones by a particular age. If you have concerns about children's development, discuss these concerns with the children's parents. They may want to consult the child's pediatrician or have you bring in a special education consultant to conduct further observation.

Add gross motor activities to your centers wherever you can. Use music from the children's home countries to march, dance, or play a game of "musical chairs". Use books in the children's home languages as well as English to inspire skits and plays.

Incorporate gross motor activities into transitions. Suggest that children gallop like gazelles when coming indoors. Or, everyone can try putting on their coats while hopping on one foot. Not only does this give children a chance to work on their gross motor skills, it is sure to bring laughs to an otherwise routine activity.

Make gross motor activities a part of your daily transitions.

Challenging Children During Gross Motor Activity

Eduardo is able to balance in place. He can even stand on one foot, with his arms extended. His caregiver, Mr. Kennedy, wants to increase his balancing skills. First, he gives Eduardo objects to hold, like beanbags, while balancing. Mr. Kennedy then challenges Eduardo to stand on stationary objects that are higher than the ground, like a sturdy bench or a tire in the outdoor obstacle course. As Eduardo's skills catch up to the challenges, Mr. Kennedy asks Eduardo to stand on various beams, even rounded ones—first alone and then holding objects.

Once he's competent in balancing, Mr. Kennedy encourages Eduardo to balance while moving. He first asks Eduardo to walk back and forth along a line on the floor, using alternate foot stepping. Next, Eduardo tries walking along an uneven surface, such as a rope on the ground. After accomplishing this, Eduardo walks along a beam. Each time he completes a walk across the beam, Mr. Kennedy raises it a bit higher.

At this point, Eduardo can balance himself both standing and moving. Because Eduardo is so adept at balance skills, Mr. Kennedy decides to make Eduardo a pair of stilts by attaching a VELCRO® Brand foot fastener atop two upside-down metal pails. Eduardo thrills himself and the other children with his newfound stilt-walking skill.

Use visual aids to teach children to throw, catch, and kick (Binelli & Yongue, 2004). Children's optic nerves are still developing, making tracking objects somewhat difficult. Try these ideas to help children keep track of the ball:

- Use bright, colorful balls.

- Use soft balls that are easy to catch, such as beach balls, balloons, balls of yarn, Koosh balls, or Nerf balls.

- Throw balls at a consistent speed and height.

Instruct children on how to position their hands and feet:

- If what they want to catch is above their waist, their thumb tips should point toward each other.

- If what they want to catch is below their waist, their pinkie tips should point toward each other.

- To throw overhand, the throwing hand should be behind the head as they step forward with the opposite foot.

Again, observe children as they work to master these skills, and keep a record of their progress. For example, watch Justin as he runs, skips, hops, throws, kicks, rides a tricycle, and performs all of the other gross motor activities discussed in this section. In which skills is he at a beginning level, mastery level, or somewhere in between? Do his skill levels increase when he plays with one or two friends? How about with the whole group? What does he think his strengths and weaknesses are?

After you have learned this information, think about how you can help children develop their skills further. If Tiffany can only throw underhand, what could you do to help her learn to throw overhand? Here are a few options:

- Work with her outdoors, showing her the correct way to throw overhand.

- Watch her throw overhand, correcting her with each try.

- Walk her through the process and give her pointers, like: "Point your shoulder of the arm that you don't throw with, toward the target. Now keep your throwing arm way behind your head and move your opposite foot toward the target. Now let your throwing arm move across your body."

- Place markers, like pieces of tape or footprints and arrows, on the ground to illustrate where Tiffany should move her feet as she throws.

- Have her practice throwing the ball against a wall.

- Encourage her to practice with a friend who has mastered this skill. Have them practice an underhand throw first, and then move on to the overhand throw. Start the children off at a relatively close and comfortable distance from one another. Then, as Tiffany gains skill, move the children farther apart.

- Have a circle of children toss balls to one another underhand, in turn. They can start with beach balls and move on to beanbags and then balls of varying sizes and softness.

Because you know Tiffany and have insight into how she learns best, you can decide which of these strategies is most appropriate for her. Practice is paramount to mastering gross motor skills. Build time into your schedule for Tiffany to practice throwing—alone, with your assistance, with a friend, or with a small group. Keep a variety of balls in various sizes, weights, and textures available for the

Plan open-ended activities that encourage movement.

children to use. The goal is to individualize your curriculum so that all of the children in your program—including Tiffany—have an opportunity to develop, refine, and master gross motor skills.

Learning and mastering gross motor skills makes children feel good about their bodies and gives them confidence in their abilities. Most children are eager to get outdoors and move. However, occasionally you will have children who do not want to participate in these activities for a variety of reasons. Perhaps they are having trouble mastering certain skills and are frustrated or embarrassed. Or they may be reluctant to participate because of illness, abuse, or overprotection at home. Maybe they do not like these kinds of activities. Gently encourage these children to join in movement activities. Try to find out why they are reluctant, and see if you can address it. Build on what interests the children.

For example, Kareem, a 4-year-old in your setting, is passionate about cars. He loves to talk about different makes and models, reads books about cars, and uses the cars in your blocks center. Think about creating a space for cars outdoors to promote Kareem's engagement in gross motor skill activity. Create roads with intersections

Play games with the children that will require them to use their large muscles.

in your outdoor space. Kareem can pretend he is a car and walk, run, or ride a tricycle through make-believe traffic.

If children do not want to be around others because they are embarrassed, find a private area to work with these children one-on-one. If they find an activity too difficult, find a way to make it less frustrating. For example, if Elizabeth cries at the thought of riding a tricycle, offer her a four-wheeled pedal toy to use until she is more confident in her ability. If she will try this toy, Elizabeth will still get the benefits of gross motor exercise in a way that meets her skill and comfort level. If children remain resistant to an activity, however, do not force their participation.

Figure 31. examines each of the basic gross motor skills that children will develop as they grow.

Figure 31. Mastering Baseline Skills at the Preschool Level

Gross Motor Skill	Physical Prerequisites for This Skill	What Constitutes Mastery
LOCOMOTOR		
Running	Walking without assistance.	Running backward and forward.
Jumping	Jumping off a step with an adult holding his/her hand.	Jumping forward from a standing position; jumping 12–16 in. on either foot and 36 in. using both feet.
Leaping	Moving through the air with an adult holding his/her hands.	Putting his/her hands on the back of a squatting child and vaulting over the child ("Leap Frog").
Standing on one foot	Standing on one foot, holding on to an adult for balance.	Standing on one foot unassisted for 10 seconds.
Hopping	Hopping on one foot in place, holding on to an adult for balance.	Hopping on either foot to a targeted landing point; hopping eight times consecutively.
Galloping	Running.	Moving by leading one foot and having the other follow; changing the lead foot.
Skipping	Running and galloping, but without changing the lead foot.	A combined leg movement of stepping and hopping; skipping 8–10 times.
Climbing stairs	Climbing upstairs with both feet on each step, no hand support; climbing downstairs with both feet on each step while holding on to a wall or railing.	Climbing up and down stairs using alternating feet and no hand support.
Rolling (somersault)	Tucking head into body while an adult pushes the child forward and turns the child over, with feet going over the child's head.	Rolling 360 degrees.
MANIPULATIVE MOVEMENT		
Throwing	Throwing a beanbag or ball underhand a short distance.	Throwing objects with controlled, smooth overhand motions; throwing a tennis ball 12 ft at target.
Catching	Trapping a thrown object with his/her whole body.	Catching an object in his/her hands with control, elbows bent.
Kicking	Kicking an object with adult holding the child's hand to maintain balance.	Kicking an object unassisted with a smooth, fluid motion of the leg.
STABILITY MOVEMENT		
Balancing	Walking along a line, sometimes on toes, occasionally stepping off of the line.	Walking forward or backward along an edge or beam for four or more steps without falling off; standing on elevated or unstable objects.
Stopping and starting	Stopping or starting with adult prompting and assistance.	Stopping and starting upon command, avoiding obstacles and changing directions.
Riding a trike	Sitting on tricycle and using feet to push forward or backward.	Using feet to pedal tricycle and handle bars to control direction and avoid obstacles.
Swinging	Sitting on swing, pushed and caught by adult positioned behind swing.	Using feet to push up on swing; moving forward and backward seamlessly.

(Goodway, Ozmun, & Gallahue, 2011)

Promoting Physical Health

According to the National Association for Sport and Physical Education (2004), only 2% of inactive children grow up to be physically active adults. Keeping children active and fit prevents childhood obesity and sets the stage for a lifetime of fitness. In addition to controlling weight, physical activity benefits children in the following ways (Benelli & Yongue, 2004):

- Builds and maintains healthy bones and muscles.

- Prevents or delays high blood pressure, cholesterol, and type 2 diabetes.

- Reduces stress.

- Increases attention spans.

- Increases academic success.

- Enhances language and social skills.

- Makes children feel confident and competent.

Be intentional about including physical movement in your lesson plans and curricula that provide young children the opportunities to strengthen gross motor skills and to promote overall good health.

Promoting Children's Fine Motor Development

Fine motor skills involve coordinating the small muscles of the hand, wrist, and fingers. These skills can be difficult to master, because they require muscular control, patience, judgment, and brain coordination (Huffman & Fortenberry, 2011). Children need to have a foundation in large muscle skills before they can develop fine motor skills. The hands and fingers need stable torso and shoulder muscles to function properly.

Like gross motor development, fine motor development is sequential and predictable. Children develop these skills at different rates. By the age of 5 years old, most children have the coordination to eat peas with a fork, use scissors to cut out collage materials, hold and turn the pages of a book, and play a kazoo, whereas newborn infants do not have the skills to grasp and hold an object. Grasping a finger or object placed in their palms is one of the first fine motor skills infants develop and is a basic reflex response. Once children can pick up a fork, zip a zipper, or pour water, they can master self-help skills like feeding and dressing themselves.

Figure 32. explains typical fine motor skill development from birth to 5 years old.

Physical

Figure 32. Fine Motor Skill Development: Birth to 5 Years Old

Age	Fine Motor Skills Developed
Young Infants birth–8 months	• Holds and shakes rattle • Eyes and head follow moving objects • Grasps objects • Looks at an object in hand while bringing it to mouth • Drops and puts small blocks into a container
Mobile Infants 9–17 months	• Transfers a block or another toy from hand to hand • Uses pincher grasp with thumb and forefinger together to pick up small objects • Pushes or pulls toys while standing or walking • Uses spoon
Toddlers 18–36 months	• Holds cup or glass in one hand • Unbuttons large buttons • Turns doorknobs • Makes lines, circles, or scribbles with fat crayons • Stacks small blocks • Pushes and pats puzzle pieces into place • Tears tissue paper into small pieces to glue onto paper • Turns pages of books, though not always one at a time
Preschoolers 3–4 years old	• Places large pegs into pegboards; strings large beads; pours liquids with some spills • Builds block towers; easily does puzzles with whole objects represented as a piece • Draws shapes, such as the circle; begins to design objects, such as a house or figure; draws objects in some relation to each other • Holds crayons or markers with fingers instead of the fist • Undresses without assistance but needs help getting dressed; unbuttons skillfully but buttons slowly • Uses scissors
Preschoolers 4–5 years old	• Uses small pegs and board; strings small beads and may do so in a pattern • Pours sand or liquid into small containers • Builds complex block structures that extend vertically; shows limited spatial judgment and tends to knock things over • Enjoys manipulating play objects that have fine parts; likes to use scissors; practices an activity many times to gain mastery • Draws combinations of simple shapes; draws persons with at least four parts and objects that are recognizable to adults • Dresses and undresses without assistance; brushes teeth and combs hair; spills rarely with cup or spoon; laces shoes or clothing and is learning to tie laces

(American Academy of Pediatrics [AAP], 2013)

Strategies for Developing Fine Motor Skills

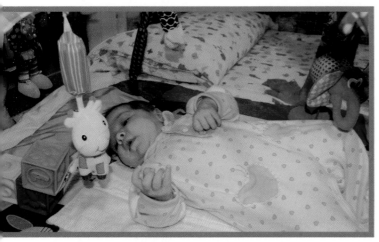

Provide plenty of space for infants to move their legs, feet, arms, and hands.

Young Infants (birth–8 months)

Provide space and opportunity for infants to move legs, feet, arms, and hands and to kick, hit, and grasp objects. Place interesting objects and toys within infants' reach to look or swipe at, hit, or kick. Be careful not to place objects into infants' hands until they are ready to grasp and release objects independently. Provide opportunities for infants to practice reaching and grasping various small objects.

Mobile Infants (9–17 months)

Provide toys and materials that encourage fine motor skills including shape sorters; containers for inserting and removing objects; and toys with pieces that separate, fit together, fit inside, and stack. Play games with infants that require physical actions, such as using different kinds of balls to roll, throw, or kick. Include a variety of books in your setting that infants can access and handle independently. Allow plenty of time for infants to explore and manipulate materials in your setting. Support infants in learning how to feed themselves independently. For example, most 1-year-old children are ready to drink from a cup. Providing appropriate cups for infants to drink from will help them develop fine motor skills as they grasp the cups and move them toward their mouths.

Let children choose activities that match their skills.

Toddlers (18–36 months)

Provide opportunities for toddlers to play and interact with other children. Provide toys and materials that help them practice fine motor skills and eye–hand coordination, such as puzzles, pegs and pegboards, blocks, construction toys, beads to string, clay, modeling clay, and lacing cards. Provide toddlers opportunities for sensory experiences using sand or water with toys, such as shovels and buckets, cups, spoons, squirt bottles, and other containers.

Preschoolers (3–5 years old)

Address a wide range of children's skills and abilities. Think about how you can offer children materials that meet differing skills and abilities in fine motor development. Provide 5- to 50-piece puzzles with and without knobs, enabling children at all skill levels to experience completing a

Physical

puzzle. Keep foam, cardboard, and wood blocks in varying sizes so that children can choose the type of block that they feel most comfortable using to build fine motor coordination.

Even though there is a wide range of what is considered typical development during the preschool years, you may become concerned if you see children continually having difficulty grasping objects or coordinating their hand and eye movements. If, for example, a 5-year-old child in your setting is still having trouble using drawing and writing tools as well as manipulating a fork and spoon, discuss your concern with the child's parents. As with gross motor difficulties, the parents may wish to consult the child's pediatrician or call in a special educator to conduct a more in-depth observation.

There may be children in your setting who have difficulty moving the small muscles in their hands or who have developmental delays. Children with cerebral palsy or those who are wheelchair-bound are most likely to need extra help. Make sure children are positioned correctly by supporting their trunks so that their heads and hands are at midpoint on their bodies (Gould & Sullivan, 2004).

Continue to observe children who have special needs. Look for ways to adapt your materials and setting to stimulate, engage, and challenge all children as they develop their fine motor skills. Some things you might try include the following (Gould & Sullivan, 2004):

- Offer the child larger beads to string on pipe cleaners.

- Attach knobs to puzzle pieces to make them easier to grasp.

- Make use of vertical planes. Place books and puzzles on easels and tape pegboards against the wall.

- Replace buttons and zippers on dress-up clothes with VELCRO® Brand closures.

- Use shower curtain rings as zipper pulls on jackets.

- Glue magnets to the backs of small blocks and toys and place them on cookie sheets.

Provide lots of open-ended experiences. Materials, like modeling clay, LEGO® building bricks, and crayons, help children continue to develop their skills and abilities. Use these materials to create open-ended activities that promote children's cognitive skills and creativity. Avoid providing a model for children to copy, as this will limit their creativity. For example, if a small group of children are drawing pictures, this is a great opportunity for you to sit and talk with them about their work. But if you begin drawing, children might copy your work instead of drawing their own pictures.

The process of working with materials, like pencil and paper, is more important than the final product.

Let children choose activities that match their skills. For example, if a group of children are working on making a collage for the bulletin board, invite children either to tear paper or to use scissors, depending on their preference and skills. Likewise, they can use glue sticks or paste—depending on their interest and skills. This allows children with varying skills to participate in the same activity and enjoy being part of the group experience.

Focus on providing children with materials to explore and manipulate. Whether children are working with clay, hammering nails, or painting at an easel, the process of working with these materials is more important than the final product. During this process, children are becoming familiar with the materials, refining small motor skills, and taking pleasure in the activities. However, forcing children to perform tasks or participate in activities before they are ready developmentally will thwart their progress. For example, children who are not yet ready to write letters or numbers will quickly become frustrated if they are required to do this task. But if they are free to experiment, children will start writing letters and numbers when they are ready.

Provide children with vertical surfaces for writing and drawing. Vertical surfaces help children develop the small muscles in their hands and wrists, as well as the larger muscles in their arms and backs. Tape pieces of paper to the wall or use easels and allow children to draw and color on the paper.

You do not need to teach children specific fine motor skills, like holding objects between their fingers and thumbs or making a circle with their thumbs and index fingers. Rather, when you encourage children to perform activities using materials that require these skills—including holding a paintbrush, tying a shoe lace, or placing a puzzle piece in a frame—they will develop these skills naturally.

By stocking your setting with materials that require small motor activity, children will not only have lots of opportunities to practice and refine their fine motor skills, but they can pick the type of activity that will interest them and motivate them to practice. For example, Charlie may choose to work in the cooking center, and Ava may choose to play with blocks. Both children will be developing fine motor skills while doing what they enjoy.

While teaching fine motor skills is not necessary, you may need to model how to use materials correctly, like musical instruments or hammers. Materials that are new to children, like digital cameras or board games, may also require modeling or direct instruction before you introduce them into play.

Figure 33. suggests materials you can add to the learning centers in your setting to promote fine motor development. These are only suggestions. Your inventory of materials may vary.

Vertical surfaces help children develop the small muscles in their hands and wrists and the larger muscles in their arms and backs.

Figure 33. Materials for Promoting Fine Motor Development in Preschoolers (3–5 Years Old)

Learning Center	Materials
Block	Foam blocks, hardwood blocks, animal figures, people figures, small cars, buses, trains, traffic signs, books, markers and chart paper, ramps, and pulleys
Art	Paints, brushes, chalk, crayons, markers, scissors, stapler, puncher, stencils, clays, wires, pipe cleaners, potholder loops and looms, feathers, paste, glue, rubber bands, and wires
Literacy	Books, felt letters and numbers, magnetic letters and numbers, puppets, letter stamps, markers, paper clips, pencil sharpener, stencils, computer keyboard, mouse, and printer
Dramatic Play	Dress-up clothing, hats, purses, jewelry, plastic foods, telephones, writing pads, cookbooks, and dolls
Music & Movement	Musical instruments (drums, kazoos, rhythm sticks, bells, triangles, maracas, etc.), headphones, and CDs/tapes/MP3s
Science Center	Seeds, prisms, magnifying glasses, eyedroppers, tweezers, tongs, magnets, food for pets, markers and chart paper, books, and egg cartons for sorting
Math & Manipulatives	LEGO® building bricks, people figures, props, beads, sewing cards, pegs and pegboards, geoboards, Cuisenaire® rods, parquetry blocks, interlocking links and cubes, lotto games, dominoes, card games, board games, puzzles, self-help frames, nesting boxes and cups, shape sorters, attribute blocks, and Unifix® cubes
Sand/Water	(Sand Center) Measuring cups, measuring spoons, pails and shovels, cookie cutters, muffin tins, ladles, magnifying glasses, shakers, toothbrushes, combs, scoops, funnels, tongs, tweezers, colander, and rakes (Water Center) Basters, squirt bottles, whisks, eggbeaters, sponges, dolls, straws, eyedroppers, fishnets, gutters, tubing, waterwheels, toy boats, and bubble wands
Cooking	Measuring spoons, measuring cups, pastry brushes, pitchers, rolling pins, can openers, mixers, mortars and pestles, graters, timers, colanders, eggbeaters, funnels, ladles, spatulas, tongs, sifters, and pastry bags and tips
Outdoors	Gardening shovels, rakes, hoes, sand and water shovels and pails, miniature animals figures, people figures, cars and trucks, books, writing paper and markers, and board games

Connecting Children's Physical Development to the Development of the Whole Child

Is building a structure out of hollow blocks an example of a physical development task? Cognitive development? Social–emotional development? Language development? All of these answers are correct.

It is almost impossible to separate physical development from the rest of children's development. With young children, social, emotional, cognitive, and language development are interrelated. Every time a child learns a physical skill, it has an impact on the other domains of development. For example, children may be able to carry and stack blocks on top of each other—a physical task. However, while they are displaying mastery of physical skills, their development is progressing in other areas, too.

Contemporary brain research proves that both gross and fine motor skill development are related to brain development. Research has also shown that the ability to skip improves reading skills (Teacher Support Force [TSF], 2011). In addition, every time children move the small muscles in their hands, brain connections are strengthened (Bredekamp, 2013).

The Interrelation of Development Skills During Play

Jessica and Cheyenne decide to build a fort out of hollow blocks together (social development). They discuss the need to take the blocks outdoors (language development). They carry the blocks outdoors and set them on a level area of ground (physical development). They devise a plan (language development; cognitive development) to make a square out of the blocks first (cognitive development) and then stack them (physical development). When they finish, they admire their fort and high-five to celebrate their success (social–emotional development).

On the other hand, the information our senses (touching, seeing, hearing, smelling, and tasting) provide us impacts our physical movements. For young children who are dependent on sensory learning, this means that their physical development is influenced by how they use the information they receive from their senses. A branch of physical development known as "perceptual motor development" focuses precisely on this relationship.

Promote perceptual motor development by offering children activities that tie sensory learning to physical movement. For example, during group time, have children sing and chant finger plays, like "Open, Shut Them" which involves physical movements:

Open, shut them, *(open and shut fists)*,

Open, shut them,

Give a little clap, clap, clap *(clap)*.

Open, shut them *(open and shut fists)*,

Open, shut them,

Fold them in your lap, lap, lap *(place hands in lap)*.

Creep them, creep them
(walk hands up body to chin),

Slowly creep them,

Right up to your chin, chin, chin.

Open wide your little mouth,

But do not put them in, in, in.

Other songs, like "Head, Shoulders, Knees, and Toes"; "Where Is Thumbkin?"; and "The Hokey Pokey" also incorporate physical movements and help children develop body awareness—a sense of their body parts and how they are connected. More active games like "duck, duck, goose" and "hide and seek" teach spatial awareness—where children are in relation to their environments. Whenever you encourage children to use their senses, you are facilitating perceptual motor development. ■

Children need to have a foundation in large muscle skills before they can develop fine motor skills.

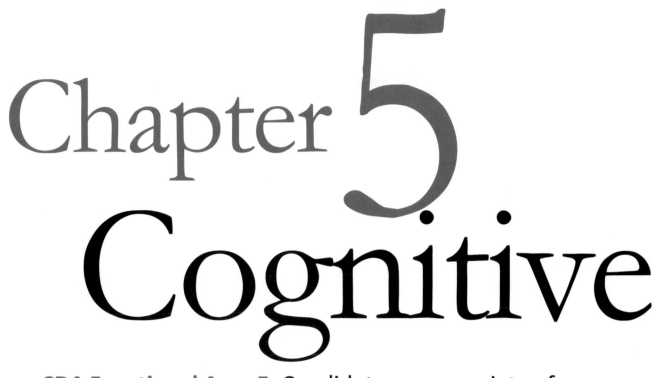

Chapter 5
Cognitive

CDA Functional Area 5: Candidate uses a variety of developmentally appropriate learning experiences and teaching strategies to promote curiosity, reasoning, and problem-solving and to lay the foundation for all later learning. Candidate implements curriculum that promotes children's learning of important mathematics, science, technology, social studies and other content goals.

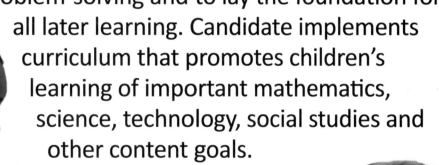

Cognitive

Introduction

Cognitive development refers to children's increasing ability to think as they grow. Children's brains develop rapidly during early childhood. They are beginning to reason, expand their memories, solve problems, think symbolically, employ logic, predict situation outcomes, understand others' perspectives, and understand cause and effect.

Your role in supporting children's cognitive growth is vital, and in this chapter, you will learn the following:

- What is Early Childhood Cognitive Development?
- Major Learning Theories.
- Executive Function and School Readiness.
- Learning Through Play.
- Children As Scientists: Content Learning.

What is Early Childhood Cognitive Development?

In 2000, the National Research Council and the Institute of Medicine of the National Academies published From Neurons to Neighborhoods: The Science of Early Childhood Development. This book explains that infants are born with millions of brain cells (neurons) that connect (synapses) as a result of experiences during the early years of life. The groups' research emphasizes the importance of four essential aspects of learning for young children (Shonkoff & Phillips, 2000):

- Loving and caring relationships with adults.
- Many opportunities to explore the world through seeing, touching, hearing, tasting, and smelling.
- Conversation and language richness in the environment.
- Play.

Young children are active learners. They learn best when they have trusting relationships with adults and can use their own experiences to make sense of their worlds. Infants and toddlers, for example, develop strong social and emotional skills when their needs are met consistently by adults they trust and when the interactions among the adults and children are positive.

What and how children learn during the first 5 years of their lives lays the foundation for successful lifelong learning. Children become confident learners when adults encourage their discoveries and explorations.

Major Learning Theories

In Chapter 4, you learned that all facets of children's development are intertwined. Separating cognitive development from social–emotional development or language development is impossible. For example, Ben and Keisha are reading a new story with Ms. Tanya. As Ms. Tanya reads, she asks both children to predict what will happen next in the story (cognitive development). She then asks them how they think the story's main characters are feeling (social–emotional development) and introduces new vocabulary (language development) throughout the tale.

As an early educator, be reflective. Observe the children in your setting and discover how they learn best. Your findings will influence the choices you make in your setting, the materials you provide, the interactions you have with the children, and the experiences you offer them.

The theorists you will read about in this chapter have influenced greatly what we know about early childhood cognitive development and our understanding of best teaching practices for young children. These professionals developed their theories after years of observing children's learning.

Jean Piaget

Swiss psychologist Jean Piaget theorized that young children think differently from adults—a theory that is the foundation for all developmentally appropriate educational practices and curricula today.

His **constructivist theory** emphasizes that thinking and learning is a dynamic, interactive process between children and their environments. In other words, children actively *construct* their own knowledge through engagement with their surroundings, and develop *schemas*, or mental concepts, to understand and think about ideas and objects.

For example, Emma, a 3-year-old in your setting, has three cats at home, but she has never seen a dog. Your group passes a dog during a community walk. Emma points to the dog and shouts, "Look at that big cat!" You explain to her that the animal she sees is actually a dog—a different animal from a cat. Emma's existing schema that identifies all four-legged, furry animals as cats is now altered.

After identifying the dog, you ask the children to tell you what they know about cats and dogs. This is a meaningful way for them to discuss their own learning and understanding about specific animals and for you to support children and their growing knowledge. With this

Cognitive

impromptu learning exercise, you have helped to expand Emma's schema about four-legged, furry animals to include dogs. She has also begun learning to categorize.

Piaget also said that children's processes of understanding new concepts involve three phases: *assimilation, accommodation,* and *equilibrium*. Children assimilate (make connections between new information and existing knowledge) and accommodate (use new information to alter their existing knowledge) to achieve equilibrium (change behavior based on altered knowledge). This idea explains how children are able to move from one stage of thought into the next (Gordon & Williams-Browne, 2013).

Through his research and observations, Piaget developed four stages of cognitive development spanning infancy to adulthood:

- **Sensorimotor:** birth through ages 18–24 months.

- **Preoperational:** toddlerhood (18–24 months) through age 7 years old.

- **Concrete Operational:** 7 years old to 12 years old.

- **Formal Operational:** adolescence through adulthood.

The sensorimotor and preoperational stages are most relevant to our work.

During the sensorimotor stage, infants are only aware of what is immediately in front of them, focusing on what they see and do and any physical interactions with their immediate environments. They are unaware of how objects react; therefore, they experiment by shaking, throwing, or mouthing these objects and learn about their worlds through trial-and-error. At about 7–9 months, infants begin to realize that an object exists, even if they can no longer see it. Known as *object permanence,* this important milestone is a sign that their memories are developing. For example, a 5-month-old infant who sees you hide an object behind your back will lose interest in the toy. She does not understand that the toy is still there, because she does not understand object permanence.

In the preoperational stage, young children start to think about things symbolically. Their language use matures. They also develop memory and imagination, which

Infants learn best when they feel safe and loved.

allows them to understand the difference between past and future and engage in make-believe. Characteristics of this stage include *egocentrism* (seeing the world from his/her perspective) and difficulty understanding *conservation* (ability to determine that quantities remain constant despite adjustments in container, shape, or size).

For example, Sean sees Patrick playing alone. "Patrick is sad because his Grandpa left," Sean says to you. After asking him some questions, you find that it is Sean who is sad because his own grandfather left the setting. Sean is in preoperational stage and assumes everyone feels sad because he does. He thinks everyone is sad for the same reason he is—their grandfathers left the setting. Children like Sean also attribute their feelings to inanimate objects and phenomena, like the weather. Sean may tell you that in addition to Patrick being sad, the falling rain means the sky is sad, too.

Understanding Conservation (preoperational stage)

You show 3-year-old Damien two equal stacks of wooden blocks. You knock down one of the block stacks, and the blocks fall into a pile on the table. You ask Damien, "Are there more blocks in the remaining stack or the fallen stack?" Although he saw you compile an equal number of blocks in each stack, he chooses the blocks that have fallen. The fallen blocks appear to take up more space, so Damien reasons that the pile must contain more blocks than the stack. You compile two equal stacks again and ask Damien, "Which stack contains more blocks?" He says that the stacks contain the same number of blocks.

Lev Vygotsky

Russian psychologist Lev Vygotsky theorized that children learn not just by interacting with objects, but also with adults and more-experienced peers. These adults and peers extend children's learning through conversations that use what the children already know to introduce new information—a concept also known as *scaffolding*. For example, Maria is learning to tie her shoelaces. She is sitting on the floor, struggling with the laces. You sit next to her and prompt her through the steps to tie her shoelace. With your verbal support, Maria is able to tie her shoelaces without you doing it for her. She will soon learn to tie them independently (Gordon & Williams-Browne, 2013).

Vygotsky also theorized that pretend play is the most important vehicle for preschoolers' learning. He observed that during imaginary play, children assume roles to regulate their behavior. For example, 4-year-old Anna understands some of the activities that a mother

Cognitive

performs. Pretending to be a mother, Anna defines her actions during play according to her knowledge of a mother's role. This teaches Anna *self-regulation,* or the ability to control her behavior, emotions, and thinking. Self-regulation is linked with children's later success in school (Spiegel, 2008).

Urie Bronfenbrenner

Russian-American psychologist Urie Bronfenbrenner is responsible for the **ecological systems theory**, which examines the impact of children's social environments on their development. He compared this theory to nesting dolls that fit inside one another. His theory comprises five ecological systems that impact learning and development:

- **Microsystem** refers to the institutions, groups, and individuals that most immediately and directly impact children's development including: family, school, religious institutions, neighborhood, and friends. For example, children are influenced by the make-up of their families. Do they have any siblings? Do they have extended relatives that live in the household?

- **Mesosystem** refers to relations between microsystems or connections between contexts, like the relationship between children's parents and early educators. If the children's parents have trusting and respectful relationships with the early educators, then those relationships will positively impact the children.

- **Exosystem** describes situations in which children do not play active roles, but are impacted nonetheless. For example, a child plays no role in his/her mother losing her job, but the child and the rest of the family will experience the impact.

- **Macrosystem** describes the culture, community, and society in which children live. Cultural contexts include developing and industrialized countries, socioeconomic status, poverty, urban versus rural environments, and ethnicity. Children, their parents, their schools, and even their parents' workplaces are all part of a large cultural context. Members of a cultural group share a common identity, heritage, and values. New generations may change these macrosystems or create new ones over time.

Observe children in your setting to determine how they learn best.

- **Chronosystem** describes the patterning of live events and transitions that occur in addition to sociohistorical circumstances, such as births of new siblings or parents divorcing or remarrying (Bronfenbrenner, 1994).

Erik Erikson

Influenced by Sigmund Freud's work, German-born American developmentalist psychologist Erik Erikson devised an eight-stage theory of psychosocial development spanning infancy to adulthood. The first three stages are most relevant to our work:

1. **Trust versus mistrust** (birth–18 months): During this stage, infants are learning whether they can trust the adults around them and the world in which they live. If infants cry, do early educators pick them up? Do infants' parents meet their basic needs? Erikson believed that there is a continuum between trust and mistrust. Infants do not learn to always trust or mistrust someone.

2. **Autonomy versus shame and doubt** (2–4 years old): During this stage of development, toddlers and young children are learning that they are competent and can perform tasks independently. Adult interactions impact children's understanding of their own skills and abilities. If children in this stage are encouraged and supported in their increased independence, they become more confident and secure in their own abilities to survive in the world. If children are criticized, overly controlled, engaged in power struggles with adults, or not given the opportunity to assert themselves, they begin to feel inadequate. These children may become overly dependent upon others, lack self-esteem, and feel a sense of shame or doubt in their own abilities.

3. **Initiative versus guilt** (3–5 years old): During this stage, children are engaged primarily in play and are further developing their relationships with peers. Children are learning how to get along independently and resolve conflicts while developing empathy, a sense of fairness, and conscience. Early educators support children in this stage by establishing a setting that supports children's interests. A small set of boundaries, limits, or rules are present in this setting and are enforced kindly but firmly (Gordon & Williams-Browne, 2013).

Abraham Maslow

Abraham Maslow developed a hierarchy of needs, in which he theorized people's basic needs must be met before they can reach their full potential. His theory is often presented as a pyramid and we will outline each set of needs in the order from basic needs to the most advanced set of needs below:

- **Basic or physiological needs:** air, food, water, sleep, and shelter.

- **Safety and security needs:** feeling safe and secure physically and emotionally within the environment.

- **Love and belonging needs:** social needs, like love, affection, and acceptance.

- **Self esteem:** the need for self-respect and esteem from others.

- **Self-Actualization:** state of harmony and understanding that exists while working to achieve full potential and reach goals (Gordon & Williams-Browne, 2013).

Be aware of children's needs in your setting. Are they hungry, malnourished, or sleep deprived? Do they feel safe and secure? Does each child have a sense of belonging in your setting?

Howard Gardner

With his theory of **multiple intelligences**, American psychologist Howard Gardner suggests that people's intelligence is multifaceted, not a one-dimensional measure of verbal and/or mathematical skill. In this theory, Gardner explains eight types of intelligences; which suggest different learning styles and preferences.

- **Linguistic:** Using language to express yourself and understand other people. Children who have this intelligence enjoy looking at books, telling stories, and using words to describe their feelings.

- **Logical/Mathematical:** Manipulating numbers, quantities, and operations. Children with this capability like to count, explore problems, and easily notice patterns.

- **Musical/Rhythmic:** Thinking in musical terms. Children with this ability hear and recognize patterns.

- **Bodily/Kinesthetic:** Using your whole body or parts of your body (e.g., hands, fingers, and arms) with great skill. Children with this ability tend to be athletic and can move with ease.

- **Spatial:** Visualizing the three-dimensional world with ease. Children with this ability enjoy puzzles, drawing, and/or painting. These children may even excel at pointing out directions from one location to another.

- **Naturalist:** Understanding living things and nature. Children with this ability enjoy hiking, gardening, or learning how to care for the environment.

- **Intrapersonal:** Understanding yourself, who you are, and what you can/want to do. Children with this intelligence have a realistic grasp of their abilities and challenges.

- **Interpersonal:** Understanding other people. Children with this intelligence can figure out other people's feelings and abilities.

Gardner also suggests a possible ninth intelligence:

- **Existential:** Questioning life, death, and spirituality. Children with this intelligence are deep, sensitive thinkers and feelers (Gardner H., Multiple Intelligences).

Figure 34. Brain Research on Cognitive Development

Neuroscientists' work over the past 25 years provides insight on how the brain works and clinical evidence of how children learn to think. Here are the major findings that impact you as an early educator (Schiller, 2010):

Research Findings	What These Findings Mean
Cognitive skills are linked to both genetics and the environment. A rich, interactive environment goes a long way in promoting brain development.	The richer the environment and the more intentional and purposeful the interactions and the experiences, the greater the number of brain connections that are made.
The primary task of the brain during early childhood is to make connections.	Experiences wire the brain. Repetition of these experiences hardwires the brain. (When connections are hardwired, they are likely to remain permanent.)
There are sensitive periods when the brain is at its peak for learning. These are known as *windows of opportunity*.	During early childhood, children's brains are developing at a rapid pace, laying the foundation for lifelong learning. Children are developing a range of cognitive skills, including cause and effect and problem-solving.
Children make use of different learning styles in different situations.	Early educators provide rich learning opportunities for children by using a variety of teaching styles and techniques that engage them in the learning experience.
Children use gestures to accompany learning.	Be sensitive to children's gestures. Exaggerated movements may indicate a breakthrough in a child's understanding of a certain concept. Regard gestures as signs that learning is taking place.
Technology can have both a positive impact on the brain (it strengthens neural connections and quickens visual recognition time) and a negative impact on the brain (losing touch with real-life relationships and the ability to be intimate with others).	Consider how children are engaging with technology in your room. Spend time speaking with children about what they are working on and learning as they use technology. Encourage children to document their learning with digital cameras or computer art programs. Avoid passive screen time.
Children process memories and solve problems during their sleep.	All young children need lots of sleep to keep their brains functioning optimally.

Executive Function and School Readiness

Children are constantly refining their *executive function*, or the mental processes needed to connect past experience with present action. These processes help children regulate their behavior so that they can concentrate, control their impulses, manage time, stay organized, and follow multistep instructions. These skills also help children filter through the stimulation they receive daily to determine which information is important at that time.

Developing these skills is crucial to children's thinking and school and life success. ZERO TO THREE: National Center for Infants, Toddlers and Families, has identified seven social–emotional skills in particular, like self-regulation, which are essential for school readiness:

- **Confidence** is developed when children expect to succeed and know that adults will help them to do so. Infants demonstrate confidence when they want to try new things and are enthusiastic about their accomplishments. For example, Jalen, a 1-year-old who has just begun walking, claps his hands and smiles when he walks five steps. He also looks to you for approval.

- **Curiosity** describes children's desires to discover new things. Curious children actively explore and investigate their surroundings, using all their senses. For example, 3-year-old David notices a new red truck in the room and runs to get it. He then sees a red ball at the corner. He abandons the truck and runs to get the ball.

- **Intentionality** describes children's determination and persistence. For example, Lili, a 7-month-old, listens attentively to her early educator and follows her face as she changes Lili's diaper. Ashley, a mobile infant, sits with a book for 5 seconds, crawls to get a doll, stays with the doll for 8 seconds, and cries to let you know she wants to be picked up.

- **Self-Control,** or self-regulation, describes children's abilities to control their actions in age-appropriate ways. For example, when Patty, a 2-year-old, is about to bite another child, her teacher calls Patty's name and offers her a toy. Or when Sam hits Sue with a book, Sue looks at her early educator and whimpers. In a loud voice, you answer: "Oh, Sue. I'm so sorry. Thanks for telling me that Sam did something inappropriate."

Provide children a wide range of experiences and materials.

- **Relatedness** is children's ability to engage with others, knowing that they will be understood. For example, Rosita, a 13-month-old, covers her face with a blanket, removes the blanket, and says, "Peek-a-boo!" You respond, "I see you, Rosita!"

- **Capacity to communicate** involves the desire and ability to exchange ideas, feelings, and thoughts with others. For example, Jamie, a 4-month-old, coos while you change his diaper. "I know you're wet, Jamie," you explain to him. "I'll change your diaper, so you'll be more comfortable." Jamie answers with more cooing. Sunny, a 2-year-old, says, "Ceeyahl pees" (cereal please). You reply, "Wow, you speak so well! You want cereal? I'll be glad to give you cereal. Thank you for asking me."

Offer children at least 1 hr of uninterrupted time for center play.

- **Cooperativeness** describes children's ability to engage in tasks or activities that balance the children's own needs with the needs of others. For example, when you begin singing the "Clean Up Time" song, some children hand toys to you while others place toys in storage boxes. Veronica, a 16-month-old, looks at you and smiles. You ask, "Do you want to help, Veronica?" She smiles more. You give Veronica a small damp sponge, and she attempts to wipe the table. You say, "Thank you so much. You are such a great helper!"

In Chapter 3, you learned to divide your setting into learning centers that allow children to choose where they explore and learn. These learning centers also support school readiness in the following ways:

- Teach children concepts such as problem-solving, cause and effect, and classification in real contexts.

- Allow children to explore their learning alone or in social groups.

- Foster imaginary play, which provides children opportunities to expand their understanding of the social world.

- Develop children's self-control.

- Increase children's attention spans and improve their memory skills.

- Provide children opportunities to sort, match, and categorize.

- Offer children opportunities to make symbolic representations of their ideas through art or movement.

Cognitive

Learning Through Play

Infants and toddlers should spend most of their days playing. Ensure that your setting is a rich (but not overstimulating) environment. Observe the children and get to know their interests. Think about other toys and materials that can build on these interests and foster their learning. Provide older infants and toddlers the opportunities to choose what materials and activities they want to play with and manipulate. Also give them the time, equipment, and experiences to use their bodies and brains in multiple ways. Help these children develop their language skills by engaging in dialogue with them while they play.

Preschoolers need ample, uninterrupted choice or free play time throughout the day to develop their memory, attention, and self-regulation skills (Spiegel, 2008). Also, because brain connections are hardwired through repetition, extended and uninterrupted play time gives children the chance to make cognitive connections repeatedly.

While children are at play, observe and scaffold their learning by stepping in intentionally when appropriate. Model curiosity and encourage children to ask and answer questions that will help them learn. Figure 35. describes ways that you can facilitate children's cognitive growth during their play.

Figure 35. How Preschool Learning Centers Impact Cognitive Growth

Learning Center	How the Child Plays	How the Early Educator Supports the Child	What the Child is Learning
Blocks	Builds towers, bridges, and airports out of hardwood blocks	• Asks questions: "How can you build your construction higher without it falling down?" • Poses problems: "What would happen if you used this small block at the base of the building?" • Allows the child to suggest and try out solutions; guides the child to success	• Predicting • Problem solving • Understanding cause and effect
Math & Manipula- tives	Plays an animal lotto game with a small group of other children and the early educator	• Reviews rules: "We can only turn over one card at a time." • Asks questions: "What book did we read that had a mole in it? Did the mole look like this one?" • Applauds children's successes	• Expanding memory, concentration, and attention skills • Matching and categorizing

Figure 35. How Preschool Learning Centers Impact Cognitive Growth (continued)

Learning Center	How the Child Plays	How the Early Educator Supports the Child	What the Child is Learning
Art	Sculpts one of the pig's houses from *The Three Little Pigs*	• Provides materials • Asks questions: "Why did you pick the house made of bricks?" • Makes comparisons: "How is this sculpture different from one of a house made of straw?" • Displays finished sculpture with a sign listing the child's name as the sculptor	• Using symbolic representation of mental ideas through art or writing
Literacy	Reads several books on the classroom tablet about animals	• Ensures that all children have access to technology • Reads an e-book aloud to the child • Asks the child to predict what will happen next in the story • Relates the story to what the child knows about elephants • Shows the child how to research information on the tablet about raccoons • Suggests that the child write a play about lions	• Using technology to develop pre-reading and writing skills

Sand/ Water	• **Sand:** Uses a collection of shells to make patterns in the sand
	• **Water:** Fills up with water and empties bottles and pails
		• **Sand:** Asks questions to guide the child's learning: "Can you add one more shell to your design?," "How does that change the pattern?," "Let's count the round shells," and "Can you put all of the round shells in one pile and the shells that are not round in a separate pile?"
		
		• **Water:** Asks questions: "Does it take more water to fill the blue bottle or the orange one?," "How can you tell how much water the red bottle holds?," and "Which bottle would you rather have in a desert?"
			• **Sand**
			  • Classifying
			  • Patterning
			  • Counting
			  • Sequencing
			  • Predicting
			
			• **Water**
			  • Categorizing
			  • Understanding volume
			  • Predicting
			  • Problem-solving
			  • Understanding cause and effect
			  • Identifying colors

Figure 35. How Preschool Learning Centers Impact Cognitive Growth (continued)

Learning Center	How the Child Plays	How the Early Educator Supports the Child	What the Child is Learning
Science	Balance rocks on a scale	• Asks questions: "Which rock is heavier?," "How many rocks do you think you'll need to weigh as much as this big one?," and "Why do you think this rock is so shiny?"	• Weighing • Measuring • Comparing • Classifying • Predicting • Problem-solving
Dramatic Play	Shop at the pretend grocery store	• Joins the children in play: "I need to get some bread. I wonder what kinds they sell here." • Asks questions: "What does a shopper do?" and "How much does milk cost? I wonder if it's more expensive than the market near my house where the milk costs $2.50 a half gallon."	• Comparing and contrasting • Pricing • Predicting • Planning • Taking on others' perspectives • Preforming self-regulation (executive function)
Music & Movement	Dance with scarves	• Dances along with the child, playing a tambourine to the beat of the music	• Experiencing rhythm and patterning
Cooking	Makes morning snack and participates in group activity of making English muffin pizzas	• Reviews knife handling and safety rules • Leads children in performing cooking tasks • Heats muffins in broiler • Leads children in tasting their muffins • Asks questions: "What happened to the cheese when it was in the broiler?," "How can we cut these muffins in half?," and "How many muffins would we need to give everyone in our class one muffin?"	• Observing physical states • Problem-solving • Following rules • Understanding one-to-one correspondence • Counting • Writing • Reading
Outdoors	Studies animal tracks on the playground after a light snowfall	• Provides magnifying glasses • Asks questions: "How many different animals were here?," "How can you tell there were three animals out here?," "How are the prints alike?," and "How are they different?"	• Comparing • Counting • Patterning • Observing with curiosity

Learning Throughout the Day

There are a number of ways to incorporate cognitive learning activities in your daily interactions with the children in your setting. Consider these examples:

Choice Time/Free Play: Leila and Reggie are playing in the dramatic play area, which the children have transformed into a make-believe clothing store. Reggie eyes a dress he would like to purchase for his mother. "It's $93, and it's on sale!" Leila says. Reggie agrees to purchase the dress, and hands Leila a few bills of play money. Leila counts the money and places it in her cash register. She gives Reggie his change, folds the dress, and hands it to him. As an early educator, observe Leila and Reggie while they utilize different learning centers during choice time. Determine the appropriate times to lend the children your support or maintain distance to let the children play and discover independently.

Transitions: Help children work on the concept of classification by having them first categorize by one trait. ("If you're wearing red, please get in line.") Then add another trait to increase the task's difficulty and challenge the children. ("If you're wearing red and your hair is black, please get your coat.")

Eating and mealtimes: Interacting with children during mealtimes fosters a sense of community in your setting. Promote the children's growing independence by getting them involved in preparing and serving the meal, modeling appropriate behavior and good manners, and recognizing new skills and accomplishments during conversation.

Tackle cause-and-effect scenarios and sharpen children's prediction skills during mealtime discussions.

During family-style lunches with toddlers or preschoolers: Use these mealtimes to introduce the children to new concepts. For example, illustrate cause and effect by noting that the fruit in the yogurt floats or that banana slices turn brown when left out of their peelings. Help children learn to predict outcomes by asking questions, like: "What would happen to the milk if we didn't have refrigerators?" or "What would we have for lunch if we ate only foods from our garden?" Ask questions that encourage children to make comparisons, like: "How are the raw carrots different from the cooked ones

Cognitive

we had yesterday?" Lead children in counting the pieces of food on their plates: "I wonder how many pieces of cucumber you took, Mario? Let's count them together."

During sleep and nap time: Sleep is necessary for children's physical, cognitive, and language development. When infants learn to fall asleep and develop a pattern to comfort themselves, they are learning to regulate their behavior. During sleep and nap time, children also develop their large muscles, become familiar with the concept of time, discover cause and effect, and learn to identify sleep as a positive experience. For example, when you sing, "Time to go to sleep, time to go to sleep" the toddlers know to move toward their cots. Provide preschoolers who choose not to sleep during these times quiet activities to perform, like working on puzzles or lying on their cots.

During diaper change and toileting: Be responsive to children during this routine and take advantage of this quality one-on-one time with the child. Initiate conversation, engage the child, and support him/her in developing a positive attitude about toileting.

During arrival to or departure from the setting: Help children manage separation from and reunions with the people they love. Make them feel understood and welcome in your setting, and help them develop self-confidence and trust. Ask families to bring familiar items from home to keep in your setting, such as photographs and other items. These items will help children settle in at your setting and remain connected to their loved ones. Play games with the children that offer opportunities for people or things to appear or disappear. Read books about separation and reunion. Ask preschoolers to sign in at your setting each morning by placing a symbol or star next to their names. Teach colors by asking Maurice, "Which backpack is yours? The green one or the black one?" Introduce sorting and word sounds by asking children, "If your name begins with the same sound as *tambourine* and *table*, please put your artwork in your cubbies."

On a neighborhood walk: Encourage children to be curious and observant. If you see Carrie staring at a ladybug on the ground, join her in a conversation about what she sees. If you see a drain on the corner of the sidewalk, talk with children about what might happen when it rains. Stimulate the children's thinking with follow-up questions, such as: "Why do you think it's good for rainwater to run down the drains?" Pose a cause-and-effect question: "What happens if water reaches a drain that is clogged with trash?"

On field trips: For example, on a field trip to a busy train terminal, ask, "Do the people here seem to be in a hurry? Why do you think that's so? Where do you think they're going?" Ask children to count the train cars, guess where the trains are arriving from or departing to, and identify the different types of train cars. On a visit to a shoe store, help children learn about classification as they observe different shoe styles, numbers as they try on different size shoes, and taking on others' perspectives as they pretend to be sales associates and customers. Allow the children to interview the real sales associates informally about their jobs.

Other teachable moments: These moments are spontaneous windows of opportunity to extend children's learning and understanding. For example, while playing outdoors, the children rush to the fence to watch high school graduates in caps and gowns walk by. Join the children at the fence and explain the significance of the graduation outfits. Likewise, you and the children see a mound of snow fall from your setting's roof onto the playground. Discuss cause and effect and ask the children to share their theories about why the snow fell to the ground. Weather-related events, like a hailstorm or the sudden appearance of a rainbow, provide opportunities to introduce science concepts.

Identifying and Building Children's Skills and Abilities

As an early educator, what you say and do—including your questions, verbal and nonverbal cues, active listening, descriptions, and suggestions—impact children's learning significantly. Your actions and words help expand children's memories and attention; develop self-regulation and executive function; recognize cause and effect; and sharpen their problem-solving and categorization skills. You also help children understand reading, writing, math, science, art, language, social studies, and technology concepts.

Observe the children in your setting and scaffold their learning. In other words, use the information the children already know to help them learn new things. Individualize your approach based on each child's skills, abilities, interests, and needs.

Scaffolding Children's Learning in Conversation

Terrell, a 4-year-old in your setting, notices that all the insects in the butterfly farm in your science center look like caterpillars, not butterflies.

You: "That's a very interesting observation, Terrell. What makes you say that?" (You want Terrell to articulate his thinking and explain what information he used to reach his conclusion.)

Terrell: "Look at all the bugs crawling on the bottom and on the leaves. They're fat like caterpillars. None of them have wings that will let them fly like butterflies."

You: "You're right about all of that, Terrell. You have made some very accurate observations. Butterflies have wings while caterpillars are chunky, cling to leaves, and crawl on the bottom and sides of the glass. They haven't yet reached the next stage where they'll make a cocoon and form a butterfly. What signs should we look for?"

Terrell: "They need to shed their skins. And hang from a branch. Like in the book we read!"

You: "That's right, Terrell. The caterpillars will continue to grow and they'll shed what's called an exoskeleton. They become too big for their skin. Sometimes they shed these skins several times. When it's time to become a butterfly, they form a final exoskeleton called a chrysalis. Inside the chrysalis is where the newborn butterfly lives. I know that you're eager to see that, but we must be patient. Why don't you make a drawing of what you think it will look like when the caterpillars form their chrysalises?"

Cognitive

In your brief conversation with Terrell, you learned and built upon his interest and knowledge. You asked him questions and repeated what he said to help him describe what he saw happening in the caterpillar's development. Terrell's vocabulary increased when you explained the scientific terms cocoon, exoskeleton, and chrysalis. You scaffold Terrell's learning by helping him relate what he already knew about caterpillars and butterflies to the new information you provided him. Finally, you helped Terrell expand the following cognitive skills:

- Curiosity about the world around him (how caterpillars and butterflies live).

- Cause and effect (what makes caterpillars turn into butterflies).

- Connections between what he already knows and what he is experiencing (how caterpillars shed their exoskeletons to become butterflies).

- Matching/sorting (figuring out which insects are caterpillars and which are butterflies).

- Predicting (imagining the new butterflies).

- Representing his thoughts symbolically (drawing what he thinks the butterfly farm will look like in the future).

Consider daily how you can best support Terrell and the rest of the children in your setting in their learning and growth. Again, observe them over time and keep individual records for each child. After you have collected sufficient data, analyze it and make conclusions about each child's progression. This information will guide you in customizing learning goals and curricular approaches both for individual children and for groups. In addition, if you need to speak with children's parents about obtaining additional assistance for their children, you will have accurate records to provide the parents and other professionals who will work with the children in the future.

For example, observe Eduardo's actions in your setting. Does he like books? Does he turn the pages for you as you are reading a book together? Can he point to the pictures as you describe them? Does he reenact the story after you read it aloud? What you observe will dictate your actions.

Sometimes children exhibit strong skills or knowledge in a particular area.

If Eduardo looks at the books in your setting with bewilderment, perhaps you would try to get him better acquainted by showing him the covers, title pages, and where the words and illustrations are in some of the texts. You might ask him to describe what he sees. On the other hand, if Eduardo is excited by books, you would ask him questions to make him think about the book and explore the plot. Ask, "What should the main character do next?," "What do you think will happen to the main character?," and "What else might the main character have done?" Knowing that Eduardo is already familiar with books, you can continue to challenge his thinking.

Suppose 4-year-old Linda is having a difficult time completing puzzles. Start her off with a puzzle with just 5–6 large pieces. If she still has difficulties, offer her puzzle pieces with knobs. Prompt her to turn a piece she is having difficulty placing in a different direction. Help her remain focused without feeling overwhelmed. Hand her one piece at a time to simplify the process. Give her tips on completing puzzles, like noting colors: "What color is this piece? Yes, it's blue. Do you see another puzzle piece that has this same color blue? Let's see if they might fit together" (Tomlinson & Hyson, 2012). Once Linda is confident assembling these puzzles, introduce her to more ones, perhaps with 10–20 pieces with no knobs. If she gets stuck, continue to work with her. Do just enough to help Linda finish the puzzle on her own.

On the other hand, sometimes children exhibit strong skills or knowledge in a particular area, leaving you wondering how to build upon this knowledge. Let these children lead the way and provide cues for what they need you to help them learn and what they are interested in.

Allowing Children to Guide Their Own Learning

Ms. Thompson observes the children in her setting as they perform an indoor gardening activity. Kenya, a 5-year-old, impresses Ms. Thompson with her depth of gardening knowledge. Kenya says that she helps her grandfather in his garden on weekends. She knows how to plant vegetables and when, the types of soil to use, and how often she should water plants. Excited by Kenya's gardening savvy, Ms. Thompson quizzes her on how vegetables grow. She challenges Kenya to predict what will happen if she waters the plants more often or places them in different areas of the room. Kenya realizes she is thinking about plants in new ways.

Days later, Kenya tells Ms. Thompson, "We moved the plant to the window so it could get more sun. Why are the red leaves green now?"

Ms. Thompson replies, "Great question, Kenya. I don't know the answer, though. Let's go to the computer and read about plants to see if we can find the answer together." After researching and discussing the information they find, Kenya concludes that too much sun exposure will turn plants green. Ms. Thompson agrees with Kenya and says, "Let's test this out to be sure." They move the plant to an area away from direct sunlight. She tells Kenya that they will watch the plant over the next few days to see what happens.

Children with special learning needs are like all children who are becoming familiar with new knowledge, objects, and skills. Observe these children in the same way, getting to know their interests, skills, and current knowledge. Then gradually scaffold their learning. For example, while 4-year-old Yvette plays with LEGO® building bricks, introduce her to a few large, 2–4 in. pieces. Yvette will learn how to fit the pieces together through trial-and-error. Eventually, she will be ready to try assembling smaller pieces. At this time, limit the number of small pieces she uses, so she is not overwhelmed. Give her the time and practice she needs to refine this skill.

Also, while working with children during play, break their tasks into small, doable steps. When children are able to work through small steps, large, difficult tasks seem possible. If children have difficulty completing small steps, perform a few steps for them, and then observe them performing the rest.

Children As Scientists: Content Learning

Not only do children refine their cognitive skills during play, but they also acquire content knowledge in areas like language/literacy, math, science, art, social studies, and technology. Learning takes place from the moment children arrive to your setting each day to the moment they leave. However, as with all areas of development, children learn through play. For example, children learn a gravity lesson (science) when they build a block tower and knock it down. In the cooking center, you help children read (literacy) the recipe you will use to cook. They may be responsible for measuring (mathematics) the necessary ingredients. When you ask Claire to add 1 tsp of *nutmeg* to the mixing bowl, she learns a new word (language). Find out what the early learning standards are in your state. Understand these standards and be intentional when teaching content.

In Chapter 6, we will discuss language/literacy content knowledge. We will explore other content areas in this section.

Mathematics

Children have an intuitive sense of math that begins in infancy, so scaffolding children's learning of math concepts is especially critical. Early childhood math researchers Sarama and Clements (2006, p. 86) emphasize that "in all activities … teachers need to help children connect their informal knowledge to their budding explicit knowledge of mathematics." Below are examples of how you can begin working with infants and toddlers to refine their math skills:

• Sing songs and finger plays that use numbers.

• Read stories that include numbers.

Observe children during play to understand where they are developmentally.

- Count all similar items that infants and toddlers see.

- Provide toys that allow children to create patterns.

- Provide toys that offer exploring different sizes.

The following examples illustrate possible methods for introducing math to preschoolers (Tomlinson & Hyson, 2012):

- Create interesting learning environments filled with math materials, like counters, puzzles, shape sorters, lotto games, beads for stringing, and pattern boards.

- Observe what children do and say to understand where they are developmentally. (Do they talk about numbers? Do they shy away from puzzles or shape sorting activities?)

- Encourage children to solve problems. (During snack time, ask, "If I have five strawberries, and I give two to Melissa, how many do I have left?")

- Ask and answer questions that encourage children's thinking. ("If this measuring cup holds ½ cup, could we use it to measure 2 cups of flour? How?")

- Pose interesting ideas for children to consider. ("The computer has a 17 in. monitor. Did you know that it's measured diagonally instead of from top to bottom?")

- Help children find and discuss the math in the world around them. ("See the interesting shape of the statue's base? How many sides does it have?")

Counting

If you ask 3-year-old Eliza her age, she will hold up three fingers. This is because counting is the first math concept she and other children grasp. In fact, finger counting is an important component of learning about numbers (Bredekamp, 2011). Also, children are grounded in the counting process when they touch the objects they count.

Children will learn to count over time with practice and repetition. The following tips will help you get the children in your setting started:

- Count everything in your setting, from the number of books in your library to the number of seats at the art table. Touch each object as you count it.

- Sing and act out counting songs and finger plays, like "There Were 10 in a Bed."

- Read and act out counting books, like *How Do Dinosaurs Count to Ten?* by Jane Yolen, numerous times.

- Point out numbers in the setting: "Let's see how many pet gerbils we have. We have one, two gerbils in the cage. The new gerbil makes three."

- Create graphs to chart the children's likes and dislikes.

- Use charts to teach number sequence. Ask the children to write their names on a numbered chart as they arrive each day. Children will be able to see who is present at the setting and the order in which each child arrived.

- Have children set the table for family-style lunch to teach one-to-one correspondence. Ask them to place one plate, one glass, one napkin, and one set of flatware on the table at each seat.

- Introduce counting during meals and snacks:

  - "You can have two graham crackers for morning snack."

  - "Do we have enough chairs for everyone? Let's count to be sure."

  - "Look at the chart to see how many slices of bananas are available for your afternoon snack."

  - "I'm going to eat one of the strawberries in the bowl. How many will be left?"

- Play number games, like Musical Chairs, counting the number of participants and chairs left to teach one-to-one correspondence.

- Ask questions during play: "How many more blocks will you need to make the towers the same height?"

- Make up problems involving numbers: "I buried three treasures in the sand. Can you find them?"

- Use counting to solve real-life problems: "There are five of you and three tricycles. How many of you can ride right now?"

- Make silly counting mistakes and let the children correct you: "Let's count the children in the circle during group meeting time—1, 2, 3, 10, 4 …"

Observe children's progress and record what you see.

Measurement

Young children ask questions constantly, like: Who's taller? Who's bigger? How much does that stone weigh? How high is the block fort? And they measure according to their own rules. The rocket ship they constructed using LEGO® building bricks is as long as the jump rope. The teddy bear weighs the same as three bean bags. Here are some ways you, the early educator, can help the children in your setting practice measurement:

Make a chart of the children's likes and dislikes.

- **Model measuring.** During dramatic play, ask the pretend party hosts for a cup of lemon tea with 2 tsp of sugar.

- **Provide real-world measurement examples.** "Let's make some modeling clay today. I have the recipe here. Who's going to help me measure out the ingredients?"

- **Pose problems for the children.** "How many cups of water do you think it will take to fill the watering can?"

- **Offer opportunities to sort objects.** Ask the children to sort flatware by size and shape. Ask them to show you which pieces are biggest and which are smallest.

- **Perform measurement activities.** "Let's line up from tallest to shortest."

Geometry, Patterning and Representing Data

Geometry, patterns, and analyzing/displaying data are math concepts that young children are exposed to already in their environments. The following activities help children grasp and apply these concepts:

- Ask questions to stretch children's thinking. "How do we arrange the pot holder loops to make a pattern where there are two blues followed by one yellow?" (patterning)

- Make graphs. Create graphs of the children's favorite foods, how much light plants need to grow the tallest, or the most popular storybooks the children like to hear you read. (data representation)

- Pose problems. "Which plant container shape will hold the most soil?" (geometry)

- Point out patterns in music and ask children to sing them. (patterning)

Cognitive

- Read aloud books about shapes (*When a Line Bends … A Shape Begins* by Rhonda Gowler Greene) and patterns (*Pattern Fish* by Trudy Harris). (geometry/patterning)

- Ask the children to clean up after block play by matching shapes. Clean up props stored on pegboards by matching objects to contact paper shapes. (geometry)

- Challenge children to create different shapes, like a pyramid, when building with hardwood blocks. (geometry)

- Help children string beads in different patterns. (patterning)

- Clap the patterns to songs and chants. (patterning)

During play, children learn geometry, patterning, and how to represent data.

- Identify objects in the room by their shapes. Children sit in a *circle* at meeting time, the block center is *square*, or the table is *rectangular*. (geometry)

- Incorporate math language into your conversations. Words like *first, bigger, heavier, above, less than, about, diagonal, approximately,* and *in between* teach children to speak and think mathematically and to see their world in mathematical terms.

Science and Social Studies

When you teach children social studies, they are learning about social relationships and societal functions. You help them understand how people coexist in their homes and communities and explore subjects like history, geography, economics, and civics. On the other hand, teaching children science encourages them to examine the physical properties of materials and objects, living things (people, plants, and animals), and the earth and environment. Here are some ways you can introduce infants and toddlers to these concepts:

- Provide opportunities for infants to hold, manipulate, and mouth toys.

Provide real-world measuring experiences.

- Offer objects of different textures for children to experiment with.

- Engage children in cooking experiences. "What happens to dough when you add in yeast?"

- Provide materials found in nature, like leaves and acorns, for toddlers to explore.

- Allow toddlers to participate in gardening experiences.

- Buy a pet fish for the setting. Keep it in a tank with a secure cover top, and allow the children to observe and feed it (with supervision).

- Help toddlers and young children plant seeds in an outdoor garden. Observe the seedlings as they grow.

- Discuss staff members' jobs with the children.

- Read stories about people with varying occupations. Discuss what these people do.

Help the children in your setting plant and tend a vegetable garden.

Again, think about how the children in your setting are exploring these topics through play and other opportunities you provide. Be intentional about tying their learning to the real world and building upon their interests and what they already know:

Teaching children science encourages them to examine the physical properties of materials and objects, living things, and the earth and environment.

- Pose challenges: "How can you turn the red paint a different color?," "What will happen to the popcorn when you put it in the microwave?" (physical properties/science)

- Suggest activities: "Today we're going to make a tornado in a bottle for our science area. Let's see how it's like the tornado we heard about in the news." (nature/science)

- Help the children make a map of the playground. (social studies)

- Ask questions that have more than one correct answer: "What do you think might happen if we put something in our compost heap besides leaves and food waste?" (nature/science)

- Plant a vegetable garden. Use the vegetables and herbs in cooking projects. (living things/science)

- Help the children form a marching band using instruments from different cultures. (social studies)

- Measure shadows at different times of day. (nature/science/math)

- Open a "repair shop" to fix broken items in the setting. (physical properties/science)

- Make family photo albums. (social studies)

- Provide opportunities for children to classify and sort different objects. (science)

- Observe animals outdoors in their natural habitats. Ask the children questions about what they see. (science)

Technology

In Chapter 1, you learned that technology—including computers and software, tablets, and smartphones—should help you create learning opportunities to support your interactions with the children in your setting. Though some technology is designed specifically for infants and toddlers, children under 2 years old should not engage in passive screen time (National Association for the Education of Young Children [NAEYC] & Fred Rogers Center for Early Learning and Children's Media at Saint Vincent College [FRCELCM], 2012). However, with your supervision and guidance, toddlers and preschoolers can use these tools to research topics you have discussed as a group, take virtual field trips around the world, create artwork, read books, write stories, and use software to document their own learning.

Technology can also help children with special needs perform tasks they are unable to complete alone. Talk and Draw software, a federally funded project, helped children with manual dexterity difficulties (difficulty using their hands) use their voices to command objects on a computer screen to draw. For some children with conditions, such as cerebral palsy, this was the first time they had ever created artwork. Though this software is no longer available, it is the precursor of similar voice recognition software products today that can fulfill this same need.

Also, computer programs can provide you the correct spelling of words in the children's home languages for labeling around your setting. These programs can also teach you the correct pronunciation of words in other languages so that you can better communicate with dual language learners. ■

Chapter 6
Communication

CDA Functional Area 6: Candidate uses a variety of developmentally appropriate learning experiences and teaching strategies to promote children's language and early literacy learning, and help them communicate their thoughts and feelings verbally and nonverbally. Candidate helps dual-language learners make progress in understanding and speaking both English and their home language.

Communication

Introduction

When we communicate, we express thoughts, ideas, information, and experiences through the way we speak, write, and display nonverbal cues, like facial expressions and crossed arms. We develop these skills at an early age. Children learn to speak and build their vocabularies through direct interaction with more competent speakers, like older children and adults.

Literacy and language development are fundamental elements upon which children build their communication skills over time. Because there are proven links between children's literacy and language development and future school success, no other subject in early childhood education has received more attention in recent years.

As an early educator, you play a pivotal role in helping the children in your setting develop a strong foundation of language and literacy so that they are prepared to start school. You achieve this through your learning environment and how you interact with the children within the environment, like reading aloud to them, small and large group meetings, and daily routines.

In this chapter, we will examine the following ways in which you can foster children's language and literacy development:

- **Creating an Environment That Supports Language and Literacy.**
- **Supporting Children's Oral Language Development.**
- **Supporting Dual Language Learners.**
- **Fostering Children's Reading Development.**
- **Fostering Children's Writing Development.**
- **Partnering With Families.**

Creating an Environment That Supports Language and Literacy

Strickland and Riley-Ayers (2006) explain that children who begin kindergarten with a foundation for early literacy are more likely to be successful students later in life. Meanwhile, children from low-income backgrounds tend to receive less exposure to language (Hart & Risley, 2003) and books. Therefore, their early literacy skills tend to be weaker (Colker, 2010a). The children in your setting come from of various backgrounds. Support their language and literacy development by creating a "literacy-rich" learning environment. Ensure that writing, books, and language are displayed everywhere in your setting for children of all ages to see.

Displaying Labels and Print

Written language becomes meaningful for children when you display print throughout your learning environment. Children will learn that print is a form of communication and begin to associate words with meanings. Include books throughout your setting and label materials so that children begin to recognize letters and words. However, do not overwhelm children by labeling every item in your setting. In addition to these ideas, here are some other ways you can make language meaningful for children at all age levels:

Young and Mobile Infants

- Display colorful pictures of familiar people and objects at eye level. Label the photos with the names of the people and objects pictured.

- Write information in front of infants so that they can see you doing it.

- Use signs, pictures, labels, and charts to communicate important information.

- Provide age-appropriate books throughout the setting that you and mobile infants can access.

- Label cubbies with photographs and names.

Toddlers

- Provide materials and toys that encourage communication and pretend play.

- Create books and sets of picture cards together.

- Include props and activities that support the development of fine motor skills children need for writing.

- Label shelves with pictures and print.

- Create a few simple areas where toddlers can explore toys and materials.

- Add books and writing materials throughout the setting.

- Write down children's ideas, stories, and words.

- Label containers with pictures of the items that belong inside.

- Create and use signs in the setting. For example, when you leave the setting, place a sign on the door that tells others where you have gone: "Gone for a walk. Be back soon."

- Provide real-world reading materials—including newspapers, magazines, and toy store catalogs.

Communication

Preschoolers

Consider the following ideas and think of other ways to ensure that you have included meaningful and intentional print throughout your environment:

- Display the following:

    - children's names, along with their photos, on cubbies;

    - books—including ones children create; and

    - children's portfolios.

- Place photos of children and their families in your setting. Label them with the names of the people pictured and their relationships.

- Post the following:

    - daily schedule with words and pictures;

    - attendance chart;

    - daily duties chart;

    - signs identifying each area of the setting and the learning centers;

    - experience charts created after field trips or nature walks;

    - signs protecting children's work (e.g., "Please do not touch");

    - handwashing chart in pictures and words;

    - recipe cards or charts; and

    - alphabet strips.

- Hang samples of children's writings.

- Label children's artwork with sentence strips.

- Label photos and other documentation of children's learning with written descriptions.

- Label children's creations with signatures or sentence strips (e.g., "This sculpture was designed by Keisha").

Dual Language Learners

- Include labels and books in each of the children's home languages.

- Color-code the labels you use for each language. For example, label the shelves in the block center with a picture of each type of block and the English word describing the block written in black ink. Include the Spanish word for the block written in green ink. Keep the colors consistent throughout the learning environment; ensure that all signs in Spanish are written in green ink. Mark books, newspapers, and cookbooks written in Spanish with green stickers.

- Represent all children's languages with your labels and signage. Children who have a strong command of their first languages can learn to speak, read, and write English more easily. This tactic also tells children that they are valued and respected in your setting and helps them appreciate each other's home languages.

- Include clear and appropriate pictures or photographs alongside written labels. Also, include the phonetic spelling of some of the words written in the children's home languages to help other adult visitors pronounce these words correctly (Nemeth, 2012).

Selecting Books

Although most children do not read independently until they reach kindergarten or first grade, the early years are critical in ensuring children's future reading success. The books you provide the children in your setting should be age-appropriate. Consider each book's length and the amount of text on each page. Think about how old a child would need to be to read or engage with each book. Children should be able to identify with the characters and plots of the books you provide. For example, children may be particularly interested in books about going to the supermarket or welcoming a baby brother. Include books that represent the setting's community and each child's culture, ethnicity, home language, and family structure. Also teach children to handle books carefully and how to repair damaged books. Instill the value of books in children and encourage them to be lifelong readers.

Here are some other ideas to ensure that you include age-appropriate books in your learning environment:

Young and Mobile Infants

Choose washable cloth or cleanable board books for infants to mouth and explore. These books should include at least one of the following:

- Stories about infants, families, animals, and everyday experiences.

- Songs, chants, and rhymes.

- Simple bright pictures and/or photographs with one or two objects per page.

- Experiences infants know, like bathing and shopping with family members.

Choose washable cloth or cleanable board books for infants to mouth and explore.

Toddlers

- Read books carefully to ensure that the vocabulary is more sophisticated than everyday speech, so children can learn new words.

- Choose board, paperback, and hardback books.

- Select books about families, infants, toddlers, everyday experiences, familiar animals, and feelings.

- Choose books about simple concepts like size, shape and color, children's interests, and self-help skills.

Preschoolers

Though they are learning to read independently, preschool children are ready to do the following (DeBruin-Parecki et al., 2005):

- Identify familiar logos, signs, and labels.

- Recognize familiar words.

- Enjoy listening to and talking about storybooks.

- Understand that print carries a message.

- Ask questions about a book's plot.

- Make evaluative comments about books.

- Pretend to read to a doll or stuffed animal.

- Identify some letters.

- Make attempts to read.

- Have a favorite author.

Preschoolers' books should be language-rich and include easy-to-follow plots, compelling characters, and aesthetically pleasing illustrations. Stock 5–8 books per child in your setting, and ensure that these books represent each child's home language. Add or rotate additional books during the year to reflect children's interests and relevant topics. For example, if there is a child in your setting who is learning to swim, a book about a character enrolled in a swim class would be relevant.

Display books so that their covers are visible.

Figure 36. Evaluating Books for Preschoolers

The following questions will help you determine whether the books you are considering are right for the children in your setting:

- Is the book free of all bias—including gender, race, age, and sexual orientation?

- Does the book contain large, bright, colorful illustrations?

- Are the pages easy to turn?

- Will the story spark conversation?

- Will children want to reread the book?

- Will children be motivated to seek out another book by this author or on the same topic?

- Is the book worthy of children's time?

- Does the book have an engaging story?

- Is this book's main purpose to promote toys, television shows, movies, or merchandise?

Figure 37. Categorizing Books

Here is a list of the types of books you will encounter when searching for titles to include in your setting:

- **Wordless books:** stories told through pictures and few or no words. For example, *A Ball for Daisy* by Chris Raschka.

- **Picture books:** including classic stories: words and pictures tell a story about real or imaginary characters and events. For example, Blackout by John Rocco; *Make Way for Ducklings* by Robert McCloskey.

- **Traditional rhymes and stories:** nursery rhymes, fairy tales, fables, and folktales from various cultures. For example, *The Wooden Sword: A Jewish Folktale from Afghanistan* by Ann Redisch Stampler.

- **Poetry:** one or several illustrated poems. For example, *Honey, I Love and Other Love Poems* by Eloise Greenfield.

- **Books with elegant writing and vocabulary:** books acclaimed for their prose. For example, *It's Mine!* by Leo Lionni.

- **Predictable/pattern books:** repeating text and predictable plots that let children join in. For example, *Brown Bear, Brown Bear, What Do You See?* by Bill Martin Jr.

- **Concept books:** pictures or photos of familiar objects or ideas such as colors, shapes, opposites, or sizes. For example, *Color Dance* by Ann Jonas.

- **Alphabet books:** fun and colorful illustrations of the alphabet. For example, *Eric Carle's ABC* by Eric Carle.

- **Counting books:** fun and colorful illustrations of numbers. For example, *Curious George Learns to Count from 1 to 100* by H. A. Rey.

- **Informational books:** realistic pictures or photographs that introduce facts about a specific topic. For example, *Bugs* by Joan Richards Wright.

- **Reference books:** resources for learning. For example, *The American Heritage Picture Dictionary*.

- **"Easy readers"/beginning chapter books:** limited vocabulary, rhyme, and repetition for beginning readers. For example, *The Foot Book* by Dr. Seuss.

(Reading Is Fundamental [RIF], n.d)

Communication

Your local children's librarian and websites like the following can also help you select age-appropriate books for your setting:

- The **Association for Library Service to Children [ALC]** (www.ala.org/alsc/) includes lists of Caldecott Medal, Newbery Medal, and Notable Children's Books award winners. The Caldecott Medal is awarded yearly to the best picture book illustrator. The Newbery Medal goes to the best children's book for school-age children. Notable Children's Books are honored for outstanding contributions to young people's literature.

- The **Charlotte Zolotow Award** (www.education.wisc.edu/ccbc/books/ detailListBooks.asp?idBookLists=221) was established in 1998 and administered by the Cooperative Children's Book Center—an examination, study, and research library of the University of Wisconsin-Madison School of Education. This award goes to the author of the best picture book published in the United States.

- **Choices Reading List** (www.reading.org/ choices) is the International Reading Association's annual list of the favorite books of children, teachers, and young adults.

Read interesting books that introduce children to new vocabulary.

Setting Up the Preschool Literacy Center

In Chapter 3, you learned tips for configuring the learning centers in your setting. Designate the literacy center as the area where children learn the fundamental skills needed to read, write, and operate a computer. Divide the center to accommodate each activity. Stock the center with materials and equipment that help to create positive language and literacy experiences for each child:

Book Area

In this area of the center, children can peruse books alone or in groups or listen to early educators read books aloud. Children can also recreate or reenact stories and perform puppet shows based on the books you read to them. Your literacy center's book area could include the following:

Children recognize books by their cover art.

- Various children's picture books that children can access and browse. Display the books so that their covers are visible. Young children cannot read book spines. They recognize books by their cover art.

- Comfortable chairs, a rocking chair, a small table and chairs, and nooks (e.g., tents or lofts) where children can look at books alone or take breaks from the group.

- Carpeting or an area rug and big pillows or cushions for reading while sitting on the floor.

- Puppets, a puppet stage, felt characters, and a felt board for dramatizing and retelling stories.

Writing Area

Include the following items in the writing area so that children can learn the alphabet, practice writing, make signs, write cards, make books, and dictate stories to you:

- Various writing tools (e.g., pencils, pens, markers, chalk, and crayons).

- Various writing surfaces (e.g., paper, stationery, chalkboard, and whiteboard).

- Journals or portfolios for children to document and record their own learning.

- Blank labels.

- Envelopes.

- Ruler, stencils, stapler, hole punch, and erasers.

- Magic Slates or doodle boards.

- Lap pads and clipboards.

- Alphabet strips.

- Sandpaper letters.

- Letter stamps.

- Index cards for making personal dictionaries of words that children use often.

- Table and chairs.

Listening Area

Include the following equipment and furnishings so that children can listen to stories, poems, or songs:

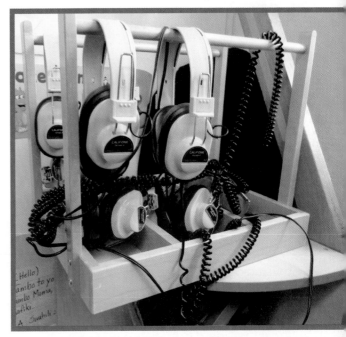

Include headphones in the listening area of the literacy center so that children can listen to stories, poems, or songs.

- Audio recordings of books, poems, lullabies, and favorite songs. This audio could be commercially produced or recorded by staff or children's parents.

- Tape recorder, CD player, or MP3 player.

- Headphones.

- Microphone.

- Comfortable seating.

Technology Area

Evaluate computer software and smartphone applications before making them available to the children in your setting.

This area may include the following equipment and materials that allow children to learn the alphabet, tell stories, listen to books read aloud, practice typing, and view websites and use software applications with early educators. This equipment list is desirable, not mandatory:

- Computer with developmentally appropriate software that can run in several languages.

- Printer and paper.

- Scanner.

- Digital camera.

- Shared computer station and two chairs per computer.

- Touch tablets like the iPad® and/or smartphones with developmentally appropriate applications.

Evaluate computer software and smartphone applications before making them available to the children in your setting. Determine whether the software and applications are developmentally appropriate and whether they foster children's learning through engagement. When evaluating these technologies, consider the following criteria:

- Application and software is interactive and engaging.

- Content is sound and interesting to children.

- Children can follow instructions and navigate program.

- Children can use the software/application independently.

- Children can experience success.

- Program is bias-free and violence-free.

- Programs can be individualized and children can use at their own pace.

- Program is flexible and can be adapted for children with special needs and dual language learners.

The following resources can assist you in locating appropriate software and applications for children 2–5 years old:

- **Children's Technology Review:** a monthly newsletter of reviews and trends in children's interactive media (www.childrenstech.com).

- **SuperKids® Educational Software Review:** evaluations of children's software by teachers, parents, and children (www.superkids.com).

Publishing Area

Children can make their own books either using the computer or tablet or by writing on paper. Illustrations can be drawn, painted, or made using photographs or clip art. Supplies for making covers and binding books are nearby.

- Access to computer/tablet/ papers, markers/crayons/paints, hole punch, and ruler.

- Cardboard or poster board.

- Laminator.

- Blank books.

- Stapler.

- Yarn or laces for binding.

- Finished books displayed.

- Table and chairs for doing work.

Be sure that all the supplies for the publishing area are nearby and easily accessible.

Figure 38. Creating Literacy-Rich Learning Centers

Incorporate language and literacy into every learning center. Label each center, include relevant books that children can easily access, and provide writing materials for children to draw or write about what they are working on and learning.

Learning Center	Language and Literacy Materials
Blocks	Materials for creating signs, wooden traffic signs, blueprints and floor plans, road maps, architectural magazines, and picture books on construction (such as *Building with Dad* by Carol Nevius and *One Big Building: A Counting Book About Construction* by Michael Dahl).
Art	Recipe cards for making play dough and cloud dough; alphabet stamps, sponges, stencils and cookie cutters; catalogs and magazines for collages; materials for creating greeting cards; sentence strips under children's art; and picture books about art and artists (such as *Beautiful Oops!* by Barney Saltzberg and *Vincent's Colors* by The Metropolitan Museum of Art).
Dramatic Play	Magazines, newspapers, books, catalogs, telephone books, address books, mail, shopping lists, greeting cards, stationery, cookbooks, calendars, business cards, healthy food containers and cans, "to do" lists, job chart for family members, pens, pencils, markers, notepads, and literacy-related props and materials for pretend scenes (such as a doctor's office, library, bookstore, clothing store, restaurant, diner, or post office).
Music & Movement	Alphabet songs on tape or CD, songbooks, sheet music and charts, books that accompany songs (like *I Know an Old Woman Who Swallowed a Fly* by Nikki Smith), books about music (like *M is for Music* by Kathleen Krull), or books about musicians (like *The Deaf Musicians* by Pete Seeger).
Science	Graphs; pens, pencils, markers; notepads, clipboards, blank books, paper; chart paper and stand; maps and globes; informational text and books; and books with pictures (such as *I Love Bugs!* by Philemon Sturges and *The Very Busy Spider* by Eric Carle).
Math & Manipulatives	Magnetic letters, alphabet puzzles, alphabet lotto, alphabet bingo, letter-sorting games, alphabet blocks, score sheets and pencils, and picture books that parallel toys and games (such as *My Book of Alphabet Games* by Kumon Publishing and *Stick to It: Toys—A Magnetic Puzzle Book* by Kate Stone and Jeff Cole).
Sand/ Water Play	**Sand:** Alphabet cookie cutters and picture books (such as *Jump Into Science: Sand* by Ellen Prager and *Dirt: The Scoop on Soil* by Natalie Rosinsky). **Water:** Alphabet sponges, chart paper and chart stand, markers, vinyl bathtub books, and picture books (such as Water Play by Leon Read and Will It Float or Sink? by Melissa Stewart).
Cooking	Recipe cards, cookbooks, snack sign-in sheet, snack menu, handwashing chart, alphabet cookie cutters, letter molds, and picture books for children such as *My Foodie ABC: A Little Gourmet's Guide* by Puck and *Hola! Jalepeno* by Amy Wilson Sanger.
Outdoors	Sidewalk chalk; paintbrushes and buckets of water; papers, crayons and markers; seed packets; bird identification charts; clipboards and paper; thermometer; rain gauge; and baskets of picture books taken outside (including books about gardening, identifying insects and birds, and taking nature walks).

Supporting Children's Oral Language Development

The Linguistic Society of America says that young children who are exposed to speech solely through TV and radio will not learn to talk. Children need human interaction to learn to speak (Birner, n.d.). Children have an innate ability to learn the rules of the languages used in their environments. Even before children can speak actual words, they communicate through cries and gestures and interpret others' sounds, body language, and verbal communication. Oral language blends the drive to speak with the desire to be social. Communication requires thinking, knowledge, and skill. Through practice, you can help children develop strong oral language skills and ensure their future reading and writing success.

Conversations

Before infants can understand or say words, they begin to communicate using gestures like facial expressions or by crying. For example, infants may cry to indicate that they want to be held. Over time, children learn to understand and respond to others' speech (receptive language) and express with their own words what they know and feel (expressive language). For example, infants begin to respond to hearing their own names and to very simple, familiar requests. Mobile infants can shake their heads or ask for an item by looking back and forth from the item to you. Their first words are ones that have a personal meaning, like *mama*. Between 18 months and 24 months, children learn hundreds of words and combine two words to form a simple sentence, like "Want juice" or "All gone."

A strong, consistent, and positive relationship exists between the amount of time a child communicates with an adult and later literacy skills (Dodici et al., 2003). The Harvard-sponsored longitudinal Home-School Study of Language and Literacy Development also documents a strong connection between early reading success and the number of complex conversations children engage in with adults in both their homes and schools (Dickinson & Tabors, 2001).

A strong, consistent, and positive relationship exists between the amount of time a child communicates with an adult and later literacy skills.

However, some early childhood experts have found that conversations that go beyond the "here and now" have the most impact on literacy development as opposed to conversations rooted in the immediate environment. For example, when you say to a child, "Put the puzzles back on the shelf" or "Try tasting the carrots," you are conveying a message, but the language you used omits elements related to literacy. Conversations that promote literacy development require language that reflects past and future as well as real and imaginary events. For example, when you talk to children about how much they enjoyed the field trip to a farm earlier in the year, or when you ask them to tell you the questions they want to ask the firefighter when he comes to visit their class next week, the children use language that goes beyond the present. These types of conversations require children to use their developing cognitive skills to represent ideas—a process that is important to the development of reading comprehension.

In addition to using language that surpasses the here and now, Dickinson, Tabors, and their colleagues found that beneficial conversations have the following attributes:

• A balance of adult and child input (taking turns).

• Attentive listening.

• Extended talk that stays on a topic of interest to the child.

• Vocabulary that is introduced in an intentional way.

As with all areas of learning, children develop at their own pace. Their experiences will influence their language and literacy development heavily. Some infants may start babbling and cooing sooner, some are more intent listeners, and others may use lots of nonverbal communication. As an early educator, use this information to figure out what to expect for the children and decide on the best ways to strengthen their language skills. Continue to think about how to best support all the children in your setting—including dual language learners and children with special needs. Use the standard dialect to prepare children for success at school.

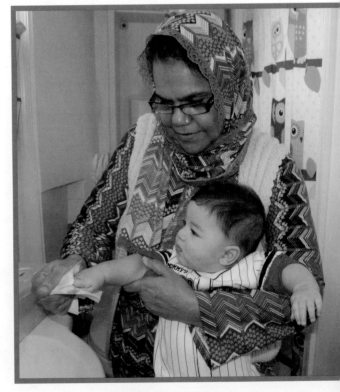

Speak gently to infants throughout the day—including during routines, like handwashing.

Using Everyday Experiences to Strengthen Language Skills

As you learned earlier, there are direct and positive relationships among the amount of time children communicate with adults, the complexity of these conversations, and literacy development. The following tips will guide you in incorporating language-building conversations into your daily interactions with the children in your setting:

Young Infants

- Speak gently to infants throughout the day—including during routines, such as diapering and feeding. These are great opportunities to strengthen your bonds with all children and incorporate additional words into their day. These "conversations" also show infants that you respect them as you describe what you are doing.

- Describe what you are doing—or provide infants a "play-by-play"—as you care for and play with them. Infants need to be surrounded by language long before they can actually produce words themselves.

- Respond to infants as if they were talking. Coo and smile back at infants, modeling the give-and-take of a conversation. Infants are learning that they can communicate with others. Mirror their expressions and use proper language. Incorporate home languages when appropriate.

- Provide pleasant sounds and music when children are likely to listen. Notice how infants respond to music and continue to play music they enjoy.

- Sing lullabies to infants as they fall asleep.

Mobile Infants

- Model language that expresses what they seem to be communicating. ("Ariel, you are getting tired, and I can help you to go to sleep.") Incorporate home language when appropriate.

- Respond to all their attempts to communicate. Talk to all infants who respond and those who do not. After speaking, wait and provide time for infants to respond. Model the give-and-take of a conversation.

- Use proper language as you describe what you are doing and what they are doing. Speak in the standard dialect.

- Show or point to materials that you are referring to as you talk about the object.

- Talk about their experiences at home.

- Sing lively versions of songs. Offer songs with motions. Make up or personalize songs.

- Tell stories.

- Recite poems.

- Sing lullabies as infants go to sleep.

- Play music when infants are likely to listen. Notice how infants respond to music and continue to play music they enjoy.

Toddlers

- As toddlers begin to use language, begin scaffolding their learning, providing them assistance as they continue to progress.

- Elaborate on their speech when they say something incorrectly instead of correcting them.

- Expand their speech. When a 2-year-old says, "Milk," reply, "Oh, you would like some milk?"

- Introduce new vocabulary and use language that will continue to build toddlers' skills.

- Show or point to materials that you are referring to as you talk about the object.

- Speak and sing in the preferred language of the child's family—including singing or cueing for those who are hearing impaired.

- Have conversations with toddlers throughout the day, every day.

- Describe and explain the child's actions and those of other people.

- Name and describe objects, actions, people, and feelings.

- Read interesting books that introduce new vocabulary.

- Offer a small collection of songs they can learn.

- Introduce music and movement opportunities when toddlers are likely to listen and participate.

- Personalize the songs as much as possible when singing individually or to the group.

- Sing silly songs.

- Recite rhymes and make up silly new ones.

- Sing songs with lots of repetitive words.

Be sure to have conversations with toddlers throughout the day, every day.

Strategies to Enhance Preschool Conversations

By approximately 4 years old, children are forming complex sentences. By kindergarten, they are using sophisticated vocabulary and grammar and have nearly accurate pronunciation. When conversations are natural and social, children are more eager to participate. The following tips will help you make your conversations more meaningful to them.

Model Conversations

Children can learn the mechanics of a conversation by observing you conversing with other adults.

- When you start or join a conversation, say something and wait for a response from the other person.

- The idea of not interrupting your conversational partner can be traced back to the writings of Cicero in 44 B.C. (The Economist, 2006). When the other person replies, look at that person, listen to what is being said, and wait at least 5 seconds after the person has stopped talking before responding.

- When it is your turn to speak again, add some information related to what was said, ask questions for clarification, stay on topic, avoid unnecessary details, and give the other person a turn.

- To keep the conversation going, say something new and interesting about the topic. You might also share your own experiences, ask open-ended questions, explain yourself, and express agreement or concern.

- When you are finished with the conversation, let the other person know. Do not end your conversation with an abrupt stop.

Support children in applying the rules of conversation by listening to them attentively. Encourage children to talk during discussions, rather than focusing on them providing you the right answers. Try to understand what it is children want to communicate and help them to express it. If children are reluctant to talk or are unhappy, offer them some extra support. Sometimes just being there and showing your concern will encourage children to express themselves. For example, you are playing and talking with 3-year-old Marcus about blocks. You say, "Your tower is very tall." Marcus places another block on his tower but says nothing. "Wow. Now it's even taller," you say. This time Marcus smiles and responds, "It's almost as tall as the ceiling!"

Modeling conversations also exposes children to correct grammar. Many of the grammatical errors that young children make in speech, such as "I wented to the store" or "I saw three sheeps," signal that they are struggling to learn the difficult rules and exceptions of the English language. Instead of correcting them, restate correctly what they say: "Did you buy anything when you went to the store?" "I saw those three sheep, too."

Scaffold Children's Language

A basic rule of developmentally appropriate teaching practice is to offer children challenges slightly beyond what they now know or can do. In Chapter 5, you learned the term *scaffolding*, which describes the way adults support children's learning by building upon children's current knowledge, providing challenges, and stepping in to support when necessary. Incorporate this idea into the way you converse with children. Speak to children using language that is more complex than the words the children use now so that they continue to build their vocabularies:

- **Ask open-ended questions that require children to respond with more than one or two words.** Open-ended questions are conversation starters, especially when they are sincere and acknowledge a child's interests. They are also effective ways to extend conversations with children. Use open-ended questions to encourage children to discuss their thinking process rather than to give a "right" answer. For example, you might ask, "What are we planning to make out of the modeling clay this morning?" Then give children time—approximately 5 sec—to reflect before restating your question or asking another one.

- **Talk with children during play.** If you are sitting with a mobile infant and see that she is taking items out of a basket or you are sitting with a group of children who are playing in the block corner, describe the children's actions: "I see that you are taking the blocks out of the basket." "You have placed three long blocks in a row on the floor." As children get older, ask questions that are both open-ended and go beyond the here and now: "What could we plant in our garden that we could serve for snack?" Ask older preschoolers to predict or form hypotheses: "What do you think will happen when you mix those paint colors together?"

Talk with children during play.

- **Make the most of reading times.** The quantity and quality of book reading are associated with literacy gains. Reading books best supports language and literacy development when you include conversations about the book you are reading. Talk with children about the main character. Exploring how the plot makes both the main character and the reader feel and comparing the story to other stories or experiences strengthens children's language and literacy skills. Reenacting stories also gives children an opportunity to expand their language and literacy skills through conversations.

- **Take advantage of children's dramatic play scenarios.** Children stretch their thinking as they imagine themselves in different scenarios. If children are taking a while to converse or are having difficulty conversing, intervene and scaffold their learning. For example, you might join the children sitting at the table in the home area and say, "Boy, am I hungry! What are we having for dinner?"

- **Retell stories.** Children enjoy hearing the same stories repeatedly, which provides you the opportunity to teach them about story elements.

- **Converse during mealtimes**. There are strong positive relationships between mealtime talk during the preschool years and children's scores on literacy measures when the children are 5 years old (Dickinson & Tabors, 2001). Sit with children throughout mealtimes and facilitate dialogue and discussion with them. During mealtime, reflect on what has happened during the day with children and discuss issues that may be on children's minds. Children are inclined to talk about subjects that interest them the most. Because young children primarily relate to the world around them from an egocentric perspective, they enjoy topics that relate to them directly.

Support Children With Special Needs

Speech and language impairments are the most common special needs in early childhood, ranging from mild (difficulty articulating certain sounds) to severe (deaf and mute). If you suspect a child's vocabulary is not developing as it should or he/she is struggling with speech, continue to observe him/her and keep a written record of your observation. Share what you have observed with the child's parents and specialists who can assist. By law, children with identified special needs can receive support services through an Individualized Education Program (IEP). As an early educator, work with specialists and the child's parents to plan appropriate learning goals.

Sometimes, many of the same strategies you have learned in this section will also work for children with special needs. Make a conscious effort to slow the pace of your own speech and employ repetition. Speak simply to children and give them one-step directions. For example, instruct a child to "Please clean your lunch plate," (one step) instead of "Please clean your lunch plate when you're done. Then go get your cot for nap time" (multiple steps).

Sign language, picture boards, and gestures may be effective ways to help children with special needs communicate. Also allow children to express their ideas through the arts—including sculpting, dance, and music.

Vocabulary Development

The term *vocabulary* refers to the bank of words we know and use to communicate effectively. This bank is divided into four types:

- **Listening vocabulary** refers to the words we understand when we hear them.

- **Speaking vocabulary** consists of the words we use when we speak.

- **Reading vocabulary** refers to the words we understand when we read them.

- **Writing vocabulary** consists of the words we use in writing.

Children's listening and speaking vocabularies develop first, just as learning to listen and speak precedes the ability to read and write. As children develop their listening and speaking vocabularies, they gain a foundation for understanding printed words. Printed words expand all four vocabularies over time.

Vocabulary is most closely linked to reading comprehension. The larger and more varied children's listening and speaking vocabularies are, the more likely that they will become readers (Tabors, Beals, & Weizman, 2001). Historically, educators regarded vocabulary development as an isolated task. They introduced children to new words and required them to memorize definitions. However, vocabulary development is a natural process. Children need to hear new vocabulary in context to understand meanings.

But most adults do not use large and varied vocabularies naturally when they speak. Oral conversations are typically limited to about 15,000 commonly used words. After analyzing 65 min of speech in more than 60 preschool classrooms, The Harvard Home-School Study of Language and Literacy Development discovered that, on average, teachers used only 43 words that researchers classified as relatively sophisticated—the types of words likely to stretch children's vocabularies (Dickinson & Tabors, 2001).

Use the book's illustrations to help children understand the story.

University of Kansas researchers Betty Hart and Todd R. Risley studied oral conversations and their impact on children from a socio-economic standpoint. The pair visited the homes of 13 high-income families, 10 families of middle socio-economic status, 13 of low socio-economic status, and 6 families who receive welfare. They observed these families for 1 hr per month, from the time the children were 7 months old until they turned 3 years old. Hart and Risley found that on average, parents from the high-income families spoke over 2,000 words per hour to their children; working class parents spoke about 1,300 words per hour. Parents whose families receive welfare spoke about 600 words per hour. Therefore, children from the high-income families gained vocabulary at a quicker rate than children from the working class or welfare-recipient families.

By 3 years old, children from high-income families possessed vocabularies that were nearly 50% greater than those of working-class children and twice as large as those of children whose families receive welfare. The high-income children even had larger vocabularies than the ones parents of welfare-recipient families used when speaking to their own children. Hart and Risley estimated that by the time all the children were 4 years old and ready to enter preschool, the children from the high-income families would have accumulated experience with 45 million words, compared to only 13 million words to which a typical child in a family receiving welfare would have been exposed (Hart & Risley, 2003).

As an early educator, be intentional in your use of sophisticated vocabulary. Continue to think about how you can incorporate new and more sophisticated words into your everyday speech throughout the day. Mealtime conversations, reading books with children, dramatic play scenarios, choice time, small group activities, and field trips are a few key situations that are most effective for introducing the rich, sophisticated vocabulary words associated with literacy development. Mealtimes are effective, because multiple people can join the conversation. Book reading provides an opportunity to learn vocabulary from two sources—the book and the early educator discussing the book. Dramatic play and field trips lend themselves to fantasy and trips to the unknown— places that are filled with exciting new words. Indoor and outdoor choice time helps you introduce new vocabulary by using new names or descriptions for items with which children are playing or working.

Developing Phonological Awareness

Beginning in 2002, the National Early Literacy Panel (NELP, 2008, p. 153) reviewed research on language, literacy, and communication in young children from birth through 5 years old. One of NELP's key findings was the significant relationship between children's knowledge of *phonological awareness*—the ability to notice and manipulate sounds in words—and success in reading and writing. Instruction in phonological awareness is critical to children's success in learning to read and write. Begin working with young children on these four skills:

- **Rhyming:** words that end with the same sound (e.g., *name* and *flame*).

- **Alliteration:** words beginning with the same sound (e.g., **br**aid, **br**ain, and **br**eakfast).

- **Sentence segmenting:** hearing each separate word in a sentence.

- **Syllable segmenting:** being aware of "chunks" in words; understanding that words can have beginning, middle, and ending sounds.

Begin working with young children on literacy skills, like alliteration (words beginning with the same sound).

Help children grasp the concept of grouping word sounds in different combinations and lengths with the following activities:

- Sing and act out rhyming songs, chants, and finger plays. Set aside time every day for children to sing silly, rhyming songs like "The Name Game." Perform chants and finger plays like "Five Little Ducks."

- Have children clap out the syllables of words.

- Experiment with rhymes. Two-word sets like *Henny Penny* are appealing to young children because the words are identical sounding except for the beginning sounds.

- Make up silly songs and substitute your own rhyming words for the actual lyrics.

- Read and memorize rhyming poems.

- Read aloud rhyming books and books that play with language, like Dr. Seuss books.

- Sing and read books that accompany rhyming songs, like "I Know an Old Lady Who Swallowed a Fly."

- Have children act out their favorite rhyming songs and chants.

- Play games in which children find objects or pictures that start with the same sound or that rhyme.

- Focus children's attention on rhymes during daily activities: "If your name rhymes with *plain, rain,* or *cane,* you may get in line now...*Jane!*"

Supporting Dual Language Learners

Eighty-four percent of Head Start programs serve children who speak two or more languages (Severns, 2010). These children are dual language learners, or "young children who are learning a second language while still developing basic competency in their first language" (Espinosa, 2010). Most infant and toddler dual language learners are able to learn English and their first languages simultaneously. Meanwhile, preschoolers may be fluent in English or have never been exposed to the language. Your goal with all dual language learners in your setting is to foster their ability to speak, read, and write in English while maintaining and supporting the learning of their home language (Tabors, 2008).

Historically, educators believed that exposing children to more than one language at a time would confuse them and hinder their mastery of English. Actually, the opposite is true:

Teaching children in their home language helps promote their speaking, reading, and writing skills in a second language. This may seem counterintuitive—wouldn't immersing children in as many hours of English instruction every day lead to the most success?—but the likely explanation is that students benefit from having solid knowledge of both languages so they can properly sort which vowels…or other parts of language can be transferred from their home language to English and (just as importantly) which ones do not (Goldenberg, 2008, p. 15).

Nemeth (2012) cites these reasons why educators should support children's home languages:

- **The home language is the foundation for cognitive growth.** Young dual language learners have acquired most of their knowledge in their home languages. Children transfer literacy skills developed in their home language to new languages. Therefore, early educators should teach these children beginning reading skills in their home languages. Children can readily learn the English alphabet once they have mastered letter and word recognition in their home languages.

- **Children feel valued when their home language is respected.** Children's self-esteem and confidence are bolstered when early educators value them for who they are. When children are free to speak their home languages with their families and within your setting, they receive the message that their home languages and cultures are important.

Work with dual language learners one-on-one or in small groups so that you can give children maximum attention.

• **Families feel valued when their home language is respected.** Families are more likely to partner with early educators when they see that their cultures are valued in the setting. Even parents who may initially feel that it is better for their children to attend a setting where only English is spoken will be relieved to find out that their home language is not only important, but essential to their child's learning.

Language and Literacy Learning

Infants and toddlers who are learning two languages simultaneously acquire them in similar ways. On the other hand, preschoolers who already understand their home languages do not learn second languages in the same way. Dual language learning experts have mapped out these steps that children undergo in acquiring a second language (Nemeth, 2012):

1. **Home language only.** First, children speak the only way they know how—in their home language—whether or not you and their peers understand them.

2. **Possible silent period.** Children stop talking as they observe and listen. They rely on gestures to communicate.

3. **Actions show understanding.** Children understand what is said to them, even though they do not speak. They can follow directions and participate in activities as directed.

4. **Formulaic speech.** Children use short phrases and words to communicate. This parallels the speech patterns of 2-year-olds learning their first language.

5. **Informal language.** Children speak in sentences and communicate well. This type of language is referred to as *playground language,* because it tends to be informal.

6. **Academic fluency.** Similarly to older preschoolers speaking their first language, dual language learners speak in more complex and sophisticated sentences.

When communicating with dual language learners in English, make eye contact with them as you speak slowly. Repeat what you say so that

Use active play activities to introduce vocabulary instead of flash cards.

children can understand. Learn a few key words in each child's home language. Ask colleagues, children's parents, and community volunteers their advice for ways to communicate with dual language learners better. Online translation services can also help you communicate more effectively.

If you are fluent in the children's home languages, think about how you can use these languages in conversations with them. Here are some other ways you can support dual language learners (California Department of Education, 2000; Espinosa, 2010; Nemeth, 2012):

- Be intentional in your use of gestures, facial expressions, and body language.

- Vary your voice inflection for emphasis.

- Work with dual language learners one-on-one or in small groups so that you can give children maximum attention.

- Use visual supports like photos, illustrations, props, gestures, and puppets.

- Learn a few welcoming words in all children's home languages.

- Post key words and phrases in all children's home languages throughout the room—including suggested questions to ask children in each learning center.

- Give children time to repeat activities over time and in different contexts.

- Narrate your actions so children can hear models of English spoken correctly: "I'm going to do a head count and send in our lunch order now."

- Assemble children who speak different home languages at various mastery levels together in small groups so that they learn from each other.

- Start conversations with simple, closed-ended questions that children can answer with a nod or other gestures.

- Use active play activities to introduce vocabulary instead of flash cards.

- Create a word wall displaying vocabulary words (in all children's home languages) the children have recently learned.

- Use books filled with predictable phrases and repetition.

- Give children plenty of examples to help them understand word meanings.

- Select books in which the illustrations closely match the text to help children discern word meanings.

- Help children notice that English letters run left to right and up and down.

- Display all children's writing samples in whatever language they used.

Fostering Children's Reading Development

After reviewing more than 10,000 research studies, the Commission on Reading of the National Academy of Education concluded that there was definitive evidence to support that reading aloud is the overall best predictor of reading success (Anderson, 1985). In numerous studies, the number of stories children had been read is the strongest variable that impacts children's school success (Braunger & Lewis, 2006).

In this section you will learn strategies to help you begin laying the groundwork for reading success for infants, toddlers, and preschoolers.

Young Infants

- Read books every day.

- Use vinyl, washable cloth and hardback picture books (thick books) infants can touch and mouth.

- Use clear speech when reading.

- Offer a toy to hold and chew while you read.

- Read books with one or two pages with stories about infants, families, animals, and everyday experiences.

- Select books with songs, chants, and rhymes.

- Provide books with simple bright pictures and/or photographs with 1–2 objects per page.

- Follow infants' interests. If they indicate that they are no longer interested in the book, then allow them to engage in other activities.

Mobile Infants

- Provide books that reflect experiences with which mobile infants are familiar, like bathing and shopping with family members.

- Encourage infants to choose the books they want to read.

- Encourage them to participate in the story.

- Allow them to touch the book while you are reading and ask questions.

- Read expressively and make sure children can see the book's pictures.

- Allow infants to "read" to you. Listen to and acknowledge their communication.

- Follow their lead. When they lose interest, let them engage in other activities.

Toddlers

- Use board, paperback, and hardback books.

- Select books about families, infants, everyday experiences, familiar animals, and feelings. Also include books about simple concepts, like size, shape and color, children's interests, and self-help skills.

- Read books to children individually and in groups of 2–3. Allow children to come or go as they gain or lose interest in the story.

- Choose books that are written with sophisticated vocabulary so that children can learn new words.

- Provide opportunities for toddlers to interact and discuss the book while you read. Conversations surrounding reading are most helpful in building language.

- Ask open-ended questions that start with why: "Why do you think the ladybug was grouchy?"

- Ask additional questions that will help children expand their thinking and relate the story to their own lives: "Have you ever been angry like the grouchy ladybug?"

- Become very familiar with the books you read.

- Vary your voice inflection and dramatize the story.

- Read the title of the book, the author, and the illustrator.

- Describe the book's plot.

- Move your finger under the words as you read.

- Stop frequently to repeat interesting words or phrases.

- Encourage children to participate in making sounds or repeating words and phrases. Ask them to predict what will happen next in the story.

- Allow toddlers to "read" to you (or recite the plot from memory). Listen to and acknowledge their communication.

Hold books so that children can see the illustrations while you read.

Reading With Preschoolers

During their research review, NELP also found that experts pinpoint four strategies early educators should employ to promote reading among preschoolers (NELP, 2008, p. 153; Espinosa, 2010):

- Teach the alphabet.

- Introduce children to rich vocabulary words that stretch their thinking.

- Help children develop phonological awareness

- Read aloud to children every day.

Although most children are not reading with accuracy until kindergarten or first grade, preschoolers are developmentally ready to do the following (DeBruin-Parecki et al., 2005):

- Identify familiar logos, signs, and labels.

- Recognize familiar words.

- Enjoy listening to and talking about storybooks.

- Understand that print carries a message.

- Ask questions about a book's plot.

- Make evaluative comments about books.

- Pretend to read to a doll or stuffed animal.

- Identify some letters.

- Attempt to read.

- Have a favorite author.

Begin engaging preschoolers in these activities early and daily. Many children enjoy hearing the same book read over and over, because they learn through repetition and are most comfortable with what is familiar. Repeated readings help children gain a sense of competence, control, and self-esteem.

Read with expression and bring the characters and events to life.

Try these techniques while reading aloud to children in your setting (RIF, n.d.):

- Establish a regular time for reading aloud.

- Find a quiet, comfortable place where children can listen to the story free from distractions.

- Invite a child onto your lap. Have at least 10 min of reading together one-on-one daily.

- Assemble groups of 4–6 children for reading aloud to ensure that all children have an opportunity to participate. Children who hear stories in small group settings have higher comprehension skills than children who are read to one-on-one or in large groups (Morrow & Gambrell, 2002).

- Select a book that you like and that you think the children will like, too. Make sure that it is appropriate and is written with rich vocabulary. Feature books in all children's home languages.

- Practice reading aloud. Read to your colleagues and in front of a mirror.

- Let children know why you selected the book. Note the similarities this book shares with other books you have read to them, like author or subject matter. Encourage children to choose which books they want you to read.

- Read the title of the book and the author's and illustrator's names. As you introduce a new book, ask children to predict what the book is about. Draw children's attention to the cover illustration.

- Read with expression and bring the characters and events to life.

- Practice contrasts with your voice, like loud and soft, fast and slow, high and low, to keep readers engaged. Also, employ pauses in your reading. The words on the page will inform your tactical choice (Fox, 2008).

- Hold the book to one side so that children can see the illustrations while you read.

- Read slowly enough for children to absorb the words and see the pictures. Use your finger to show children the words they are interested in. Move your finger as you read to them and point out that print in English is read from left to right.

- Use the book's illustrations to help children understand the story. Incorporate children's experiences to help them relate to the plot.

- Stop throughout the reading to ask children questions about what might happen next or how they believe a character is feeling. Ask them how they would react in a similar situation.

- Watch the children's body language. They may need a break or even to end a session early. Try to determine whether the children's need to fidget or the book choice is causing the problem.

- Talk about the book afterward and elicit the children's reactions. Ask and answer questions.

- Pose open-ended questions that will spark conversations about the book: "What do you think the bears did to Goldilocks?" Highlight the rich or new vocabulary words. Help children make connections.

- Ask the children to retell the story in their own words.

- Have children act out the story.

- Encourage children to draw, paint images, or write about the story.

- Keep the book available in the literacy center for children to view alone or in small groups.

- Create an audio recording of the book for children to enjoy in the listening area of the literacy

Shared Reading

"Shared-reading activities are often recommended as the single most important thing adults can do to promote the emergent literacy skills of young children" (NELP, 2008, p. 153). This activity transfers the responsibility for reading from the adult to the children. To spark shared reading, select a big book or other large-text book to share with a group of children. Predictable books, in particular, encourage children to participate in the reading. As you read, point out the words. This action helps children learn the concepts of words and print and that the eye moves from left to right while reading. During subsequent readings of the book, ask new questions and challenge children to predict the plot and chant predictable phrases. Focus on building and extending their understanding of the book. During other readings, focus on decoding (learning and applying knowledge of letter-sound relationships) or the book's language and vocabulary. As children become more familiar with the story, invite them to "read" the text (or recite the plot from memory) out loud to the group.

Find a quiet, comfortable place where children can listen to the story free from distractions

Figure 39. How Reading Aloud Benefits Children

In this chapter, you have learned that reading aloud fosters children's literacy and language development. Here are some additional ways that reading aloud benefits the children in your setting:

- Sends children the message that reading is a valued activity. The pleasurable feelings associated with reading aloud are essential to creating lifelong readers.

- Creates a social event, filled with discussion and involvement.

- Teaches children book awareness. They learn that pictures provide clues to stories, books and print go from left to right, print represents written language, and stories have a beginning, middle, and end.

- Helps children make sense of their worlds and understand why things happen and how things work.

- Scaffolds children's learning, making connections between what children know and have experienced and the ideas and information that are read to them.

- Promotes empathy and understanding as new characters and subjects beyond the child's immediate sphere of reference are introduced.

- Improves children's attention spans and ability to listen.

- Increases children's vocabulary by exposing them to new words that they do not hear in conversation. For example, when an adult converses with a 3-year-old, the adult uses only nine rare words per thousand words spoken. While reading a 3-year-old a picture book for preschoolers, that same adult reads about 27 new words to the child.

- Increases children's abilities to comprehend written texts. Listening and reading comprehension are directly related. Because children can listen on a higher level than they can read, reading aloud makes complex ideas more accessible.

- Teaches children how to read expressively as they imitate your emotion and enthusiasm in reading.

- Encourages children to stretch their minds.

- Stimulates children's imaginations, hones their observation skills, enhances listening skills, promotes curiosity, and allows them to practice solving problems.

- Models for children how fluent readers read and reflect on what is read.

(Trelease, 2006)

Alphabet Knowledge

Children's first exposure to the English alphabet is usually through the alphabet (or "ABC") song. Help children relate the letters they sing in the song to the letters on an alphabet strip. Point out the letters on the strip as they sing. Encourage them to begin the song in the middle or sing it backward.

Make learning the alphabet meaningful and fun for children and incorporate their learning into your natural interactions. The following list of tactics will also help you to begin familiarizing children with the letters of the alphabet:

Communication

- Read alphabet books aloud with the children, pointing out the letters as read.

- Sing songs with letter play, such as "B-I-N-G-O."

- Play alphabet-related lotto and concentration games that require children to identify and name letters.

- Display alphabet strips at children's eye level in areas where children are likely to use them, like the writing area of the literacy center.

Include items like sandpaper letters in the writing area of your setting's literacy center.

- Incorporate alphabet props in their learning environment (e.g., alphabet cookie cutters in the cooking center; sandpaper letters and rubber stamp letters in the writing area; alphabet sponges in the sand and water play center; magnetic letters, alphabet blocks, and alphabet puzzles in the math and manipulatives center; and alphabet stencils in the art center.)

- Point out letters as you help children write sentence strips, record their words on chart paper, read a book, or see signs on a neighborhood walk.

- Give children lots of opportunities to develop their writing skills, like making signs, publishing their own books, and creating writing samples.

- Teach children to read and write their names. Once they know the letters in their names, other letters may become more familiar to them. For example, Carl sees that *cat* begins with *c*, like his name does, and that *rabbit* begins with *r*, like the third letter in his name.

Fostering Children's Writing Development

In this chapter, you have learned that children develop their reading and writing skills simultaneously. Furthermore, vocabulary development, phonological awareness, and hearing books read aloud also help to develop their writing skills. Before they are fully able to write, children experiment with writing in three stages:

- **Scribbling:** Children explore markers, crayons, and other writing tools to see what effect they have on paper. Though they make marks and squiggles that look like scribbling, these beginning attempts at writing are quite different from scribbling in children's minds. These marks, which are children's first writings, differ from their beginning attempts at drawing. Children are able to distinguish between their early writings and their art even when adults may not.

- **Scribble writing and letter-like forms:** In this stage, scribbles morph into marks. A recognizable letter will emerge among the rows of little marks. These first attempts at letters are sometimes referred to as "mock letters," because they resemble real letters. Typically, the first letter of a child's name is the first real letter he/she writes. Initially children write these first real letters in all capitals, because they are easier for children to form. Over time and with practice, mock letters will all transform into real ones.

- **Letters that represent sounds in words:** By the end of the preschool years, children start organizing the letters they write. Instead of randomly writing letters on paper, children write in rows, often writing row after row of a single letter.

When they start learning letter sounds, children shift to writing letters according to these sounds. For example, a child may write a note that reads "I LV U." This is the start of "real" writing, even though it uses invented spelling (writing words according to the way the letters in the words sound). This is a natural stage in children's writing development. When you acknowledge and accept children's writing, they will see themselves as competent and confident learners and will continue to refine their writing skills.

Supporting Children's Writing

Model writing to demonstrate that print has meaning and motivate children to begin scribbling and writing. Young children are egocentric (seeing the world from their perspectives), so help them learn to write the most important word in their vocabularies—their names. Children develop this skill in stages:

1. Using scribbles to represent their names.

2. Using actual letters from their names (one letter, the first few letters, or the first and last letters).

3. Writing their names in ways that others can recognize, but not always ordering the letters correctly.

4. Writing the letters, generally, in conventional order, but with some letters reversed or transposed.

5. Writing their first and last names conventionally.

Model writing to demonstrate that print has meaning and motivate children to begin scribbling and writing.

As they learn to write their names, encourage children to sign their artistic masterpieces or create nameplates for their books. Children can practice writing their names on the attendance sheet or by signing up for turns for snacks, using the computer, or riding a tricycle.

When children are aware of the letters in their names, they begin to use these letters in writing other words. Here are some additional ideas for facilitating children's writing skills:

- **Be a writing role model.** When children observe you writing, they learn that this is a valuable skill. Let them watch you filling out forms, sending in the lunch order, or writing notes to send home to families. Because you do it, writing becomes something they want to do, too.

- **Give children practice developing the fine motor skills they need for writing.** Encourage children to practice grasping writing tools appropriately in the "tripod grasp." The pads of a child's thumb and index finger should encircle the pencil, which rests on the middle finger near the first knuckle. All fingers should apply equal (but not heavy) pressure.

Some preschoolers have trouble correctly positioning writing tools in their hands. They may hold a pencil with their fists or wrap their thumb around the pencil and tuck it between their first two fingers. Their grasping problems are sometimes due to undeveloped hand muscles. However, inefficient grasps can prevent the development of appropriate muscles and place stress on children's finger joints. Preschoolers can easily develop writer's cramp, which keeps them from wanting to try to write.

Help children develop the needed fine motor skills to hold a pencil correctly through both modeling and direct instruction. Maintain a relaxed attitude so children are not self-conscious. Handwriting experts provide the following tips (Colker, 2010b):

- Place a sticker or rubber band on the part of the pencil where children should grasp.

- Have children practice with small pieces of chalk or miniature-golf pencils to gain control.

- Encourage children to write on vertical surfaces, such as easels or chalkboards, to strengthen muscles and position their wrists appropriately.

Include journals in the literacy center's writing area so that children can document and record their own learning.

- Work with children on writing projects.

    - Create charts and graphs of experiments in the science center.

    - Post documentation panels of children's work.

    - Publish books and stories with children.

    - Ask children to dictate stories to you that you record on chart paper, in journals, or in children's portfolios.

    - Send class thank-you notes to program visitors.

    - Develop, write, and post a set of rules for your setting.

Figure 40. Supporting Reading and Writing Skills for Children With Special Needs

- Provide children with dexterity problems a variety of materials, such as shaving cream, sawdust, or hair gel. These materials allow them to practice tracing letters with their fingers instead of holding a writing tool.

- Provide letters with texture—made of sandpaper, glitter, or other materials— for children who learn by touch.

- Provide hand-over-hand guidance (place your hand over the child's hand).

- Use large, simple, and bright letters.

- Encourage children with fine motor challenges to look at books independently to gain practice holding books and turning pages.

- Ensure that all children are seated comfortably for read-aloud sessions. If a child has gross motor problems, ask a specialist for help in finding a comfortable seating position.

- Give children with concentration problems a small, soft toy to hold.

- Give children with attention problems individual copies of the book you are reading aloud to look at independently. Explain to the other children, "This helps Sophia understand the story better. You can understand by looking at the big book I'm holding."

- Begin with simple, wordless or photograph-based books.

- Select books that appeal to the senses, such as texture or scratch-and-sniff books.

- Modify existing books by adding texture to illustrations and outlining numbers and letters in glue.

- Select books with cardboard pages that are easy to turn. Or glue ice-pop sticks to the pages as an aid.

- Children must keep their bodies stable in order to write. Ensure that their feet are solidly on the floor and that the table height falls between the child's waist and chest.

- Place sponge rollers on the handles of brushes or pencils so that children can hold them more easily.

- Use voice-activated software programs to allow children to use their voices—instead of their hands—to write.

- Tape paper to the table or to a dining tray to keep the paper stable.

- Let children know consistently that you value any and all of their "attempts" at writing.

- Use technology. Children can use a computer to listen to stories and type at their own pace and levels of ability. Work with the children's families and specialists to match appropriate technology to children's needs.

(California Department of Education, 2000)

Communication

Partnering With Families

Language and literacy development are major concerns for parents with young children. Parents want to do everything they can to ensure their children enter kindergarten prepared to be successful readers and writers. Creating a partnership with each family strengthens the quality of education you provide and deepens your understanding of each child's interests, skills, and needs. Learn about favorite stories, books, and songs that are shared at home and incorporate them into your learning environment. This will help young children transition into the setting and feel a sense of belonging. This information will also assist you in helping children make connections between the stories, books, and songs they engage in at home and those they engage in at your setting.

Also share with families the research and successful strategies for promoting language and literacy development and let them know what their child's favorite books, stories, poems, and songs are. This provides parents with additional ideas for fun activities at home and information for supporting their child's language and literacy development in meaningful ways.

Weikle and Hadadian (2003) found that successful readers tend to have parents or other family members who did the following:

- Served both as reading and writing models.

- Regularly read aloud to their children.

- Took time to interact with their children.

- Provided reading and writing materials for youngsters to use.

- Believed themselves to play an important role as their child's teacher.

Share with your children's families the following practices that promote literacy:

- Creating a literacy-rich home environment with plenty of reading materials and a quiet space that is comfortable for reading.

Successful readers tend to have family members who read aloud.

- Reading with children every day.

- Talking with children about their day.

- Taking family outings and discuss them.

- Joining children in pretend play.

- Singing and rhyming with children.

- Writing with children.

Early educators play a critical, foundational role in supporting children's language and literacy development in their first years. Fill your environments with language and print. Engage in conversations that are meaningful to children's interests, inserting new vocabulary whenever possible. Read aloud every day. Support their attempts at writing. Pay special attention to children with special needs or who are dual language learners. Partner with families to promote language and literacy learning for every child at home and in your setting. The choices you make now will impact children's literacy development for years to come. ■

Chapter 7
Creative

CDA Functional Area 7: Candidate uses a variety of developmentally appropriate learning experiences and teaching strategies for children to explore music, movement, and the visual arts, and to develop and express their individual creative abilities.

Creative

Introduction

Creativity involves generating novel ideas in alternative, previously unimagined ways, and it engages curiosity, risk taking, and imagination. Creative behavior must be original, relevant, fluent (occurs frequently and with ease) and flexible (uses nontraditional approaches) (Isenberg & Jalongo, 2010).

As an early educator, your job is to discover and nurture the creativity in every child so that they grow to be creative problem-solvers. In her article, "Your Creative Brain at Work," Evangelia Chrysikou (2012, p. 26) explains that "innovation matters in an enormous variety of professions. The contributions of creative thought can directly translate into career advancement as well as financial rewards. In an unfavorable economic climate, raising your creative game may even mark the difference between survival and failure."

Chrysikou adds that for many years, we thought that creativity was rare—a gift that only a lucky few of us possessed. True, we are naturally drawn to children who paint realistically, sing with perfect pitch, or dance with grace and flexibility. However, the figures in some children's paintings are unrecognizable. Some children sing off-key and move with less grace. Nonetheless, these children are learning to experiment, risk failure, try new things, and think with flexibility and originality. Although your role is not to be a "talent scout," you can foster every child's creativity—regardless of its perceived degree—in your early childhood setting (Isenberg & Jalongo, 2010).

In this chapter you will learn the following ways to support children's creativity:

- **Environments That Promote Creativity.**

- **Creativity Through Daily Interactions and Experiences.**

- **Promoting the Visual Arts.**

- **Creativity Through Music, Movement, and Dance.**

- **Creativity Through Dramatic Play and Story Retelling.**

Although your role is not to be a "talent scout," you can foster every child's creativity.

Environments That Promote Creativity

The learning environment you create—the setting itself, the people within the setting, and any routines and schedules you establish—and the amount of uninterrupted time children have to explore it dictate the types of experiences they will have in your setting. Children's creative possibilities are limited when they rotate learning centers every 15 min or when they cannot retrieve materials independently, explore and mouth materials, or get messy.

Design your learning environment in a way that supports creativity. Children should know that they are free to be themselves, take risks, and stretch their minds and ideas in your setting.

Creativity in Infant and Toddler Settings

There is a strong connection between curiosity and creativity. As humans, we have an innate sense of curiosity about the world around us.

Infants and toddlers explore the use of all of their senses. As they test new materials and objects and develop and explore the use of different body parts, these children are attempting to make new discoveries and learn about the physical world. In their settings, create spaces and incorporate a variety of sensory materials that will promote exploration. Include toys, such as teething rings, balls, rattles, squeaky toys, various containers, stacking toys, and blocks. Place materials where infants can explore them. Place objects near young infants who are not yet mobile but are able to grasp. Place materials, including various toys, containers, blocks, shakers, and books so that mobile infants can reach and use them independently. Exploring these items helps infants learn about the toys' physical properties and learn that toys have different purposes.

Toddlers, on the other hand, tend to be highly creative in the way they explore and manipulate objects. They express themselves using a variety of symbols and media. With encouragement, toddlers enjoy solving problems and are motivated to learn new things. This encouragement also fosters the development of children's positive self-concept. As they start to feel confident about what they can do and discover, they become more motivated to develop creative solutions to problems.

Reflect on the different ways children can use or manipulate a toy or object.

They also begin to express their ideas and feelings through imaginary and dramatic play, paint, crayons, clay, blocks, music, and movement.

Provide toddlers with a range of materials that engage all five senses, like crayons, collage, clay, and finger paint in the art center and different sizes, shapes, and types of blocks in the block center. As you observe infants and toddlers at play, continue to note which materials interest them the most and which materials they never use. Reflect on the different ways children can use or manipulate a toy or object. Ask: Are you providing materials that engage all five senses? How long do children want to spend exploring different materials and new objects? Where do they spend the most time engaging? Can you incorporate objects with multiple uses, purposes, or ways they can be manipulated? How can you support children to use materials in different ways? For example, allow a toddler to use pegs from a pegboard to march across the table, promoting creative thinking.

Also, evaluate the learning environment configuration. Does it allow infants and toddlers to roam and explore freely? Can children access materials for different purposes independently?

Figure 41. Fostering Creativity in Preschool Settings

This chart provides specific ideas for materials you can include in your setting's learning centers to promote creativity, curiosity, and exploration. Later in this chapter, we will discuss how your interactions with preschoolers throughout the day also support these skills.

Learning Center	How Materials Promote Creativity
Blocks	• Offer children open-ended unit blocks for building. • Create opportunities for young toddlers to use rake motions with hands to pick up blocks. • Make sure there is ample, traffic-free space for children to build constructions. • Encourage children to make signs to keep their creations on display after center time has ended. • Challenge children with problems: "How can these cars get across the river?" or "The tower keeps falling down, what do you think we need to do to ensure that it stays upright?"
Art	• Provide open-ended materials for painting, drawing, and making collages or sculptures. • Emphasize the process over the final product. • Encourage children to express their thoughts and feelings through their art. • Frame and display children's artwork.
Literacy	• Encourage children to create rhymes, poems, and books. • Encourage older toddlers to respond to more complex questions. • Encourage infants to explore books and paper by crumpling, patting, and banging. • Read and share books with small groups of infants/toddlers daily. • Invite children to act out stories from books and finger plays. • Have children write and act out their own plays. • Encourage children to use computers for drawing and creating stories.

Creative

Figure 41. Fostering Creativity in Preschool Settings (continued)

Learning Center	Ways to Promote Creativity
Dramatic Play	• Provide dress-up clothing and accessories so that children can assume various roles. • Provide prop boxes for role-playing scenarios at a doctor's office, beach, or hair salon. • Provide props that will stimulate children's imaginations, such as a telephone or a cash register. • Enter the children's play on occasion to stimulate the action or pose a problem to solve ("I'm hungry. When will you be serving lunch?").
Music & Movement	• Dance and perform creative movements with children using various props indoors and outdoors. • Help children create homemade instruments to play. • Sing spontaneously and during transitions. • Make up songs and dances with the children. • Ask children to draw pictures of how different types of music make them feel. • Include a variety of musical instruments and support children in playing them.
Science	• Create opportunities for children to explore and discover. • Incorporate natural materials for exploration. • Encourage children to brainstorm ways to solve problems. • Help children conduct experiments. • Challenge children to discover interesting ways to display data.
Math & Manipula-tives	• Provide opportunities to use tools. • Provide children with open-ended materials. • Provide both table and floor space for assembling puzzles. • Create puzzles and toys with children. • Allow children to devise their own rules for games.
Sand / Play	• Have children discover, from touch, what objects are buried in sand. • Encourage children to predict what objects will sink or float in water. • Provide open-ended props. • Ask lots of open-ended questions to stimulate children's thinking.
Cooking	• Encourage children to create and record their own recipes. Try these new recipes during your cooking experiences using fresh and healthy ingredients. • Provide garnishes for children to decorate dishes. • Encourage children to put their own "stamp" on recipes. • Ask children to create placemats, centerpieces, and inviting table settings.
Outdoors	• Invite children to help with landscaping. • Bring process-oriented activities, such as art and woodworking. • Provide straws, wires, strawberry baskets, six-pack rings, and plastic hangers for children to use as wands while blowing bubbles. • Invite children to make up outdoor games they can play. • Provide necessary equipment for infants, toddlers, and preschoolers with special needs to interact with their peers. • Create opportunities for young toddlers to develop strength, balance, and coordination by repeating movements.

Creativity Through Daily Interactions and Experiences

In Chapter 5, you learned that young children think differently than adults. These children's creativity also differs from creativity adults exhibit (Runco, 2012). Children tend to be less inhibited than adults, focus less on finding the "right" answer, and be unable sometimes to distinguish between reality and fantasy. For example, as they use open-ended materials and new media, children are less concerned with the final product and more interested in enjoying and learning from exploration. They are less concerned with what their painting or drawing looks like or whether their block structure really is a spaceship. Because of these characteristics, creativity is natural for children.

Because they are less concerned with what their painting or drawing looks like, children are naturally creative.

As you observe and interact with children during play, think about the following tips for engaging with them as they explore:

- **Ask lots of open-ended questions.** Observe and think about how you can scaffold children's learning by focusing on how and what they are learning. Describe their actions aloud: "I see that you are placing orange paint right next to the blue paint on the paper." However, do not worry about children learning specific facts or figures.

- **Instead of "copying" models or examples, focus on children's interest and their own explorations and originality.** What activities are children choosing to engage in? What materials do they prefer to use? Is a child scribbling on pieces of paper because they are exploring holding a pencil, a large crayon, or the properties of paper? Are they applying glue to paper to learn about consistency and the properties of glue? Are they mixing different colored paints on paper to witness its effects? Avoid asking a child, "What is it?" This question conveys to them that their work has to be labeled or identifiable and that they must have a product in mind when working and creating. Instead, think about how you can encourage children to explain and express their experiences and ideas with you.

- **Think of how to help children use materials in new and exciting ways.** Could you allow children to move materials from one area to another? Can children "save" their artwork or constructions and continue working on them tomorrow?

- **Provide children time to explore.** Do not rush young children from one activity to the next. Allow them to focus on the activities and materials in which they are most interested and curious. The more time you allow children to solve problems, create, explore, and learn, the more time you are able to observe them.

Creative

Figure 42. Supporting Creative Thought

- Encourage children to consider possibilities. (Creativity involves identifying problems and solving them.)
- Respect all children's responses and ideas.
- Create an atmosphere where children are free to take risks.
- Let children know that messes are not only tolerated but, sometimes, invited.
- Give children lots of "practice" time to test their ideas and thoughts and experiment with materials.
- Help children deal with failure and learn from their mistakes.
- Offer children constructive feedback and encourage them to provide each other the same.
- Limit competition.

- Offer ongoing encouragement, not empty praise.
- Teach children strategies for creative thinking, and place few restrictions on their ideas.
- Do not expect children's art to be representational. Instead, value their scribbles, splatters, and blobs as artwork. Instead of asking what it is, ask children to describe their work.
- Allow children time to revisit (and rethink) their work. When people are allowed time to return to an idea, they often see things in a new way and experience a breakthrough in their thinking.
- Ask children to identify sounds and materials in the setting.

(Isenberg & Jalongo, 2010; Chrysikou, 2012)

Promoting the Visual Arts

Drawing, painting, sculpting, working with clay, and creating collages and mobiles are all expressions of children's creativity. The visual arts allow children to create something new, be original, and fulfill their need to communicate their ideas and feelings. You have learned that you should design your art center to promote creativity. Keep open-ended materials accessible to children of all ages. Offer diverse, open-ended colorful materials for infants and toddlers to explore, as well as materials with different patterns, textures, and colors. Encourage toddlers to use various media to express themselves, such as large sheets of paper and fat crayons for drawing; ribbons and dried flowers for weaving; and glitter and buttons for collages. Children's creative expressions and continued interest in the arts vary greatly according to the quantity and quality of their early experiences (Denac, 2008; Kemple & Nissenberg, 2000).

Children's artistic explorations begin with drawing and painting.

Drawing and Painting

Children's artistic explorations begin with drawing and painting in an attempt to discover what tools, like crayons and paintbrushes, can do. As an early educator, be aware that children go through distinct stages when learning to draw and paint (ZERO TO THREE, n.d.):

1. **Random scribbling (15 months–2.5 years).** Children grab hold of a crayon or marker and find that it will leave a mark on paper. Marks grow into squiggles, which children find exciting.

2. **Controlled scribbling (2–3 years).** As children gain hand control over a marker or crayon, they perch them between their thumbs and forefingers rather than grabbing the writing tools in a fist. Scribbles turn into circles and lines. Instead of touching the paper randomly, children place marks on paper with intentionality.

3. **Lines and patterns (2.5–3.5 years).** Children realize that they can convey meaning through their drawings. They work hard to include in their art the curves and lines that they see in real objects.

4. **Pictures of objects or people (3–5 years).** Children are now able to put circles and lines together. Because these early drawings are often unplanned, children frequently do not know what they will be drawing until it happens. Later, as they gain both physical control over drawing tools and the intellectual skill to understand that their thoughts can be represented visually, they plan their art. Children now draw with intentionality and have a finished product in mind.

Knowing and understanding these stages will help you support children in exploring and experimenting with drawing and painting tools. Again, your observations of children's interests and skills are critical. Each child is unique and will master different skills at different times.

Figure 43. Other Art Activities

After children are familiar with drawing and painting, they will embrace other art forms eagerly. Most young children enjoy experimenting with art forms such as the following:

- **Collages**—tearing or cutting tissue and magazine photos to paste onto paper or cardboard; embellishing the design with feathers, confetti, ribbons, or sequins.

- **Clays or dough**—molding clay or play dough into sculptures or mounds; rolling dough or cutting out letters or shapes with cookie cutters.

- **Three-dimensional constructions**—building and creating three-dimensional structures that stand (stabiles) or hang (mobiles).

- **Weaving**—using potholder loops or freestanding looms to create potholders, fabrics, and designs.

- **Woodworking**—sawing and gluing wood pieces together to create constructions and projects (under adult supervision).

Early educators can help children move through these steps and help them learn how to hold and use drawing and painting utensils. Crayons and markers are held in the "tripod grasp." The pads of a child's thumb and index finger should encircle the tool, which rests on the middle finger near the first knuckle. All fingers should apply equal (but not heavy) pressure.

Help children learn paintbrush techniques and ensure that you have a variety of brushes available to best meet children's needs. For example, while all children may benefit from using seamless brushes with metal bands, older toddlers and younger preschoolers work better with flat, 1-in. brushes. Older children can use round or flat brushes.

Invite children to use a variety of drawing and painting media—including water-based paints, finger paints, and dyes. Also offer children alternative painting materials, such as squeeze bottles, squeegees, string, marbles, or straws. Children can try drawing and painting on cardboard, Styrofoam™, wood, and other surfaces. Even "painting" the side of the building with water on a sunny day gives children an opportunity to express themselves and then watch these expressions evaporate.

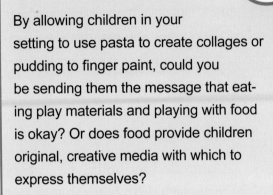

Should Food Be Art?

By allowing children in your setting to use pasta to create collages or pudding to finger paint, could you be sending them the message that eating play materials and playing with food is okay? Or does food provide children original, creative media with which to express themselves?

Is this an example of finding new ways to use and manipulate materials, or are you teaching children to waste resources when other children like them go hungry every day?

The use of food as an artistic medium is a complicated issue with no clear-cut, right, or wrong answer. Find out your setting's policy regarding the use of food as art. If there is no policy in place, encourage staff and parents to discuss this issue and devise a policy together.

Supporting Children's Exploration

Set the tone for creativity by designing your setting to support art exploration and introducing children to different media and tools: "Today I'm going to introduce you to a new tool for working with clay and dough. It's called an 'extruder.' See what happens when you put clay in it and push down. You'll have lots of time to explore and experiment with it."

Through art exploration, children at any age learn about creative self-expression and about themselves as individuals. Do not direct these experiences. Avoid worksheets and coloring pages. Instead, let the children's imaginations take charge. If 18 children in your setting are painting today, then the day should conclude with 18 distinct paintings. The styles, colors, and subjects of each painting should reflect the personalities of the artists. Encouraging children to explore with art materials however they see fit is the best way to nurture creativity.

Encourage toddlers to use various media to express themselves.

Hands-on, open-ended explorations, like painting and drawing, allow children to explore and experiment with art media at their own pace. The creative process children undergo is more important than the final products. This process is an opportunity to acknowledge the child's creative use of materials. For example, a toddler may make a fist and rub his knuckles through a glob of paint before punching several holes in the paper.

As children paint or draw, describe their actions or ask respectful questions about their work: "I see that you are placing red paint next to the green paint." "How did you make that blue shape?" "You filled up the whole paper with your drawing." "It looks like you added some texture to the clay." If children indicate that they are drawing pictures of their homes or sculpting blue jays out of play dough, encourage their creative thinking. Ask them to describe their work or tell you how they made their creative decisions.

Avoid asking children, "What is it?" or making assumptions about their artwork. Treat all children's artwork with respect, and let them know that you appreciate their creations. Ask the children to tell you which pieces they want to display, which they want to place in their portfolios, and which they want to take home. Have the children sign their masterpieces and display this work (in actual frames or construction paper edging) throughout the setting as documentation of their learning. Make signs or sentence strips to describe the art or to make a statement about the artist's creative intent: "Louis wanted his mobile to look and feel like a windy day." When their artwork is displayed at their eye level, children have the opportunity to revisit and discuss it.

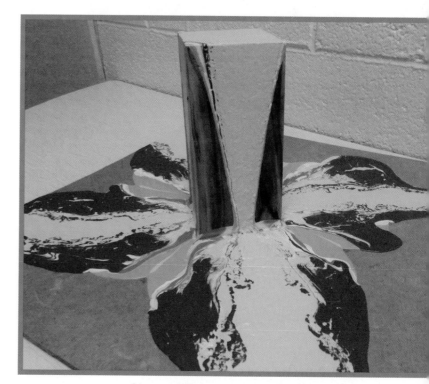

Most young children enjoy experimenting with art forms.

Creativity Through Music, Movement, and Dance

Music and movement experiences support children's physical, language and literacy, cognitive, and social–emotional development. These experiences encourage them to move their bodies in new ways, explore new sounds and songs, and explore musical instruments. Because young children make strong connections between movement and understanding, some of them actually learn through movement. When introduced to music and movement at early ages, these kinesthetic learners become more adept at and comfortable with moving their bodies.

If you or a colleague plays an instrument, play it to accompany the children's singing.

Singing

Singing is a simple way to introduce children to the creativity of music and movement. For example, infants respond to musical sounds by cooing and moving (Kenney, 1997). You can soothe infants by rocking and swaying them gently in your arms while singing lullabies. When you sing, you expose infants to new vocabulary, sounds and rhythms, facial expressions, and creative expression.

As children get older, they sing and shout words they know and make up their own silly verses to songs. They do not care whether they or you can carry a tune, stay on key, or keep time to the beat. They just want to sing with you or anyone else who wants to join in.

Make singing an opportunity for both group fun and individual expression. The following are ways to make singing a regular part of your day:

- Sing songs as part of your routines (e.g., to alert children of cleanup time or to demonstrate for how long children need to wash their hands).

- Incorporate singing into group meetings.

- Play games that include singing, like "the hokey pokey" and "London bridge."

- Read/sing song-based books, such as *There Was an Old Lady Who Swallowed a Fly* by Simms Taback.

- Make up songs with children that narrate what they are doing.

- Record audio versions of songs to play for the group or for children to listen to alone.

- Invite parents to teach the children songs from their culture or in the family's home language.

- Sing from a class songbook of favorite songs.

- Encourage spontaneous singing.

- If you or a colleague plays an instrument, play it to accompany the children's singing.

- Let children stand up when they sing to help them "feel" the music.

Sparking Musical Creativity

Your setting design and the materials and resources you provide all foster children's creative thinking and exploration. Designate a spacious area in your setting for music and movement, and send children the message that these expressions of creativity are valuable. In this space, include the following:

- Accessible music, instruments, and movement props.

- Space for in-depth exploration and experimentation through music and movement.

- Various musical instruments representing the children's home cultures and instruments, like steel drums or rain sticks, which are featured in music of their cultures.

- Various instruments, both homemade (drums from oatmeal boxes, cymbals from metal pie plates, and maracas from shakers) and purchased (triangles, bells, and xylophones).

- Software for listening to and composing music and learning about dance.

- A wide range of music—including children's music, music representing children's cultures, classical, rock, pop, country, hip-hop, jazz, and show tunes.

- Props like streamers, scarves, ribbons, flags, costumes, low stilts, and hula hoops for moving and marching to music. These props exaggerate movements and help children stretch their creativity.

- Quiet areas for listening to music in private.

Allow children to move in ways that reflect their moods.

Creative

In addition, here are some ideas for spurring children's musical creativity (Colker, n.d.; Parlakian & Lerner, 2010):

- Sing songs with infants.

- Sway with infants in your arms as you listen to music with different tempos and rhythms.

- Provide infants with movement experiences, like finger plays.

- When infants are lying on their backs, gently move their arms and legs to music.

- Incorporate songs with hand gestures. This helps infants who are learning to coordinate hands and fingers to explore their bodies through music. They may imitate your movements and will begin to sing and make sounds around 10–12 months old.

- Play music to create moods, like classical during nap time and rock music during exercise.

- Allow children to choose music and move in ways that reflect their moods (e.g., marching to drums to show excitement).

- Help children begin to choreograph dances. Work with children to pinpoint what the music tells them. Then, brainstorm ways of communicating these ideas to others through movement.

- Encourage children to create *interpretive dances* (movements that express feelings and emotions).

- Have children recreate the sounds of their worlds through music and their voices.

- Encourage children to compose music to accompany a play or puppet show.

- Invite children to make musical instruments.

- Challenge children to recreate music using classroom instruments.

- Encourage children to play instruments in different ways, such as pounding maracas instead of shaking them.

The Reggio Emilia Approach to Art and Creativity

Since the 1940s, the people of Reggio Emilia, a town in northern Italy, have believed that children are best educated when teachers and families work together closely. In the Reggio classroom, children—not lesson plans—drive the curriculum. Teachers deem any topic the children are interested in worthy of study. They follow these interests closely to conduct long-term studies and investigations that are documented in photographs, pictures, and the children's words. After teachers and parents, the Reggio classroom itself is considered the children's third teacher. These classrooms are flooded with natural light and contain beautifully crafted materials.

Creativity lies at the heart of the Reggio program. Part of the famous philosophy is that there are "100 languages of children," meaning that children need to express their ideas and feelings not just through words, but through all the arts—visual, music, dance, and dramatic play. Observers of a Reggio program note the sophistication of preschoolers' artwork. As they express themselves artistically, observe their surroundings, and predict outcomes, these children produce remarkable creations.

- Ensure children know that there is neither a right nor a wrong way for their music to sound.

- Seek out music that supports literature or art; for example, playing reggae or Creole music during or after reading *Cendrillon: A Caribbean Cinderella* by Robert D. San Souci.

- Help children differentiate music by tone, tempo, genre, and pitch.

- Give children opportunities to conduct while their friends play instruments.

- Introduce children to computer programs and websites that will help them compose music, such as PBS's *Maya & Miguel.*

Music, Movement, and Culture

When you incorporate children's cultural dances and movements, you provide them opportunities to learn more about themselves and each other. You also encourage them to express themselves in an environment in which they feel respected and valued. Ask: What dances are children are engaged in at home or in their communities? Do children enjoy practicing these dances and movements? Can these dances be incorporated in meaningful ways? As a culturally responsive early educator, understand that music and movement carry various meanings

Help children differentiate music by tone, tempo, genre, and pitch.

among specific religious, ethnic, and cultural groups. Some religions may prohibit certain types of music, instruments, and movements. Communication with families is critical to ensure that children know that they are respected and valued in your program.

Figure 44. Questions That Promote Music and Movement Creativity

- How do you feel when you hear this music?

- How can you show others how this music makes you feel?

- Can you show me with your body what this music wants you to do?

- Do you see colors in your mind when you hear music?

- How can you dance to this music?

- What props would you like to move with to this music?

- What images do you see?

- What would you like your friends to do to this music with you?

- How would you use this music when playing with blocks? With puzzles? Outside?

- What changes would you make to this music?

- What is it about your favorite music that appeals to you?

- Should all music sound like your favorite music?

Creativity Through Dramatic Play and Story Retelling

During play, children can act out and reenact their experiences. As Isenberg and Jalongo explain (2010, p.198):

> Children learn about their world not only from their interactions with it, but also from the way the world interacts with them. These concrete, personal experiences provide the basis for their developing abstract thinking. Because drama is always concrete, specific, and personal, it helps children more easily understand how their physical and social worlds work and connect. In other words, dramatic play provides a wonderful vehicle for children to explore and learn about the social and physical world they live in.

Play fosters imagination, new ways of thinking, and problem-solving. *Dramatic play*, in particular, helps children understand and experiment with social roles. It can also give them countless opportunities for acquiring social skills as they play with others. Through dramatic play, children gradually learn to consider others' needs and appreciate different values and perspectives.

All play allows children to take on roles, see things from others' perspectives, and act as adults and feel grown up. It provides an arena for children to face their fears. For example, a child who is afraid of shots can pretend to be a doctor administering shots to others. Play also helps children develop abstract thinking skills as they use objects to represent or symbolize other things or ideas. For example, " This marker is my pretend hotdog." Play stretches children's imaginations as they pretend to act as people and animals in their world might act.

As infants, children begin to imitate facial expressions, an action that lays the foundation for later dramatic play. The quality of experiences for infants and toddlers will impact their creative thinking and play as they get older. Secure and happy children

Although children are the stars of dramatic play scenarios, early educators facilitate and sometimes play along.

will begin to develop more extended and imaginative play episodes. Around 18 months, children begin to engage in symbolic play, where a block can be used to represent a car or other object. As children grow, their pretend play experiences become more intricate. By 3 years old, play scenarios generally have three components: plots, roles, and props. Children make plans, assume roles, and use objects to express their feelings and ideas.

Although it is the children who are the "stars" of dramatic play scenarios, early educators serve as facilitators. You are the children's play director, ensuring that dialogue and action do not end abruptly. As the director, you might enter the action when children's play has lost momentum. For example, 2-year-old Derek is pretending to make soup and appears to not know how to progress the scenario. Suggest that he pour some soup into two bowls so that each of you can taste it. Or you might ask open-ended questions that spark the children's thinking, like: "What's for dinner?" "What did you do at work today?" "What books do you have that I might borrow?" "Can you show me how to train the dog so she doesn't bark so much?" "Can you help me plan a tea party for tomorrow?" "Whom should we invite?" During play, there are no right or wrong answers, so questions like these offer children situations in which they can be creative.

In addition to directing children's play, you can support their imaginary and dramatic play in the following ways:

- Provide a variety of dress-up clothing that children are free to wear that represent genders, ages, and a range of occupations with which children are familiar.

- Offer a variety of accessories (e.g., shoes, hats, jewelry, ties, and boas) for children to add to their outfits.

- Make prop boxes available that contain unique props for new settings, like a beach, vet's office, school, or a hair salon.

- Provide real props such as aprons, dishes and flatware, magazines, and books that can make imaginary settings feel more real.

- Allow children time to get involved in their scenarios.

- Offer children opportunities to revisit scenarios over time.

- Encourage children to try new and different activities.

You are the children's play director, ensuring that dialogue and action do not end abruptly.

- Pose problems for children to solve and encourage them to devise a variety of solutions.

- Introduce children to new materials.

- Offer specific comments, like "You gave the children a good start to the day by making them breakfast."

Story retelling also facilitates children's creative thinking and problem-solving skills. When children retell a story they have heard, read, or created, their understanding of the story is deepened. For example, children can retell and reenact a favorite story or book or dictate a story idea to you. In these instances, they know the gist of what they want to say, if not the exact wording, and the sequence of events.

The creativity in story retelling rests in the presentation of the story. Children's expressions, timing, enthusiasm, and interpretation display their creative thinking. Promote creativity during story retelling by allowing children to choose the books or stories. This builds their personal motivation and support for the story. Help children secure appropriate props and costumes, and give them time and space to plan and practice. Prepare questions in advance to focus children's attention on how their characters feel and act. Revisit the reenactment afterward and link back to the story. Instead of acting out the plot of a favorite story, some children may opt to use puppets to tell the stories. Help children build a stage, announce the story on a chalkboard, and collect tickets to the special performance. ■

Competency Standard III:

To support social and emotional development and to provide positive guidance

Developmental Contexts

Functional Area 8: Self

Young infants *(birth–8 months)*, during the first few weeks and months of life, young infants begin to build a sense of self-confidence and security in an environment where they can trust that an adult will lovingly care for their needs. Infants are only emerging in their ability to regulate their temperature and recognize signs of discomfort such as hunger or feeling cold. An adult who cares for a young infant provides immense support for future abilities in self regulation by being consistently available. The adult feeds the child when hungry, keeps he child warm and comfortable, soothes the child when distressed and offers learning opportunities by providing interesting things to look at, taste, smell, feel, hear and touch.

Mobile infants *(9–17 months)*, a loving provider is a resource or "home base" who is readily available and provides warm physical comfort and a safe environment to explore and master. This emotional stability is essential for the development of self-confidence as well as language, physical, cognitive and social emotional growth.

Toddlers' *(18–36 months)* sense of self and growing feelings of independence develop at the same time that they realize the importance of parents and other providers. The healthy toddler's inner world is filled with conflicting feelings and ideas — independence and dependence, confidence and doubt, fear and curiosity, hostility and love, anger and tenderness, aggression and passivity. Understanding the wide range of toddlers' feelings and how they might be expressed can help support the adult's ability to provide a calm and emotionally secure environment.

Preschoolers *(3-5 years old)* experience many conflicting feelings and ideas: independence and dependence, confidence and doubt, fear and power, hostility and love, anger and tenderness, and aggression and passivity. They continue to need a reliable environment and secure relationships with adults as they deal with these feelings and learn more about themselves in an expanding world: peers,school, neighborhood, and society. They are proud of their new skills in caring for themselves, developing friendships, building and making things work, understanding and achieving. Adults can support them by respecting and recognizing the strengths and needs of each child and by providing experiences that help them grow as individuals.

Functional Area 9: Social:

Young infants *(birth–8 months)* enter the world with an innate capacity and need for social contact. Yet each baby is unique in styles of interacting and readiness for different kinds of interactions. Infants need both protective and engaging social interactions with a few consistent, caring adults who get to know

Competency Standard III (continued)

them as individuals. When adults respond to the cues and signals of young infants, they model social interactions. It is through these early experiences that infants learn to read and respond appropriately to the cues of others.

Mobile infants *(9–17 months)* are curious about others but need assistance and supervision in interacting with other children. They continue to need one or a few consistent adults as their most important social partner(s) and as a bridge to creating additional social partners.

Toddlers *(18–36 months)* social awareness is much more complex than that of younger children. Toddlers can begin to understand that others have feelings too — sometimes similar to and sometimes different from their own. They imitate many of the social behaviors of other children and adults. As toddlers become increasingly interested in other children, adults should guide and support their interactions, recognizing that they continue to rely upon familiar adults for emotional stability.

Preschoolers *(3-5 years old)* welcome social interactions with adults and children. Their social skills develop rapidly, first through parallel play, near other playing preschoolers, and gradually through more cooperative play, with them. Adults can promote understanding and respect among preschool children by providing experiences in sharing materials, responsibilities and social problem solving. Preschoolers can begin to learn about differing individual and group needs in a positive way.

Functional Area 10: Guidance

Young infants *(birth–8 months)* begin to adapt their rhythms of eating and sleeping to the expectations of their social environment through the gentle guidance of sensitive early educators who meet their needs. Infants basic trust in adults and their environment that is established at this time directly affects the child's responsiveness to positive guidance later and promotes the development of self-regulation.

Mobile infants *(9–17 months)* want to do everything but they have little understanding about what is permissible and may not remember rules. Adults can organize the environment in ways that clearly define limits and minimize conflicts. While respecting the child's experiments by saying "no," they can reinforce positive social interaction (for example, hugging) and discourage negative behaviors (for example, biting).

Toddlers *(18–36 months)* move through recurring phases of extreme dependence and independence as they gain new skills and awareness. They require an understanding provider who remains calm and supportive during their struggle to become independent. Adults must be resourceful in recognizing and encouraging self-regulatory behavior while setting consistent, clear limits.

Preschoolers *(3-5 years old)* can participate in the process of setting group rules and can benefit from learning why those rules are necessary. They require an understanding adult who remains calm and supportive as they continue to become self-regulated. They will continue to "test" limits from time to time as they grow more confident and independent. Adults can support them by acknowledging their feelings and remaining consistent about expectations, routines, and limits.

Chapter 8
Self

CDA Functional Area 8: Candidate develops a warm, positive, supportive, and responsive relationship with each child, and helps each child learn about and take pride in his or her individual and cultural identity.

Self

Introduction

In Chapter 5, you learned about Abraham Maslow's hierarchy of needs, which includes basic or physiological needs (air, food, water, sleep, and shelter), safety and security, love and belonging, self-esteem, and self-actualization. Maslow theorized that all these needs must be met before people can reach their full potential. As an early educator, work to meet children's self-esteem and self-actualization needs by observing and getting to know each child individually and acknowledging, respecting, and appreciating who each child is. When you help children build their self-esteem and meet their needs for self-actualization, you help them develop a solid sense of self and empower them to take on challenges.

Children are motivated to learn when their interests, preferences, and backgrounds are reflected in their learning environments. Help children appreciate the characteristics that define them uniquely—such as their temperament, strengths, and approaches to learning—and support them in valuing who they are as members of families, cultural groups, communities, and society as a whole.

In this chapter, we will explore the following ways in which you can help children develop a strong sense of self:

- **Appreciating Each Child.**
- **Promoting Children's Sense of Self.**
- **Developing a Sense of Racial Identity.**
- **Guiding Children in Expressing Their Feelings.**
- **Helping Each Child Flourish.**

Appreciating Each Child

Experiences shape our identities over time. During early childhood, we develop our self-concept, or the at-tributes, abilities, attitudes, and values that define us. Children learn about themselves and construct their own identities within the context of their families, communities, relationships (with people, places, and things), and the actions and responses of others. Positive experiences help children understand that they are important, valued, and respected. From birth, children develop a sense of belonging when they feel accepted, develop secure attachments, and trust those who care for them. When children feel safe, secure, and supported, they develop the confidence to explore, take risks, and solve problems. The relationships among you, the children, and their families play a key role in building children's identities.

Also, view children as active participants and decision-makers in the learning environment. Respect and work with each child's unique skills, qualities, and abilities. Understanding children's developmental milestones will help you select materials and employ teaching strategies that will meet children's needs and ensure their progress, growth, and learning. Also, understand each child's gender, temperament, personality, approaches to learning, strengths and challenges, and family circumstances. Each of these factors contributes to the development of the whole child.

Truly knowing and understanding the children in your setting requires observation, time, and commitment. This knowledge allows you to customize the environment, materials, curriculum, and your interactions with individuals and groups to best serve each child.

The following are ways you can bolster children's developing self-concept and strengthen your relationships with each child:

Infants

- Respond to each infant's needs. Infants develop a sense of trust when they know that their needs will be met.

Allow children to bring their favorite items from home.

- Help infants understand and develop their physical capabilities (e.g., encouraging them to clap hands, reach, smile, wave, point, and talk using gurgles and sounds).

- Help infants distinguish themselves from others (e.g., saying the infants' names and the names of family members and viewing and pointing to photographs).

- Provide opportunities for infants to be with, watch, and listen to other children.

- Set up spaces for infants to practice self-help skills, like grooming and dressing.

- Nurture and respond to each child during daily routines.

- Hold infants and give them one-on-one positive attention.

- Include photos of infants and their families within the setting.

Self

- Hang mirrors on the walls so that mobile infants can see themselves and explore.

- Ask families to bring in the child's favorite items—including blankets, toys, and teething rings.

Toddlers

- Respond to each toddler's needs.

- Provide safe opportunities and spaces for toddlers to be independent and develop self-help skills.

- Provide opportunities for toddlers to be with, watch, and listen to other children.

- Nurture and respond to each child during daily routines and transitions.

- Provide each toddler one-on-one positive attention.

- Include photos of toddlers and their families within the setting.

- Post documentation of children's learning—including artwork and photographs of toddlers' experiences within your setting.

- Hang mirrors on the walls so that toddlers can see themselves and explore.

- Allow children to bring their favorite items from home—including stuffed animals and books.

Which Impacts Children's Development More: Nature or Nurture?

Scholars have debated for centuries the impact of genetics versus environmental influences on human development. Both *nature* (our genetic or inherited make-up) and *nurture* (the influence of the physical and social environment) impact our physical and social traits. For example, consider a malnourished child whose growth is stunted due to lack of food or inadequate diet. Then consider a child who is surrounded by supportive and nurturing family members. How are the children's development and sense of self impacted in each situation?

Preschoolers

- Create "All About Me" books with children that feature photos of their families, pets, and friends and include documentation of the work and learning that they select.

- Chart children's favorite foods, books, and toys. Post these charts on the wall at children's eye level.

- Ask children to determine which pieces of art, writing samples, and photos they would like to display in the setting, place in their portfolios or "All About Me" books, or take home.

- Allow children to bring their favorite items from home—including stuffed animals and books.

Gender

Early educators can help children develop a positive sense of both genders by allowing them to experiment with gender roles through play. Around 2 years old, children begin to form their own ideas concerning gender. By the time they are 3 years old, most children know whether they are boys or girls and will begin to form opinions about gender roles (Martin & Ruble, 2004). By 3 years old, children begin to apply gender stereotypes to toys, so provide a wide variety of dolls and dress-up clothes that appeal to both boys and girls.

While temperament does not define or predict behavior clearly, it can help you understand how children react and relate to the world around them.

Children learn about gender by observing others' behavior, absorbing societal norms, and processing media and environmental messages. When using shared bathrooms (as most toddlers and preschoolers do), children collect data on what makes a girl different from a boy physically. However, for young children, gender is more about behavior than anatomy (Derman-Sparks & Edwards, 2010). In fact, it is not unusual for children to believe that they can change genders simply by adopting new behaviors.

If you send children the message that they are free to try out different roles, they will feel comfortable doing so. This includes having a welcoming attitude about girls doing woodworking or playing with blocks and boys tending to dolls or playing a mom or a baby in the housekeeping area. Early educators who are familiar with factors that influence gender identity can critically analyze their learning environments and all materials provided and effectively counteract and minimize gender bias in their settings (Zaman, 2007).

Temperament

Temperament (the way a person approaches and reacts to the world) influences a person's behavior and the way they interact with others. It is driven by both *nature* (genetic or inherited make-up) and nurture (the influence of the physical and social environment). While temperament does not define or predict behavior clearly, it can help you understand how children react and relate to the world around them. Temperament can also help you and parents identify children's strengths and determine what support these children will need to succeed in their relationships and environments.

Understand and know how to handle the three major temperaments in young children: easy or flexible; difficult, active, or feisty; and slow-to-warm-up or cautious (Oliver, 2002). Your awareness

Self

will help you increase your understanding of the children; create stronger connections with them; and facilitate their social, emotional, and cognitive growth. For example, if you know that Ricardo is easily distracted, provide him with a nook or corner where he can read or work alone. Similarly, if Elizabeth is shy and reluctant to enter groups, teach her language to make joining others at play easier: "Can I build with you?" or "This is my favorite puzzle. Would you like to do it with me?" Model how to enter a social situation, such as during dramatic play: "Elizabeth and I would like to join you for tea today. What are you serving?"

Understanding how children are likely to react to the people and events in their lives makes you more of a responsive and effective early educator. Give children your full attention and reflect on how you can support each child in developing an easy or flexible temperament. For example, when working with infants, observe their facial expressions and body language. Learning to distinguish cries will enable you to meet the infant's needs—including diaper changes, feeding, and soothing.

Approaches to Learning

Beginning at birth, young infants are able to form relationships with adults, develop trust, and explore the world. With a developmentally appropriate learning environment and nurturing

responsive adults, young children can explore and learn. As they gain knowledge and skills across the physical, cognitive, language, and social–emotional domains, children also develop *approaches to learning*, or specific skills that help direct their learning. There are specific characteristics that determine a child's approaches to learning (Hyson, 2008):

• Intrinsic motivation to learn.

• Interest and joy in learning.

• Engagement.

• Persistence.

• Planning.

• Ability to focus.

• Flexible problem-solving.

• Inventiveness.

• Tolerance for frustration.

Give children time to become fully engaged in an activity.

Children's approaches to learning are closely linked to school readiness. Children who can plan, focus, and remain persistent, curious, and engaged tend to be more successful in school and are more likely to graduate from college. Each child's approaches to learning are different. For example, some children are problem-solvers and others are naturally persistent. Evidence that boys and girls differ in their approaches to learning also exists. For example, girls are more persistent and are more likely to plan than boys. Early educators can best support children's approaches to learning in the following ways (Hopkins, 2004; Hyson, 2008):

- Focus on children's efforts, not their capabilities.

- Give children specific feedback when something does not work.

- Help children learn that failure is a part of learning, not a cause for shame.

- Offer children choices to pique their curiosity.

- Nurture their creativity by asking lots of questions. Suggest new ways of viewing things or using materials.

- Help children finish what they start and provide time to do so.

- Give children time to become fully engaged in an activity.

- Help children appreciate challenges and find pleasure in solving difficult problems.

- Instill a love of learning.

Strengths and Challenges

Every child in your setting will excel at some skills and struggle to master others. For example, Amanda may be able to sing beautifully, but she cannot roll the ball in a straight line during kickball. Understanding children's strengths and challenges helps you customize activities to work on specific skills, encourage children to learn, and promote their success.

Howard Gardner's theory of multiple intelligences, which you learned about in Chapter 5, details nine ways in which children's abilities are represented by unique talents and personality traits. Children will typically excel sharply in one or two areas that may represent their individual learning styles. To maintain these children's engagement, challenge them in the

Focus on children's efforts, not their capabilities.

areas in which they excel and the areas in which they struggle. The skills, knowledge, and abilities of some children in your setting may be stronger or weaker than what is expected for the age group. In both scenarios, intentionally plan meaningful activities and opportunities that will challenge children and build on their specific skills.

In some instances, children will benefit from additional screening and support from specialists. Approximately 8% of all children 3–5 years old receive federal special education services free of charge through the public school system under the Individuals with Disabilities Education Act (IDEA) of 2004 (Office of Special Education Programs [OSEP, 2008]). The same law provides early intervention services for infants and toddlers (Part C of IDEA), preschoolers (Section 619 of Part B of IDEA), and school-age children in grades K–12 (Part B of IDEA).

From birth to 3 years old, children are eligible for free assessment and evaluation and are provided an Individualized Family Service Plan (IFSP) through an early intervention program. This plan is developed with the focus on families as the greatest resource for infants and toddlers.

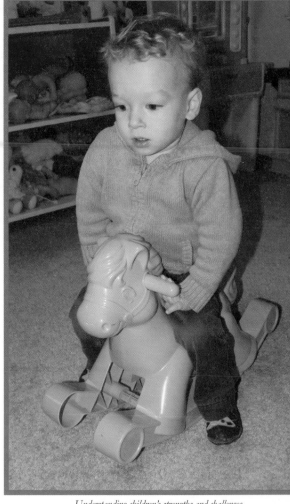

Understanding children's strengths and challenges helps you customize activities.

All preschoolers who are eligible for special education services are provided an Individualized Education Program (IEP). (Many people and even official documents refer to an IEP as an *Individualized Education Plan.* Even though the document is a plan, the official term is *program* [Hayslip, 2012].) The IEP, which is developed by educational staff in concert with parents, specifies the goals for each child and the services that will be provided. These services typically include speech, occupational, and physical therapy. Staff, with the help of special educators and related service professionals, implement the IEP.

When you know what the children's services and goals are, you are better equipped to offer them the special education services they need.

Family Circumstances

Families provide children with bonding and first relationships and contribute to children's developing sense of self-concept. Successful families preserve children's innocence with protection, love, and encouragement. Consider how the following family circumstances impact children:

- Family composition characteristics (e.g., the relationships and ages of family members, including birth order).

- Family culture and religious beliefs.

- Home language.

- Parents/family income, education level, occupations, work hours, military/civilian status, and marital status.

- Family member disabilities or mental health issues (including substance abuse).

- Exposure to domestic violence.

- Special circumstances, such as marital separation, divorce, deployment, moving, homelessness, illness, or death in the family.

Be aware of children's family circumstances so that you can offer appropriate support. For example, children whose parents battle substance abuse may need extra stability and comfort to counteract their parents' unpredictable behavior. Or a child whose home language is not English will need support in learning to read and write in both languages. Here are some ways you can gather the information you need to fully understand a child's family situation:

- Observe continually. Observe children playing alone, in small groups, and with everyone at meeting time. Record observational notes and create a snapshot of what each child is like over time.

- Take photos of children and their accomplishments. Hang these on the wall and keep these in the children's portfolios as records of their progress.

- Keep samples of each child's work. Children will reveal a lot about themselves through their art, writing, and projects.

- Form an information-sharing relationship with parents. Through regular meetings, morning drop-off/afternoon pick-up, e-mail, and informal conversations, develop a system for ensuring that you are aware of changes in children's lives.

Observe children playing alone, in small groups, and with everyone at meeting time.

Self

- Ask parents/guardians to complete an initial questionnaire about their home and family when their child enrolls in your setting.

- Conduct parent workshops.

- Meet with parents regularly to discuss children's progress.

- Conduct home visits so you can see children's families. Take photos to display at the program that will show the children and their siblings interacting.

- Greet each child personally at the start and end of each day.

- Talk to children at their eye level and use their names during your conversations.

- Interact one-on-one with children daily to get to know them better, observe their skill levels, and bond with them.

- Consult specialists for additional insight.

Once you are aware of the particular family circumstances that may be affecting children, help them feel appreciated and supported in the following ways:

- For children who have nontraditional family compositions, avoid using the terms mommy and daddy or even parents. The general term *family* is more inclusive.

- To lessen any emphasis on family income, avoid such practices as asking children to "show and tell" their possessions. Instead, ask children to share new experiences.

- Whether children come from affluent, home-less, or immigrant families, let families and children know that you hold the same high expectations for all children.

- Read books to children that feature main characters dealing with the same things that children in your program are facing, such as being in foster care (*Murphy's Three Homes* by Jan Levinson Gilman), having to move (*Melanie Mouse's Moving Day* by Cyndy Szekeres), parents' pending divorce

Interact one-on-one with children daily to get to know them better, observe their skill levels, and bond with them.

(*Two Homes* by Claire Masurel), or siblings with special needs (*My Brother Charlie* by Holly Robinson Peete and Ryan Elizabeth Peete). As you read and discuss these books with children, make sure that children experiencing these situations feel secure and encourage them to express themselves.

- Reassure children who have survived violence and abuse or who are experiencing parental separation or divorce. Use your words and body language to communicate that none of these circumstances is ever the children's fault. Consult experts if you feel children need additional support or you need ideas on how to support them within your setting. Offer children lots of dramatic play and sand and water play experiences where they can express their emotions and regain some control. Report any suspected abuse to your supervisor and local authorities.

- In cases of suspected sexual abuse, consult experts on what you can do to support and protect children. Even if there has been no abuse, introduce all children to the concepts of good touching and bad touching, using dolls, puppets, or books, like *Please Tell! A Child's Story About Sexual Abuse* by Jessie. Report any suspected abuse to your supervisor and local authorities.

- Regard children's irrational fears as rational ones. Both fears are just as troubling to children. Do not dismiss these fears with phrases like, "There's nothing to be afraid of." Acknowledge their fears and offer comfort.

- Help children overcome their fears by exposing them to the feared object or person in small increments. For example, if Eduardo is afraid of dogs, introduce plastic dogs into his dramatic play. During play, Eduardo can command the toy to behave and do what he wants. When Eduardo has control over the dogs during play, real dogs will become less threatening to him over time. Also, read picture books about children who are comfortable around dogs such as *Clifford the Big Red Dog* by Norman Bridwell. When you think he is ready, introduce Eduardo to a real dog, perhaps one that is older and mellow. Prepare him for the dog's sniffs and licks. With time and safe encouragement, Eduardo can overcome his anxiety.

- Help parents support children who experience toileting accidents. For example, after eliminating medical causes, develop a schedule (at least every 2 hr) in which you regularly remind Mariah to go to the bathroom. Once there, teach her the 20-second rule. After she has urinated, ask her to count aloud to 20 and then try to urinate again. If Mariah wets her clothes, involve her in cleaning herself while reassuring her that accidents happen.

- Children's coordination skills vary. For example, some preschoolers, like Kenny, experience constant clumsiness. Support him while you help him refine his coordination skills. If he knocks over the art display every time he heads to the dramatic play area, let him know that you will find a better place for the display—then move it.

Promoting Children's Sense of Self

Self

Sense of self, or identity, includes the roles, behaviors, and attributes we associate with ourselves from infancy—including descriptions, such as "I'm strong," "I'm tall," or "I'm good at figuring things out." *Self-esteem* refers to people's perceptions of their own self-worth. Children's self-esteem may be impacted by their perceptions of being lovable ("I am a good friend.") and capable ("I make beautiful paintings.") (Bredekamp, 2011).

Early educators can promote children's sense of self by becoming familiar with understanding the different aspects of self-esteem. For example, self-esteem does not involve boasting or immodesty. Rather, it is about people's feelings concerning who they are and what they can do. *Earned self-esteem* is tied to action and accomplishment. If children complete tasks successfully, then they feel good about themselves. *Global self-esteem* refers to a general sense of pride and involves making children feel good about being themselves.

Senses of self and self-esteem develop and change over time and are heavily influenced by individual perceptions and how others' perceive us. For instance, as an early educator, when you send children messages that they are valued members of your setting and that they are capable, you help to grow their self-esteem. With self-esteem comes confidence and increased competence. Children with healthy self-esteem are able to withstand setbacks and accept new challenges and responsibilities.

There are a number of ways you can boost children's self-esteem:

- Build on children's strengths. Find activities that will showcase children's skills and help them feel competent.

- Help children develop their talents and explore their interests.

- Encourage children to engage in tasks that involve skills they have mastered, like dressing, serving snacks, cleaning up, writing their names, or solving problems. Then, set challenges for children that are slightly above their skill levels to build confidence.

- Use job charts to assign children helper roles. Make them feel good about their accomplishments.

Children's self-esteem may be impacted by their perceptions of being lovable and capable.

Be a Coach Instead of a Cheerleader

Praise conditions children to work for accolades instead of working toward accomplishing goals. Or, as Galinsky (2012, p. 2) points out, some children will stop trying to complete tasks altogether for fear that they will not be able to repeat their performances:

> It is clear that when adults praise children for seemingly in-born characteristics like being smart, it creates the opposite effect. Children become less willing to take on challenges because they don't want to lose their label of smartness. Praising children for their effort and their strategies is much more effective. . . Self-esteem is a by-product of trying hard, making mistakes, failing, and learning to go forward toward a goal.

Encourage and acknowledge children rather than praising them. Instead of saying, "Good job," keep your feedback specific to children's actions. By describing what they have done, you can help them understand it: "Thank you for putting all of the plates and glasses on the table. Now all the children sitting down for lunch at the table with Ms. Andersen will have their own plate and glass to use."

- Listen carefully to children and be attuned to what they may be communicating about their sense of self-worth. Be patient with toddlers who say, "No," or "Mine," constantly. They are becoming aware of their senses of self and identity.

- Respond to children in a supportive, kind, and positive tone of voice. Practice by recording your conversations to make sure your tone is appropriate.

- Offer children choices that support their learning styles. This offers all children the opportunity to gain confidence and build independence.

- Prepare children for new experiences.

- Spend one-on-one time with each child. Giving young children your attention sends the message that they are valuable.

- Help children make friends.

- Laugh at your mistakes so that children will understand that making a mistake is part of learning.

- Greet children affectionately every day, and show them you enjoy being with them.

- Celebrate with children as they learn how to roll over, sit up, crawl, and walk.

- Show your delight when infants coo, babble, and learn to speak their first words.

- Help children set goals. This will teach planning skills and help children notice their accomplishments.

- Focus on what each child contributes individually. Avoid comparing him/her to other children.

- Acknowledge and understand that every child is competent.

Successful experiences help children develop a sense of personal competency and self-esteem. Children need to feel worthy if they are to become confident, competent, and independent. As an early educator, create an environment where children can express positive feelings and ideas about themselves as they move through childhood into adulthood. Create opportunities for children to take risks and experience success, which will help them develop a sense of self-worth. When children make mistakes, they need supportive adults who do not rescue them from the consequences, but teach them to solve problems and express confidence that they will do better next time.

Valuing Children's Families

In Chapter 3, you learned that culture refers to the way we eat, sleep, talk, pray, play, and value things and concepts (Derman-Sparks & Edwards, 2010). These rules, passed down from generation to generation, tell us what to believe in and which values to hold.

Culture includes outward symbols, like the way we dress or eat or the languages we speak, and a deep behavioral structure. Cultural rules dictate how we show respect; what constitutes spirituality; our concepts of time and personal space; our values and goals of schooling; and, in essence, the kinds of people we want our children to become.

Early educators have a responsibility to help children develop positive cultural and personal identities specifically through valuing a child's family. Here are some ways you can make children feel that their families' behaviors and beliefs are acceptable and valued:

- Pronounce all family members' names correctly.

- Represent all families in the children's books, toys, music, and recipes you choose for the setting.

- Display pictures of the children's families prominently throughout the setting and in homemade books.

- Learn the "rules, traditions, and expectations" of all the families in the setting to develop meaningful relationships and support each culture within the learning environment (Derman-Sparks & Edwards, 2010).

- Determine which early childhood practices may conflict with families' cultural beliefs and resolve those differences.

While you cannot compromise on anything that will negatively impact children's health and safety, it is important to show respect and consideration for cultural practices like the following:

- Modeling tasks rather than allowing children to do things independently.

- Valuing interdependence and finding it impolite to single out one child for praise.

- Emphasizing that children share rather than take turns.

- Deeming eye contact between children and adults while speaking as disrespectful.

- Deeming boys serving their own meals as disrespectful.

Should any of these or other culture-based challenges arise, work together with the children's families to devise a plan that will respect individual cultural values and blend them with your setting's best practices.

Developing a Sense of Racial Identity

Though children do not understand the concept of racial groups, they notice differences among people. For example, one child may touch another child's hair, because it appears different. Children may understand that their skin is a certain color but not that they belong to a collective racial group. Even when using formal terms that refer to skin color, children understand the meanings of these words very differently. With their limited experience, they often use other words to describe racial skin tones, such as those related to the things around them.

Studies show that toddlers as young as 2 years old use racial categories to predict people's behaviors. Three- to five-year-olds not only categorize people by race, they express bias based on race (Aboud, 2008; Hirschfeld, 2008; Katz, 2003; Patterson & Bigler, 2006).

Although children often attach meaning to race without adults directly telling them to do so, it is important to note that "the biases children exhibit are not random." In fact, they often "reflect both subtle and not so subtle messages about the relative desirability of belonging to one social group as opposed to another" (Katz & Kofkin, 1997, p. 62). In other words, children notice the ways in which whiteness is normalized and privileged in American society. This is a prime reason why all children need to see themselves and their cultures represented in your learning environment.

Children from diverse families expect a degree of variation in how people look, feel, and sound. They begin to understand that their world comprises much diversity and begin to associate the human face, voice, and touch with a particular race. By 3 years old, many children can put their reactions to skin color into words from images of their daily interactions (Wardle, 2008). They not only notice the color of their own skin, but also mention how theirs is different from that of other people.

Determine which early childhood practices may conflict with families' cultural beliefs and resolve those differences.

Just as they are learning about differences between colors and shapes at this age, children are also beginning to categorize people. Many 3- and 4-year-olds discuss physical differences between themselves and others, specifically between boys and girls.

Children of color receive conflicting messages from society, which impacts the development of positive racial identities. *All people are equal, but some people are more equal than others.* Children's self-identities originate from their names, genders, and familial relationships—not from racial identification. Your goal as an early educator is to help children learn tolerance and acceptance of people of different races, cultures, and ethnicities.

If these children are not supported in positive identity formation, they can easily incorporate racist or stereotypical messages unconsciously into their view of themselves and others.

Children who learn from the world that they are feared or looked down upon because of racism, xenophobia, and other biases learn to feel shame about who they are. As an early educator, ensure that the learning environment shows evidence of diversity with which young children can easily associate. Ask: Does each child in your class identify with the learning environment? Do the children see themselves and their families represented throughout the setting and throughout the day? Are the materials present in proportion to the children in your setting? Do you have strategies for speaking with children who may inadvertently make comments that are inappropriate? Create a learning environment that represents all the children in your setting.

Guiding Children in Expressing Their Feelings

When you help children communicate their feelings effectively, you foster their social–emotional development. In turn, these children feel good about themselves and are further developing positive self-concept. The Center on the Social and Emotional Foundations for Early Learning at Vanderbilt University (n.d.) details a number of strategies you can employ to help children learn to express their emotions effectively:

- Help children associate a name with the way they feel. Often, children get frustrated when they cannot articulate the way they feel. They act out physically, because they are unable to use words. For example, Sarah is frustrated that she is having trouble stacking blocks in a tower. She throws a block across the room, because she does not know how to communicate her frustration.

- Give children lots of opportunities to identify feelings in themselves and others. For example, you might say to a child, "Riding the bike is so much fun. I see you smiling. Are you happy?" Or you might point out a situation and ask the child to reflect on what someone else may be feeling: "Joey bumped his head on the slide. How do you think Joey feels?"

- Start identifying basic emotions, such as happy, sad, and angry. Then introduce more descriptive words, such as lonely, frustrated, or grateful. This technique is known as *emotional literacy*. By providing children with more descriptive labels for emotions, they can express their feelings more specifically. For example, Leila is not only *sad* that her grandfather will not be visiting the setting today, she is *disappointed*. Amir is not just *happy* that today is his birthday, he is *excited*.

- Use feeling charts and picture books to help children match facial expressions with feelings. For example, while reading *David Gets in Trouble* by David Shannon, discuss David's expressions when he is caught doing things he has been told not to do. How does his facial expression change after he apologizes?

- Acknowledge when children talk about their feelings, and make your praise specific: "I'm very proud of you, Mike, for telling me that your feelings were hurt when you didn't get a turn at the computer. It's important to let me know what your feelings are. Now I can do something about it."

- Let children know that everyone has negative feelings sometimes. While they are not allowed to hurt or insult another child, children should not be ashamed of feeling angry. Explain to children that there are positive ways of expressing these negative feelings. For instance, they can calm down by sitting on comfortable pillows and reading a book or spending time individually with pets in the setting.

- Give children space to work through negative emotions. Offer them a book to read, a turn at the sand or water table, or an opportunity to be alone. This is not "time out"; it is space and time to resolve conflict internally.

- Model calmness and reason when discussing feelings with children. Children will learn from your example that emotions are best discussed calmly and straightforwardly.

- Encourage children to resolve peer conflicts independently and put into words how their peers' actions made them feel. Encourage children to devise solutions either individually or in groups, and support them in resolving the conflict.

Give children space to work through negative emotions.

Self

- Practice feeling-related activities, such as drawing "feeling faces," playing with puppets and dolls, or playing games such as "feeling face bingo" where children cross out feeling faces once they identify the emotion the face demonstrates (Joseph & Strain, 2010).

Figure 45. Emotion Words to Teach Young Children*

• Angry	• Proud	• Friendly	• Relieved
• Calm	• Disappointed	• Stubborn	• Interested
• Brave	• Frustrated	• Generous	• Peaceful
• Tense	• Embarrassed	• Shy	• Jealous
• Cheerful	• Silly	• Ignored	• Overwhelmed
• Bored	• Excited	• Satisfied	• Lonely
• Confused	• Uncomfortable	• Impatient	• Loving
• Surprised	• Fantastic	• Safe	• Comfortable
• Curious	• Worried	• Important	• Concerned

*Children with certain special needs and children from low-income families may possess limited vocabularies. These children, in particular, may need you to introduce them to emotion-related words and their meanings (Joseph & Strain, 2010).

(Center on the Social and Emotional Foundations for Early Learning, n.d)

Helping Each Child Flourish

If we were to ask parents what they want most for their children, they might say that they want their children to be happy, healthy, loved, and well-balanced. Parents want their children to flourish (Seligman, 2011). In recent years, educators have come to appreciate the role of two factors in helping children flourish: optimism and resilience. In this section, we will identify ways in which you can help children be confident that they will succeed. When they confront problems, one of their first thoughts should be, "I can figure out what to do." When they meet challenges, they should know, "I can do it."

Optimism

The Mayo Clinic defines *optimism* as "the belief that good things will happen to you and that negative events are temporary setbacks to overcome" (Brody, 2012). Suzanne Segerstrom of the University of Kentucky says that optimism involves motivation and persistence. Resilient people have healthy self-esteem; optimists gladly accept challenges.

Optimists are, by nature, motivated and believe that they are in control of their lives. They are healthier than pessimists and live significantly longer. Pessimists, in contrast, are prone to depression, even as young as preschool age (Seligman, 2007). Though optimism can be taught (the human brain can actually be rewired for optimism), the nature versus nurture debate may explain why all people are not optimists (Fox, 2012). The relationship between children's temperaments and environments is linked to optimism and pessimism.

Here are some ideas for helping children become more optimistic:

- Ask children to reflect on the positive things in their lives. Help them keep a gratitude journal to document good things that happen to them.

- Help children avoid common thinking traps, such as the following:

  - **jumping to conclusions** ("Brooklyn's playing with the puzzles again. I bet she won't want me to be in the math and manipulatives center with her.");

  - **always thinking the worst** ("I spilled paint on the carpet. My teacher will hate me."); and

  - **overemotionalizing** ("Anthony won't share with me. I'm never going to talk to him again.").

- Use humor and laughter to encourage positive feelings.

- Use dramatic play and puppet skits to work through difficult or scary scenarios, like an impending hurricane.

Often, children get frustrated when they cannot articulate the way they feel.

- Read and discuss children's books that feature optimism. For example, *Art From Her Heart* by Kathy Whitehead tells the story of 1950s African American folk artist Clementine Hunter. Hunter overcame numerous obstacles to create her art. Her work was even displayed in a gallery she was not allowed to enter because of her race.

- Teach children exercises such as meditation and yoga that help them relax and view situations from different perspectives.

- Consistently acknowledge each child's feelings.

- Challenge children to be open-minded and think optimistically. Through conversations, role playing, and play exercises, children can alter their pessimistic thinking.

- Model optimistic thinking.

Self

Resilience

Reaching In…Reaching Out (RIRO) is a Canadian resiliency training project established in 2002 for children under 8 years old. The Child & Family Partnership sponsored the program on the belief that *resilience* (the ability to recover from or adjust easily to change) helps children overcome disadvantages and reach out for new opportunities. "More than thirty years of research shows that people who are resilient are healthier, live longer, are more successful in school and at work, are happier in relationships, and less prone to depression" (RIRO, 2012, p. 1).

Children who learn to be resilient possess the 3 Cs (RIRO, 2012):

- **Control:** These children believe that they are in charge of their lives.

- **Challenge:** They view mistakes as opportunities for learning.

- **Commitment:** Active engagement and follow-through provide meaning for their lives.

Resilient children resemble children with a healthy self-concept (Brooks & Goldstein, 2003). They feel valued and appreciated, and they understand both their strengths and weaknesses. They are able to set realistic goals, solve problems, and view mistakes and challenges as learning opportunities. Children who are resilient focus on the aspects of their lives that they can control.

Researchers identify specific factors that lead to resilience, such as: trusting relationships, emotional sup-port outside the family, self-esteem, encouragement of autonomy, hope, responsible risk taking, a sense of being lovable, school achievement, belief in God and morality, and unconditional love. As an early educator, there are a number of strategies you can employ to promote the resiliency of all the children in your setting. Resilience is a component of self-esteem, so these strategies will overlap with the ones suggested earlier in this chapter (APA, 2011; Hurley, 2012; Brooks & Goldstein, 2003):

- Let children experience failure and learn from their mistakes. Allow them to keep trying and experience their inner strength.

- Help children create a *mantra* (a word, sound, or statement repeated to aid concentration). Saying words of encouragement to themselves, like, "Slow and steady wins the race," reminds them that even though life can be hard, they can still be successful.

Use humor and laughter to encourage positive feelings.

Self

Resilient children feel valued and appreciated.

- Have a positive attitude and support a child's efforts to try new things.

- Offer guidance to and support children who are learning to solve problems. Encourage them to offer solution ideas before you offer your own.

- Emphasize the importance of doing nice things for other people. "Scientists have found that doing a kindness produces the single most reliable momentary increase in well-being of any exercise we have tested" (Seligman, 2011, p. 20).

- Teach children to take personal responsibility for their own well-being. When children can dress and feed themselves, they can assert their independence and feel confident in their abilities.

- Make every child feel special. Children need to have at least one adult who gives them the strength to persevere through difficult times.

- Promote persistence, not perfection.

- Model resilience and allow children to see how you deal with stress. Convey self-confidence and show children how to defuse tension with humor.

- Provide children lots of opportunities to work through stress and frustration, like during pretend play or while drawing, painting, or using the sand or water table.

- Read and discuss books with children that feature resiliency themes, such as *I Can Do It* by Dana Lehman. ■

Chapter 9
Social

CDA Functional Area 9: Candidate helps each child function effectively in the group, learn to express feelings, acquire social skills, and make friends, and promotes mutual respect among children and adults.

Social

Introduction

Being social is a learned behavior that involves feeling comfortable around other people, enjoying their company, understanding their cultural norms and values, forming mutually respectful relationships, and understanding how to resolve conflicts. As an early educator, you play a major role in the development of children's social skills by arranging your setting to promote social activities throughout the day, fostering play, facilitating small and large group activities, and promoting authentic friendships. You also promote *prosocial behaviors* (behaviors intended to benefit another person, like helping, sharing, and comforting) and support children's development of skills needed to resolve conflict independently.

We will examine five basic components involved in helping children develop social skills:

- **Encouraging Successful Social Interaction.**

- **Supporting Children's Play.**

- **Forming Friendships.**

- **Helping Children Resolve Conflict.**

- **Building Prosocial Skills.**

Encouraging Successful Social Interaction

As children grow, they watch the world around them, noting people's similarities and differences. Children also learn how social groups operate and determine ways to join and participate in groups successfully. You can help children engage in successful social interaction by developing positive, secure, and respectful relationships with each child and fostering a tight-knit community within your setting.

Develop positive, secure, and respectful relationships with each child. The quality of young children's relationships with their early educators is related both to children's future academic success and future social relationships (Hyson & Taylor, 2011). Young children who grow up experiencing more secure attachment relationships are more likely to get along with peers, develop empathy and make friends easily and are less likely to become bullies or the victims of bullies (Riley, San Juan, Klinkner, & Ramminger, 2008).

As an early educator, you can form secure attachments with children beginning in infancy. These attachments help you understand their development, provide the appropriate environment for them, and respond to the cultural and individual needs of children and their families. When you create strong bonds with children, you make them feel safe and secure, help them form relationships with peers and other adults, and give them the confidence to take risks and solve problems. Children are also more likely to imitate respectful relationships once they see these relationships modeled.

Children develop attachments not with the adults who simply feed and diaper them, but with the adults who talk with them, nurture them, and meet their social and emotional needs. Use both verbal and nonverbal communication to let the children in your setting know that you care about them and that they are special. Call children by their names, give children appropriate hugs, spend time with them, and talk and laugh with them often. Ask them about their families or home lives. Talk with their parents regularly and make home visits when appropriate. As an early educator, you share a significant part of children's lives, and they come to rely on you for strength and support. They need to believe that you care about what happens to them and their family members.

The relationships you form with the children in your setting are established by the many interactions you have with them throughout the day that show that you care about, appreciate, and value them unconditionally. Three practices fuel these types of relationships (Dodge, Colker, & Heroman, 2002):

- Talking and listening to children respectfully.

- Being sensitive to children's feelings.

- Validating children's accomplishments and progress.

Also low child-to-educator ratios, small groups, primary caregiving, continuity of care, responsive routines, and engaging learning environments all encourage the formation of your relationships with each child and their relationships with each other.

Create a classroom or group community. Your setting is where staff, children, and their parents all connect. Though these connections define the dynamics of your

Reaching out to others through play is a skill that develops as children grow and mature.

learning community, you set the tone for the ways children relate to others and others relate to the children. Establish a strong learning community to help children develop the necessary skills they need to participate in groups. Through your relationships with the children, you help them understand rules and expectations, play cooperatively with others, and participate fully in the learning community. Providing children with these positive experiences fulfills a core philosophy and ensures that they have the opportunity to be successful and reach their potential.

Supporting Children's Play

Play, particularly pretend play, is a unique and effective learning medium that paves the way for academic and social success. Studies confirm the superiority of play-based models in comparison to academic curriculum models (Trawick-Smith, 2009). These study results are especially pronounced for children with language delays, perceptual impairments, and autism. In addition, play has been found to be one of the best predictors of children's later language and learning (Lewis et al., 2000). Dual language learners use more elaborate first and second language during their free play, which leads to increased language learning.

Psychologists view pretend play as the "intersection of cognitive development and social experiences" (Seifert, 2004). While pretending to engage in social interactions, such as eating a family meal or dressing a doll for bed, children use social cues to fill in the blanks. For example, during Gerard and Emma's tea party, they envision the bevy of foods and teas on the table and figure out together the best way to serve the treats. When Donald lifts a unit block to his ear like a telephone and pretends to talk to someone on the other end of the line, his pretend play represents a real-life experience. Donald's understanding of this symbolism is a leap of cognition.

During play, children use social circumstances to make cognitive gains. By learning to read others' expressions, children determine how they should respond. This is called social referencing. For example, when Bruce enters a pretend classroom scenario, Emily, his pretend teacher, eyes him and nods toward the chair. Bruce sits down and remains quiet. In this pretend play session, Emily and Bruce understand the roles they are assuming, how they have been integrated into the scenario, and how they should react to each other.

You promote play in your setting with the materials you provide to children and the design of the learning environment.

Social

Play develops in stages, and reaching out to others through play is a skill that develops as children grow and mature:

Solitary play. Very young children play by themselves. They might look at books, play with toys, or assemble puzzles.

Onlooker play/behavior. An onlooker is a child who watches others at play but does not engage. Though onlooker behavior is not a stage of play development, it is a normal role for many children who are still developing the social skills needed to interact with others at play.

By the time children are preschoolers, they are able to participate in cooperative play.

Parallel play. This type of play—common among toddlers—involves two children sitting near each other but performing two independent tasks. For example, two children may sit side by side in a sandbox. However, one digs and the other pans sand through a sieve. Even though the children are sitting side by side, neither child shows much interest in what the other child is doing.

Cooperative play. By the time children are preschoolers, they are able to participate in cooperative play. Two or more children work together to complete a common goal, such as planting a garden or painting a mural. The children are able to discuss their common goal, devise a plan to achieve it, and celebrate the accomplishment together. For toddlers, playing with more than one other child can be a challenge. As they get older, they develop the skills for three-way play. Cooperative play comes naturally to preschoolers who are able to extend themselves to others. For example, Irene and Thaddeus are sitting next to each other in the block center. They notice that they both enjoy building, so they decide to build together. They combine their individual skills and plan to build a racing boat. They learn to listen to each other and to communicate, negotiate, and compromise. Although these skills are new to the children, they understand that the skills can benefit them in reaching their goal. Irene and Thaddeus refine their plans. They test out hypotheses and solve problems. Most of all, they learn how others in the world act in similar circumstances. For some children, play gives them the opportunity to shine as leaders.

Configuring the environment for play.

As you learned in Chapter 3, you promote play in your setting with the materials you provide to children and the design of the learning environment. Again, think about the materials you provide

Assembling Prop Boxes

Prop boxes are filled with materials that you can use to encourage dramatic play among the children in your setting. Create them based on your children's interests and experiences to help them form connections with new knowledge. For example, one of the children in your setting recently visited the optometrist. You want to expose the rest of the children to this experience. Inside a large, lidded empty box, gather the materials that you think would complement a pretend optometrist visit—including pads of paper, calendars, magazines, eye charts, eyeglass frames, and mirrors on stands.

Ask the children to draw and write about their experiences using the items in the box. Read books about visiting the optometrist, like *The Adventures of Anthony as Seen through His Eyes* by David B. Miller. Plan a field trip to an optometry center or invite an optometrist to your setting. Make the imaginary experience as realistic as possible, and continue to reflect on how you will extend children's learning through your descriptions and questions.

both indoors and outdoors. Ensure that there are multiples of popular items so that children can play simultaneously.

Also consider including materials and objects that multiple children can use at the same time to play together. For example, include large wagons outdoors that multiple children can sit inside and practice pulling or oversized pails that several children can work together to fill.

Think about the learning centers in your preschool setting. Are they configured to foster independent activities and cooperative play? Would Louis be able to help himself to water and graham crackers, and then sign off on a list that he has had his snack? Could LeShawn, David, and Karen make mini meatloaves together, using the same mixing bowl and taking turns mixing the ingredients?

Carefully arranging the learning environment and focusing on different aspects of play are essential to promoting peer interaction and future school success.

Infants and Toddlers in Play

Infants use all their senses to learn about their surroundings. They enjoy play that involves lots of physical contact, singing and dancing, and using materials with a variety of textures. While playing with infants, provide them with interesting objects and materials, respond to their cues, follow and imitate their actions, and take turns making faces and sounds. Offer infants activities that are interesting—but not too challenging—and follow their interests and pace.

In addition to learning from active involvement and the exploration of materials, infants and toddlers learn when adults talk and play with them. Gradually build older toddlers' attention spans by pointing out new and interesting ways to use the same object. Alternate introducing children to new possibilities ("If you turn the box over, you'll see how it opens!") and acknowledging and praising them for doing something new ("You opened the box!"). Also demonstrate imaginative play, like rocking a baby doll to sleep or saying vroom, vroom while moving a toy car.

Children also learn from their observations and interactions with other children. Mobile infants might enjoy imitating each other's behavior as they begin to relate to one another. Demonstrate for infants what other children are doing within the setting to help these infants gain awareness of the other children. This engagement in play helps infants learn about relationships, social interactions, and the world around them.

Preschool Children in Dramatic Play

In Chapter 7, you learned that dramatic play helps children understand and experiment with social roles, consider others' needs, and appreciate different values and perspectives. *Self-regulation* (control of emotions, behavior, impulses, and focus) is linked closely to and develops through dramatic play. Self-regulation allows children to focus and learn across all domains of learning and is considered the single best predictor of children's success in school and life (Spiegel, 2008). Children who have developed strong self-regulation skills can play and relate well without adult intervention. When children talk to themselves during play about the tasks they will complete and how to complete them, this is evidence of developing self-regulation skills. Once children can self-regulate, they are open to mastering and employing social skills, like sharing and taking turns.

Each time children enter a dramatic play scenario, they learn more about how others live and work in the world. The home area is the focus of most dramatic play learning centers. Here, children assume family roles, like mom, dad, children, grandchildren, and pets. Using plastic toy foods and child-sized furnishings, dishes, and glasses, children prepare, serve, and clean up after meals. They engage in family discussions over meals and dress for school and work.

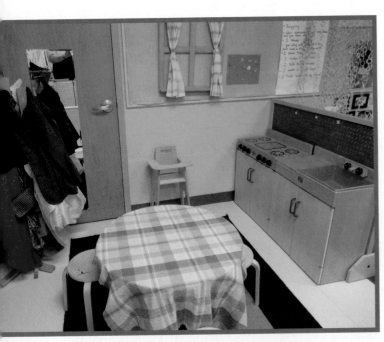

The learning centers in a preschool setting should be configured to foster independent activities and cooperative play.

On the other hand, add other settings that are relevant to children's lives and experiences, such as a grocery store, a parent's office, a veterinary clinic, the post office, a hair salon, or a doctor's office. In each new setting, children learn more about how people live, work, and interact with one another. By assuming the roles of cashiers, hair stylists, or corporate executives, children can explore these relationships further.

Ask children to help select and create a new dramatic play learning center. See what experiences and materials excite or interest them. For example, if Shantel tells you about her experience at a doctor's office and is afraid of receiving shots, work with her to create the design and materials for the new doctor's office setting. If Shantel can choose what she engages in and how she engages, then participating in creating this new setting can empower her. You are providing her the opportunity to control what she fears, even if it is just for pretend. The more details included in the setting, the more realistic and fun the experience will be.

Also create fantasy scenarios that will foster children's imaginations and creativity, like a giant bird's nest, pirate ship, rocket ship, castle, or prehistoric cave. Engaging children in determining the topics and designs of dramatic play settings will both scaffold children's learning and engage them in the learning process.

The opportunity for children to engage in free play is a critical feature of every early childhood setting. Not only is it linked to school readiness and language development, it supports children's understanding of the world around them. Although children's play is authentic and meaningful when self-directed, there are times when you, the early educator, can enter their play to scaffold their learning. For example, Sarah is shy and afraid that the other children will not want to play with her. Sit next to Sarah at the table in the dramatic play learning center and announce to the children, "Sarah and I have had a long day at the office. What can we make for dinner?"

At other times, model cooperation during play. For example, Kyle has been having trouble cooperating with the other children. Go into the house area and announce to them, "What can I do to help? Is there any cleaning or ironing I can do?" Or, if Trey has been continually rejected, partner with him and announce, "Trey and I would like to make our secret omelet recipe for you. Get ready to treat your taste buds." This partnership will give Trey a successful social experience with other children on which he can build later. Also think about how you are extending children's learning and modeling language through your participation.

Children's Group Interaction

Children develop physically, intellectually, and emotionally through play. In particular, group play and peer interactions help children learn about their social roles naturally. Within the learning community you foster in your setting, both groups of children will form and change throughout the day. The cooperative activities they engage in teach them *prosocial behavior* (voluntary behavior intended to benefit another person). As children work together to achieve common goals, they learn how to work as a team, support one another, and value and respect each other's thoughts and feelings. Think about projects children can complete in groups, like decorating the setting, writing thank you notes to guests, tending to pets, or tending a garden.

Even games can encourage cooperation rather than competition. Play expert Rae Pica (n.d.) says that if given the choice, most children prefer to play cooperative games over competitive ones. Competition pits children against one another, raises stress levels, and reduces group trust and motivation. Cooperation, on the other hand, makes children feel good about themselves and each other, increases self-esteem, fosters group trust, and increases motivation. When children cooperate during games, they develop critical listening skills, support and encourage each other, take turns, and find pleasure in others' successes.

A game like "musical chairs" does not make sense in countries, like Japan, where cooperation is emphasized. When these children play the game, they scurry to make room for each other when music stops. Pica suggests that early educators can readily convert "musical chairs" and other competitive games into cooperative ones in which there are no "losers" and all children develop positive group social skills. The following are additional ways in which you can support children working in groups throughout the day:

Choice time: (indoors and outdoors): Children can choose to play or work alone or with others in small or larger groups depending on interest. They are learning about sharing, taking turns, entering groups of children already in play, and observing how other children use and manipulate materials and objects.

Group meetings: These meetings should be engaging and short in duration. With a new community of learners, start your days with a short daily group meeting that lasts about 10 min. Extend the

Parallel play involves two children sitting near each other but performing two independent tasks.

duration of meetings over time until meetings last 15–20 min. Children can sit in assigned spots. They should keep their arms and legs to themselves and respond when called upon. Encourage participation throughout the meeting and in whole group activities with group songs, finger plays, and dances. If children cannot sit still or do not want to participate in group meetings, excuse them to play or read alone quietly. If children are regularly opting out of group meetings, consider different tactics to make meetings more engaging.

Small groups: If you or a volunteer are leading a small group activity, children can work individually or in groups to follow along with the activity. For example, while making applesauce with a group of four children, each child sits around the table and participates in preparing the applesauce. They all dice one or two apples, measure the correct amount of cinnamon, and take turns stirring.

Mealtimes: During mealtimes, children develop friendships and learn about others in the setting. Children can set the table or retrieve their own or other children's lunches from cubbies. They can also talk with each other and with staff and volunteers sitting at the table. Children can discuss their weekend activities or their favorite foods. During family-style dining, children take turns in serving themselves and passing items to each other.

Outdoors: Children can participate in small group activities, such as gardening, picnicking, or woodworking. They can study leaves, read, or use climbing equipment, bikes, and the sandbox independently or with other children.

Forming Friendships

Laura Berk, a developmental psychologist who has published widely on the effects of children's development, defines *friendship* as "a mutual relationship involving companionship, sharing, understanding of thoughts and feelings, and caring for and comforting one another in times of need" (2002, p. 377). The friendships children establish during preschool years create a sense of belonging and security. Successful friendships in early childhood contribute to children's quality of life and give children what Lilian Katz and Jean Mendoza (2011) call a sense of "having a place." Friendships are essential for mental health and social–emotional well-being.

Learning how to start and maintain friendships is a critical life skill. Model and create an environment within your setting that promotes interacting and working together. When working with small groups of children, mix the groups so that children can learn from each other in a variety of contexts. Give children who are shy or reluctant additional support and coaching. Help children find the right words to express interest in playing with other children: "Jimmy, Andy was wondering if you'd like to work with him on our new alphabet puzzle." "Jimmy, let's get these cars ready for the race. Miguel, may we join you in racing our cars?" By equipping children with the language they need, they can reach out to potential friends.

Sometimes children act out when they are upset. They have difficulty taking turns, sharing, or being close to other children. The following are ways you can support these children in making friends:

Children who have developed strong self-regulation skills can play and relate well without adult intervention.

- **Give children acceptable choices.** For example, "McKenzie, I can't let you hurt Star. I know that you want to play with the dolls with her, but when you grab the dolls and push Star down, that hurts her. Let's think about what you might do when you get angry like this. You could try another activity, like playing at the water table. Or you can talk to me about how you feel."

- **Offer children a "safe" phrase or gesture they can use when they feel themselves losing control.** For example, shouting the word rabbit will alert you and Jasmine that she is losing control. Jasmine can sit in the quiet area until she feels she has regained composure, preventing her from acting out or hurting someone.

- **Help children develop socially acceptable ways of behaving.** Use appropriate and welcoming language and describe your actions. Gently provide suggestions or ideas if children are having difficulties or ask questions that inspire them to create their own rules and solutions.

Children with special needs may not have yet developed an understanding of another person's social cues. They may need your help to make friends. Children with developmental delays, however, are able to reach out to others much like the rest of their peers (Yu, Ostrosky, & Fowler, 2011).

While getting to know each other, children are able to focus on only one aspect of another person at a time. This may hinder a person with physical disabilities from making friends. Help children see beyond physical impairments by reading books that feature children with physical disabilities, such as *Rolling Along: The Story of Taylor and His Wheelchair* by Jamee Riggio Heelan and *Some Kids Wear Leg Braces* by Lola M. Schaefer.

It is important for each child to develop prosocial skills, begin friendships, and treat each other with respect, compassion, and kindness. However, it is not realistic or authentic to teach children that everyone is friends with every single other person they encounter. Though it is beneficial for all children to get along, they should develop several friendships independently and not be forced to become friends with everyone.

If you are leading a small group activity, children can work individually or in groups to follow along with the activity.

Figure 46. Encouraging Friendships

Here are a few things you can do to help children make friends:

- Discuss the subject of making friends during group time to spark children's interest in the idea. Remind them that though they may have friends who look the same as and different from them, their friends should care about and enjoy being with them.

- Read and discuss books about friendships, such as *My Friend Isabelle* by Eliza Woloson and *How Do Dinosaurs Play with Their Friends?* by Jane Yolen.

- Suggest that children work together to complete a task, such as setting the table for lunch or cleaning a specific part of the learning environment. This will give children the opportunity to see whether the child they are working with could be a potential friend.

- Coach children when they are working together on a task. Acknowledge their shared success and en-courage them to feel good about their teamwork. Sometimes friendships are formed just by sharing common experiences.

- Model friendship. Talk to the children about your own friendships and the pleasure they bring.

- Host special events where children can play together—for example, a picnic or a group art project, such as painting a mural. Again, the motivation is to help children feel close to those they are working with cooperatively.

- Take and post photos of friends. Encourage children to publish their own books about friendship.

- Guard children against rejection and exclusion. Consider a setting rule that children cannot reject other children who want to play. Early childhood education researcher Vivian Paley had one rule in her classroom: "You can't say you can't play." Children had to play with partners they might never have played with otherwise, out of which unexpected friendships were born (Paley, 1993). Children with strong social skills are resilient in the face of rejection (Dewar, 2009). They are able to explain their rejection ("Perhaps Rachel already had too many friends to play with."), bounce back, and reach out again ("Rachel's playing alone with the dolls. Maybe I can play with her now.").

Helping Children Resolve Conflict

Conflict is a normal part of children's lives. Having different needs or wants, or wanting the same thing when only one is available, can easily lead children into conflict with one another. For example, "She won't let me play," "He took my __," or "Tom's being mean!" are complaints that you and parents will often hear when children are unable to resolve conflict. Having different needs or wants, or wanting the same thing when only one is available, can easily lead children into conflict. These disputes primarily involve toys, relationships, ideas, space, and power. Children commonly respond by arguing, acting out physically, or backing off and avoiding each other. Help children learn to cooperate by teaching them effective ways to resolve conflict independently. With these skills, children are much happier and maintain better friendships.

Social

Until they develop the skills to manage conflict effectively, most children need specific guidance to help them reach resolutions. Adult responses to children's conflicts have powerful effects on children's behaviors, attitudes, and skills. Your goal is to help them see conflict as a shared problem that they can solve by understanding both points of view and finding a solution with which everyone can agree.

Some situations give children opportunities to learn how to become better problem-solvers, negotiators, and communicators, especially through *conflict resolution* (a process of resolving disputes or disagreements). HighScope (2012) developed a six-step approach for conflict resolution among children:

1. **Approach calmly, stopping any hurtful actions.** Make sure that everyone is safe by inserting yourself between the children. Work to manage the children's anger so that everyone can calmly assess the situation.

2. **Acknowledge children's feelings.** Let the children know that you understand that they are angry, upset, or hurt by the situation.

3. **Gather information.** Let the children know that you are going to help them solve their problem, but first you must know what is wrong.

4. **Restate the problem.** Use the children's own words to repeat each child's side of the situation and to let them know that you heard them. "Lindsey, Emilio says that he was riding the tricycle, and you pushed him off and took it. Can you tell me what happened?"

5. **Ask for solution ideas and choose one together.** Each time that children offer a solution, repeat their words aloud. "Lindsey, you suggest that Emilio rides the tricycle this morning, and then you ride after lunch. What do you think, Emilio?" Encourage children to reflect on their feelings, plan alternative solutions, predict the consequences, and determine which idea makes the most sense (Epstein, 2003). If children cannot devise a suitable solution, or if they suggest a solution that is too punitive or unrelated to the problem, step in and propose your own solution.

Use the children's own words to repeat each child's side of the situation and to let them know that you heard them.

6. **Be prepared to provide follow-up support.** Everyone needs to understand the reasons behind the conflict and resolution. If a similar problem occurs in the future, the children can reach a resolution more easily. Evaluate how well the chosen resolution worked and consider whether the children could reach a more effective solution in the future.

Ultimately, the goal is for children to resolve conflicts on their own, acknowledging each other's feelings and devising possible solutions that will satisfy both parties. You can link to previously resolved conflicts or situations in stories that you read to the children. By using their experiences you can help them understand how to prevent and resolve conflicts independently.

Building Prosocial Skills

Early childhood development and education expert Marilou Hyson says that adults often forget that prosocial behaviors are voluntary (Hyson & Taylor, 2011). For example, Ricky apologies to others only when you tell him to do so. His actions are not prosocial, because they are involuntary. However, prosocial behavior can be taught, supported, and facilitated. Traits like compassion, empathy, and sympathy fuel prosocial behavior, so to behave prosocially, children must know how to empathize (identify with what another person is feeling) and understand another person's perspective. Establishing positive

Children who behave prosocially in early childhood settings continue to behave this way throughout their lives.

interactions among all children and adults creates an atmosphere of mutual respect and support, encourages prosocial behaviors, and develops a supportive community of learners. Moreover, children who behave prosocially in early childhood settings continue to behave this way throughout their lives.

The following are ways in which you can help children understand someone else's feelings:

- **Help children put their feelings into words.** For example, "When you threw the puzzle pieces on the floor, you looked very frustrated. It's upsetting when a puzzle seems too difficult."

- **Read books where you can discuss or ask children to describe the characters' feelings.** For example, "Mr. Worm is sad that no one came to Baby Worm's party." Ask children why a character may be feeling a certain way once the emotion is identified. "Yes, Mr. Worm looks sad. Why do you think he feels this way?"

- **Help children to interpret facial expressions.** "Look at Mr. Worm's eyebrows and mouth. Does he look sad?"

- **Encourage children to reenact their favorite stories with puppets.**

Once children have learned empathy, they can relate to others' feelings, which begets kindness. These children can now be caring and comfort their peers. Model kindness for the children in your setting and be respectful and caring toward others. Children's development of these skills and attributes will be uneven. Continue to support them all in the development of these skills and attitudes.

When the children have established a caring learning community within the setting, work with them to expand this concept to their communities outside your setting. Think about how they might project caring, respect, and kindness, and ask them for their thoughts. You might be surprised by the sophistication of their responses. Try organizing acts of kindness like the following:

- Collect used toys for children who do not have many of their own.

- Make drawings for children in the hospital.

- Cook snacks to bring to a homeless shelter.

Chapter 10
Guidance

CDA Functional Area 10: Candidate provides a supportive environment and uses effective strategies to promote children's self-regulation and support acceptable behaviors, and effectively intervenes for children with persistent challenging behaviors.

Guidance

Introduction

As you observe the children in your setting during choice time, they all seem to be playing peacefully. Suddenly, you hear a loud screech. Melissa and Brian are engaged in a tug-of-war over a toy train. Within seconds, all the children are focused on Melissa and Brian's conflict. In Chapter 9, we discussed creating a caring community of learners, and you learned HighScope's six-step approach to conflict resolution. In this chapter, we will focus on supporting and guiding children's specific behaviors, covering seven important things you can do to maintain a responsive, caring environment:

- **Setting Effective Rules.**
- **Addressing Challenging Behaviors Positively.**
- **Employing Positive Guidance Techniques.**
- **Understanding Time-Out and Effective Alternatives.**
- **Addressing Ongoing Challenging Behavior.**
- **Stopping Bullying.**
- **Partnering With Families.**

Setting Effective Rules

Set positive, clear, and developmentally appropriate rules for the children in your setting. These rules provide a common framework that keeps everyone safe and helps children focus on play and learning. Follow the following tips to ensure the effectiveness of your rules:

Model appropriate behavior. Build a trusting relationship with each child in your setting. Young children view you as their role model and are attentive to the ways in which you interact with other people.

Provide space in your setting for children to be alone or assemble in small groups. Though children—especially infants—need one-to-one interaction with you, they also require social interactions with other children.

Acknowledge individual children and their positive behaviors. When infants coo, respond by cooing, too. Let mobile infants know you approve of their behavior when they move to sit next to other children. "Lucy you are sitting next to Joe. You're becoming friends. That's wonderful!" The infants will begin to understand the importance of relating to others.

Provide opportunities for success. Young children begin to understand positive behavior when they accomplish simple tasks that get your approval. For example, encourage children to get their own mats at nap time, and praise their efforts. Remember to make your praise specific to this task.

Establish routines and rituals. Individualize rituals to reflect what children do at home so that they begin to regulate and organize their own behavior. For example, sing the same song (in the same language) at the start of nap time or rub toddlers' backs to lull them to sleep.

Praise and encourage children's sense of independence. Toddlers need to participate in many routines and receive numerous opportunities to perform tasks independently, like washing and drying their own hands, selecting a book to be read, and holding a sign for the "red light, green light" game.

Understand that children may not be ready to share. Children's sense of ownership is just developing. Ensure that your expectations of children sharing are reasonable. They acquire the ability to share over time, but still benefit from opportunities to experience and practice taking turns. However, provide duplicate toys to minimize the probability of conflict.

Provide opportunities for young children to say, "No." Play games where you say, "Yes," and they say, "No." Sing songs that include the word *no* and read books that ask yes/no questions. This gives children opportunities to explore and experiment with control.

Provide children with better options. For example, Alicia makes attempts to color on the wall. Though she enjoys writing on a vertical surface, writing directly on the walls is against your setting's rules. Consider encouraging Alicia to color on a section of the wall covered with paper or providing her with other paper or materials for drawing.

Be attentive to behavioral patterns. Observe and document challenging behaviors. Look for patterns to discover triggers that may prompt these behaviors.

Create and enforce clear and simple rules. Toddlers can understand and follow a few simple, clear rules (no more than three or four at one time). For example, "We wash our hands before we eat." or "We sit at the table when we eat."

Often, children get frustrated when they cannot articulate the way they feel.

Use the word *no* in extreme situations. Reserve the word no for very dangerous situations. For example, if Kevin is about to swing a baseball bat, which could accidently hit Thalia, you would say, "Kevin, no!"

Involve preschoolers in establishing rules. Children are most invested in rules that they have suggested. Participating in the rule-making process motivates preschoolers to enforce the setting's rules.

Start with a few rules. Do not overwhelm the children with rules—especially very young children whose memories are just beginning to develop. Start with just four or five rules, like the following:

1. Walk inside; run outside.

2. Talk in regular voices inside; use loud voices outside.

3. Be kind to each other.

4. Put away everything you play with.

Once the children master these rules, introduce more.

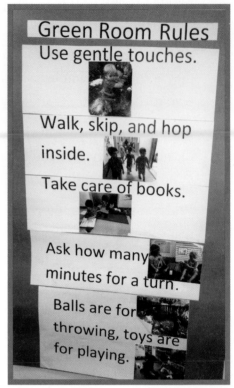

Most children in your setting are still learning to read, so represent rules with pictures.

Do not overwhelm the children with rules; start with just four or five.

Scaffold children's learning to help them understand new rules. When you relate rules to ideas children are already familiar with, these rules will make more sense to them. For example, children know that if a tricycle is broken, it means that the toy no longer works properly. A rule that stipulates that broken toys and equipment are stowed away until they are fixed builds on an idea with which children are already familiar. Therefore, the rule makes sense.

Explain the "why" behind a rule. For example, preschoolers are starting to understand cause and effect. They can predict that if they run indoors, they might knock down and hurt another child or trip and hurt themselves. Therefore, children can understand why indoor running is not allowed.

Keep all rules positive. Young children understand positive wording more easily. If the rule's intent is for children *not* to do something, state the beginning of the rule positively: Use blocks only for building, not throwing.

Display setting rules in all the languages the children speak. Write and speak the rules in each child's home language to ensure that all children understand the setting's rules.

Illustrate rules with pictures. Most children in your setting are still learning to read, so represent rules with pictures. Take photos of children implementing the rules in the setting, and use these photos to remind the children of the rules. Post the rules and photos at the children's eye level.

Let children practice following the rules. Give children lots of opportunities to put the rules into action. Encourage them to commit to following the rules and discuss together how the rule keeps children safe. Encourage children to role play following the rules during dramatic play. For example, they could act out what they should do if they burn themselves while cooking or how to add a seat belt and booster seat to a car they are building with hollow blocks.

Apply rules consistently. Help children understand that the rules *always* apply to them, not just when they remember or when it is convenient.

Gently remind children of rules when they forget. When children fail to follow a rule, discuss with them—in a nonjudgmental tone—the consequences and how the situation would have been better had they remembered to follow the rule. Remind them to remember and follow the rule in the future.

Acknowledge children when they follow rules appropriately. For example, Leah spills paint on the floor near the easel and immediately gathers wet paper towels. You say, "Thank you, Leah, for cleaning up the spill. Now we don't have to worry that anyone will slip on the paint. Plus, you are helping to keep our art center clean."

Addressing Challenging Behaviors Positively

"Challenging behavior is any behavior that interferes with children's learning, development, and success at play; is harmful to the child, other children, or adults; [and/or] puts a child at high risk for later social problems or school failure," including aggressive, disruptive, and antisocial behaviors (Kaiser & Rasminsky, 2012). It is developmentally appropriate early in life for all children to exhibit challenging behaviors as they grow and learn (Kaiser & Rasminsky, 2010). Beginning in infancy, all children can demonstrate challenging behavior as they are learning about their bodies, self-regulation, their feelings and emotions, and the adults and peers around them. As an early educator, your role is to

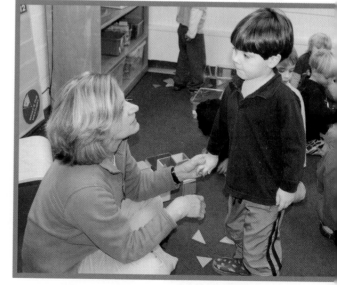

Positive guidance is the best approach for you to support children and help them maintain control of their behavior and emotions.

guide and support children as they develop the skills to manage their feelings and emotions, share materials and resources, treat others with respect and kindness, and care for their surroundings.

Terms like positive guidance, discipline, and punishment all relate to the prevention and handling of children's challenging behaviors. *Discipline* (training that corrects, molds, or perfects) is commonly associated with *punishment* (a penalty for rule violations). However, punishment rarely corrects children's behavior, because it is often hurtful, shameful, arbitrary, and unrelated to

Building trust between early educators and children.

the behavior itself. "Punishing children for their wrongdoings will not create change—just a need for more punishment" (Bailey, 2001, p. 8).

For example, if Conner bites Danny, a punitive approach to the situation would be to allow Danny to bite Conner. The reasoning behind this approach is that Conner will understand what it feels like to be bitten and stop biting other children. However, this approach models aggression—not problem-solving—and only humiliates and enrages Conner. Similarly, discipline systems that are based on rewards or stickers do not model problem-solving. Some early educators employ these systems, because they believe children will change their behaviors to receive the rewards. In the short term, these systems appear to work. Over time, children become dependent upon these external rewards and behave just to obtain them—not because they have developed internal self-discipline or emotional regulation. When children no longer receive the rewards, their behaviors regress.

Both punishment and discipline-based reward systems fail to teach children what to do instead of the challenging behavior. Children are bombarded with negative messages about what they *cannot* do, which weakens the emotional bond between early educators and children. Children are unable to feel secure when they are constantly scrutinized for what they do "wrong."

For young children, learning appropriate behaviors is a process. They need lots of practice before they can master these skills. *Positive guidance* is the best approach for you to support children and help them maintain control of their behavior and emotions. It focuses on instilling a desire in children to behave by doing the following:

- **Building trust between early educators and children.** Early educators spell out expectations for children's behavior, emphasize children's positive qualities, and believe in children's abilities to make appropriate choices.

- **Developing children's social and emotional skills.**

- **Teaching children problem-solving skills.** "Guidance teaches children to solve their problems, rather than punishing them for having problems they cannot solve" (Gartrell, 2001, p. 9).

- **Developing self-regulation through consistency.** Children learn to control their emotions when you, the early educator, offer them security through understood rules and clear limits. Dramatic play also empowers children to reenact and practice situations requiring self-control.

- **Encouraging independence as children accept responsibility for their own behavior.**

- **Inviting reflection as children try to understand their peers' points of view.**

- **Serving the best interests of both the child and the group.**

Your strongest ally in promoting positive behaviors in children is the relationships you form with them. These strong relationships govern children's behavior and give them the desire to solve conflicts (Bailey, 2001). With your support and encouragement, children can learn to behave appropriately out of choice—not coercion or manipulation—inside and outside your setting.

Figure 47. Positive Guidance Versus Punishment

Positive guidance and punishment impact children differently:

Positive Guidance	Punishment
Builds self-esteem.	Makes child feel worthless and angry.
Gives confidence.	Embarrasses.
Respects children.	Shames children.
Focuses on what children *can* do.	Focuses on what children *cannot* do.
Examines causes of behavior.	Focuses on eliminating undesirable behavior.
Empowers children.	Intimidates children.

(Kersey & Masterson, 2013; Gartrell, 2004; Klein, 2008)

Employing Positive Guidance Techniques

The following approaches will support you in positively guiding the children in your setting (Adams & Baronberg, 2005; Klein, 2008):

Reconfigure the setting to prevent and correct challenging behaviors. By adjusting your setting's environment, you can address problems before they occur. For example, provide duplicates of popular toys and dolls to prevent conflicts over who uses the toy when. These children are just learning to share. When you make the toy available to them all, you can then work with them to develop their sharing skills without the distraction of conflict. Also, if children can access the fire trucks without walking through the block center, they will no longer accidently topple other children's creations. During family-style dining, the children at your table pass the food clockwise, wait for everyone to be served, and are courteous. However, you notice that the two youngest children keep spilling their cartons of milk. You observe that these children are having difficulty opening their cartons. Before lunchtime the next day, you pour the milk from all the children's cartons into a glass pitcher and place it on the table. The children then pass the pitcher around the table so that they can successfully pour milk into their own glasses.

In addition, ensure that you provide an area for a child to be alone or with only one other child. This helps young children decrease stimulation, calm down, and self-regulate their behavior and emotions. Place pillows or comfy seating in this space with books, puzzles, or other quiet toys that children can use while in this area. Bring young children to this space if they are having a tantrum. Support them and speak with them softly as they calm themselves.

Should I Reconfigure My Setting?

Though you cannot prevent all challenging behaviors, reconfiguring your setting may correct many problem situations. If you find that an area of your setting or a learning center becomes too noisy or prompts conflicts, observe children's behavior in these areas, and ask yourself the following questions:

- Should I limit the number of children allowed in this area of the setting or the number of children who use this learning center at one time?

- Are the materials and activities age-, individually, and culturally appropriate for the children in my setting?

- Are the materials so familiar to the children that they are bored?

- Are the children disinterested in the activities?

- Are the activities overstimulating for children?

- Do the children have enough play time to become fully engaged?

- Do I require children to play in several learning centers when they really want to remain involved in just one?

- Do I give children advance warning of transitions?

Determine the root causes and motivation for children's challenging behaviors. Eliminate the causes of challenging behaviors instead of just treating the symptoms. Even when you know that children are acting out of anger or a need for attention, find out the underlying cause of this anger or need by observing them. For example, Owen kicks Seth's cot during nap time. When Seth asks Owen to stop, Owen kicks the cot harder. You intervene by sitting quietly with Owen and asking him to talk with you about what is making him so angry. He tells you that he cannot sleep and that he does not like lying on his cot. You offer him the options of either looking at a book while lying on his cot or assembling a puzzle quietly.

When children do not know why they behave a certain way, look for patterns in their behavior. Discover what happens before and after the challenging behavior occurs to identify its cause (Miller, 2013). For ex-ample, Tyler sits down for lunch, starts rocking in his chair, and does not eat. He could be sick, tired, nervous, upset, or reacting to an issue at home. Perhaps Tyler's medication is affecting his appetite. However, through observation, you discover that Tyler normally plays happily with Marcus before lunchtime. Tyler seems annoyed when it is time to clean up and prepare for lunch. He cleans up and walks to the table, muttering to himself.

Could Tyler be upset that lunchtime interrupts his play time with Marcus? Now that you think you have determined the cause of the problem, ask: What should I do about this? Perhaps you could find more opportunities during the day for Tyler and Marcus to play. Or seat Marcus and Tyler at the same table or next to each other during lunch. Experiment with a few solutions to see what works.

Also, children may exhibit challenging behaviors because they are still learning how to express their feelings and emotions. Use this opportunity to coach them. For example, Meesha knocks down Daria's block structure. Daria bites Meesha's arm. Kneel to Daria's eye level and coach her to express how she is feeling.

Provide children with developmentally appropriate choices. Empower young children to make good choices by offering them appropriate and acceptable alternatives. For example, Zora is upset that there is no spot for her at the water table. Acknowledge how she feels, "I know that you want to play at the water table, but right now it's full. Only four children can play here at one time

If children are struggling to resolve a conflict, kneel to the children's eye level and help them devise a resolution.

to keep it safe. I do see that there's space at the art easel, at the sand table, and in dramatic play. Which one of those do you want to try?"

Phillip has been hitting and pushing Miguel. After talking to Miguel and determining that he is not hurt, talk to Phillip and give him options. "Phillip, I can't let you hurt Miguel. We need to keep everyone's body safe. By hitting and pushing Miguel that will hurt his body. If you feel you need to hit and push something, you can go over to the beanbag chair, and hit and push the chair as much as you like. You also can go to the sand table and play there until you've calmed down. Which option are you going to choose?"

When you give children safe choices, also give them the opportunity to dictate the terms of their choice, like how long they want to stay engaged in the activity and when they want to do something else. Offering children choices puts them in charge of their own behavior and builds self-regulation.

Use natural consequences when appropriate. A *natural consequence* is the inevitable result of a child's behavior that is not imposed by an adult. Natural consequences can be effective guidance techniques, especially when children are unhappy with these consequences. For example, if Maureen throws her favorite doll on the floor in anger and the doll breaks, then Maureen must deal with the natural consequences of her behavior—her doll is broken and she can no longer play with it.

Coach children and support them in resolving conflicts independently. If children are struggling to resolve a conflict, kneel to the children's eye level and help them devise a resolution. The resolutions must be acceptable to each child who is involved. You can coach and support them through this process. In Chapter 9, you learned HighScope's six-step approach to conflict resolution. Also, gently remind the children of previous conflicts they resolved or link this situation to stories you have read together.

Focus on the positive. For example, if Rebecca bangs on the floor during circle time, or if Jade keeps making faces at everyone working on puzzles, ask both children to stop. Keep your comments positive and explain *why* to help them make better choices in the future "Rebecca, we want to ensure that everyone can hear the story, can you please keep your hands in your lap so everyone can hear?"

If these behaviors continue after you firmly and respectfully ask the child to stop, intervene if there is a safety issue, such as Jade aiming a puzzle board to throw at

Kneel to a child's eye level and coach him/her to express how he/she is feeling.

Rebecca. However, if no one is at risk and you think that the child is seeking attention, your best response is to ignore the behavior in the short term. Children who misbehave for attention crave your intervention. Without reinforcement in the form of attention, the behavior will end. In the meantime, work to treat the cause of the behavior and find out what was causing the children to seek attention in this way. If you do not address the children's longer-term needs for attention, they will find some other way to fulfill their needs.

Acknowledge children individually and in front of the group. Give children the chance to shine. This helps reinforce positive behaviors and reaffirm for children that you care about them and that they matter. Ensure that each child gets uninterrupted, individual attention from you each day.

Spending time with children helps you strengthen your relationship with each child.

Help children do the right thing. For example, 3-year-old Tony removes a block that Lisa has set aside for a wall she is building and adds it to his own structure. Lisa sits on the floor and begins to cry. Because 3-year-olds still have trouble understanding others' point of view, Tony's behavior might not have been intentional. Explain to him how his actions affected Lisa, and listen carefully to his reaction. Devise a plan for Tony to resolve the situation. Perhaps Tony can help Lisa find a block for her wall. Tony will feel better having done something helpful for Lisa.

Observe all children and continue to learn new things about them each day. Record notes daily and reflect on children's behaviors and actions so that you can learn how to best support each child—including children who are too young or otherwise unable to speak. Recording notes and reflecting will also help you discover events that could be triggering children's challenging behaviors.

Individualize your approach to meet children's needs. No "one-size-fits-all" approaches exist in early childhood education. Every child has unique interests, temperaments, personalities, knowledge, skills, and family situations. One strategy may be effective with one child, but not with other children.

Teaching children to solve problems, giving appropriate encouragement, listening actively, and modeling appropriate behaviors are all effective positive guidance techniques as well. If you have formed strong relationships with the children, then you have a good idea about the strategies that work best with each of them. For instance, you know that 3-year-old Louisa has a hard time staying focused and sitting still during group times because of her age and temperament. You ask her if she would prefer to go to the art center or pick a book to look at quietly. You also know that Mario, who has a developmental delay, throws things when he is upset. Because he is on an IEP (Individualized Education Program), you follow the strategies the special educator suggests for calming him down, and then give him choices. The following practices will enhance effectiveness of any strategy you employ (Kaiser & Rasminsky, 2012):

- **Spend time with children.** Children need consistent and ongoing guidance. Spending time with children helps you increase your knowledge and understanding of their interests and skills and strengthen your relationship with each child.

- **Maintain control.** You cannot expect children to control their emotions if you cannot control your own. Speak to children in a low, steady voice, maintain distance between you and them, and keep your arms at your sides. Communicate warmth and understanding to children. If their actions overwhelm you or test your patience, ask a colleague to relieve you until you feel calm enough to face the children again.

- **Support the whole child.** If children struggle with challenging behaviors, focus on their positive attributes and target the specific challenging behaviors. Avoid labeling children. For example, never refer to or label them as "troublemakers."

- **Talk with the child privately.** Young children embarrass easily. If they feel humiliated in front of the group, then they will not be receptive to what you say.

- **Believe in the children.** Positive guidance can almost always be successful if you are respectful, firm, clear, and caring toward children. Give children time to develop the self-control and motivation to want to behave appropriately. Let children know that you are always there for them and that they can talk to you whenever they are upset.

Understanding Time-Out and Effective Alternatives

The term *time-out* is actually short for the phrase "time out from positive reinforcement from the group," meaning the early educators and community of learners. This tactic, which is a form of discipline, is typically employed when children have been acting out, ignoring rules, or disrupting the group. Though children remain in the same room with the group, they are asked to sit outside of the activity area where they are causing the problem. This isolates children from the

The term time-out is actually short for the phrase "time out from positive reinforcement from the group."

activity and gives them time to calm down and think about their behaviors. During time-out, the early educator remains calm, objective, nonthreatening, and respectful. Originally, time-out was meant to last for 1 min per year of a child's age. For example, a 4-year-old would remain in time-out for 4 min. Children take the opportunity to calm themselves. These children can then rejoin the group after time-out, ready for a successful experience.

Time-out has a role in an early educator's guidance repertoire, with certain caveats (Dunlap, 2004):

> Time-out is only effective when used in the context of a comprehensive approach to behavior support that is designed to teach, nurture, and encourage positive social behaviors. Time-out should be used only by well-trained teachers and educators when less intrusive discipline procedures have been tried and deemed unsuccessful and only in combination with positive procedures designed to teach new skills and prevent challenging behaviors from occurring.

Time-out can work, if used carefully and infrequently. However, the tactic rarely works as intended and the warnings Dunlap outlines are rarely heeded. Early educators are not trained regularly on how to effectively use the time-out approach after they have exhausted all other positive guidance techniques. Instead, time-out has become the primary strategy early educators employ, even when other positive child guidance strategies would be more effective. In some situations, early educators assign half the group to extended time-out periods.

Because time-out is misused and overused, some children cease to take it seriously. Instead of calming down and thinking about their actions, children make faces at the group, fidget in their chairs, or simply zone out. Other children may spend their time justifying their behaviors or feeling shamed or defeated, not understanding the reason for their isolation. When time-out is over, they go back to the group refreshed and ready to try new behavioral stunts. The child's lack of respect for the time-out tactic can lead to a power struggle between the early educator and the child, which is detrimental to the child and the community of learners. Time-out often turns into punishment. Instead of experiencing it as redirection or guidance by logical consequences, children experience a painful interlude. Time-out can damage children in the following ways (Kaiser & Rasminsky, 2012):

Positive guidance can almost always be successful if you are respectful, firm, clear, and caring toward children.

- Children can become more aggressive, possibly using the minutes they spend in time-out to plot revenge.

- Children receive the message that you can control others if you have power.

- Children feel that their early educators and their peers do not like them.

- Children from cultures that value group participation feel that they are being shunned.

- Time-out interferes with learning.

- Time-out violates children's sense of safety and security.

- Time-out severs the relationship educators have with children.

Sending children to time-out can reduce their confidence and self-esteem and can cause them to feel worthless. When children feel hurt or humiliated, it is difficult for them to think about how to alter their behavior to avoid being sent to time-out again. Often children in time-out are labeled as "troublemakers" and are the first accused of misconduct. Once children accept this label, it is easier for them to be "troublemakers" than to fight the misnomer.

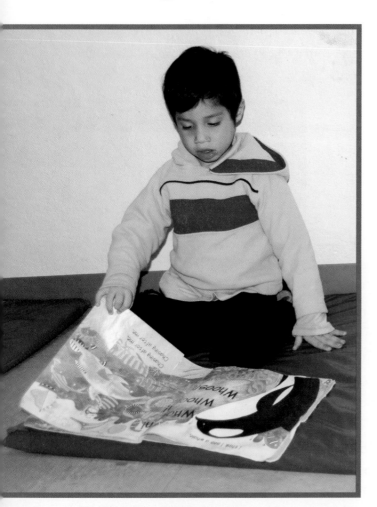

Give children a choice to choose a quieter activity to engage in.

Because of time-out's misuse, overuse, and possible negative effects, most guidance experts recommend phasing out time-out. The following are some strategies you can employ instead:

- **Child choice.** Inform children that they have one more chance to stop their disruptive behavior or else they will have to choose a quieter activity to engage in, away from the group (Saifer, 2003). If the disruptive behavior continues, find them a quiet area, like the literacy or math & manipulatives center, in which to play. Instead of telling them to stay in the quiet area for a certain period of time, tell them that they can return to the group when they are calm and able to participate. During this time, encourage and support the children and help them devise a plan for rejoining the group. There is no punishment in this approach, and the children are empowered to make better choices and take control of their actions.

- **Time away.** Sometimes called "cool-down" or "private time," time away performs the function that time-out should with very important differences. Time away puts the power in the child's hands and is proactive, not reactive. For example, Katie feels angry, upset, and the urge to do something she is not allowed to do. She tells you that she wants to move to a quiet area, such as the sand table or literacy center, where she remains until she feels better. Katie determines how long she remains in this area, and returns to the group when she is ready (Kaiser & Rasminsky, 2012).

- **Bringing Children in Close.** Dubbed the "anti-time-out," the "bringing children close" technique involves children coming to you for hugs when they feel out of control or they are disturbing the group. The purpose of the cuddle is not to reward children for bad behavior. Your hugs provide them a safe space to calm down. If children are flailing (and you are certain they are not having a seizure), you might keep a warm hold using your arms and knees. It is tough for an overwrought child to listen, so say nothing during this time except, "I'll hold you until you feel calm" (Porter, 2008).

- **Teaching democratic life skills.** According to Gartrell, time-out, like all forms of discipline that shame children, must be abolished. He argues that early educators should replace these practices with positive ones that build on "an encouraging classroom." The goal of positive guidance, in his view, is for children to learn *democratic life skills*, or the social–emotional skills they need to become healthy individuals and contributing members of society. These skills include the following abilities (Gartrell, 2001, p.14):

  - Seeing one's self as a worthy individual and a capable member of the group.
  - Expressing strong emotions in nonhurting ways.
  - Solving problems ethically and intelligently.
  - Understanding others' feelings and viewpoints.
  - Working cooperatively in groups while accepting the human differences among members.

This strategy lets children know that you care about them even if you dislike their behavior. It also unites you and the children and strengthens trusting and respectful relationships. Most importantly, it gives children the support they need to be in control of their emotions. Most early educators report that as children gain self-control, calming takes less time, and the challenging behaviors disappear.

Learning democratic life skills is an ongoing process for children. The challenge, according to Gartrell (2001, p. 14), is "for teachers—and children—to recognize conflicts as opportunities for teaching and learning." Early educators should teach children these skills through all of the day's events—not just when problem behavior exists.

Addressing Ongoing Challenging Behavior

Dealing with children's challenging behaviors has become a national concern among educators and administrators. In a study of 4,000 preschool settings in 40 states in America, 10.4% of teachers reported that they had expelled a child in the previous year due to behavioral problems (McCabe & Frede, 2007). In Chapter 8, you learned that children's family circumstances impact their behaviors. Some children may exhibit ongoing challenging behaviors when there is stress at home, parents are separating or divorcing, a new baby arrives, or a parent loses a job or becomes ill. Although most children eventually manage to cope with these experiences, they usually benefit from extra support and understanding from you and their families. Other children may exhibit repeated challenging behaviors when they get frustrated, do not have the skills to communicate their emotions and feelings, or are struggling to make friends.

If not addressed, children's challenging behaviors could continue, multiply, and lead to lifelong problems. For instance, research has found that children with challenging behaviors are unlikely to have success in school and will be burdened with social and emotional problems later in life—including mental illness. Challenging behavior in preschool is one of the strongest predictors of delinquency, drug abuse, and antisocial behavior in adults (McCabe & Frede, 2007).

Ideally, no child would ever be expelled from an early childhood setting and early educators would prevent and handle challenging behaviors using positive child guidance techniques consistently. Treat children with respect and focus on their positive actions. Though challenging behaviors may test your patience and even anger you, never let your anger and frustration show. Be calm, objective, and professional at all times. Your relationships with the children are your greatest aids. When early educators and young children have strong bonds, children have better interactions with their

What's Causing Challenging Behavior?

To help identify what is causing a child's challenging behavior, follow these three steps:

1. **Observe what happened before the challenging behavior occurred.** Was there a "trigger"?

2. **Document the problem.** How often did the offending behavior occur?

3. **What happened afterward?** What did the child gain or avoid from acting this way?

This process is known as a *functional analysis*. Your analysis should help you determine what the child is trying to obtain (your attention or perhaps a toy), what the child is trying to avoid (taking a nap or sitting for a story), or what level of stimulation the child is trying to change (boredom while waiting). With this information, you can discover patterns in the child's behavior and anticipate and change the situations that led to the behaviors. For example, if Naomi hits others during transitions, make sure to position yourself to help her prepare for the upcoming transition. Give her your attention for being cooperative rather than disruptive.

peers and are more eager for positive attention (Powell, Dunlap, & Fox, 2006). Gartrell (2008) says that early educators should "reach out to children at risk for stigma and help them turn around their lives by building positive attachments with them, assisting them to find membership in the class, and teaching them democratic life skills" (2002, p. 41).

In some cases where children's challenging behavior is recurring and not readily resolved, Gartrell recommends that you develop an Individual Guidance Plan (IGP). For example, 2-year-old Jake's tantrums are becoming increasingly frequent, which warrants a pediatrician's attention. Like an Individualized Family Service Plan (IFSP) or Individualized Education Program (IEP) for a child with special needs, the IGP brings together everyone who is concerned about the child—staff, family members, and sometimes specialists. Similar to an IEP, participants agree on what the problem is, what needs to be done about the problem, how to implement the guidance strategies, and how to monitor progress and evaluate the plan. Gartrell (2011) explains that the meeting is positive, because everyone shares a common purpose—the good of the child.

Stopping Bullying

Dan Olweus (1997), who has studied bullying problems among youth for nearly 40 years, defines bullying as the continual and damaging actions of one child against another that are not provoked by the target. Direct bullying is physical or verbal, involving hitting, kicking, name-calling, or teasing. Indirect bullying is less obvious, involving threatening and teasing. Children as young as 2 and one-half years old have been known to bully. Boys tend to be physically aggressive, direct bullies while girls tend to be indirect bullies who are sophisticated in rumor-spreading, telling secrets, excluding other children, and making threats. In preschool, bullying occurs most frequently in social play, with playmates as the targets.

Bullying among young children occurs at all socioeconomic levels and in all settings in all geographic regions. Kaiser and Rasminsky (2012) cite research that estimates that 17% of all children are bullies and 18% of all children are targets. However, because bullying occurs out of adults' sight and often goes unreported, these numbers could be underestimated.

Researchers have learned that, unlike most children who exhibit challenging behaviors, bullies tend to have high self-esteem and social skills. They are also popular, often surrounded by friends and admirers. Bullies have an uncanny ability to understand others' minds and emotions. They can easily take advantage of their targets because bullies know what makes others tick. These children lack empathy, have little regard for authority, and view violence positively. They do not care if they inflict pain, and may even enjoy hurting other people. Olweus (1993) found that 60% of boys who had been bullies were convicted of at least one crime by early adulthood.

Bullying targets, on the other hand, have low self-esteem and experience social isolation. They are often timid and do not defend themselves. Children who are different—because of looks, disability, or ethnicity—from the others in their settings seem to be at greatest risk of bullying. Bullied children lack focus and experience difficulties in school. Over time, these children typically develop depression and anxiety and can become suicidal.

Pearce & Thompson (1998) explain that "every time an act of bullying is successful, it represents failure for children, adults, school, and community." Though bullying cannot be ignored, there are no easy solutions to the problem. Penalties and punishment are ineffective and usually lead to harsher attacks on the targets. Positive guidance, again, offers the best approach. Here are some positive suggestions for combatting bullying in your setting (Kaiser & Rasminsky, 2012; EDC, 2008):

Whatever method you employ to end bullying in your setting, be positive and compassionate.

- **Teach needed social skills.** Bullies lack empathy, problem-solving, self-regulation, and calming skills. Bullied children lack assertiveness. All of these social skills can be taught through direct teaching, modeling, and role playing.

- **Speak to children positively.** The old model of comforting the victim and punishing the aggressor is ineffective. Both children need to be treated with care and respect. Work with children to express their feelings and observe them carefully to get at the heart of what is causing the problem. For the child who is bullying, find positive outlets for leadership abilities. For the target, reassure this child that it is your job to keep the child safe.

- **Use books and puppets to help children work through their feelings** (bibliotherapy). You can use these books to help children see how their lives relate to the characters in the story. The children can use puppets to help them express their thoughts and feelings. Here are some recommended books to encourage discussions:

  - *The Bully Blockers Club* by Teresa Bateman.
  - *Alley Oops* by Janice Levy.
  - *Stand Tall, Molly Lou Melon* by Patty Lovell.
  - *The Recess Queen* by Alexis O'Neill.
  - *The Juice Box Bully: Empowering Kids to Stand Up for Others* by Bob Sornson and Maria Dismondy.

Whatever method you employ to end bullying in your setting, be positive and compassionate. Get to the root cause of the behaviors and offer bullies choices that will have a positive outcome.

Partnering With Families

Begin the guidance conversation with parents positively. Spell out your guidance philosophy in a guidebook or manual, or as part of your setting's orientation materials. At the start of the year or whenever a new child enrolls in your setting, invite families to meet and discuss the policy.

- **Keep research available that supports the positive guidance strategies and techniques you use.** This evidence will help you explain how your policy and practice is rooted in best practices. For example, instead of announcing to parents that punishment is a bad practice, explain that your setting's staff do not employ punishment, because researchers have found that not only is it ineffective, but it can also make a problem worse. Families that use punishment may feel defensive or feel the need to resist what you say. Distribute to parents copies of brief research about punishment so that they can read about the subject themselves.

Some parents may disagree with your policies, because the policies differ from the way parents were raised. For example, a father might say, "I spank my child so the world won't," and tell you that you have his full permission to spank his child. Respect his perspective, but do not spank the child. Politely but firmly let the parent know you cannot comply with his request and that you have a no-hitting policy in your setting. Explain to him the strategies you will be using and why. Solicit his help in working together to prevent and address any challenging behaviors. Perhaps the parent has other practices that are aligned with your philosophy that you can incorporate into your practice.

- **Keep communication with parents ongoing and two-way.** Check in with them during drop-off and pick-up, and communicate through e-mail, newsletters, or regular meetings. If an ongoing challenging behavior exists, discuss it with the child's family privately, politely, and nonjudgmentally. Begin the conversation discussing the child's positives. Also share information with parents that you think they will find helpful. For example, send home tip sheets on positive guidance, information on active

Invite families to meet and discuss your settings guidance policy.

listening, or pamphlets about how to help children express their feelings. Understanding appropriate expectations will help parents know when children are acting appropriately for their age or when they are having a true behavior problem. Keep families abreast of what is happening in the setting and offer parenting resources such as books, classes, or workshops when appropriate.

• **Discuss children' challenging behaviors with parents.** If children's behaviors are severe, meet with their parents in person. In cases of bullying, meet with both the bullies' and targets' parents. Conduct these meetings separately to prevent conflict among parents. During these meetings, listen intently and contribute to the conversation. Hearing what happens at home will help you perform a functional analysis and get to the root of the problem.

The best outcome of these meetings is for you and the child's family to brainstorm a common approach for addressing challenging behaviors. If children receive the same message in your setting that they do at home, your approach has a much higher likelihood of success. ■

Competency Standard IV:

To establish positive and productive relationships with families

Developmental Context

Functional Area 11: Families

Young infants *(birth–8 months)* are establishing patterns of sleeping, waking, eating, playing, and social activity. They can be supported in developing some stability in these routines by the sensitive and consistent responses of adults. Families and providers can anticipate needs and respond more appropriately to the infant's signals when they share details with each other about the baby at drop off and pickup times.

Mobile infants *(9–17 months)* may have difficulty separating from the family members even when the provider is a familiar and trusted person. Providers can support infants and their families by recognizing that it may be upsetting both for the adults and the child and providing strategies to ease the separation. Providers should recognize the potential for competition between themselves and parents and work to avoid it, remembering that infants can have more than one important adult in their lives. Providers and families also need to agree on reasonable and safe limits as children begin to explore and wander.

Toddlers *(18–36 months)* develop their own special routines and rituals in order to feel safe and secure. It is essential that families and providers share their experiences and understanding of the child's patterns and provide consistent, dependable support for the toddler's developing sense of self competence and confidence.

Preschoolers *(3-5 years old)* move back and forth from their family to the child care program more independently than younger children. They are also more sensitive to the differences between the two environments and observe carefully the interactions between their parents and educators/providers. Educators/providers should build a "partnership" with each family to best support the needs of each child. They should keep each other informed of important developments in children's lives and provide mutual support in nurturing each child's physical, social, emotional, and cognitive development.

Chapter 11
Families

CDA Functional Area 11: Candidate establishes a positive, responsive, and cooperative relationship with each child's family, engages in two-way communication with families, encourages their involvement in the program, and supports the child's relationship with his or her family.

Families

Introduction

Partnering with children's families is a recurring theme in this textbook. Research and advocacy organizations, like the National Association for the Education of Young Children (NAEYC), agree that early care and education should be a collaborative effort between parents and early educators. "The experts have been polled and the results are in: a positive parent–educator relationship contributes to school success" (PBS Parents, n.d.). The two most stable presences in children's lives are you and their families. When true partnerships exist among early educators and families, children feel safe and secure and trust the environment you have established. These partnerships also ease children's transitions between home and school.

In this chapter, we will discuss the components involved in forming a positive bond with families:

- **Defining Family.**
- **Establishing Partnerships With Families.**
- **Encouraging Family Participation.**
- **Communicating With Families.**
- **Meeting Formally With Families.**
- **Supporting Families in Their Child's Development.**

Defining Family

When we think of families, the traditional nuclear and extended families whose members are biologically related typically come to mind.

The American family model depicted in television shows during the 1950s and 1960s—a father who works outside of the home and a mother who stays home to raise the children—now applies to just 15% of all families (Hare & Gray, 2008). The U.S. Census Bureau (n.d.) defines the term *family* as "a group of two people or more (one of whom is the householder) related by birth, marriage, or adoption and residing together." However, in a 2010 survey, 60% of Americans said people can be family simply because they deem themselves to be. Fifty-one percent of those surveyed even thought that pets should be a part of the definition of a family, too (Hare & Gray, 2008).

Families share emotional bonds, common values, goals, and responsibilities and contribute significantly to each other's well-being. When a family includes children, one or more adults may assume an involved role in the children's lives and become their parents. These adults can include biological parents, grandparents, stepparents, aunts and uncles, foster parents, adoptive parents, and any other person who fulfills a significant portion of the parenting and care for the child. These adults may not necessarily be biologically related to the child or even live with the child all the time.

Types of Family Structures

Today's families exist in various forms, like the following:

- **Nuclear families:** About two-thirds of families—including the 15% of families who fit the model depicted on television decades ago—fall into this category. Some nuclear families consist of mothers who work and fathers who stay at home or two parents who are unemployed. These families can include two heterosexual or two homosexual parents. The children in these families are either biologically related to one or both parents or adopted.

- **Cohabiting families:** These families resemble nuclear families, but the parents are not married.

- **Single-parent families:** Single parents head one-fourth of all families. Though both men and women may head these families, women head 88% of these families. It is estimated that 60% of all children will spend some part of their lives in this family configuration (Hare & Gray, 2008).

- **Blended families:** These families are products of divorces and remarriages. Children in these families may be biologically related to one parent or both.

- **Grandparent-led families:** Eight percent of children live with a grandparent for a variety of reasons, from death of a parent to a parent's inability to care for the child.

Today's families exist in various forms.

- **Interracial or transracial families:** In interracial families, the parents are of different races and the children are typically biracial. Transracial families consist of parents and adopted children of different races.

- **Foster- and group-home families:** These temporary families are formed in the best interest of the children, who are often placed with the families by the courts or other government agencies.

- **Kinship care families:** In these families, an arrangement (either legal or informal) exists for relatives, instead of parents, to care for children.

- **Commuter families:** These nuclear or cohabitating families include parents who live and work away from the rest of the immediate family. These situations usually exist because of job responsibilities, educational needs, or military obligations. For example, a woman's husband and children may live in one city, but she lives and works in another during the workweek.

- **Transnational families:** These families live part of each year in different countries. This dynamic can exist in various forms:

  - **Children reside with the same set of parents in both countries.** For example, the family's primary residence is in the United States, but they live in China in the summer.

  - **Children reside with one parent in both countries.** For example, a mother and children's primary residence is in the United States, but they live in India in the summer.

  - **Children reside with one parent in one country and the other parent in another country.** For example, the children's primary residence is in the United States, but their father works in Brazil. The children live with their father in Brazil in the summer and with their mother in the United States the rest of the year.

  - **Children reside with parents in one country and grandparents in a different country.** For example, the family's primary residence is in the United States, but the children's maternal grandparents live in Ethiopia. The children live in Ethiopia with their grandparents in the summer and the United States with their immediate family the rest of the year.

You will notice that in this chapter, the words *families* and *parents* are used interchangeably. Both words refer to the people who are primarily responsible for the children in your care—whether they are parents, stepparents, grandparents, aunts and uncles, cousins, guardians, foster families, or other members of the children's households.

Represent all families in your setting and within your learning environment. Consider these family structures when choosing the books, materials, photos, and activities that you provide each day. Children will benefit from seeing their families represented on a daily basis in your setting. They will know that they are respected and valued and that they can trust your setting.

How Culture Impacts Family Dynamics

As an early educator, your role in building and maintaining positive relationships with children and their families is not always easy. It helps to have good communication and strong listening skills, flexibility, and creativity to manage these situations and maintain positive connections.

Each family's relationships, communication styles, expectations for children's learning and behavior, and parental roles are unique. Parents' and early educators' own family experiences and cultures influence their perceptions of roles and relationships. For example, some cultures do not value independence and feel that giving a child too much

Children will benefit from seeing their families represented in your setting.

responsibility is not appropriate. Or some families deem it appropriate to punish or spank their children, which can be harmful to children and is against your setting's policies.

Although some families' cultural practices may not comply with your setting's policies, work to respect and build trusting partnerships with all families. Listen to parents' concerns and respectfully discuss your setting's policies and practices. For example, respectfully decline Rashida's parent's request to punish the child by explaining your policies and sharing information about other techniques, like positive guidance. You might even schedule a meeting with her parent to discuss the topic in detail. Listen intently to John's mother's reasons for why she believes it is inappropriate to teach a child to be independent, and then ex-plain why your setting values this principle. Even though both parents' views conflict with your setting philosophy, or with child development research, respect and listen to the parents' concerns and show that you value and respect them.

On the other hand, the standards of behavior that families expect children to uphold at home may not be the same as the standards you set for them in your setting. Anti-bias educators Louise Derman-Sparks and Julie Olsen Edwards (2010, p. 40) explain that children in your setting may not be exhibiting "deviating behavior that needs adjustment." Rather, their behavior may be a product of cultures at home that clash with the culture in your setting. In these situations, your first reaction should be to carefully examine your values and experiences. When discussing children's behavior with their parents, hear and understand their viewpoints, even if they disagree with you by offering evidence that seems unreasonable or unsupportable by research. Understand the origin of these beliefs and values so that you can strengthen your relationships with both the family members and their children. Do not expect families to abandon their fundamental values. Instead, be prepared to compromise or discover another acceptable solution.

Think about ways that you and parents can respect and honor both points of view. Schedule a formal one-on-one meeting with parents to discuss the issue. After the meeting, continue to follow up with the parent by sharing the child's experiences each day at your setting. If a family finds that the setting's philosophy conflicts greatly with their own values, they may choose to withdraw their child from your setting and enroll the child in one that fits their needs better. However, some parents will welcome a chance to learn about the developmentally appropriate practices that influence your setting's policies and procedures. In turn, hearing the families' viewpoints can expand your thoughts and support you in clearly articulating your teaching practices.

Establishing Partnerships With Families

The relationships in our lives—whether they are with family members, friends, or neighbors—transform into partnerships when the people involved all share a common goal and the responsibility for reaching it. Your relationships with parents transform into partnerships because you all want to support their children developmentally and will work together to achieve this. "Family engagement occurs when there is an ongoing, reciprocal, strengths-based partnership between families and their children's early childhood education programs" (Halgunseth, Peterson, Stark, & Moodie, 2009, p. 3).

All partnerships stem from positive relationships and require all partners to do the following:

- Regard each other as equal and contribute to the partnerships in different ways.

- Value and respect each other for what they think, even if there are differences.

- Listen and talk to each other.

- Make an effort to understand and trust each other's points-of-view.

- Confer with each other when making important decisions.

Most parents find their setting visit so rewarding that they are eager to return.

Parents may be anxious about leaving their children in the care of adults outside their networks of families and friends. Developing strong partnerships with parents will help them feel secure throughout the day knowing that their child is in a safe and nurturing setting. Through strong partnerships and clear two-way communication, parents will have a deeper understanding of your setting's configuration and your daily schedule and routines. They will understand the "why" behind teaching practices and setting policies. Their confidence in the quality of your setting may prompt them to encourage other parents to enroll their children.

Your ability to articulate the importance of play and how and what children learn will build parents' confidence in you as a professional and will give them ideas for things to do at home that reinforce your work. It will also open the door for parents to share more information about their child and their values to help you understand the child better. Use this information to reflect on how you can tailor your teaching practices to support their child. Sharing with parents documentation of their child's learning on a regular basis will encourage parents to share their thoughts and engage in the learning process. Parents can contribute their own observations and descriptions to their child's portfolio, which the child can revisit throughout the day.

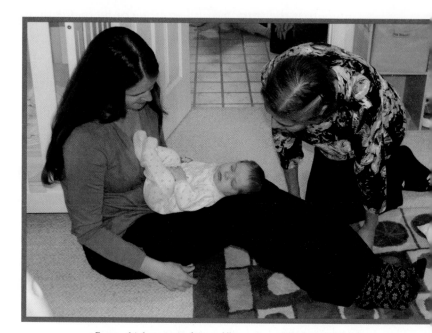

Parents of infants can spend time cuddling, cooing, and playing with their infants.

In addition, children will transition into your setting much more easily if they understand clearly what is expected of them and they feel safe and secure. When you incorporate children's interests and experiences from home into your setting, you create strong links between the children's homes and your setting. For example, Andre went to the beach with his family last week. During the trip, his parents took photos of the sand castles Andre built. They brought the photos to the setting to include in Andre's portfolio. Andre can revisit the photos and describe his vacation. You can link his experience building sand castles at the beach with his experience playing at the sand table or in the sandbox outside. Andre can look at the photos throughout the day or even try to build another castle using blocks or LEGO® building bricks.

When you build strong partnerships with families, you gain a clearer understanding of each child's strengths. Information, like family values, parenting styles, and events in the child's life, equips you to identify why children react or behave in a certain way. You are more likely to develop stronger bonds with children if they feel that you are connected to their families.

Initiating Partnerships

Once families enroll their children in your setting, let them know that you want to partner with them on behalf of their children. Communicate this message through your words and your actions. The following are a few suggestions for how to initiate these partnerships:

Develop a setting welcome packet for parents. The bulk of this welcome packet should focus on policies, program hours of operation, sick child policies, emergency plans, and field trip rules (including back-up plans in cases of inclement weather). Also include your setting's mission, the philosophy of your setting's approaches to learning, and a description of the curriculum you use. Use the packet to communicate your vision for partnerships with parents, invite parents into your setting, and create opportunities for safe and respectful dialogue. Consider including a list of frequently asked questions to address common parent concerns. Include an acknowledgement form in the front or back of the packet. Ask parents to sign the form to ensure that they have received a copy of the welcome packet. If you change policies during the course of the year, notify family members and provide them with the updates in writing. Review the welcome packet each year to ensure that the content is current and that the text and photos or illustrations welcome families and illustrate the setting's diversity. Get the packet translated into each language spoken by children's families. (Head Start and Early Head Start programs are required to issue parent welcome packets or handbooks in accordance with the Head Start Program Performance Standards.)

Hold an orientation open house. Invite families to tour your setting before their child's first day to establish a friendly and respectful rapport with families. Demonstrate your commitment to professionalism by speaking with them in a serious and friendly manner. Review the welcome packet with families and answer their questions. Introduce your curriculum and walk families through a typical day in the setting. Show them how transitions occur between activities, and explain the importance of play in children's learning. In addition, use this opportunity to feature the ways that you welcome families into your program. Let them know that the following are available:

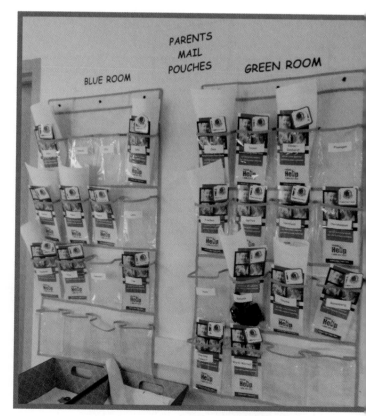

Be sure to show families where they can find their mailboxes.

- Facility that is accessible to all families enrolled in the setting.

- Mailboxes for communicating with families.

- Signage in every family's home language that includes the children's names and critical signs, such as the names of the interest areas and a job chart.

- Family bulletin board for displaying notices of interest to families.

- Sign-in and sign-out sheets for families dropping off children in the morning and picking them up in the evening.

- Locked cabinet where family members can store their coats, purses, and other personal belongings while they are visiting the program.

- Adult-sized chairs for if they want to read a story or join children for lunch.

- Documentation panels that feature what children are learning.

- Digital camera for taking photos to include in homemade books and around the setting.

- Sample questions family members might ask children during activities, posted on the sides of divider shelves in each of the centers.

- Resources families can borrow.

- Book bag children can borrow filled with favorite books, toys, or puppets.

Conduct an intake/enrollment interview. Upon enrollment, all settings conduct a brief initial meeting with families to complete written forms and obtain critical information about the child and family. Conduct this meeting in person and in a comfortable area. Make snacks and beverages available during the meeting. If the family does not speak your home language and you are not fluent in theirs, a staff member or interpreter who is fluent in both languages should also attend. Even if this person is present, learn a few words in the family's home language, such as "welcome" and "thank you," beforehand to show respect for their culture. Pose open-ended questions, such as, "What are Michael's sleeping habits at home?" These questions will help you get the most information from the family. The following is a list of important questions you should ask families:

Developing strong partnerships with parents will help them feel secure knowing that their child is in a safe and nurturing setting.

- Who are the members of the family? Describe their relationships with the child. Do extended family members live in the household or nearby? Does the child have any special relationships with family members or family friends? If the parent is in a romantic relationship, does the romantic partner live in the household or visit frequently? Are there any family pets?

- What language do they speak at home? Is the child exposed to any other languages?

- Does the family have any traditions they would like to see honored in the setting?

- What individuals are allowed to pick up the child from the setting? What is their relation to the child? What are their phone numbers?

- Do you—the early educator and your staff—have permission to photograph the child for educational use in the setting or for use in publications or videos publicizing the setting?

- Does the child have permission to take supervised field trips for educational purposes? Does the child have permission to ride on buses or in private vehicles for these activities?

- What is the child's health history? In Chapter 2, you learned all the information that you should collect—including the name and phone number of the child's physician, emergency contacts, and procedures in case the child gets sick or injured. Does the child have any food allergies? Is the child on medication?

- What activities do the children like best? Do they have favorite toys? What are their favorite books?

- Describe children's nap time/bedtime routines. How long do they sleep? Do they have any bedtime rituals? Are they grumpy, enthusiastic, or confused when they wake up?

- Describe the child's mealtimes. If the mother nurses the child, at what times does she do so? Will she be nursing at the setting or sending milk or formula? Will the child be transitioning to solid foods at the setting? For older children, does the family eat together during mealtimes? Are there any family traditions or rituals? What are the child's favorite foods? What foods does the family eat?

Make parent involvement an important component of your setting's philosophy.

- Do children have any fears? How do they deal with them?

- How do the families comfort children when they are upset?

- What would the family say are their child's greatest strengths?

- What would the family say are their child's greatest challenges?

- Has the child ever been diagnosed with a special need? Is the child on an IFSP (Individualized Family Service Plan) or an IEP (Individualized Education Program)?

- What are the family's goals for their child in your setting? What are their wishes and dreams for their child in the future?

- What kind of role would the family like to play in the setting?

Parents of toddlers can explore the setting with their child and other toddlers and play games.

You might not get all of the information you need during this initial intake interview. This experience may even overwhelm some family members. For others, you may be the first early educator they have met, and they may feel intimidated by your position. Others may be embarrassed to share what they feel is private information. For example, a family may be reluctant to share that they live at a homeless shelter or are dealing with immigration worries (Derman-Sparks & Edwards, 2010). Some families may think you are insinuating that they are not good parents.

If parents resist your questions, pick and choose which answers to push for, like ones that involve permissions or signing off on policies. Answers that focus on parental hopes and dreams can wait. Parents are just getting to know you. Perhaps once you have developed a stronger relationship, they will be more forthcoming with additional information.

Handling Personality Conflicts With Families

Collaborating and establishing positive relationships with families helps you gain their trust and respect as you interact with their children. Parents will feel comfortable talking to you about issues and concerns they may have about their child. Families will also actively participate in any events or experiences in your setting and become more involved in programming and planning.

However, you may encounter families who are difficult for you to embrace because of their personality traits. Or you may discover that you are not a particular parent's favorite person, and you may sense hostility from this parent. Some families may limit their contact with you out of intimidation. Others may be suspicious of your intentions. Despite family members' feelings or actions, be open and proactive in forming relationships with them. If you are having a problem connecting with a child's family, figure out a better approach. Find a way for you to get to know each other. You will benefit from your heartfelt efforts to learn all you can about families and their beliefs and desires for their children.

Encouraging Family Participation

Families should know that they are welcome in your setting at all times to observe and participate in meaningful ways. Some settings, like Head Start, have a long history of parent involvement. Other settings, like co-ops or the Sure Start program operated by the Department of Defense Dependents Schools, require parent participation. Make parent involvement an important component of your setting's philosophy.

Involving families in meaningful ways takes careful thought. Some families may be reluctant to participate. Being in your setting may intimidate them. They may lack confidence that they will know what to do, or feel they do not have time to devote to visiting your setting. Gently encourage these parents to get involved in the activities they are comfortable doing and have time to do. See what interests a parent and build on that. Families can get involved in your setting by simply engaging in play with their child and other children. Parents of infants can spend time cuddling, cooing, reading stories, and playing with their infant. Parents of toddlers can explore the setting with their child and other toddlers, play games, describe what the toddlers are doing, and read stories. Preschoolers' parents can ask open-ended questions and engage children in their learning.

Assist parents in helping children learn through play by introducing the specific strategies you use to scaffold children's learning. For example, explain how you describe children's actions as they are engaging with the learning environment. Provide some examples of what this looks like and model it. Give parents sample open-ended questions that they might ask children to extend their learning. These questions may help parents think of their own questions.

Once parents do get involved, they are usually pleasantly surprised and excited by what happens daily in the setting. Seeing how proud their child is to have them there is often all it takes. Most parents find the experience so rewarding, they are eager to return.

The following are a few activities that parents can engage in while visiting the setting:

- Playing with their child and other children during choice time.

- Leading a small group activity, such as playing a game, putting together a puzzle, or blowing bubbles outdoors.

- Reading a story.

- Helping script a puppet show.

- Singing with the children or leading a finger play during meeting times.

- Making materials, such as play dough, with the children.

- Introducing children to the music of their culture.

- Cooking a family's favorite recipe with the children.

- Talking to the children in the dramatic play center about their occupations.

- Eating lunch with the children.

- Helping children plant a garden.

- Overseeing a woodworking project.

- Accompanying the group on a field trip.

- Attending setting celebrations.

Families can also assist with administrative tasks, such as brainstorming lesson activities or planning the curriculum. Though it is helpful to have parental help with these tasks, encourage parents to spend time in the setting with their children.

Figure 48. Reading Aloud

The following are tips for parents who are reading aloud to children in your setting:

- Select a book that you like (and have read before) and that you think the children will like, too.

- Hold an infant or toddler in your lap. Or gather a group of 2–3 toddlers or 4–6 preschool children in a comfortable area where everyone can sit on the floor. Sit on a chair so all the children can see the book.

- Point out the names of the book's author and illustrator and the cover illustration. See whether the children can predict what the book will be about.

- Have fun bringing the characters and plot to life. Read with expression.

- Read slowly enough for children to take in the words and look at the pictures.

- Stop during the reading to invite children to complete a predictable phrase or sentence, to guess what might happen next, or to think about how they might react in a similar situation in real life. Ask older children open-ended questions about how a character might be feeling or why they think the situation occurred.

- If children lose interest or decide they want to do something else, allow them to follow their interests and leave the group.

- Watch the children's body language. Children may need a break or even to end the session.

- Talk about the book afterward. Encourage children to retell the story in their own words.

Many family members are unable to visit the setting during the day because of work obligations. However, these parents can still contribute in some way. For example, if a parent is willing to sing, ask him/her to record some favorite children's songs for the music & movement or listening center. A family member who can sew can make curtains and a tablecloth for the home area of the pretend play or dramatic play center. Or this person could make a puppet stage or pillows for the literacy center. Parents who are artists could make signage or design displays for the setting. Family members experienced at woodworking might make frames for the children's artwork or extra shelving for storing materials. Bilingual parents can translate materials or make signage for the setting in their home languages. All parents can assemble items at home, such as empty paper towel rolls, baby food jars, buttons, keys, packing peanuts, or plastic trays for children in the setting to use for art or science projects. Continue to brainstorm with family members about creative ways they might contribute to the setting.

Preparing Families for Visits to the Setting

Remember, parents may be meeting the other children in your setting for the first time. Prepare them in advance to engage in activities successfully with your community of learners:

1. Share your goals for the activity.

2. Give the family member a chance to observe you or another staff member doing the activity.

3. Review the activity with the family member. Answer any questions.

4. Allow the family member to lead the activity while you observe.

5. Review the activity with the family member. Answer any questions.

6. Let the family member lead the activity on alone, but stay nearby in case this person needs your support.

7. Review the activity with the family member. Answer any questions.

Create one-page tip sheets for activities that parents may want to do, and get them translated into all of the home languages spoken by family members.

Through strong partnerships and clear communication, parents will have a deeper understanding of your daily schedule and routines.

Figure 49. Sample Questions/Comments for Infants and Toddlers

Include individual charts throughout the setting to guide parents' interactions with each age group. Translate them into the families' home languages.

Center	What Children are Learning	Sample Questions/Comments
Blocks	Geometry (shapes, sizes); balancing; developing fine motor skills; writing	• "I see that you put three rectangular blocks on top of each other." • "You placed the longer block on top of the shorter block."
Art	Expressing feelings and ideas; exploring textures, colors, and different mediums; developing fine motor skills; developing aesthetic sense	• "Do you want to post your painting on the wall here, in your portfolio, or would you rather take it home?" • "I see that you are using orange paint on the paper."
Books	Print has meaning; pictures are related to the text of the book; how to correctly handle books	• "Do you want me to read this story?" • "Can you touch the rabbit's furry tail? How does it feel to you?" • "I wonder what will happen if the four monkeys jump on the bed."
Dramatic Play	Trying out roles; working through experiences; developing executive function and self-control	• "May I join you for dinner? What are we eating?" • "You are pushing the stroller very fast." • "Who is calling on the telephone?" • "Peek-a-boo! I see you!"

Figure 50. Sample Questions/Comments for Preschoolers

Post sample questions on the side of a divider shelf where parents can consult them during play for preschool aged children.

Center	What Children are Learning	Sample Questions/Comments
Blocks	Geometry (shapes, sizes); balancing; developing fine motor skills; writing	• "Which blocks would be best to put at the bottom of your tower?" • "How might you keep the building from falling down?" • "How many of these small blocks will it take to make a large block?" • "What should we write on the sign next to your construction?"
Art	Expressing feelings and ideas; using color and texture; developing eye–hand coordination; developing aesthetic sense	• "Why did you choose to use dark colors?" • "How does this collage make you feel?" • "If you tell me about your drawing, I'll write down your words on this sentence strip." • "Do you want to post your painting on the wall here, or would you rather take it home?"
Literacy	Learning about letters, words, and print awareness; discovering how books work; gaining an appreciation of books; learning to write their names	• "There's a picture of three rabbits eating carrots on the cover of this book. What do you think this book might be about?" • "This word begins with a *P* sound? Can you think of any other words that begin with a *P* sound?" • "This book is by Eric Carle. Do you remember any other books you've read by this same author—Eric Carle?" • "Let's act out the story we just read using puppets. Who would like to be the little boy?"
Dramatic Play	Trying out roles; working through experiences; developing executive function and self-control	• "May I join you for dinner? What are you serving?" • "What does your little girl need to do to get ready for school?" • "Would you like to be the doctor who gives children shots? You can make sure that you don't hurt them." • "May I join your tea party? I'd like to bring my friend Maria with me."

Figure 50. Sample Questions/Comments for Preschoolers (Continued)

Center	What Children are Learning	Sample Questions/Comments
Music & Movement	Patterns and relationships; expressing themselves; music appreciation; phonological awareness	• "How would a rhinoceros move?" • "How could we make a drum out of this oatmeal box?" • "Why does this bell make such a high sound?" • "Which songs on the CD did you like best?"
Science	Applying scientific method; experimenting; graphing; observing	• "How do these leaves look the same? How are they different?" • "What colors do you see when you hold the prism in the light? Are the colors always in the same order?"
Math & Manipula-tives	Counting; seriation; matching; more than/less than; fine motor skills	• "How did you know where to put that last puzzle piece?" • "What other card has a picture that looks like this piece of fruit?" • "Tell me about your Lego® construction." • "How many pegs are on the pegboard now?"
Sand & Water	Expressing feelings; experimenting; observing; predicting; fine motor skills; volume; patterning	• "Do you think this rock will sink or float in the water?" • "How did you use the shell to make these patterns in the sand?" • "If we were to turn the water table into an ocean, what should we put in the bottom of the table?" • "What happens to the sand when it gets wet?"
Cooking	Learning about letters, words, and directionality with recipe cards; observing properties change; measurement, volume, and number	• "How many steps are there in this recipe for pine-apple salad?" • "What happened to the popcorn kernels when they were heated?" • "How do we know when the bread is done?"
Outdoors	Developing large muscle skills; exploring nature	• "How did you feel when you got to the top of the climber?" • "Why don't you take the magnifying glass and see whether you can discover what the ants are doing?" • "How will you know when the tomatoes in your gar-den are ready to be eaten?" • "Let's see how long our shadows are. What should we use to measure them?"

Families

Communicating With Families

Strong two-way communication is imperative to maintaining effective partnerships with families. Communicate with all families daily. As parents describe their experiences and perspectives, encourage two-way communication with active listening and empathy. When communicating with families, admitting that you do not know the answer to a question and being willing to seek the information demonstrate keen self-awareness (Gillespie, 2006). Though you are knowledgeable about early childhood development, the National Association for the Education of Young Children (NAYEC, 2011, p. 23) agrees that as an early educator, you are not expected to know all the answers to parents' questions:

> Parents do not feel like partners in the relationship when staff members see themselves as having all the knowledge and insight about children and view parents as lacking such knowledge. In reciprocal relationships between practitioners and families, there is mutual respect, cooperation, shared responsibility, and negotiation of conflicts toward achievement of shared goals. Practitioners work in collaborative partnerships with families, establishing and maintaining regular, frequent, two-way communication with them.

Here are some suggested mediums and times through which you can communicate effectively with parents:

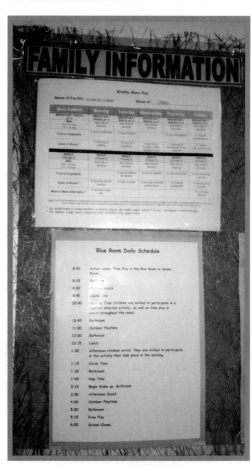

- **Welcoming mail:** Before children's first day, send families a one-page letter that lets them know that you and the staff are excited that the children are joining your setting. Describe briefly your setting's philosophy and what your goals are for the children. Alert families to the setting welcome packet they will receive, which spells out your responsibilities and the responsibilities parents will need to agree to assume. Let them know the date and time of setting orientation and when you will be conducting a home visit. Reassure them that you will be available to answer all of their questions. Also consider sending the children postcards to welcome them personally to the setting.

- **Morning drop-off:** When parents accompany children into the setting, this affords you the opportunity to meet with families daily. Informal meetings like these help you forge bonds with families. Greet family members by name and ask about their night or weekend. Listen attentively to what family members

Direct families to bulletin boards within your setting so they can obtain important information.

tell or ask you. Share anecdotes about their children and ask families any questions you have. Avoid using any technical jargon in these conversations. Your goal is to communicate with families—not to impress them with your knowledge.

In addition, if there are upcoming field trips or events parents should know about, share this information with them either in-person or by written invitations you deliver to them personally. Also direct them to the family bulletin board. Let family members know what your plan is for the day and what learning objectives you will be working on with their children. Ask whether they have time to stay for a while before leaving for the day. If so, encourage them to stay for as long as they would like to.

- **Afternoon/evening pickup:** This brief meeting time, like morning drop-off, is an opportunity to converse with families. Parents will want to know how their child's day went, so share something positive. Describe children's actions or what specific activities they performed. For example, "Aaron tried hard to crawl today." Respectfully listen to parents as they respond to the information you provide. For example, a parent who enters your setting may be upset to see his/her son playing in the cooking center. Listen to parents as they articulate their concerns before you respond and explain early childhood education practices and the reasons supporting them. Provide parents of infants and toddlers with detailed information regarding their children's diapering and feeding each day.

  Remind children of the things they need to take home and wish them a good evening. Some children may cling to you when their parents arrive. Other children may be engrossed in an activity. Gently remind the children that their parents have arrived and that they will be able to engage in the activity the following day. Children who cling to you may be unhappy that their parents left them that morning or stayed away for so long. They may say that they are angry with or do not like their parents. Give all the children a warm goodbye so that everyone will be eager to return to your setting the next day.

- **Phone calls and e-mail:** Depending on families' preferences, set up a regular schedule for contacting them. During this check-in, talk about their children's progress, discuss any concerns, and chat about future plans. Include specific examples of children's learning and work or whether you are noticing any changes in children's sleeping and eating patterns. Sending families photos of their children engaging in play during the day is another way you can regularly communicate with families and strengthen the partnership.

  Encourage family members to contact you via phone or e-mail if they have concerns or want to discuss something with you. An e-mail request affords you time to gather records or other material you might need for your discussion. If parents have no access to either a computer or phone, arrange to meet them in person.

- **Newsletters:** Consider distributing weekly or monthly newsletters to families that include information, such as a review of what happened last week/month and mealtime menus.

You might also present short, informative articles, like an article about how you resolve conflicts in your setting or a "family volunteer of the month" feature. Feature stories might inspire some reluctant family members to become more involved in the setting. Desktop publishing and web-based software can help you produce a professional-looking newsletter with photographs. The newsletter does not need to be grand, and can be distributed in print or via e-mail.

- Website: Consider creating a website for the setting, or asking a colleague or family member for help. A website can help you keep families informed through stories, photos, and videos and document children's project work in the setting. Since these photos/videos will be posted to the Internet, obtain permission from families before posting. Anyone around the world can view your website, so think carefully about the information you post. You'll also want to think about the images you are displaying, since the whole world can see them. See Figure 51. for a list of websites that can help you create your own.

- **Blogs:** Depending on your time, interest, and technical skill, you and staff could contribute to a blog about life in your setting. A blog presents an opportunity to tell families about daily happenings in your setting. Limit your blog posts to objective observations only. Do no say anything controversial, embarrassing, or hurtful about the children and families in your care. Focus your blog on factual information while telling stories with humor and personality.

- **Children's portfolios:** Encourage children to take their portfolios home and share their learning with their families. Families can also reinforce children's learning by contributing to portfolios and documenting learning at home.

Communicating with families will improve the quality of care you are providing for their children. Encourage family members to reach out to you with any questions or concerns, and make it easy for them to contact you. Always inform parents of all special occasions—especially when you and the children take field trips. Even if parents provide written consent for their children to go on field trips, make sure that parents know where their child is that day.

Generally, you should share all information with families about their children's time in your setting. However, if infants in your care take their first steps in your setting, hold off on informing the parents of this major milestone until they inform you that they have seen infants take a few steps.

As an early educator, when you support the family, you also support the child.

Figure 51. Resources to Help You Create Setting Websites and Blogs

Here are a few websites that will guide you through creating and hosting a website for your setting:

Websites

- education.weebly.com
- www.shutterfly.com/share-photos/classroom-websites.jsp
- www.classicwebsites.org
- www.educatorpages.com
- doodlekit.com/home

Blogs

- edublogs.org
- education.weebly.com
- classblogs.us
- classblogmeister.com

Some of these sites will connect you to fellow early childhood bloggers around the world. You can communicate with them about your setting and share ideas about meaningful activities and experiences and how you use technology to communicate with families.

Meeting Formally With Families

Sometimes you will need to arrange a formal meeting, such as a home visit or parent–educator conference, with family members to speak about their children openly, confidentially, and at length. Parent meetings and workshops, on the other hand, allow you to discuss and share setting information and ideas as a group.

Home Visits

Home visits help you get better acquainted with families and understand the children's home environments. Conducting these visits before children enroll reduces their anxiety, eases their transition into the setting, makes the transition less emotional, and gives them an opportunity to meet early educators in their own spaces. Home visits also help you deepen your understanding of parents' values and child-rearing practices. For example, if you know the child-rearing beliefs of infants' parents, you will then be aware of the pattern of responses each infant has already learned.

Arrange the home visit with families ahead of time. Send them a postcard letting them know your intent, which is to spend time getting to know them and their child before the child's first day in your setting. Follow up with a phone call arranging a date and time for you to arrive that is convenient for the family and when the child is likely to be awake. Reassure family members that there is no need for them to make special arrangements or accommodations. Bring a colleague along with you on these visits for safety reasons and to have an extra set of eyes and ears during the conversation. If you do not speak the family's home language, choose a colleague who does. One of you can engage with the child while the other speaks with family members. When you arrive at a family's home, be friendly, open, respectful, warm, and non-judgmental. This may be a family's first impression of you, so make it a good one. Be able to pronounce their names and their child's name correctly. Help them pronounce your name, if necessary.

Smile and be welcoming. Work to put everyone at ease. Consider bringing a welcome gift for the child—something from the setting that he/she can engage with at home. This gift could be a book about the child's new early educators with photos of the different areas within the setting's learning environment. This links the child to your setting and makes the idea of being there seem like less of an unknown.

During the home visit, give the family an overview of your policies and philosophy. Introduce the welcome packet and ensure that they know about the orientation meeting. Answer their questions, address concerns, and let family members know that your goal is to work with them to ensure their child's success. Determine which family member will be dropping off the child in the morning. Discuss how the family member will stay with the child at the setting on the first few days, what the family member might do, and what he/she expects. Ask the parent to be sure to say "goodbye" to his/her child and to let the child know when he/she will return. Reassure the parent that his/her child will be safe and secure in your setting.

Discuss the first day of attendance and strategies for reducing separation anxiety. Bring a camera with you to take pictures of family members that you can display in the setting. Let parents know that having these photos in the room where the child can look at them is a

Regular parent–educator conferences allow you to speak in-depth with children's family members about their child's progress.

proven strategy for comforting children and for dealing with separation anxiety. If a family member is absent from the home, think about how you can represent him/her in your setting. For example, Orlando's father is in the military and has been deployed to another country. Get the details of Orlando's father's deployment. Ask Orlando's family for a photo of his father or video of him singing or reading to Orlando. If Orlando's feelings about his father's deployment surface at your setting, you can talk with him while looking at the photo or recording. These items reaffirm the father's place in Orlando's life.

With the parents' permission, ask the child to give you a tour of the home. Many children like to show off their rooms. As you tour the home, discover the child's favorite playthings, pets, music, and foods. This information will help you make him/her more comfortable in your setting.

On the other hand, sometimes scheduling a home visit may not be possible. Perhaps safety issues prohibit your visit. Or families may not want you to come, feeling that your visit would be an invasion of their privacy. Others may be embarrassed by their homes. Some families may be homeless. Respect families' wishes. If you cannot go to their homes, then arrange to meet at a neutral place, like a local coffee shop, community center, or library room where you can talk.

In addition to the initial home visit, we recommended that you conduct two other visits, one at midyear and another a month before the end of the program year. During the midyear home visit, focus on the child's progress and how well the setting is serving the child. Review and plan for the coming year during the end-of-year visit.

The Council for Professional Recognition offers a Child Development Associate Home Visitor credential. This nationally recognized accreditation demonstrates the competence of home visitor professionals. Visit www.cdacouncil.org and click on "Child Development Associate (CDA) Credential™" to learn more.

Parent–Educator Conferences

Regular parent–educator conferences provide you the chance to meet with children's family members, speak in-depth about the children's progress, and plan for their future time in your setting. Though the number of conferences you conduct during the year may vary, settings typically hold two or three conferences per year. You will conduct fewer conferences if you also conduct home visits. Home visits give you an opportunity to cover much of the same information.

Here are some tips that will help you conduct effective parent–educator conferences:

Schedule parent–educator conferences for dates and times that are convenient for family members. It may be difficult for them to take time off from work, so prepare for evening or weekend meetings. Offer families three date/time options that fit your schedule, and allow them to choose the one that works best for them. Once you agree on a meeting time, follow up with a reminder note. Ask parents to think about any questions or concerns they would like to discuss at the meeting. Consider suggesting topics you would like them to think about beforehand. If parents are having difficulty securing transportation or child care, do what you can to assist them.

Develop your agenda for the meeting in advance. The focus of the meeting should be the child's progress, so gather all the necessary data—including notes from your observations, formal assessments, and the child's portfolio. Summarize this information into a one-page fact sheet. This sheet will provide you with talking points for the conference and a handout for parents to take home. Organize all materials and information prior to the meeting.

Choose a comfortable, distraction-free area to conduct the conference. Choose a welcoming, comfortable area where you and the parent can be alone without distractions, such as a conference room or staff lounge. Sit on adult-sized chairs and use a table to hold your papers. Avoid sitting behind a desk opposite family members. This seating arrangement sends parents the message that you are in charge and that they are there to listen to you.

Choose a comfortable, distraction-free area to conduct the conference.

Begin the parent–educator conference with a positive anecdote about the child. Show the parent one of the child's drawings or paintings or a photo of the child's block construction from the previous week. Keep conversation natural and make sure the parent is at ease.

Be aware of cultural considerations. Maintain distance from parents and avoid physical contact if it is not culturally appropriate. If they do not speak English and you do not speak their home languages, arrange for a staff person or interpreter who speaks the language to attend the meeting as well.

Reassure families that the purpose of the meeting is to promote the interests of the child. Let them know that they can ask questions at any time and that you are both there to listen, talk, share, and plan. Inform them that you will be taking notes so that a record of the meeting and topics discussed exists. Ask family members how they think their child is progressing in your setting. Then follow parents' cues to discuss the following topics:

• How the child is adapting to the setting.

- The child's interests and engagement.

- Description of the child's growth and learning.

- The results of your observations and assessments.

- Where the child stands in relation to goals that have been set.

- Any concerns you or the child's family might have.

- What goals you and the child's family have for the child in the future.

- Next steps to take.

Reflect on how much progress the child has made. Point out changes in the child's work—including art and writing samples that indicate the child's growth. Share and refer to written and dated observations that you have taken of the child. Ask parents about growth and progress that they have noticed in the child.

Indicate any behaviors that have prompted specific concerns about a child. Avoid using labels, such as *aggressive, destructive, slow,* or *hyperactive.* Concentrate instead on concrete, documented examples of behaviors. Keep your observations objective and factual.

Although parents may be reluctant to acknowledge their children's challenges, draw out this information gently. Ask them what they have observed at home. If you think it would be helpful to provide them with information about child development, have these resources available during your meeting. Likewise, suggest materials and activities families can do with children at home. Devise a plan of action together.

If the child is on an IFSP or IEP with an identified disability, allow family members to share their feelings and experiences. Let them know what you and your colleagues are doing to ensure that the child gets the best services possible. Be open and positive in discussing the child's hard work and growth. Provide family members with the support they need, and reassure them that you are there as an advocate on their child's behalf.

End the parent–educator conference on a positive note.

Share and discuss ideas each of you has for the future, like activities, trips, the transition to the next year, or changes to the setting. Base future action steps on goals that you and family members set.

End the parent–educator conference on a positive note. Remember, you and family members are partners in supporting the child's growth and development. After the parent–educator conference, give family members a written copy of the agreed-upon next steps to help families monitor what is being done for their child and monitor progress. These steps will also serve as the starting point for the next parent–educator conference.

Parent Meetings and Workshops

At times, you will gather all the children's family members at your setting for parent meetings, which are informational or educational, and workshops, which engage family members in hands-on activities, like making musical instruments for the setting.

Planning for these group meetings is similar to your preparations for parent–educator conferences. Workshops often involve creating materials for the setting. Aim to hold workshops at your setting so that participants can use setting tools and see where the materials will be placed. This also ensures that the location is ideally located and accessible to families. However, if your setting is not large enough to accommodate the group, consider reserving a community room with adult-sized seating in a nearby library or church. Arrange for refreshments and child care, if possible. Also arrange for a translator to be pre-sent.

Publicize the meetings and workshops well in advance using flyers, e-mails to families, your website, and word of mouth. Check with family members a few days ahead of time to get an approximate head count so that you can set up the room accordingly and order enough refreshments. Ensure that everyone has directions to the meeting location and knows what time the meeting will begin.

Invite subject matter experts to speak to the attendees about the meeting topic. They lend the content extra credibility and may make the meeting seem more important to some parents. For example, invite a nutritionist to speak to parents about planning menus for children and weaning infants from the bottle. Or invite a child development specialist to speak about employing developmentally appropriate practices in child care. Allow plenty of time at every meeting and workshop for questions and answers.

During workshops, tap into family members' creativity, and make the gathering fun. Offer refreshments and play music while the parents work.

See Figures 52. and 53. for topic ideas for your next parent meeting or workshop.

Figure 52. Topic Ideas for Parent Meetings

- Positive child guidance
- Getting children ready for bedtime
- Children's allergies
- Meal planning/healthy nutrition
- Reading to children/choosing books
- Technology and young children/choosing software and applications
- Video games and young children
- Family life: dealing with separation, moving, divorce, and death
- Handling stress
- Appreciating diversity
- Fire prevention, safety, and sanitation
- Academics in the early childhood setting

- The value of play
- Ages and stages of early childhood
- Buying toys for children
- Learning opportunities for children in everyday household tasks and routines; activities to do at home with children
- Infant, toddler, and preschool development— what is and is not typical development
- Supporting dual language learning
- Supporting children with special needs
- Supporting gifted children
- Community, state, and federal resources for families
- Preparing for kindergarten

Supporting Families in Their Child's Development

During the intake/enrollment interview you conducted with each family prior to their child's first day, you may have learned the family's hopes and dreams for their child. They may have also requested information about child development. First-time parents or parents of infants and toddlers may ask you what they should be doing to facilitate their child's growth and development or whether their child is developing typically. They will want to know when they should be concerned about their child's development and what resources are available to them if they suspect their child has special needs. Here are a few things that will help address some of these concerns:

Create a resource library in your setting. Your setting's resource library should include simple child development texts with milestone charts that explain typical child development. If your setting does not have these types of books, refer parents to credible websites or borrow books from your local library on behalf of family members.

Offer parenting assistance. Conduct meetings about parenting issues or suggest reading material on specific parenting issues. Suggest local parenting classes or support groups for family members to join. Work with your supervisor to collect a resource file that includes suggested reading or local

Figure 53. Topic Ideas for Parent Workshops

- Setting up a lending library for toys, books, CDs, and prop boxes
- Computer literacy classes
- Family literacy classes
- Making milk-carton blocks
- Making lotto games
- Making family books for children
- Making musical instruments
- Planting a garden
- Landscaping the outdoor play area
- Woodworking
- Turning family recipes into recipe cards and cookbooks
- Creating science projects
- Making a puppet stage and puppets
- Journaling with children
- Planning wellness fairs with specialists, such as pediatricians, nutritionists, dietitians, and other health professionals

resources that you can share with family members. If an issue arises that involves more than one family, convert this topic into a parent meeting. Invite a pediatrician, developmental psychologist, or parent educator to lead the session and answer families' questions.

Allow parents to participate in child screenings. If your setting performs screenings of children, encourage parents to participate in this activity so that they can see how specialists assess child development. Having family members present also puts children at ease while they are being tested.

Supporting Children With Special Needs

A family with a young child who has special needs will require lots of support from you. Most likely they are new to this situation and feel overwhelmed. They will have numerous questions and few answers and will need assistance to secure the best services for their child. Family members may look to you for help in balancing their lives while caring for their child. Always begin conversations with these families by listening and being open to their insights. Be positive in discussing the child's efforts and growth. Share information and plan in partnership with the family and the child's support services team.

A family with a young child who has special needs will require lots of support from you.

Figure 54. Organizations That Support Families With Children Who Have Special Needs

Every family that has a child with a special need should become familiar with these government-funded organizations:

- National Dissemination Center for Children with Disabilities *(nichcy.org)*.

- State-level Parent Centers that are part of the Parent Technical Assistance Center Network [every state has at least one Parent Training and Information Center] *(www.parentcenternetwork.org)*.

In addition, there are organizations that focus on specific disabilities:

- The Autism Society *(www.autism-society.org)*.

- National Center for Learning Disabilities *(www.ncld.org)*.

- Learning Disabilities Association of America *(www.ldanatl.org)*.

- LD OnLine *(www.ldonline.org)*.

- United Cerebral Palsy *(ucp.org)*.

- National Down Syndrome Congress *(ndsccenter.org)*.

- National Down Syndrome Society *(www.ndss.org)*.

- Alexander Graham Bell Association for the Deaf and Hard of Hearing *(listeningandspokenlanguage.org)*.

Maintaining Confidentiality

Keep confidential any information families share with you. While your primary concern in your partner-ship with families is the child, sometimes parents will need your assistance. For example, when family members confide in you about financial or health problems, remember that these conditions will also impact their children. Awareness of this issue can help you understand children and improve their care. When you support the family, you also support the child. However, this information should remain between you and the parent.

In addition, store in locked file cabinets all paper copies of family records—including meeting and conference notes, intake summaries, child observation records, and information families share with you. If family members volunteer to help you or other staff manage paperwork, do not allow them access to any children's or family members' records other than their own. Likewise, if parent's reveal information (positive or negative) about other families or children, thank them and let them know that you maintain contact with those children's families. Also inform parents that you are unable to discuss other children or families with them. You are able to share personal data only with individuals whom family members have given you written permission to inform. For example, a support specialist may need additional information about Deanne and ask to see the child's records. Even if you know and trust the specialist, do not grant him/her access without Deanne's parents' written consent.

Keeping information confidential is not only ethical, it also builds bonds between you and families and helps you maintain their trust. ■

Chapter 12
Program Management

CDA Functional Area 12: Candidate is a manager who uses observation, documentation, and planning to support children's development and learning and to ensure effective operation of the program or group. The Candidate is a competent organizer, planner, record keeper, communicator, and a cooperative co-worker.

Program Management

Introduction

Throughout this textbook, we have discussed the various roles you play in fostering children's development and learning. You also fulfill a management role within your setting—even though you are not an administrator, director, or principal. Consider your primary responsibilities: configuring the learning environment, planning your day, implementing the curriculum, assessing and documenting children's learning, and evaluating both children's learning and the setting's successes. To perform these tasks effectively requires you to regularly manage time, space, resources, activities, and records—the same aspects of the workplace that managers handle to ensure efficiency. In this chapter, we will explore the managerial tasks that early educators need to perform to work successfully and effectively with young children:

- **Observing Children Within the Setting.**
- **Documenting Children's Learning.**
- **Planning and Evaluating.**
- **Working With Colleagues and the Community.**

Observing Children Within the Setting

Though we all observe our surroundings naturally, what is it that we really see? What are we looking for? How do we ensure that we gather the information we need?

For example, you may have observed that the children in your setting seem unusually antsy today, and no one has played in the dramatic play center. But did you also observe that it is well after 1:00 p.m.? That the children could not have outdoor time because of the torrential rain? Or that they may be bored with the items in the dramatic play center, because the inventory has not been changed in 6 months?

It is imperative to observe with purpose and from more than one vantage point. In their book *The Power of Observation*, authors Jablon, Dombro, and Dichtelmiller (2007, p. 1) define *observation* as "watching to learn." Determine what it is you want to learn and observe to gather the necessary information.

Observing With Purpose

The key to planning and implementing your curriculum successfully is your ability to take time to see what is really happening with the children in your setting. When you observe your learning environment, you obtain clear and detailed information about what works well and what needs improvement. Ask yourself the following questions as you observe the children. Use the answers to plan for individual children and the whole group, guide the children's behavior, document their learning and development, and report progress to families and colleagues.

- What the children like? How do they approach learning? For how long do they attend to a task? Do they persevere? What is their temperament like? What is their personality like?

- How can I form a relationship with each child? How can I facilitate relationships between infants, toddlers, and preschoolers? What are they interested in? What materials do they like to play with? How do they interact with family members? How do they like to be comforted?

- What cognitive, math, language/literacy, social–emotional, and physical skills does each child possess?

- What specific skills do I see children developing and working on? Has each child demonstrated growth in specific areas over time?

- Does the curriculum support child-directed speech, self-talk, and parallel talk?

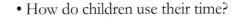

- How do children use their time?

- Are we meeting the curriculum's goals?

- Are any of the children gifted? Do any of the children have developmental delays or special requirements?

- What triggers a child's challenging behavior?

- How does this child interact with peers?

- How do the children interact with their families?

- How does the child interact with other adults?

- How well is the environment working? Are quiet areas separated from noisy areas? Are children able to play undisturbed? Are there any areas that invite children to run or create "traffic" problems?

Keep a clipboard available in the learning environment so that you can record observational notes at any moment.

- Does my setting promote inclusivity for infants, toddlers, and preschoolers?

- Does my environment encourage active exploration and play? Does my classroom arrangement allow for children to move at their own pace? Do children stay engaged? Are there areas of the room that children use regularly? If so, why? Are materials accessible to children? Do children return materials to their designated places on shelves when they are through playing with them?

- How effectively are transitions working? Is there a lot of downtime while children move from one activity to another? Does any learning take place during transitions?

- Does my setting provide consistent, predictable, and positive experiences for infants and toddlers? How effective are group care strategies? Is there an opportunity for gross motor activity? Does each child have a role?

- Are all children eating? Are children developing self-help skills?

- Is nap time working? Do most children fall asleep? Do the children who are awake keep themselves occupied? Does the layout promote children's sleeping and comply with health regulations?

Observation and Assessment

Assessment is "an ongoing process that includes collecting, synthesizing, and interpreting information about children, the program, and their instruction" (Epstein, Schweinhart, DeBruin-Parecki, & Robin, 2004). As an early educator, you assess children's learning and development to plan, implement, and evaluate the effectiveness of the experiences you provide them in your setting (Copple & Bredekamp, 2009, p. 21–22).

Subjecting children to tests or asking them to perform certain tasks only allows you to evaluate children individually. Rather, ongoing and authentic (meaningful, real-world learning experiences) assessment helps you evaluate which parts of your setting work well for the children and which parts need improvement. Evaluate children on tasks that have meaning for them in real-life contexts and in multiple ways over time. Incorporate the voice of the child, the voice of the parents, and your voice as you document children's learning. Your assessments are tied to the curriculum and/or standards you are using and are consistent with your goals and instructional practices (Losardo & Notari-Syverson, 2011).

As you observe young children's engagement throughout the day, document their learning across all do-mains to obtain complete, clear information on each child. Build on this information daily, and review it regularly to determine your setting's effectiveness and make necessary changes. This approach is known as *formative assessment*.

Observing Consistently and Effectively

Throughout this textbook, we have emphasized the significance of observation within your setting. Regularly recording your observations enables you to effectively plan and implement your curriculum for the children individually and as a whole. Your daily teaching practices are so deeply rooted in observation that you cannot perform your job effectively without it.

The purpose of your observation will drive when, where, and how you will conduct it. Observations occur in natural settings and are integrated into children's daily activities. In other words, observe children's typical behaviors during typical activities, like during personal care routines, interactions, and play. For example, if you want to examine how Brandon interacts with peers, observe him during indoor and outdoor choice times and document his interactions. Likewise, if you want to observe Jessica to monitor the development of specific fine motor skills, observe her engaged in art projects, working on puzzles, and eating lunch.

Provide early childhood staff with places to conduct their observations, like a chair in the corner of the room away from the areas where educators and children normally congregate. Some university settings are equipped with adjacent observation labs. A one-way mirror is built into the wall adjoining these rooms. Children and staff in the setting only see their reflections in the mirror. However, this mirror allows staff in the observation room to see what is happening in the setting.

Observe children regularly and frequently to get an accurate reading of their behavior. The more frequently you observe, the greater the likelihood that your observations will be truly characteristic of the child. As you conduct these regular observations, consider linguistic and cultural differences. For example, you observe that Skylar has difficulty stacking blocks to form a tower. Record this information, even though you have seen her stack blocks without difficulty before. A more accurate picture of Skylar's abilities will develop as you observe her over time. Perhaps she is not yet proficient in stacking blocks and is working to refine this skill. Therefore, your observations of her successfully stacking blocks and having difficulty make sense.

The idea of observing regularly while focusing on children's learning and development can seem over-whelming and you may wonder how you will find the time to do both. Though observation should be frequent and regular, it is not a continual task. Rather, it happens in predetermined blocks of time. Work with your colleagues to build short, informal and longer, formal observations into your daily schedule. Spend no more than 10 or 15 min on informal observations. The time period is short, but it is long enough to gather helpful data that only require quick notation. Over time, these types of observations will become a part of your daily routine. Here are some tips that will help you record observations more efficiently:

- Record the date and time of every observation and include the names of the children you observed.

- Abbreviate commonly used terms.

- Place address labels on a clipboard. String a pin through the loop in the board's clip. Keep this clipboard available in the learning environment so that you can record notes at any moment.

- Wear an apron, and store pens and index cards in the front pockets. Use a pen and index card at any time to record an observation.

- Use a tablet or smartphone app to help you write, track, and sort your observations by child, activity, or learning center.

Use a tablet or smartphone app to help you write, track, and sort your observations by child, activity, or center.

- Use checklists to observe your setting or routines quickly.

On the other hand, for more time-consuming observations, you can divide the labor among your colleagues, parent volunteers, and even other children. For example, devise a rotation schedule for your colleagues that divides your observation duties and assigns each of you to four or five children daily. While some colleagues perform observations, others work with the rest of the children. Or if you are performing an activity that involves *time sampling* (following and observing a child every 30 min), ask a parent volunteer for help. Preschoolers can assist you with *event sampling* (observing how long children engage in a particular activity). If you want to know how often children engage in art or have a snack, give them a token to drop inside a jar every time they enter the art center or have a snack. Or ask them to sign their name on a sign-up sheet when they use the writing center.

With time and practice, you will become more skilled and efficient at performing daily observations. You will be able to observe more children each day, and the time it takes you to record your observations will decrease.

Objective and Subjective Observation

You can perform various types of observations, depending on your purpose and the time you have allotted for the observation. Figure 56. lists some of those observations and the best means for recording your findings. Some of the observations you conduct will require objectivity (expressing or dealing with facts or conditions) (Carr, 2001; Carr & Lee, 2012).

To be objective in your observation, do not make assumptions or assign causes to what you observe. Avoid words, like the ones in Figure 55., that indicate that you have made any judgment about what you have seen.

Figure 55. Words to Avoid While Recording Observations

• Happy	• Mean	• Ugly	• Nice	• Artistic
• Sad	• Selfish	• Creative	• Kind	• Needy
• Angry	• Generous	• Bored	• Aggressive	• Curious
• Funny	• Sloppy	• Helpful	• Smart	• Intelligent
• Lonely	• Neat	• Lazy	• Shy	• Excited
• Bossy	• Beautiful	• Talented	• Scared	• Pretty

The words in Figure 55. represent things that are not observable. They denote abstract emotions occurring inside of a child or reflect your opinion or interpretation of the behaviors you are observing. None of the words denote actual skills or behaviors.

Objective writing is straightforward and can be challenging. Examine the following sample narratives:

> **Warren is contentedly playing at the sand table. Eduardo comes over to join him. Eduardo looks around to see whether anyone's watching (he doesn't realize that I am) and deliberately throws sand in Warren's face. Poor Warren starts crying, so I drop everything to go comfort him.**

This narrative includes opinions and judgment words, like *contentedly, deliberately,* and *poor.* Also, the observer has interpreted what he/she believes are Eduardo's motivations. However, he/she has no way of knowing why Eduardo went to the sand table and is unable to prove that he was looking around "to see whether anyone is watching."

> **Warren is at the sand table. He is making circular shell patterns in the sand. After 3 min, Eduardo takes a vacant place at the table. He picks up a shovel and then puts it down. He looks around the table and digs his hand in, pulling out a stone and putting it down. He again looks around the table. Warren picks up the stone and adds it to his pile of shells. Eduardo looks at Warren and says, "That's my stone" and throws sand at Warren's face. Warren begins to cry.**

This objective narrative provides insight into Warren's interests and skills as well as the possible roots of a conflict.

Record all your observations accurately, documenting what you see and hear in the exact order that it happens. Ensure that you capture language and dialogue verbatim.

Figure 56. Recording Your Observations

Type of Observation	Description	How to Record the Information*
Brief Notes	These quick, noteworthy entries are used to provide data on a child's interests or progress.	Note this information on an index card, an address label, a sticky note, or a log sheet. For easy access, keep these tools on a clipboard to which a pen is tied, so that you can access them quickly. Jot down a short note and date the entry.
Anecdotal Records	These records are short descriptions of incidents involving one or more child. These records provide data on a child's interests, interactions, and progress.	In addition to the description, the notations include the date of the observation, the names of the children observed, and how long the observation lasted. Record comments on index cards.
Running Records	This is the most common type of formal observation. Running records are descriptions of children's behavior recorded objectively, accurately, and chronologically over a specific length of time, typically 10–15 min. Record children's verbalizations as they occur. Use running records to provide data on a child's interests, interactions, language development, and progress.	In addition to the running record, this documentation includes the names of the children observed, the location of the observation, and how long the observation lasted.
Diary/ Journal Observations	These observations are descriptions of a child's behavior sequentially over time. They are performed with a specific purpose in mind, such as discovering what triggers a child's aggressive behavior or why a child is suddenly withdrawn.	Make entries on index cards or in a notebook.
Matrices	These grids are specific to a skill or skills. List the names of all the children you are observing. Take brief notes next to children's names regarding their skill levels. Use this format to study group progress in specific areas of development.	Record observations on the grid described.

Figure 56. Recording Your Observations (continued)

Type of Observation	Description	How to Record the Information*
Event Sampling	This observation documents the number of times a child engages in a particular behavior (such as reading books, getting into arguments, and cleaning up after free play) in a specified time period.	Make tally marks on forms designed for this purpose.
Time Sampling	Time sampling records the number of times something happens (whether or not a child socializes with others or how many times a child uses the computer or plays with LEGO® building bricks) during a specified time period (typically 30 min).	Make tally marks on forms designed for this purpose.
Checklists	Checklists allow you to gather observational information about children's skills, behaviors, or attitudes.	Place check marks on a prepared form whenever you observe the noted skill, behavior, or attitude.
Rating Scales	A way of evaluating a child's observed skill, behavior, or attitude from high to low proficiency or frequency. This type of instrument can also be used to observe the environment. Often rating scales include rubrics that specifically describe each point of a rating scale.	A number is selected that corresponds to the proficiency or frequency of the observations on each item in a prepared form.

* Although early educators have used these traditional recording methods with great success, some educators are now using tablets and smartphones to record their observations. Applications exist that allow you to speak your observations into your device.

Other observations, like learning stories, use storytelling that is subjective (based on personal feelings, prejudices, or interpretations) (Carr, 2001; Carr & Lee, 2012). Early childhood expert Margaret Carr introduced the concept of learning stories in her 2001 book, *Assessment in Early Childhood Settings: Learning Stories*. She discusses the concept further in the 2012 publication she co-authored with Wendy Lee titled *Learning Stories: Constructing Learner Identities in Early Education*.

A learning story is a narrative about infants', toddlers', or preschoolers' learning. The stories incorporate the voices of the storyteller or observer, the child, and the parent. From the perspective of the storyteller or observer, learning stories describe what is happening with the children, document what learning is taking place throughout the experience, and end with examining next steps. Storytellers will share their observations with parents and ask them to contribute to the story. Children also discuss their own experiences, feelings, and learning. See Figure 57. for a sample learning story.

Figure 57. Sample Learning Story

Building Together With Anthony and Rosie
March 2, 2013

Today, during choice time, I watched you two work together to build a tunnel for trains to go through in the block center. I could hear you developing a plan for which blocks you were going to use and where you were going to place each block to create your tunnel. You also built a very large train station that had a waiting room for passengers. It took you quite some time, but you both kept working on it until you were happy with what you created. You showed me your train station when you finished, because you were so proud of your success. You couldn't wait to tell me all about the train station and how it functioned. I then left the block center, and you continued to build the station and add more detail. Again you were so proud of your success and brought me over to see the additions that you made.

What Does This Tell Me?

As you were working together to build the tunnel and the train station, I learned that you enjoy working together. You were using your oral language skills as you were talking to each other, asking questions, and discussing what to do. You also used clear language to articulate your thoughts and ideas to each other. This ensured that you both understood each other. It took you a long time to build both the tunnel and the train station, and this demonstrated persistence and motivation. You used your knowledge of mathematics, science, and technology to build your tunnel and train station and demonstrated creativity and innovation through your novel design.

Where to Next?

I hope that you continue to work with each other. There will be lots of different activities during which you can work alongside each other. You both have an enthusiasm for building using the blocks, and it will be interesting to see whether you continue to use your creativity and innovation to make different things.

Child's Voice

[Anthony] Me and Rosie were making buildings for the trains. It was hard, because sometimes the blocks fell over, but then we got them to stand up. We made a tunnel and a train station so that the people did not get wet when they were waiting to ride the train, because it's raining.

Parent's Voice

[Early educator asks Anthony's parents whether Anthony likes to build at home.]

Anthony loves to build with LEGO® building bricks at home. He will spend hours with his big brother creating spaceships and rocket ships that they are going to send to the moon. He loves to show his dad his creations and is hoping that we can get new blocks for him to work with.

Summarizing Observational Information

After completing your observations and recording your findings, reflect on the information you have collected and determine next steps. You have already completed this work if you used your observations to complete rating scales or rubrics. Further interpretations are not necessary.

At this time, view your objective observations through a subjective lens. Review the purpose of your observations, and ask yourself the following questions:

Objective writing is straightforward and can be challenging.

- Looking at the observations as a whole, what have I learned about this child?

- Do any patterns appear?

- What might cause or explain the child's behavior?

- Does this explanation cover everything that was observed? If not, what else might be at work?

Once you have made your best guess about why a situation or behavior is occurring, devise an action plan.

How frequently you summarize your observations depends on how you will use the information. At the end of each day, you may want to review the data you collected and modify your future daily plans to incorporate what you observed. Or you may choose to review and summarize your observations weekly to distance yourself from the information, which may help you view the information objectively (Jablon, Dombro, & Dichtelmiller, 2007).

Documenting Children's Learning

Documentation refers to "the process of collecting and recording evidence about children's learning and development" (Bredekamp, 2011). Part of being a conscientious early educator is being able to effectively document the progress of both individual children and the group using a set of recorded observations. This is important for you in planning and evaluating your setting. It also enables you to share information with families and colleagues.

Portfolios

The informal and formal observations that you have performed, recorded, and stored are a significant part of documenting children's learning. Organize and store observational notes, anecdotal records, learning stories, and running records that relate to children's learning in their portfolios. *Portfolios* house information that showcases each child's interests, knowledge, attitudes, skills, and behaviors and documents a child's learning over time. Also include any observation-based checklists, tallies, rating scales, and rubrics that offer insight into the child's growth and development.

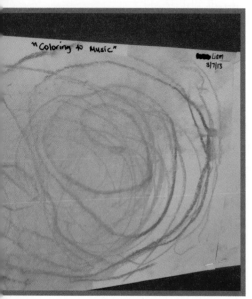

Include children's drawings and paintings in their portfolios.

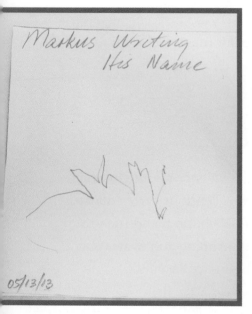

Children's portfolios should include writing samples that show the child's scribbling, letters, and words.

The bulk of children's portfolios consists of actual samples of children's work that represent development over time. These samples may be real or photographed, depending on their size and fragility. Include the following in each portfolio:

- Children's artwork—including drawings, paintings, and collages.

- Writing samples that show the child's scribbling, letters, and words.

- Number samples that show the child's mastery of counting over time.

- Books/stories the child dictated and illustrated.

- Printouts of art, writing, book publishing, and other creative experiences done on the computer.

- Lists of books read.

- Graphs of science-related experiments.

Also include photos of the following:

- Artwork—including sculptures, murals, and mobiles.

- Dishes children created during individual and group cooking activities.

- Dramatic play scenarios and puppet show skits.

- Science experiments.

- Playground feats.

- Block creations.

- Routines—including brushing teeth, washing hands, having a meal, napping, and putting on/taking off a jacket.

- Examples of the child working and interacting with others.

- The child on field trips.

Date these samples and write notes on them (e.g., "Chandler is sorting leaves by color, which she was not able to do a month ago"). In addition, incorporate children's voices. For example, you might want to also include the following in children's portfolios:

- Notes and comments from children about their work—including audio descriptions of artwork recorded by staff.

- Recorded discussions with children about favorite things to do at home and at the setting.

- Transcripts of recorded conversations among children, their peers, and adults.

- The child's personal reactions to learning experiences.

- Children's evaluations of their work and experiences.

Finally, a child's portfolio might contain information about the child that family members or specialists have contributed. This information should be relevant to the child's growth, learning, or development.

Portfolios—like all forms of learning documentation—should tell a complete story (Seitz, 2008). In this case, the story is about an individual child's learning and development over the course of the year. Having this information will help you plan for the children and share information with families. It will also help children revisit their learning.

Documenting the Group's Learning

Use documentation to illustrate the learning and development of a group of children. For example, this documentation could summarize a project investigating children's interest in rain, describe a memorable field trip to a farm, or highlight how children have mastered a specific concept, like *measurement*. You can also incorporate all the children's voices in a learning story.

Use bulletin boards, presentation boards, or documentation panels to prepare this documentation to display at children's eye level. You can also use web diagrams, maps, photographs, slide shows, video clips, or artifacts to tell the story. For example, if you wanted to show children learning to measure, display photos of them measuring plants they have grown, marking their own height against a wall, and using a ruler to measure each other's feet in a shoe store dramatic play scenario. You could also include videos and photos of children using other objects to measure, such as twine to measure a sand-table toy or their own feet to determine the dimensions of a cage for a pet guinea pig. Children can narrate these photos, explaining what object they used to measure

Program Management

and how their methods worked. The idea is to track children's thought processes as they use and refine this skill. The more media you use, the richer your story will be.

This form of storytelling "shows children that their work is valued, makes parents aware of class learning experiences, and allows teachers to assess both their teaching and the children's learning. In addition, dialogue is fostered with other educators. Documentation becomes a tool for teacher research, reflection, collaboration, and decision making" (Institute for Early Childhood Education and Research [IECER], 2012, p. 1).

Planning and Evaluating

Early educators need to plan for both individual children and the group. They also need to observe and evaluate the plans as they are being implemented to know if they are serving the children optimally. Planning and evaluation should be part of a never ending cycle of curriculum planning, with each feeding into the next:

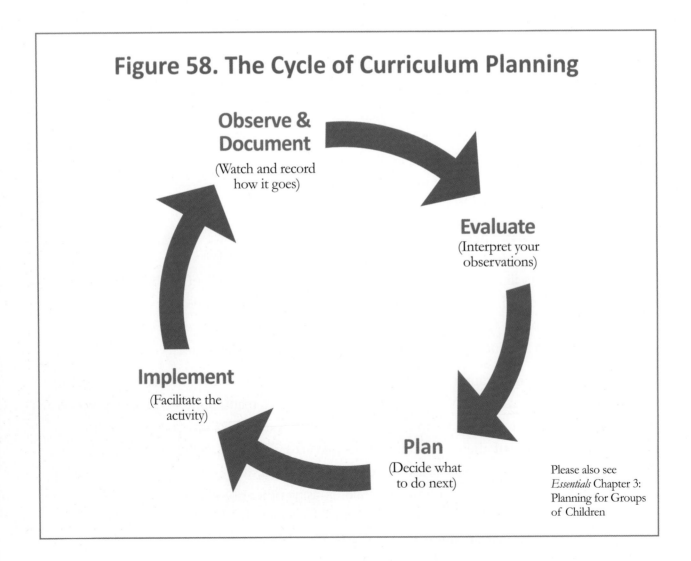

Figure 58. The Cycle of Curriculum Planning

Observe & Document
(Watch and record how it goes)

Evaluate
(Interpret your observations)

Implement
(Facilitate the activity)

Plan
(Decide what to do next)

Please also see *Essentials* Chapter 3: Planning for Groups of Children

Planning for Individual Children

All the observations, assessment data, parental input, and work samples you have collected provide you with a wealth of information about each child, including the following:

- **Specific skills, behaviors, and attitudes across the domains of development and learning.** Document whether children are meeting specific standards, regardless of which standards you follow—state, Head Start, or your own setting's standards. At least one of the rating scales, rubrics, or observational scales you have administered will provide you data on each child's physical, social–emotional, cognitive, math, language, and literacy skills in relation to the standards your setting uses. Samples of a child's work, transcripts of conversations with the child, and input from families provide examples of these skills in action that enrich your observations.

For example, you know that Miranda has strong fine motor and prosocial skills and that she is knowledgeable of print concepts in both English and Spanish. This information will help you plan and implement a curriculum that will build on her many abilities, challenge her, and honor her home language while increasing her English literacy. Similarly, you also know that Mohammed has good gross motor and social skills, but he needs help refining his fine motor skills. You can create meaningful opportunities for him to work specifically on his fine motor skills, like using scissors to cut construction paper or plastic knives to cut apples. You could also help Mohammed continue to work on his gross motor and social skills with activities that will challenge him just enough to keep him engaged.

- **The child's interests.** Your observational records will reveal in which area of the setting children most of their time; the materials they like to use; their favorite books, stories, and games; and any other likes and dislikes. This information tells you how to effectively plan for children's

Observation, evaluation, planning, and implementation are all parts of an ongoing cycle.

learning, set up the learning environment, engage them in conversation, plan meaningful experiences, and make them feel valued and validated.

- **The child's temperament and learning style.** Your observational records will reveal the contexts in which each child learns best, letting you know the best approaches for teaching individual children. As a responsive early educator, create opportunities for one-on-one interactions with the children throughout the day and respond to children's verbal and nonverbal cues. Adapt the learning environment so that all children can move freely according to their own abilities and interests.

- **The child's friendships.** Observational notes and family members' input will reveal details about a child's relationships with peers and adults. Use this information when planning for small group activities, conducting group meetings, and supporting children during meal and snack times.

- **Special requirements.** Screening and family input forms, parental conversations, and observations will help you provide a child with needed support during situations, like divorce, or if a child has an identified special need addressed in an IFSP or IEP. You can also accommodate parents' requests concerning their children, like dietary restrictions.

Organize this information with a planning form, like the one in Figure 59., that gathers and summarizes the observational and supporting data you have collected on a child. Moreover, defining the learning objectives for each child guides your teaching practices. You will focus on what is important for children to learn and help them master these objectives in a developmentally and culturally appropriate way.

Your program should designate how often you will set learning goals for children and complete individual planning forms. At a minimum, perform these tasks three times a year—a month after the child's first day in your setting, midyear, and at the end of the year. If you conduct assessments on children's learning more often, complete a planning form each time you gather new data. Understanding children's interests, knowledge, skills, and abilities allows you to set appropriate goals and customize your teaching practices accordingly.

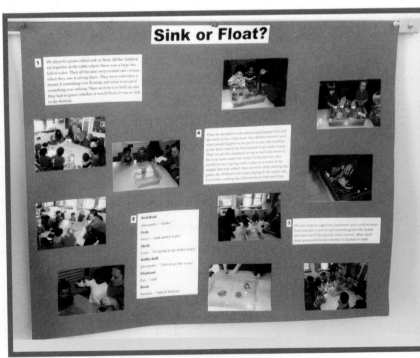

Use bulletin boards, presentation boards, or documentation panels to illustrate the learning and development of a group of children.

Figure 59. Individual Planning Form

Child's name: _____ Date of birth: _____

Child's home language: _____ Class/group: _____

Early educator's name: _____ Date: _____

Developmental Summaries (include sources of information for each)

Gross motor skills: _____

_____

_____

Fine motor skills: _____

_____

_____

Social-emotional skills: _____

_____

_____

Language skills: _____

_____

_____

Math skills: _____

_____

_____

Science and social studies skills: _____

_____

_____

Figure 59. Individual Planning Form (continued)

Other cognitive skills: _____

_____

_____

Child socializes with: _____

_____

_____

This child's interests are: _____

_____

_____

Summary of major strengths: _____

_____

_____

Summary of areas for growth: _____

_____

_____

Special needs/supports (if applicable): _____

_____

_____

Learning standards to work on with this child:

1. _____

2. _____

3. _____

Goals for this planning period:

1. _____

2. _____

3. _____

Planning for Children on an IFSP or IEP

Through your screenings and other observations of children, you may suspect delays or other disabilities. Discuss your observations with your supervisor and then with the children's families. Specialists will then evaluate the child to determine whether they have disabilities in accordance with the Individuals with Disabilities Education Act (IDEA). If disabilities are present, specialists, along with you, children's parents or guardians, special educators, and any teaching colleagues in your setting, will write an Individualized Family Service Plan (IFSP) or Individualized Education Program (IEP) for the children.

Some children may enroll in your setting with an IFSP or IEP already in place which states their strengths, specifies learning goals, and designates what services your setting must provide. In accordance with children's IFSPs/IEPs, make accommodations that will enable them to fully participate in the setting's curriculum. This may mean rearranging the setting or providing children with adapted toys, eating utensils, and computer software and hardware. Or you may need to present information differently or repeatedly. You may need to work with a special educator to learn how to interact with the children in the best way.

Resources

According to the National Dissemination Center for Children with Disabilities (NICHCY, 2010), consult the following resources to learn more about children's specific special needs:

- United Cerebral Palsy (UCP) *www.ucp.org.*

- Autism Society *autism-society.org.*

- The Arc *www.thearc.org.*

- Division for Early Childhood (DEC) through the Council for Exceptional Children *www.dec-sped.org.*

- National Association for the Education of Young Children (NAEYC) *www.naeyc.org.*

- The Early Childhood Technical Assistance Center (NECTAC) *ectacenter.org*

Planning for Groups of Children

In Chapter 3, you learned that spending time with small groups of children allows you and other early educators to engage more deeply with a few children at a time, working on specific skills or knowledge. For example, you may notice that a few children need help refining their fine motor skills. Other children may be interested in cars. This information will help you choose new materials, like books, songs, rhymes, and stories, to include during large group time with preschoolers and small group activities with all children. Reflect on your observations and documentation of children's learning to support and evaluate your planning and implementation. Following the planning cycle will increase your effectiveness each day. Posting your weekly planning on the wall informs parents of the learning that children are engaging in each day. Refer to Chapter 3 for additional information on planning for infants, toddlers, and preschoolers.

Working With Colleagues and the Community

Consider all the adults involved in your setting—family members, colleagues and other staff, program volunteers, community service personnel, licensing staff, special educators, social workers, substitute early educators, supervisors and other administrators, trainers, medical and dental personnel, and consultants. When you think about all your responsibilities, remember that you are not alone. All these adults play a role in your setting, are influenced by the way you manage it, and are personally invested in the children's and the setting's success. Establish and manage successful, cooperative, and respectful relationships with all of these individuals. Be an exemplary early educator and set a good example for the children.

Colleagues and Supervisors

Professional relationships are integral to program management. Present yourself with professionalism and be open to others' opinions, beliefs, and ideas. You work with your co-workers, supervisor, and setting director every day, and you have established relationships with each of them. Work to maintain strong relationships and partnerships with these colleagues. Collaborate to ensure that the children are supervised appropriately. This helps maintain order in the learning environment and keep everyone safe and healthy. For example, if two toddlers are playing in a small wading pool outdoors, two adults must supervise the children. In infant and toddler settings, ensure that the same staff members work with the same infants and toddlers to support the development of strong emotional bonds.

How frequently you summarize your observations depends on how you will use the information.

Handling Disagreements and/or Criticism

If you observe an early educator doing something that conflicts with early childhood best practices, express your concern to this person in private. Discuss the situation to see whether there might be an explanation. If there's not an explanation, monitor the situation before discussing it with a supervisor—unless what you observed is harmful to another person. If you have an issue with what a colleague has said, even if it is in a group setting, speak to this person in private and discuss the matter calmly. Tell the early educator in a nonaccusatory way what upset you. State the facts, avoid blame, and manage your emotions to help you reach a resolution.

If your supervisor gives you negative criticism or feedback, avoid blame and manage your emotions. You may think that your supervisor has misunderstood something or made a conclusion based on incorrect or incomplete information. Try to supply your supervisor with correct or additional information. However, you are responsible for managing the setting, and your supervisor is responsible for managing you. Consider the situation from this person's perspective. Your supervisor may be offering you this feedback constructively to help you become a better early educator, so do not be offended. Accept this person's feedback for what it is: a different perspective on which you can reflect. Upon reflection, decide whether your supervisor offered valuable feedback that will help you improve in the future.

Substitute Early Educators

Substitute early educators are often introduced into the setting without spending any time with you or your children. Prepare to make their time in the setting effective. Create a binder for them that includes the following:

- A class list, with the names of every child and family member (preferably with photographs).

- All appropriate paperwork, including necessary forms (e.g., injury report forms).

- The list of who is authorized to pick up each child at the end of the day.

- A copy of your setting's rules, daily schedule, and lesson plans that cover the time period the substitute educator will work at your setting.

- A list of any of the children's special needs (e.g., who has an IFSP/IEP, who has food allergies, or who might need to leave the setting early that day).

External Community

Special educators, social workers, trainers, community service representatives, and consultants are all there to offer you, families, and children support and supplemental services. In essence, they are there to enhance the services you provide. Meet the specific community members who support your setting and the families you serve. Among the organizations that you may want to contact are those that handle the following:

- Domestic violence, including child abuse and neglect and spousal abuse (e.g., organizations like Parents Anonymous, Child Protective Services, and local shelters).

- Homelessness (e.g., local shelters).

- Nutrition (e.g., the local extension office).

- Screening children for disabilities (e.g., Child Find).

- Translation/interpretation.

- Resources for families.

Figure 60. lists some of the typical resource agencies that serve families. Add to this list by searching the Internet or collaborating with your supervisor. Speak with your licensing representative if you need help locating the services your local community offers. ■

Figure 60. Community Resources

- Parenting programs
- American Red Cross
- Easter Seals
- Safety groups
- Mental health clinics
- Medical clinics
- Dental clinics
- Supplemental Nutrition Assistance Program (SNAP)
- WIC— Special Supplemental Nutrition Program for Women, Infants, and Children
- Financial planning

- Child care resource and referral
- Cultural resource groups
- Resale shops
- Educational supply stores
- Food cooperatives and farms
- Public library
- Children's bookstores
- Early and periodic screening programs
- Local children's museums and the zoo
- Any service organization that might contribute resources or funds to your program

Chapter 13
Professionalism

CDA Functional Area 13: Candidate makes decisions based on knowledge of research-based early childhood practices, promotes high-quality in child care services, and takes advantage of opportunities to improve knowledge and competence, both for personal and professional growth and for the benefit of children and families.

Professionalism

Introduction

Everything that you do as an early educator—including keeping children safe and healthy, fostering their learning and development, maintaining strong partnerships with their families, and managing a successful setting—commands a commitment to professionalism. Your conduct should always reflect early childhood education best practices and illustrate your dedication to your career and the children in your care. In this chapter, we will focus on the following skills and traits that contribute to your professionalism:

- **Educating With Intentionality and Reflection.**
- **Making Ethical Decisions.**
- **Articulating Values, Vision, and Passion.**
- **Continuing Your Professional Development.**
- **Advocating for Children and Families.**

As an early education professional, you are a lifelong learner—meaning that you are engaged in an ongoing process of remaining abreast of the latest industry research and best practices, refining your own education practices, and growing in your profession.

Educating With Intentionality and Reflection

As an early childhood education professional, you must possess a firm knowledge of childhood development, remain abreast of current research in the field, and have a desire to support and scaffold each child's learning. These characteristics help you educate with purpose and reflect on the effectiveness of your teaching practices.

Intentional Early Educators

Ann Epstein, author of *The Intentional Teacher* (2007, p. 4), explains that "to be 'intentional' is to act purposefully, with a goal in mind and a plan for accomplishing it." Intentional early educators observe the children in their care, determine their needs, employ best teaching practices based on these needs, and reflect on the experience as a whole. They avoid employing certain practices simply because they were trained to do so or because other early educators or colleagues employ

Council for Professional Recognition • 800-424-4310

the same practices. Instead, intentional early educators continue to question and think about how and why a teaching practice supports children's learning. They are problem-solvers and independent thinkers. These educators ask themselves questions like the following:

- What do the children in my setting need?

- What information do I need to gather to determine this need?

- What are my goals for the children in my setting?

- What is the plan for achieving these goals?

- What additional information do I need to meet these goals?

- In what areas do I need to develop professionally to support my teaching practices?

Educators Deb Curtis and Margie Carter (2009, p. 299) say that intentionality is a disposition:

> Intentional teachers. . .have certain qualities that distinguish them from teachers who depend on curriculum activity books, follow the same theme plans year after year, or struggle daily to get the children involved in anything productive. The knowledge and skills of master teachers are not necessarily different from those of other teachers. Rather, these professionals have become improvisational artists. They have developed a set of attitudes and habits of mind that enable them to respond readily to the classroom dynamics and multiple needs of children.

The National Association for the Education of Young Children says that successful early educators are always intentional (Copple & Bredekamp, 2009, pp. 33–34):

> Whenever you see a great program, one in which children are learning and thriving, you can be sure that teachers (and the administrators who support them) are highly intentional. In everything good teachers do—creating the environment, considering the curriculum, and tailoring it to the children as individuals—they are purposeful and thoughtful. As they make myriad decisions, big and small, they keep in mind the out-comes they seek. Even in responding to unexpected opportunities—"teachable moments"— intentional teachers are guided by the outcomes the program is trying to help children reach and by their knowledge of child development and learning.

> Having their objectives and plans in mind, intentional teachers are well prepared to tell others—parents, administrators, colleagues—about what they are doing. Not only do they know what to do, they also know why they are doing it and can describe their purposes.

Epstein (2007; 2009) adds that knowledge of child development, curriculum, observational assessments, and proven instructional strategies distinguish intentional educators from nonintentional ones.

To become a more intentional early educator, Schiller (2007) recommends the following three-step approach:

1. **Familiarize yourself with child development and research knowledge to understand which outcomes are best suited to the children in your care.** Be knowledgeable and observant. Understand how children of different ages, dispositions, and interests learn best and the accommodations you need to make to foster their learning.

2. **Select targeted, desired outcomes for children while planning.** Intentional early educators must be exceptional planners who configure the environment, choose materials, and question children in ways that promote learning.

3. **Learn from the children you teach. Understand that teaching involves following *and* leading.** This may mean that you let the children decide what they will engage in and learn. For example, some children might enjoy sorting leaves, so allow them to do so. At times, you also facilitate adult-guided learning while exploring materials or technology, like a new microscope. To follow up, intentional educators might then lead small groups in playing a lotto matching game or allowing children to create their own matching games.

Figure 61. Characteristics of Intentional Education

- **High expectations.** Early educators believe that children are capable. They expect children to challenge themselves and try harder. This expectation leads children to want to be capable and competent.

- **Planning and management.** Early educators set appropriate learning objectives for each child, but are flexible enough to alter plans to include the children's new interests and unexpected needs.

- **Learning-oriented classroom.** Early educators and children are dedicated to the processes of learning and value the progress.

- **Engaging activities.** Early educators choose activities that are meaningful, related to children's lives, and designed to challenge children without frustrating them.

- **Thoughtful questioning.** Early educators customize questions for children to learn what they are thinking and to help stimulate their ideas.

- **Feedback.** Unlike praise, which signifies approval, feedback helps children evaluate their work by presenting information, identifying problems in thinking, helping children make predictions, and challenging children to use their imaginations and creativity.

Reflection

Intentionality and reflection coincide. When you analyze your teaching approach through reflection, you can improve your approach and become even more effective *and* intentional.

Reflection is a process of observation and self-evaluation. Reflective early educators analyze how they have responded to past experiences and how other involved individuals reacted. These educators then use this analysis to make changes in their setting, alter their teaching practices, and make decisions in the future.

Reflection not only provides insight about your learning community and your practices, but it also helps you learn more about you and what makes you "tick." As an intentional early educator, you understand who you are as a human being and as a professional. This self-awareness helps you become more objective and thoughtful about your relationships with children and the way you approach teaching. Reflection helps you to better understand the following characteristics about yourself:

- Your values and beliefs.

- Your strengths and weaknesses.

- Your teaching philosophy.

- Your teaching and learning styles.

- How past experiences have influenced you.

- Your understanding and appreciation of diversity.

- Your understanding and appreciation of dual language learners.

- Your understanding of individual children and their learning and behaviors.

- Your role in the teaching process.

- Your "authentic" self.

Early educators who regularly practice reflection find that it also helps them uncover hidden biases and dispositions. Anti-bias educators Louise Derman-Sparks and Julie Olsen Edwards (2010) challenge early educators to reflect on how their personal biases might affect their practices. For example, they explain that through reflection, an early educator realized that 4-year-old Jack always "got on her nerves," because his facial expressions were similar to her father's, with whom she had a difficult relationship. Once she made this connection, she became aware of her tendencies and bonded with Jack in a way she had not been able to before. Another early educator realized that Annette and DeMarcus's tardiness annoyed her, because she had been raised to believe tardiness was disrespectful. She ignored their parents when they tried to explain that the bus was often late arriving at the bus stop. However, she realized that she had not considered that the children's families could not afford cars and that public transportation, though unreliable, was their only means of transportation. Once she was able to view the situation from their perspective, she was able to change her own perspective about the children's tardiness and become more supportive of their families' needs.

Reflective early educators are better able to do the following:

- Slow down and take a better look at how they teach.

- Discover patterns in children's behaviors.

- See how they translate theory into practice.

- Determine whether they act with professionalism.

- Recognize and change behaviors that are not consistent with their standards of effective teaching.

- Determine whether their teaching addresses the learning standards.

- Uncover issues that impact children's learning.

- Use multiple sources of information to inform their practice.

The type of reflection improves your planning and teaching practices. Ask yourself *what* and *why* questions to increase your own awareness about your teaching practices and the impact they have on children. Questions like What am I doing? and Why am I doing it? will lead you to ask: How effective is my teaching? What are the children learning? What can I do better? When planning weekly, your reflections on children's learning and growth will help you plan your environment and all experiences throughout the day. For example, you might note that Trey's rapidly developing body and nerves may be causing his fussiness, so you may develop a plan for providing constant soothing primary care when he is at the setting and communicate this strategy with his family.

Reflective early educators are better able to discover patterns in children's behaviors and uncover issues that impact children's learning.

Realizing the Truth During Reflection

Today, in the dramatic play center, you joined the children's "dinner" and talked with them about what they were eating. You and the children laughed and they vied for your attention. You introduced new words, like *spatula* and *seafood*.

As you reflect on the activity that afternoon, you remember it being a success. You remember thinking to yourself that the children's parents would be very pleased to hear them using these more advanced vocabulary words. However, your original intent for entering the children's play was to observe firsthand how they were assuming roles and learning skills, such as following rules and regulating their emotions. As you talked with the children, you planned to talk about foods and introduce new words. When you analyze the experience, though, you realize that you lost track of these goals and were caught up in having fun with the children. You realize that you were flattered that the children were vying for your attention and that you began performing for them. At the time, you considered the experience a success, but the experience was more of a success for you than for the children. They received less out of the experience than you did. Realizing these facts convinces you that in the future, you will need to remain focused on the children to be the best educator you can be for them.

Reflective early educators take a step back and decide whether they are executing plans as effectively as possible. They also tend to be more flexible and open to change than early educators who are not reflective (Stewart, 2010). The following are some tips to help you become a better reflective early educator (Beal, n.d.; Carter, Cividanes, Curtis, & Lebo, 2010; Pappas, 2010; Neas, 2012):

- Make time in your schedule for reflection. Just as you made a commitment to observe children every day, commit to reflection time as well. Once you build reflection consistently into your regular schedule in an organized, systematic way, the process will become automatic.

- Focus your reflections. Begin reflecting by focusing on a specific concept, like how you teach individual children, rather than a broad, abstract concept, like how you teach in general.

- Work with a mentor or coach who can guide and critique your work.

- Choose several children each day to focus your reflection on, much like your observations.

- Try journaling/keeping a diary. These daily or weekly entries will help you maintain a healthy perspective. Describe your immediate reaction and the children's reactions to experiences. Pose questions for yourself that you can reflect on in future entries.

- Try collaborative journal writing. Ask your fellow early educators to join you in keeping diaries that you can share and critique while writing feedback for each other.

- Hold regular discussion groups with peers about their observations

- Record video of yourself teaching. Watch and critique this recording.

- Ask a colleague to observe your teaching and give you feedback.

- Ask the children for feedback about their day. Listen carefully—they know success when they experience it.

- Use learning stories, which you learned about in Chapter 12. Write these stories as first-person narratives and focus on a specific child or group of children in your setting with whom you have been working. Write about your experiences interacting with the child or group and discuss your thinking along with your interpretations of the child's actions and thoughts. Think about your actions and goals, offer interpretations, and describe your feelings. Once you have written your story, invite the children and their family members to incorporate their voices into the story.

Making Ethical Decisions

Throughout the day, you make decisions about everything that happens within the setting—including the following:

- What materials should I make available?

- Is it too cold to go outside today?

- Who should be the helpers who will set the tables for lunch?

- Should I extend outdoor play, since the children are having so much fun discovering worms?

- Should I let Charles keep napping or wake him for snack, since he ate so little for lunch today?

While all of these decisions require thought and consideration, once you make them, you will probably give them little additional thought. However, other situations, like the following, require you to reflect on what you believe and what you know is best for children before making a decision:

Finding a Mentor

Consider asking a skilled early childhood professional whom you trust and respect to serve as your mentor. Many professionals choose mentors to guide and support them as they face challenges, celebrate successes, and grow professionally. The National Association for the Education of Young Children and Child Care Aware® of America (2011, p.10) define "mentoring" as a "relationship-based process between colleagues in similar professional roles, with a more-experienced individual with adult learning knowledge and skills, the mentor, providing guidance and example to the less-experienced protégé or mentee. Mentoring is intended to increase an individual's personal or professional capacity, resulting in greater professional effectiveness." This relationship should be mutually beneficial. You and your mentor should be clear about the nature of the relationship and the expectations you have of each other so that you can learn and grow together.

Figure 62. Reflective Questions

Devise a list of questions to guide your reflection. There are no *right* or *wrong* questions. Just choose those that will be most useful to you. Here are some suggestions:

- What captures my attention as the children engage, explore, and talk with each other and with me?

- What do I notice in the children's faces and actions?

- What is the child drawn to and excited about?

- How do schedules and routines influence this experience?

- How might the child's culture be influencing the experience?

- What learning goals can be addressed?

- Was the instructional objective met? How do I know children learned what I intended them to?

- Were the children productively engaged? How do I know?

- Did I alter my instructional plan as I taught the lesson? Why?

- What additional assistance, support, and/or resources would have further enhanced this lesson?

- If I had the opportunity to teach the lesson again to the same group of children, would I do anything differently? What? Why?

(Carter & Curtis, 2009; Sesay-St. Paul, n.d.)

- DeVon has been very aggressive lately, shoving and pushing other children. You want to consult with his parents so that you can devise a plan of action. However, you believe DeVon's father will punish him severely if he hears how his son has been behaving.

- Four-year-old Austin's dad tells you that he does not want his son wearing any of those "sissy" dress-up clothes anymore. "If Austin grows up to be a homosexual, it will be your fault," his father says.

- Aaliyah's mother has volunteered to help you with filing. You accept her offer and give her the keys to the filing cabinets. When you check to see whether she needs your help, you find her looking at other children's portfolios.

- At a staff meeting, your supervisor Tony tells a joke about a particular ethnic group. A few people laugh. Most, like you, look uncomfortable.

- Eddie, a 4-year-old on an IEP for emotional disturbance, exhibits screaming outbursts. By constantly working with him in ways his specialists suggest, his screaming has lessened somewhat, and he is contributing more to the program. You are very pleased by this progress. However, by devoting so much time to Eddie, you have devoted less time to many of the other children.

- At a parent conference, Sean's mother tells you that her boyfriend is rough with Sean when he talks back to him. After confiding in you, she begs you not to tell anyone.

- Maddy's father arrives at your setting wanting to spend time with his child, though a court order restricts his access.

What would you do in these situations? To some early educators, the solutions may be readily apparent but difficult to implement. Other early educators may be unsure about the best course to follow and need guidance.

For those instances in which the answer is not obvious, The National Association for the Education of Young Children (NAEYC, 2005) has developed a *Code of Ethical Conduct* (www.naeyc.org/positionstatements/ethical_conduct) that outlines early educators' professional responsibilities. As Feeney (2010, p. 72), one of the document's authors, writes, "Professional ethics helps us as early childhood educators to think about our responsibilities to children, families, communities and society and to address some of the difficult situations we face every day." Because the document applies to all members of the profession, it represents the values and moral responsibility of the field, not of any one individual. It thus relieves early educators from concerns that they are acting alone. When you apply the *Code of Ethical Conduct*, you represent the early childhood field to society.

Using the *Code of Ethical Conduct* as a moral compass in decision-making is straightforward. It is divided into four areas of ethical responsibility:

- **Children:** "Our paramount responsibility is to provide care and education in settings that are safe, healthy, nurturing, and responsive for each child."

- **Families:** "Because the family and the early childhood practitioner have a common interest in the child's well-being, we acknowledge a primary responsibility to bring about communication, cooperation, and collaboration between the home and early childhood program in ways that enhance the child's development."

- **Colleagues:** "In a caring, cooperative workplace, human dignity is respected, professional satisfaction is promoted, and positive relationships are developed and sustained."

- **Community and society:** "Our responsibilities to the community are to provide programs that meet the diverse needs of families, to cooperate with agencies and professions that share the responsibility for children, to assist families in gaining access to those agencies and allied professionals, and to assist in the development of community programs that are needed but not currently available."

Each area provides early educators with ideals and principles they can use in decision-making. One principle, P-1.1 (in "Ethical Responsibility to Children," Section 1), presides over all others:

> Above all, we shall not harm children. We shall not participate in practices that are emotionally damaging, physically harmful, disrespectful, degrading, dangerous, exploitative, or intimidating to children.

Much like a physician's Hippocratic oath, this principle is the early childhood field's credo. It guides your teaching practices and how you support children in learning, growing, and thriving.

As an early educator, consult the Code for help in making decisions in difficult situations, like one of the situations presented earlier:

> *Four-year-old Austin's dad tells you that he does not want his son wearing any of those "sissy" dress-up clothes anymore. "If Austin grows up to be a homosexual, it will be your fault," his father says.*

While your immediate reaction may be to address the father's veiled threat or to explain your personal views to Austin's parents, neither response is appropriate. Section 1, Principle P-1.3 of the Code states the following:

> We shall not participate in practices that discriminate against children by denying benefits, giving special advantages, or excluding them from programs or activities on the basis of their sex, race, national origin, immigration status, preferred home language, religious beliefs, medical condition, disability, or the marital status/family structure, sexual orientation, or religious beliefs or other affiliations of their families.

As an early educator, you treat girls and boys equally according to this principle. Children of both genders have access to all materials within the setting. Therefore, children can try on whatever clothes they want as they explore male and female roles. Trying on clothing of the other gender is very typical behavior for children under 5 years old and an opportunity for them to learn social skills, rules, and roles.

Section 2, Ideal I-2.6 states, "to acknowledge families' childrearing values and their right to make decisions for their children." Acknowledge Austin's dad's right to hold different values about what his child should be exposed to in your setting.

Principle P-2.2 provides further guidance, "We shall inform families of program philosophy, policies, curriculum, assessment system, cultural practices, and personnel qualifications, and explain why we teach as we do—which should be in accordance with our ethical responsibilities to children."

According to the Code, you might decide that the best course of action is to find a quiet place in the setting to meet informally with Austin's parents and respectfully discuss the setting's philosophy toward pretend dress-up play. Acknowledging their concern, explain why you do what you do and gently reassure Austin's father that there is no relationship between dress-up play and later sexual identity. To reinforce your position, give him copies of research papers to take home and read. Many parents will accept what you have to say when they see there is research and sound reasoning behind the practice.

Another one of the previous situations presents a real dilemma:

> *At a staff meeting your supervisor Tony tells a joke about a particular ethnic group. A few*
> *people laugh. Most, like you, look uncomfortable.*

You are offended that Tony is telling a joke that stereotypes an ethnic group. This joke, in your opinion, is racist. However, Tony is the offender. On the one hand, you want to confront him at that moment before the entire group. On the other hand, you fear that a confrontation would get you fired.

One of the core values in the *Code of Ethical Conduct* "Preamble" is, "Respect diversity in children, families, and colleagues." Your supervisor's joke was disrespectful to that particular ethnic group and to all people who value diversity.

Section 3, Principle P-3A.2 provides sound advice: "When we have concerns about the professional behavior of a co-worker, we shall first let that person know of our concern in a way that shows respect for personal dignity and for the diversity to be found among staff members, and then attempt to resolve the matter collegially and in a confidential manner."

Perhaps you could make an appointment to speak to Tony privately. During this meeting, tell him in a factual, nonaccusatory way that you were offended by the joke he told at the staff meeting and that it made you uncomfortable. Let him know that you wanted to bring it to his attention, because he may not have been aware of how the joke was received. Communicate your own reaction to the joke, not the reactions of others. Tell your supervisor that you felt that it was important to discuss the situation with him because of the principles outlined in the *Code of Ethical Conduct*.

The *Code of Ethical Conduct* will help alleviate some of the stress involved in making decisions in difficult situations. This does not mean that the situations will be less difficult or that the decisions will be less painful to implement. What it does mean, though, is that your decisions will be ethical and professional.

As an early educator, you treat girls and boys equally according Section 1,
Principle P-1.3 of the NAEYC Code of Ethical Conduct.
Children of both genders have access to all materials within the setting.

Articulating Values, Vision, and Passion

The ability to confidently and clearly explain how children learn, what children learn, and your developmentally appropriate teaching practices that support learning will strengthen your outreach and relationships within your community.

Become familiar with the early learning standards that govern your setting. Search the Internet to find your state's official early learning standards. These standards represent the learning outcomes that all children in your setting need to master. Be prepared to explain how your setting addresses these goals.

Be prepared to articulate additional state and federal laws, like the Individuals with Disabilities Education Act (IDEA) that emphasizes the strengths and abilities of children and their families. Knowing what IDEA requires will help you work with families and explain how you will continue to support them.

Explain the following when discussing your setting's best teaching practices with families or others in the community:

- Configuring and using your learning environment.

- Valuing play.

- Scheduling activities for the day.

- Programming for dual language learners.

- Fostering community partnerships in support of children and families.

- Guiding young children's behavior.

- Assessing children's development and learning.

- Fostering creativity.

- Scaffolding learning with a variety of teaching strategies.

- Enhancing problem-solving abilities.

- Making the curriculum accessible to children with disabilities.

- Partnering with families.

- Preventing child abuse.

The more active you are in a professional group—attending meetings and volunteering for committee or board positions—the more you will get out of your membership.

Professionalism

Specify the age groups of the children you work with to help others visualize these experiences.

Your ability to explain these practices will strengthen you as a spokesperson for the setting and as a valued communicator for families and community programs. This ability places you in a position of responsibility, and designates you as the voice of your setting—and of early childhood education—to your community.

Continuing Your Professional Development

As an early education professional, you are a lifelong learner—meaning that you are engaged in an ongoing process of remaining abreast of the latest industry research and best practices, refining your own education practices, and growing in your profession.

The early childhood education field, like many other industries, does not remain static. New research informs our practice. As the knowledge base grows, the field's thinking around how children learn shifts. For example, there was a time when early childhood educators depended on scripted lessons, and nearly all preschool activities were educator-directed. Research determined that child-directed activities driven by children's discoveries are more effective. Today, the intentional early educator opts for a balanced approach, where learning is scaffolded.

Education trends emerge because research supports them. These trends reflect the research of the time period. While we are confident that our practices today are best, research may lead us in another direction in the future, and the field will need to make accommodations. If you are not aware of new research, you will not be able to shift your teaching practices and provide what children need at that time.

Professional development opportunities help you stay current in the field, improve your teaching practices continually, and work toward being a better early educator. Lilian Katz (n.d.) believes that early educators' needs for professional development will vary as they mature in their jobs and gain confidence working with children. While beginning early educators are in survival mode, they need on-site support and mentoring. After a year or two at the job,

Resource & Referral Agencies

Ninety-nine percent of zip codes in the United States have a local, government-funded Child Care Re-source and Referral agency (CCR&R) that serves two primary purposes:

1. To assist parents in finding child care programs in their area that match their needs.

2. To raise the quality of child care by providing professional development opportunities and various resources to local early educators and early childhood professionals.

Search the Internet to find the name of your local CCR&R and learn about all the ways that it can support you and your work.

though, most early educators are confident and are improving their teaching practices. They benefit from attending conferences, reading journals, and meeting with colleagues. In contrast to beginning early educators, seasoned early educators—with at least 3 years of on-the-job experience—are able to take a step back and look at their job performance in perspective. They crave depth and insight. For them, journals, conferences, seminars, and continuing education offer the kind of information they need to excel in their careers.

Early childhood professional development opportunities come in various forms:

- Journals, books, newsletters, and websites.

- On-site training and technical assistance.

- Self-training courses (DVD or online).

- Meetings, trainings, and conferences offered by local, state, regional, and national or international professional organizations and associations.

- Observation visits to other settings.

- Seminars and institutes.

- Community college, university, and graduate degree courses/programs.

Attend meetings and activities that will help you perform your job more effectively. Being able to connect and talk with other early childhood professionals can be invigorating. Check with your supervisor to see whether your setting recommends specific professional development opportunities and whether financial support for these opportunities is available. If your setting is unable to support you financially, there may be additional funding available from the state or your community.

Connecting With Professional Groups

Each day, most early educators are only in contact with the colleagues at their settings. However, there is value in connecting with the professional groups in your community and networking with others in the early childhood education field. Some professional groups may be local chapters of national organizations. Others are state groups or groups of locally active early educators.

Find out what early childhood education professional groups are active in your area. Contact several of these groups to learn more about their activities and membership. Visit their websites and peruse their newsletters, journals, or other literature. Select one or two organizations, attend a few of their meetings, and join the group if you think that it and the members are a good fit for you. The more active you are in the group—attending meetings and volunteering for committee or board positions—the more you will get out of your membership.

See Figure 63. for a list of the major groups dedicated to serving early childhood professionals:

Figure 63. Early Childhood Education Professional Groups

Organization	What It Does/ It's Mission
Association for Childhood Education International™ (ACEI) www.acei.org 1101 16th St. NW, Ste. 300 Washington, DC 20036 (202) 372-9986 • (800) 423-3563	ACEI's mission to promote child well-being continues to strengthen and evolve with the changing world environment. The organization commits to bridging the gap between global initiatives and local needs.
Child Care Aware® of America (formerly the National Association of Child Care Re-source and Referral Agencies [NACCRRA]) www.childcareaware.org 1515 N. Courthouse Rd., 11th Floor Arlington, VA 22201 (800) 424-2246	Child Care Aware® of America works with more than 600 state and local Child Care Resource and Referral agencies nation-wide. These agencies help ensure that families in 99% of all populated ZIP codes in the United States have access to high-quality, affordable child care. To achieve its mission, Child Care Aware® leads projects that increase the quality and availability of child care, undertake research, and advocate child care policies that positively impact the lives of children and families.
The Division for Early Childhood (DEC) www.dec-sped.org 27 Fort Missoula Rd., Ste. 2 Missoula, MT 59804 (406) 543-0872 3415 S. Sepulveda Blvd. Suite 1100, Unit 1127 Los Angeles, CA 90034 (406) 543-0872 • (310) 428-7209	The Division for Early Childhood promotes policies and advances evidence-based practices that support families and enhance the optimal development of young children who have or are at risk for developmental delays and disabilities.
Military Child Education Coalition (MCEC) www.militarychild.org 909 Mountain Lion Circle Harker Heights, TX 76548 (254) 953-1923	The MCEC's work is focused on ensuring quality educational opportunities for all military children affected by mobility, family separation, and transition. The organization performs research, develops resources, conducts professional institutes and conferences, and develops and publishes resources for all constituencies.
National Association for Bilingual Education (NABE) www.nabe.org 8701 Georgia Ave., Ste. 700 Silver Spring, MD 20910 (240) 450-3700	NABE's mission is to advocate for the nation's bilingual and English language learners and families and to cultivate a multi-lingual, multicultural society by supporting and promoting policy, programs, pedagogy, re-search, and professional development that yield academic success, value native language, lead to English proficiency, and respect cultural and linguistic diversity.

Figure 63. Early Childhood Education Professional Groups (continued)

Organization	What It Does/ It's Mission
National Association for the Education of Young Children (NAEYC) www.naeyc.org 1313 L St. NW, Ste. 500 Washington, DC 20005 (202) 232-8777 • (800) 424-2460	NAEYC is the world's largest organization working on behalf of young children. The organization's mission is to serve and act on behalf of the needs, rights, and well-being of all young children with a primary focus on the provision of educational and developmental services and resources.
National Black Child Development Institute (NBCDI) nbcdi.org 1313 L St. NW, Ste. 110 Washington, DC 20005 (202) 833-2220 • (800) 556-2234	Since 1970, the National Black Child Development Institute has remained steadfast in its mission "to improve and advance the quality of life for Black children and their families through education and advocacy." As a membership organization with volunteer-based affiliate networks in over 20 communities across the country, NBCDI serves as a national resource agency providing strengths-based programs, publications, policy, and trainings focused on the following areas: health and wellness, early childhood development and education, elementary and secondary education, literacy, child welfare, and family engagement.
National Head Start Association (NHSA) www.nhsa.org 1651 Prince St. Alexandria, VA 22314 (703) 739-0875 • (866) 677-8724	The National Head Start Association is a nonpartisan, not-for-profit organization committed to the belief that every child, regardless of circumstances at birth, has the ability to succeed in life. The organization's mission is to coalesce, inspire, and support the Head Start field as a leader in early childhood development and education. The opportunities offered by Head Start lead to healthier, empowered children and families and stronger, more vibrant communities. NHSA is the voice for more than 1 million children, 200,000 staff, and 1,600 Head Start grantees in the United States.
Southern Early Childhood Association (SECA) www.southernearlychildhood.org 1123 S. University Ave., Ste. 255 Little Rock, AR 72204 (501) 221-1648 • (800) 305-7322	Since 1948, the Southern Early Childhood Association has brought together preschool, kindergarten, and primary teachers and administrators; caregivers; program directors; and individuals working with and for families, to promote quality care and education for young children. Over 20,000 individuals working in every aspect of child care and early childhood belong to SECA.

Figure 63. Early Childhood Education Professional Groups (continued)

World Organization for Early Childhood Education (OMEP-USA) www.omep-usnc.org Southern Illinois University Carbondale, IL 62901 (618) 453-4246	OMEP-USA is one of more than 70 national committees (chapters) in World OMEP, a nonprofit child advocacy organization associated with the United Nations, UNICEF, UNESCO, the World Health Organization, and others working for healthy, peaceful, equitable, sustainable, and just environments for the world's children today and in the future.
ZERO TO THREE: National Center for Infants, Toddlers and Families www.zerotothree.org 1255 23rd St. NW, Ste. 350 Washington, DC 20037 (202) 638-1144	ZERO TO THREE is a national, nonprofit organization that provides parents, professionals, and policymakers the knowledge and know-how to nurture early development. The organization's mission is to ensure that all babies and toddlers have a strong start in life.

Approach your professional development with intentionality and reflection. Analyze your professional development and ask: Is the training I have received useful to me and the job that I perform? Is my teaching improving? Am I getting what I want out of my professional development? Are there other areas that I want to explore further or that are challenging in my professional practice? If you are not satisfied with the answers to these questions, consider making some changes to your professional development plan. Reconsider the groups you have joined and your level of involvement, and ask your colleagues, supervisor, and mentor for advice.

Advocating for Children and Families

The early childhood education field needs professionals like you to join the ranks of advocates who work to rally societal support for the industry. Until society values early childhood education—and those who teach young children—our work will always be undervalued.

Being an early childhood education advocate means that you continually educate the public about the early childhood field—much in the same way that you educate them about your setting—and work with groups to influence legislation in support of the industry. These groups often have the staff, resources, and experience to help you advance the cause more effectively. For example, organizations like NAEYC and the Ounce of Prevention Fund (www.ounceofprevention.org), a Chicago-based group that funds and advocates for nationwide access to high-quality early childhood programs, have toolkits that help you frame your message, target elected officials, and work with the media. These organizations supply you with factsheets and data to help you present your position to your intended audience.

Figure 64. lists some of the other leading organizations that advocate for children and families.

Figure 64. Advocacy Organizations

Organization	What It Does/ It's Mission
Alliance for Justice (AFJ) www.afj.org 11 Dupont Circle NW, 2nd Floor Washington, DC 20036 (202) 822-6070	Alliance for Justice is a national association of over 100 organizations, representing a broad array of groups committed to progressive values and the creation of an equitable, just, and free society. AFJ works to ensure that the federal judiciary advances core constitutional values, preserves human rights and unfettered access to the courts, and adheres to the even-handed administration of justice for all Americans.
Alliance for Early Success (formerly the Birth to Five Policy Alliance) www.earlysuccess.org PO Box 6756 Leawood, KS 66206 (913) 642-3490	The Alliance for Early Success (formerly the Birth to Five Policy Alliance) is a catalyst for putting vulnerable young children on a path to success. As an alliance of state, national, and funding partners, the organization's goal is to advance state policies that lead to improved health, learning, and economic outcomes for young children, starting at birth and continuing through age 8.
Center on the Developing Child at Harvard University developingchild.harvard.edu 50 Church St., 4th Floor Cambridge, MA 02138 (617) 496-0578	Since 1969, CLASP has been a trusted resource, a creative architect for systems change, and one of the country's most effective voices for low-income people. The organization develops and advocates for federal, state, and local policies to strengthen families and create pathways to education and work.
Children's Defense Fund (CDF) www.childrensdefense.org 25 E St. NW Washington, DC 2001 (800) 233-1200	The Children's Defense Fund is a nonprofit child advocacy organization that has worked for 40 years to ensure a level playing field for all children. The organization champions policies and programs that lift children out of poverty; protect them from abuse and neglect; and ensure their access to health care, quality education, and a moral and spiritual foundation.
Council for Exceptional Children (CEC) www.cec.sped.org 2900 Crystal Dr., Ste. 1000 Arlington, VA 22202 (888) 232-7733	The Council for Exceptional Children is the largest international professional organization dedicated to improving the educational success of individuals with disabilities and/or gifts and talents. CEC advocates for appropriate governmental policies, sets professional standards, provides professional development, advocates for individuals with exceptionalities, and helps professionals obtain conditions and resources necessary for effective professional practice.

Professionalism

Figure 64. Advocacy Organizations (continued)

Organization	What It Does/ It's Mission
First Five Years Fund www.ffyf.org 33 W. Monroe St., Ste. 2400 Chicago, IL 60603 (312) 453-1835	The First Five Years Fund helps America achieve better results in education, health, and economic productivity through investments in quality early childhood education for disadvantaged children from birth to age 5. The organization provides knowledge, data, and advocacy, helping federal policymakers make investments in the first 5 years of a child's life that create greater returns for all.
National Center for Children in Poverty (NCCP) www.nccp.org 215 W. 125th St., 3rd floor New York, NY 10027 (646) 284-9600	Founded in 1989 as a division of the Mailman School of Public Health at Columbia University, NCCP is a nonpartisan, public interest research organization. The organization is one of the nation's leading public policy centers dedicated to promoting the economic security, health, and well-being of America's low-income families and children. NCCP uses research to inform policy and practice with the goal of ensuring positive outcomes for the next generation.
National Council of La Raza (NCLR) www.nclr.org Raul Yzaguirre Building 1126 16th St. NW, Ste. 600 Washington, DC 20036 (202) 785-1670	The National Council of La Raza—the largest national Hispanic civil rights and advocacy organization in the United States—works to improve opportunities for Hispanic Americans. Through its network of nearly 300 affiliated community-based organizations, NCLR reaches millions of His-panics each year in 41 states, Puerto Rico, and the District of Columbia. To achieve its mission, NCLR conducts applied research, policy analysis, and advocacy, providing a Latino perspective in five key areas: as-sets/investments, civil rights/immigration, education, employment and economic status, and health.
National Women's Law Center www.nwlc.org 11 Dupont Circle NW, #800 Washington, DC 20036 (202) 588-5180	Since 1972, the National Women's Law Center has expanded the possibilities for women and girls in the United States. The organization has succeeded in getting new laws on the books and enforced, litigating groundbreaking cases all the way to the Supreme Court, and educating the public about ways to make laws and public policies work for women and their families. Today, an experienced staff of nearly 60 continues to advance the issues that cut to the core of women's lives in education, employment, family and economic security, and health and reproductive rights—with special attention given to the needs of low-income women and their families.
Voices for America's Children www.voices.org 1000 Vermont Ave. NW, Ste. 700 Washington, DC 20005 (202) 289-0777	Voices for America's Children is the nation's largest network of multi-issue child advocacy organizations. The organization's nonprofit, non-partisan network spans almost every state, the District of Columbia, and the U.S. Virgin Islands. It leads advocacy efforts at the community, state, and federal levels to improve the lives of all children, especially those most vulnerable, and their families.

Figure 65. Ways to Advocate for Children

- Be the spokesperson for your setting. As an early childhood education professional, you should be able to communicate your program's story—its philosophy and research-based practices. Because you already represent your setting to families and community organizations, you are well-equipped to explain the importance of quality early childhood education to funders and policymakers.

- Team up with your colleagues to form your own advocacy group.

- Join forces with school boards and other local organizations.

- Promote and help plan local events for NAEYC's Week of the Young Child™ (www.naeyc.org/woyc). The purpose of this event is to focus public attention on the needs of young children and their families and to recognize the early childhood programs and services that meet those needs.

- Vote to elect candidates who support children and families.

- Attend town meetings and ensure that early childhood issues get on the agendas.

- Introduce the families you serve to advocacy opportunities.

- Start or join letter writing campaigns to urge all elected officials to support stronger and better child care legislation.

- Write letters to the editor or *op-eds* (feature articles usually opposite the editorial page) to magazines, journals, and newspapers offering your point of view.

- Start a blog about your work in the field. Include photos of children playing and learning. Remember to get prior written permission from parents to use their children's photos in this way.

- Invite policymakers to visit your program.

- Hold an open house where visitors can visit your setting and witness developmentally appropriate practices in action.

- Identify a specific children's issue for which to advocate (e.g., obtaining more services for children with disabilities or homeless children, promoting diversity, or increasing salaries in child care).

Identify the many opportunities around you to become a champion for early childhood education. You have the option to lead efforts, like those listed in Figure 65., or work behind-the-scenes writing brochures or grant proposals, gathering data for policy papers or surveys, or developing advocacy videos. See where your talents and passions lead you, and find a way to show your support for children and families. Young children need **you**. Families need **you**. The profession needs **you**.

You are the ideal advocate because you have completed this textbook and are putting the concepts you learned into practice. ■

References

Chapter 1 Safe

American Academy of Child and Adolescent Psychiatry. (2012). Lead exposure in children affects brains and behavior. Retrieved from http://www.aacap.org/App_Themes/AACAP/docs/facts_for_families/45_lead_exposure_in_children_affects_brain_and_behavior.pdf

American Academy of Pediatrics, American Public Health Association, & Health Resources Association. (2011). *Caring for our children: National health and safety performance standards—Guidelines for early care and education programs* (3rd ed.). Washington, DC: American Public Health Association.

Centers for Disease Control and Prevention. (2012). Lead: Prevention tips. Retrieved from http://www.cdc.gov/nceh/lead/tips.htm

Centers for Disease Control and Prevention. (2013). Sudden unexpected infant death (SUID). Retrieved from http://www.cdc.gov/sids/

National Association for the Education of Young Children. (2011). *Code of ethical conduct: Supplement for early childhood program administrators.* Retrieved from http://www.naeyc.org/files/naeyc/file/positions/Supplement%20PS2011.pdf

National Safe Kids Campaign. (2004). Drowning fact sheet. Retrieved from http://www.preventinjury.org/PDFs/DROWNING.pdf

Pesheva, E. (2010, March 22). A dangerously tasty treat: The hot dog is a choking hazard. Retrieved from http://www.hopkinschildrens.org/A-Dangerously-Tasty-Treat-The-Hot-Dog-is-a-Choking-Hazard.aspx

Savage, M. A., Kawanabe, I. T., Mejeur, J., Goehring, J. B., & Reed, J. B. (2002). *Protecting children: A guide to child traffic safety laws.* Retrieved from National Highway Traffic Safety Administration website: http://www.nhtsa.gov/staticfiles/nti/enforcement/pdf/ProtectingChildren.pdf

Skin Cancer Foundation. (n.d.). Sun safety tips for infants, babies, and toddlers. Retrieved from http://www.skincancer.org/prevention/sun-protection/children/sun-safety-tips-for-infants-babies-and-toddlers

State of New York Department of Health. (n.d.). What child care providers need to know about lead. Retrieved from http://www.health.ny.gov/publications/2517.pdf

University of Nebraska Cooperative Extension.. (n.d.). Toxicity of common houseplants. Retrieved from http://lancaster.unl.edu/factsheets/031.htm

U.S. Fire Administration. (2003). A fact sheet on fire safety for babies and toddlers. Retrieved from http://www.usfa.fema.gov/campaigns/usfaparents/downloads/508/USFA_FireFacts_508.pdf

Chapter 2 Healthy

American Academy of Pediatrics. (2009). **Caring for your baby and young child: Birth to age 5** (5th ed.). New York, NY: Bantam Books.

American Academy of Pediatrics, American Public Health Association, & National Resource Center for Health and Safety in Child Care and Early Education. (2011). *Caring for our children: National health and safety performance standards—Guidelines for early care and education programs* (3rd ed.). Elk Grove Village, IL: American Academy of Pediatrics.

American Academy of Pediatrics, American Public Health Association, & National Resource Center for Health and Safety in Child Care and Early Education. (2011). Important information about new bleach concentration. *In Caring for our children: National health and safety performance standards—Guidelines for early care and education programs* (3rd ed.). Elk Grove Village, IL: American Academy of Pediatrics. Retrieved from http://cfoc.nrckids.org/Bleach/Bleach.cfm

Aronson, S. S. (2012). *Healthy young children: A manual for programs* (5th ed.). Washington, DC: National Association for the Education of Young Children.

Centers for Disease Control and Prevention. (2010). Proper handling and storage of human milk. Retrieved from http://www.cdc.gov/breastfeeding/recommendations/handling_breastmilk.htm

Centers for Disease Control and Prevention. (2012). Vaccine safety: Thimerosal. Retrieved from http://www.cdc.gov/vaccinesafety/concerns/thimerosal

Colker, L. J. (2009). *Sure start program guide.* Arlington, VA: Department of Defense Education Activity.

Dixon, S., & Rosas, A. (n.d.). Just a spoonful of sugar: Tips for giving medicine to kids. Retrieved from http://www.pampers.com/just-a-spoonful-of-sugar-tips-for-giving-medicine-to-kids

Karageorge, K., & Kendall, R. (2008). *The role of professional child care providers in preventing and responding to child abuse and neglect.* Washington, DC: Office on Child Abuse and Neglect, Children's Bureau.

National Association for the Education of Young Children. (2011). *Code of ethical conduct and statement of commitment.* Washington, DC: Author

The Nemours Foundation. (2012). Breast or bottle? Retrieved from http://kidshealth.org/parent/pregnancy_newborn/formulafeed/breast_bottle_feeding.html#

Santos, A. (2010). New Massachusetts regulation requires tooth brushing in child care settings. Retrieved from http://www.examiner.com/working-moms-in-boston/new-massachusetts-regulation-requires-tooth-brushing-child-care-settings

University of Michigan Health System. (2012). Children with chronic conditions. Retrieved from http://www.med.umich.edu/yourchild/topics/chronic.htm

U.S. Department of Agriculture, & U.S. Department of Health and Human Services. (2010). *Dietary guidelines for Americans, 2010* (7th ed.). Washington, DC: U.S. Government Printing Office. Retrieved from http://health.gov/dietaryguidelines/dga2010/DietaryGuidelines2010.pdf

Chapter 3 Learning Environment

Colker, L. J. (2009). *Sure Start program guide.* Arlington, VA: Department of Defense Education Activity.

Copple, C., & Bredekamp, S. (Eds.). (2009). *Developmentally appropriate practice in early childhood programs serving children from birth through age 8* (3rd ed.). Washington, DC: The National Association for the Education of Young Children.

Derman-Sparks, L., & Edwards, J. O. (2010). *Anti-bias education for young children and ourselves.* Washington, DC: The National Association for the Education of Young Children.

Dodge, D. T., Colker, L. J., & Heroman, C. (2002). *The creative curriculum for preschool* (4th ed.). Washington, DC: Teaching Strategies.

Early Head Start National Resource Center. (2010). *Create an environment of YES!* Retrieved from http://eclkc.ohs.acf.hhs.gov/hslc/tta-system/ehsnrc/Early%20Head%20Start/early-learning/curriculum/environment_nycu.htm#CreateanEnvironmentofYES

National Infant & Toddler Child Care Initiative. (2010). *Infant/toddler curriculum and individualization.* Retrieved from ZERO TO THREE: National Center for Infants, Toddlers and Families website: http://www.zerotothree.org/public-policy/state-community-policy/nitcci/multidisciplinary-consultant-module-3.pdf

Nemeth, K. N. (2012). *Basics of supporting dual language learners: An introduction for educators of children from birth through age 8.* Washington, DC: National Association for the Education of Young Children.

Owocki, G. (1999). *Literacy through play.* Portsmouth, NH: Heinemann.

Chapter 4 Physical

Albrecht, K., & Miller, L. G. (2000). *Innovations: Infant toddler development.* Beltsville, MD: Gryphon House.

American Academy of Pediatrics. (2013). Ages & stages: Baby 0–12 mos. Retrieved from http://www.healthychildren.org/english/ages-stages/baby/Pages/default.aspx

Benelli, C., & Yongue, B. (2004). *Supporting young children's motor skill development.* Farmington Hills, MI: The Gale Group.

Berk, L. E. (2012). *Child development* (9th ed.). New York, NY: Pearson.

Bredekamp, S. (2013). *Effective practices in early childhood education: Building a foundation* (2nd ed.). Boston, MA: Pearson.

Centers for Disease Control and Prevention. (2012). Developmental milestones. Retrieved from http://www.cdc.gov/ncbddd/actearly/milestones/index.html

Gallahue, D. L., Ozmun, J. C., & Goodway, J. D. (2011). *Understanding motor development: Infants, children, adolescents, adults* (7th ed.). Dubuque, IA: McGraw-Hill.

Gould, P., & Sullivan, J. (2004). *The inclusive early childhood classroom: Easy ways to adapt learning centers for all children.* Beltsville, MD: Gryphon House.

Huffman, M., & Fortenberry, C. (2011). Helping preschoolers prepare for writing: Developing fine motor skills. *Young Children, 66* (5), 100–103.

National Association for Sport and Physical Education. (2004). *Active start: A statement of physical activity guidelines for children from birth to age 5* (2nd ed.). Reston, VA: Author.

Shonkoff, J. P., & Phillips, D. A. (Eds.). (2000). *From neurons to neighborhoods: The science of early childhood development.* Washington, DC: The National Academies Press.

Teacher Support Force. (2011). *Brain exercises and physical coordination are benefits of physical education.* Robbinsville, NC: Author. Retrieved from http://www.teacher-support-force.com/brainexercises.html

Chapter 5 Cognitive

Bronfenbrenner, U. (1994). Ecological models of human development. *International Encyclopedia of Education, 3* (2), 1643-1647.

Center on the Developing Child at Harvard University. (2011). *Building the brain's "air traffic control" system: How early experiences shape the development of executive function* (Working Paper 11). Retrieved from http://developingchild.harvard.edu/index.php/resources/reports_and_working_papers/working_papers/wp11/

Cohen, J., Onunaku, N., Clothier, S., & Poppe, J. (2005). *Helping young children succeed: Strategies to promote early childhood social and emotional development.* Retrieved from ZERO TO THREE: National Center for Infants, Toddlers and Families website: http://main.zerotothree.org/site/DocServer/help_yng_child_succeed.pdf

Copple, C., & Bredekamp, S. (Eds.). (2009). *Developmentally appropriate practice in early childhood programs serving children from birth through age 8.* Washington, DC: National Association for the Education of Young Children.

Gordon, A. M., & Williams-Browne, K. (2013). *Beginnings & beyond: Foundations in early childhood education* (9th ed.). Independence, KY: Cengage Advantage Books.

Hart, B., & Risley, T. R. (1995). *Meaningful differences in the everyday experience of young American children.* Baltimore, MD: Brookes Publishing.

National Association for the Education of Young Children, & The Fred Rogers Center for Early Learning and Children's

Media at Saint Vincent College. (2012). *Technology and interactive media as tools in early childhood programs serving children from birth through age 8.* Retrieved from http://www.naeyc.org/files/naeyc/PS_technology_WEB.pdf

Nemeth, K. N. (2012). *Basics of supporting dual language learners: An introduction for educators of children from birth through age 8.* Washington, DC: National Association for the Education of Young Children.

Sarama, J., & Clements, D. (2006). Mathematics in kindergarten. *Young Children, 61*(5), 38–41.

Schiller, P. (2010). Early brain development research review and update. *Exchange,* 26–30.

Shonkoff, J. P., & Phillips, D. A. (Eds.). (2000). *From neurons to neighborhoods: The science of early childhood development.* Washington, DC: The National Academies Press.

Spiegel, A. (Presenter). (2008, February 21). Old-fashioned play builds serious skills. In National Public Radio (Producer), *Morning edition* [Radio program]. Retrieved from http://www.npr.org/templates/story/story.php?storyId=19212514

Tomlinson, H. B., & Hyson, M. (2012). Cognitive development in the preschool years. In C. Copple (Ed.), *Growing minds: Building strong cognitive foundations in early childhood* (pp. 13–23). Washington, DC: National Association for the Education of Young Children.

Chapter 6 Communication

Anderson, R. C. (1985). *Becoming a nation of readers: The report of the national commission.* Champaign-Urbana, IL: University of Illinois.

Birner, B. (n.d.). Language acquisition. Retrieved from http://lsadc.org/info/ling-faqs-lang_acq.cfm

Braunger, J., & Lewis, J. P. (2006). *Building a knowledge base in reading* (2nd ed.). Newark, DE: International Reading Association.

California Department of Education. (2000). *Prekindergarten leaning development guidelines.* Sacramento, CA: Author.

Colker, L. J. (2010a). America's early childhood literacy crisis. *Teaching Young Children, 3* (4), 27–29.

Colker, L. J. (2010b). Getting a grip on things: Building fine motor skills. *Teaching Young Children, 3* (5), 26–28.

DeBruin-Parecki, A., Perkinson, K., & Ferderer, L. (2005). *Helping Your Child Become a Reader.* Washington, D.C.: U.S. Department of Education. Retrieved from http://www2.ed.gov/parents/academic/help/reader/reader.pdf.

Dickinson, D. K., & Tabors, P. O. (Eds.). (2001). *Beginning literacy with language: Young children learning at home and school.* Baltimore, MD: Brookes.

Dodici, B. J., Draper, D. C., & Peterson, C. A. (2003). Early parent–child interactions and early literacy development. *Topics in Early Childhood Special Education, 23* (3), 124–136.

The Economist. (2006, December 19). The art of conversation: Chattering classes: The rules for verbal exchanges are surprisingly enduring. *The Economist.* Retrieved from http://www.economist.com/node/8345491

Espinosa, L. M. (2010). *Getting it right for young children from diverse backgrounds: Applying research for improved practice.* Upper Saddle River, NJ: Pearson.

Fox, M. (2008). *Reading magic: Why reading aloud to our children will change their lives forever.* New York, NY: Mariner Books.

Goldenberg, C. (2008). Teaching English language learners: What the research does—and does not—say. *American Educator, 32* (2), 8–23, 42–44.

Hart, B., & Risley, T. R. (2002). *Meaningful differences in the everyday experiences of young American children.* Baltimore, MD: Brookes.

Hart, B., & Risley, T. R. (2003). The early catastrophe: The 30 million word gap by age 3. *American Educator, 27* (1), 4-9.

Morrow, L. M., & Gambrell, L. B. (2002). Literature-based instruction in the early years. In S. B. Neuman &. D. K. Dickinson (Eds.), *Handbook of early literacy research* (pp. 348–360). New York, NY: The Guilford Press.

National Early Literacy Panel. (2008). *Developing EARLY LITERACY: Report of the National Early Literacy Panel. A scientific synthesis of early literacy development and implications for intervention.* Washington, DC: Author.

Nemeth, K. N. (2012). *Basics of supporting dual language learners: An introduction for educators of children from birth through age 8.* Washington, DC: National Association for the Education of Young Children.

Reading Is Fundamental. (n.d.). Choosing good books for young children. Retrieved from http://rif.org/us/literacy-resources/articles/choosing-books-for-young-children.htm

Severns, M. (2010). Dual language learners: What early educators need to know [Blog post]. Retrieved from: http://earlyed.newamerica.net/blogposts/2010/dual_language_learners_what_early_educators_need_to_know-28196

Strickland, D., & Riley-Ayers, S. (2006). *Early literacy: Policy and practice in the preschool years.* New Brunswick, NJ: National Institute for Early Education Research at Rutgers University.

Tabors, P. O. (2008). *One child, two languages: A guide for early childhood educators of children learning English as a second language* (2nd ed.). Baltimore, MD: Brookes.

Tabors, P. O., Beals, D. E., & Weizman, Z. O. (2001). You know what oxygen is? Learning new words at home. In D.K. Dickinson & P.O. Tabors (Eds.), *Beginning literacy with language: Young children learning at home and school.* Baltimore, MD: Brookes.

Trelease, J. (2006). *The read-aloud handbook* (6th ed.). New York, NY: Penguin Books.

Weikle, B., & Hadadian, A. (2003). Emergent literacy practices among parents of preschool children with and without disabilities. *International Journal of Special Education, 18* (1), 80–99.

Chapter 7 Creative

Chrysikou, E. G. (2012, July). Put your creative brain to work. *Scientific American Mind*, 24–31.

Colker, L. J. (n.d.). Creative arts: Child development tracker: 3 to 4. Retrieved from http://www.pbs.org/parents/childdevelopmenttracker/three/creativearts.html

Denac, O. (2008). A case study of preschool children's musical interests at home and school. *Early Childhood Education Journal, 35* (5), 439–444.

Isenberg, J. P., & Jalongo, M. R.. (2010). *Creative thinking and arts-based learning: Preschool through fourth grade* (5th ed.) Upper Saddle River, NJ: Merrill.

Kemple, K. M., & Nissenberg, S. A. (2000). Nurturing creativity in early childhood education: Families are part of it. *Early Childhood Education Journal, 28* (1), 67–71.

Kenney, S. (1997). Music in the developmentally appropriate integrated curriculum. In C. H. Hart, D. C. Burts, & R. Charlesworth (Eds.), *Integrated curriculum and developmentally appropriate practice: Birth to age eight.* Albany, NY: SUNY Press.

Parlakian, R., & Lerner, C. (2010). Beyond twinkle, twinkle: Using music with infants and toddlers. *Young Children, 65*(2), 14–19.

Runco, M. A. (Ed.). (2012). *The creativity research handbook: Volume 2.* New York, NY: Hampton Press.

ZERO TO THREE. (n.d.). Learning to write and draw. Retrieved from http://www.zerotothree.org/early-care-education/early-language-literacy/writing-and-art-skills.html

Chapter 8 Self

Aboud, F. E. (2008). A social-cognitive developmental theory of prejudice. In S. M. Quintana & C. McKown (Eds.), *Handbook of race, racism, and the developing child* (pp. 55–71). Hoboken, NJ: John Wiley & Sons.

American Psychological Association. (2011). Resilience guide for parents & teachers. Retrieved from http://www.apa.org/helpcenter/resilience.aspx#

Bredekamp, S. (2011). *Effective practices in early childhood education: Building a foundation.* Boston, MA: Pearson.

Brody, J. E. (2012). A richer life by seeing the glass half full [Blog post]. *The New York Times.* Retrieved from http://well.blogs.nytimes.com

Brooks, R., & Goldstein, S. (2003). 10 ways to make your children more resilient. Retrieved from http://www.familytlc.net/resilient_children_preteen.html

Center on the Social and Emotional Foundations for Early Learning. (n.d.). Teaching your child to: Identify and express emotions. Retrieved from http://csefel.vanderbilt.edu/familytools/teaching_emotions.pdf

Copple, C., & Bredekamp, S. (Eds.). (2009). *Developmentally appropriate practice in early childhood programs serving children from birth through age 8.* Washington, DC: National Association for the Education of Young Children.

Derman-Sparks, L., & Edwards, J. O. (2010). *Anti-bias education for young children and ourselves.* Washington, DC: National Association for the Education of Young Children.

Dombro, A., Jablon, J., & Stetson, C. (2010). Powerful interactions begin with you. *Teaching Young Children, 4* (1), 12–14.

Fox, E. (2012). *Rainy brain, sunny brain: How to retrain your brain to overcome pessimism and achieve a more positive outlook.* New York, NY: Basic Books.

Galinsky, E. (2012). Success in parenting—Avoiding the happiness and self-esteem traps. Retrieved from http://www.huffingtonpost.com/ellen- galinsky/parenting-advice_b_1651941.html

Hirschfeld, L. A. (2008). Children's developing conceptions of race. In S.M. Quintana & C. McKown (Eds.), *Handbook of race, racism, and the developing child* (pp. 37–54). Hoboken, NJ: John Wiley & Sons.

Hopkins, G. (2004). How can teachers develop students' motivation—and success? Retrieved from http://www.education-world.com/a_issues/chat/chat010.shtml

Hurley, K. (2012). Building resiliency in preschoolers. Retrieved from http://practicalkatie.com/2012/05/18/building-resiliency-in-preschoolers/

Hyson, M. (2008). *Enthusiastic and engaged learners: Approaches to learning in the early childhood classroom.* New York, NY: Teachers College Press.

Joseph, G. E., & Strain, P. S. (2010). *Enhancing emotional vocabulary in young children.* Nashville, TN: Center on the Social and Emotional Foundations for Early Learning.

Katz, P. A. (2003). Racists or tolerant multiculturalists? How do they begin? *American Psychologist, 58* (11), 897–909.

Katz, P. A., & Kofkin, J. A. (1997). Race, gender, and young children. In S.S. Luthar, J.A. Burack, D. Cicchetti, J.R. Weisz (Eds.), *Developmental psychopathology: Perspectives on adjustment, risk, and disorder* (pp. 51–74). New York, NY: Cambridge University Press.

Martin, C. L., & Ruble, D. N. (2004). Children's search for gender cues: Cognitive perspectives on gender development. *Current Directions in Psychological Science, 13,* 67—70.

Office of Special Education Programs. (2008). Thirtieth Annual Report to Congress on the Implementation of the Individuals with Disabilities Education Act, Parts B and C. 2008. Washington, DC: Author.

Oliver, K. (2002). Understanding your child's temperament. Retrieved from http://ohioline.osu.edu/flm02/FS05.html

Patterson, M. M., & Bigler, R. S. (2006). Preschool children's attention to environmental messages about groups: Social categorization and the origins of intergroup bias. *Child Development, 77,* 847–860.

Pearson, J., & Hall, D. K. (2012). Guide 1: Resilience—a brief overview. In D. Smith (Ed.), *Reaching IN. . .reaching OUT resiliency guidebook: "Bounce back" thinking skills for children and adults* (pp. 1–3). Ontario, Canada: Child & Family Partnership.

Seligman, M. E. P. (2006). *Learned optimism: How to change your mind and your life.* New York, NY: Pocket Books.

Seligman, M. E. P. (2007). *The optimistic child: How to change your mind and your life.* New York, NY: Mariner Books.

Seligman, M. E. P. (2011). *Flourish: A visionary new understanding of happiness and well-being.* New York, NY: Free Press.

Wardel, F. (2008). Diversity in early childhood programs. Retrieved from http://www.earlychildhoodnews.com/earlychildhood/article_view.aspx?ArticleID=548

Zaman, A. (2007). Gender-sensitive teaching: A reflective approach for early childhood education teacher training programs. *American Association of Colleges for Teacher Education, 129* (1), 110–118.

Chapter 9 Social

Berk, L. E. (2002). *Infants, children, and adolescents* (4th ed.). Boston, MA: Allyn & Bacon.

Dewar, G. (2009). Preschool social skills: A guide for the science-minded parent. Retrieved from http://www.parenting-science.com/preschool-social-skills.html

Dodge, D. T., Colker, L. J., & Heroman, C. (2002). *The creative curriculum for preschool* (4th ed.). Washington, DC: Teaching Strategies.

Eisenberg, N., Fabes, R. A., & Spinrad. T. L. (2006). Prosocial development. In W. Damon & R.M. Lerner (Eds.), *Handbook of child psychology,* 6th ed, Hoboken, NJ: John Wiley & Sons.

Epstein, A .S. (2003, September). How planning and reflection develop young children's thinking skills. *Beyond the Journal: Young Children on the Web.* Retrieved from http://journal.naeyc.org/btj/200309/Planning&Reflection.pdf

HighScope. (2012). Social development. Retrieved from http://www.highscope.org/Content.asp?ContentId=294

Hyson, M., & Taylor, J. L. (2011). Caring about caring: What adults can do to promote young children's prosocial skills. *Young Children, 66* (4), 74–83.

Katz, L. G., & Mendoza, J. A. (2011). Introduction to the special section on social-emotional issues in the lives of young children. *Early Childhood Research & Practice, 13* (1). Retrieved from http://ecrp.uiuc.edu/v13n1/

Lewis, V., Boucher, J., Lupton, L., & Watson, S. (2000). Relationships between symbolic play, functional play, verbal and non-verbal ability in young children. *International Journal of Language & Communication Disorders, 35* (1), 117–127.

Paley, V. G. (1993). *You can't say you can't play.* Cambridge, MA: Harvard University Press.

Pica, R. (n.d.). When kids cooperate. Retrieved from http://www.maternitycorner.com/mcmag/articles/child0004.htm

Riley, D., San Juan, R. R., Klinkner, J., & Ramminger, A. (2008). *Social & emotional development: Connecting science and practice in early childhood settings.* St. Paul, MN: Redleaf Press.

Seifert, K. L. (2006). Cognitive development and the education of young children. In B. Spodek & O. N. Saracho (Eds.), *Handbook of research on the education of young children* (3rd ed., pp. 9–22). Mahwah, NJ: Erlbaum.

Spiegel, A. (Presenter). (2008, February 21). Old-fashioned play builds serious skills. In National Public Radio (Producer), Morning edition [Radio program]. Retrieved from http://www.npr.org/templates/story/story.php?storyId=19212514

Trawick-Smith, J. (2009). *Science in support of play: The case for play-based programs* (White Paper). Willimantic, CT: Eastern Connecticut State University.

Yu, S. Y., Ostrosky, M. M., & Fowler, S. A. (2011). Children's friendship development: A comparative study. *Early Childhood Research & Practice, 13* (1). Retrieved from http://ecrp.uiuc.edu/v13n1/

Chapter 10 Guidance

Adams, S. K., & Baronberg, J. (2005). *Promoting positive behavior: Guidance strategies for early childhood settings.* Upper Saddle River, NJ: Pearson.

Bailey, B. (2001). *Conscious discipline: 7 basic skills for brain smart classroom management.* Orlando, FL: Loving Guidance.

Dunlap, G., Fox, L., Hemmeter, M. L., & Strain, P. (2004). *The role of time-out in a comprehensive approach for addressing challenging behaviors of preschool children* (What Works Brief 14). Retrieved from Center on the Social and Emotional Foundations for Early Learning website: http://csefel.vanderbilt.edu/briefs/wwb14.pdf

Education Development Center. (2008). What you can do: Recommendations and strategies for adults. Retrieved from http://www.eyesonbullying.org/cando.html

Gartrell, D. (2001). Replacing time-out: Part one—Using guidance to build an encouraging classroom. *Young Children, 56* (6), 8–16.

Gartrell, D. (2002). Replacing time-out: Part two—Using guidance to maintain an encouraging classroom. *Young Children, 57* (2), 36–43.

Gartrell, D. (2004). *The power of guidance: Teaching social-emotional skills in early childhood classrooms.* Clifton Park, NY: Delmar.

Gartrell, D. (2008, January). Guidance matters: Comprehensive guidance. *Beyond the Journal: Young Children on the Web.* Retrieved from http://www.naeyc.org/files/yc/file/200801/BTJGuidanceGartrell.pdf

Gartrell, D. (2011, February/March). Good guidance. The goals of guidance: Democratic life skills. Handout 1: The individual guidance plan. *NEXT for TYC, 4* (3). Retrieved from http://www.naeyc.org/files/yc/file/201107/IndividualGuidancePlan.pdf

Kaiser, B., & Rasminsky, J. S. (2010). What is challenging behavior? Retrieved from http://www.education.com/reference/article/what-challenging-behavior/?page=3

Kaiser, B., & Rasminsky, J. S. (2012). *Challenging behavior in young children. Understanding, preventing, and responding effectively* (3rd ed.). Boston, MA: Pearson.

Kersey, K., & Masterson, M. (2013). *101 principles for positive guidance with young children: Creating responsive teachers.* Upper Saddle River, NJ: Pearson.

Klass, C. S., Guskin, K. A., & Thomas, M. (1995). The early childhood program: Promoting children's development through and within relationships. *Zero to Three, 16,* 9–17.

Klein, A. S. (2008). Guiding young children: 21 strategies. Retrieved from http://www.earlychildhoodnews.com/earlychildhood/article_view.aspx?ArticleID=578

McCabe, L. A., & Frede. E. C. (2007, December). *Challenging behaviors and the role of preschool education* (Preschool Policy Brief, Issue 16). Retrieved from National Institute for Early Education Research website: http://nieer.org/resources/policybriefs/16.pdf

Miller, D. F. (2013). *Positive child guidance* (7th ed.). Stamford, C.T.: Cengage Learning.

Olweus, D. (1993). *Bullying at school: What we know and what we can do.* Oxford, England: Blackwell.

Olweus, D. (1997). Bully/victim problems in school: Facts and intervention. *European Journal of Psychology of Education, 12,* 495–510.

Pearce, J. B., & Thompson, A. E. (1998). Practical approaches to reduce the impact of bullying. *Archives of Disease in Childhood, 79* (6), 528–531.

Porter, L. (2008). *Guiding children's behaviour* [DVD]. Adelaide, Australia: Small Poppies SA.

Powell, D., Dunlap, G., & Fox, L. (2006). Prevention and intervention for the challenging behaviors of toddlers and preschoolers. *Infants & Young Children, 19* (1), 25–35.

Powell, D., Fixsen, D., Dunlap, G., Smith, B., & Fox, L. (2007). A synthesis of knowledge relevant to pathways of service delivery for young children with or at risk of challenging behaviors. *Journal of Early Intervention, 29* (2), 81–106.

Saifer, S. (2003). *Practical solutions to practically every problem*. St. Paul, MN: Redleaf Press.

Chapter 11 Families

Copple, C., & Bredekamp, S. (Eds.). (2009). *Developmentally appropriate practice in early childhood programs serving children from birth through age 8* (3rd ed.). Washington, DC: National Association for the Education of Young Children.

Derman-Sparks, L., & Edwards, J. O. (2010). *Anti-bias education for young children and ourselves*. Washington, DC: National Association for the Education of Young Children.

Gillespie, L. G. (2006, September). Cultivating good relationships with families can make hard times easier! *Beyond the Journal: Young Children on the Web*. Retrieved from http://www.naeyc.org/files/yc/file/200609/RockNRollBTJ.pdf

Halgunseth, L. C., Peterson, A., Stark, D. R., & Moodie, S. (2009). *Family engagement, diverse families, and early childhood education programs: An integrated review of the literature*. Retrieved from National Association for the Education of Young Children website: http://www.naeyc.org/files/naeyc/file/research/FamEngage.pdf

Hare, J., & Gray, L. A. (2008). All kinds of families: A guide for parents. Retrieved from http://www1.cyfernet.org/prog/fam/nontradfam.html

National Association for the Education of Young Children. (2011). *Code of ethical conduct: Supplement for early childhood program administrators*. Retrieved from http://www.naeyc.org/files/naeyc/file/positions/Supplement%20PS2011.pdf

PBS Parents. (n.d.). The parent–teacher partnership. Retrieved from http://www.pbs.org/parents/goingtoschool/parent_teacher.html

U.S. Census Bureau. (n.d.). Frequently asked questions. Retrieved from http://www.census.gov/hhes/www/income/about/faqs.html

Chapter 12 Program Management

Bredekamp, S. (2011). *Effective practices in early childhood education: Building a foundation*. Upper Saddle River, NJ: Pearson Education.

Carr, M. (2001). *Assessment in early childhood settings: Learning stories*. Thousand Oaks, CA: SAGE Publications.

Carr, M., & Lee, W. (2012). *Learning stories: Constructing learner identities in early education*. Thousand Oaks, CA: SAGE Publications.

Copple, C., & Bredekamp, S. (Eds.). (2009). *Developmentally appropriate practice in early childhood programs serving children from birth through age 8* (3rd ed.). Washington, DC: National Association for the Education of Young Children.

Epstein, A. S., Schweinhart, L. J., DeBruin-Parecki, A., & Robin, K. B. (2004, July). Preschool assessment: A guide to developing a balanced approach. *Preschool Policy Matters,* (7). Retrieved from http://nieer.org/resources/policybriefs/7.pdf

Illinois Early Learning Project. (n.d.). Tip sheets: The project approach for preschoolers. Retrieved from http://www.illinoisearlylearning.org/tipsheets/projects-overview.htm

Institute for Early Childhood Education and Research. (n.d.). Research into practice: Reggio Emilia. Retrieved from http://earlychildhood.educ.ubc.ca/community/research-practice-reggio-emilia

Jablon, J. R., Dombro A. L., & Dichtelmiller, M. L. (2007). *The power of observation* (2nd ed.). Belmont, CA: Wadsworth Publishing.

Losardo, A., & Notari-Syverson, A. (2011). *Alternative approaches to assessing young children.* Baltimore, MD: Brookes.

National Dissemination Center for Children With Disabilities. (2010). Special education services for preschoolers with disabilities. Retrieved from http://nichcy.org/schoolage/preschoolers

National Dissemination Center for Children With Disabilities. (2012). Categories of disability under IDEA. Retrieved from http://nichcy.org/disability/categories

Seitz, H. (2008, March). The power of documentation in the early childhood classroom. *Young Children, 63* (2). Retrieved from http://www.naeyc.org/files/tyc/file/Seitz.pdf

Chapter 13 Professionalism

Almon, J., & Miller, E. (2011). *The crisis in early education: A research-based case for more play and less pressure.* Retrieved from Alliance for Childhood website: http://www.allianceforchildhood.org/sites/allianceforchildhood.org/files/file/crisis_in_early_ed.pdf

Beal, J. (n.d.). How to become a reflective teacher. Retrieved from http://www.ehow.com/how_5011663_become-reflective-teacher.html

Bredekamp, S. (2011). *Effective practices in early childhood education: Building a foundation.* Boston, MA: Pearson.

Carter, M., Cividanes, W., Curtis, D., & Lebo, D. (2010). Becoming a reflective teacher. Teaching Young Children, 3(4), 1–4.

Carter, M., & Curtis, D. (2009). *The visionary director: A handbook for dreaming, organizing, and improving your center.* St. Paul, MN: Redleaf Press.

Copple, C., & Bredekamp, S. (Eds.). (2009). *Developmentally appropriate practice in early childhood programs serving children birth through age 8* (3rd ed.). Washington, DC.: National Association for the Education of Young Children.

Curtis, D., & Carter, M. (2011). *Reflecting children's lives: A handbook for planning your child-centered curriculum.* St. Paul, MN: Redleaf Press.

Derman-Sparks, L., & Edwards, J. O. (2010). *Anti-bias education for young children and ourselves.* Washington, DC: National Association for the Education of Young Children.

Duncan, S. (2010, January/February). Intentional and embedded professional development: Four steps to success. *Exchange,* 70–72.

Epstein, A. S. (2007). *The intentional teacher: Choosing the best strategies for young children's learning.* Washington, DC: National Association for the Education of Young Children.

Epstein, A. S. (2009, January/February). Think before you (inter) act: What it means to be an intentional teacher. *Exchange,* 46–49.

Feeney, S. (2010). Celebrating the 20th anniversary of NAEYC's Code of Ethical Conduct—Ethics today in early care and education: Review, reflection, and the future. *Young Children, 65* (2). Retrieved from http:// http://www.naeyc.org/yc/pastissues

Golinkoff, R. M., & Hirsh-Pasek, K. (2012). Hold on to your hobby horses: Fueling the debate on playful learning. Retrieved from http://www.huffingtonpost.com/roberta-michnick-golinkoff/children-play-learning-_b_1884281.html

Hyson, M. (2012). What's too scary? Retrieved from http://families.naeyc.org/learning-and-development/child-development/whats-too-scary

Katz, L. G. (n.d.). The developmental stages of teachers. Retrieved from http://ceep.crc.uiuc.edu/pubs/katz-dev-stages.html

Lillard, A. S., Lerner, M. D., Hopkins, E. J., Dore, R. A., Smith, E. D., & Palmquist, C. M. (2012). The impact of pretend play on children's development: A review of the evidence. *Psychological Bulletin*. Advance online publication. doi:10.1037/a0029321

McIvor, C. (2011, July 26). Learning by experiment is all in a day's play: Rudiments of the scientific method seen in four-year-old children. Nature. doi:10.1038/news.2011.442

National Association for the Education of Young Children. (2005). *Code of ethical conduct and statement of commitment*. Washington, DC: Author.

National Association for the Education of Young Children, & Child Care Aware of America. (2011). Early childhood education professional development: Training and technical assistance glossary. Retrieved from http://www.naeyc.org/GlossaryTraining_TA.pdf

Neas, L. M. R. (2012). Ideas to begin reflective teaching strategies in your classroom. Retrieved from http://www.brighthubeducation.com/teaching-methods-tips/92097-reflective-teaching-strategies/

Ounce of Prevention Fund. (2009). The Ounce of Prevention Fund early childhood advocacy toolkit. Retrieved from http://www.ounceofprevention.org/advocacy/pdfs/EarlyChildhoodAdvocacyToolkit.pdf

Pappas, P. (2010). The reflective teacher: A taxonomy of reflection (part 3). Retrieved from http://www.peterpappas.com/2010/01/reflective-teacher-taxonomy-reflection.html

Schiller, P. (2007, November/December). More purposeful and intentional infant and toddler care. Exchange, 10–13.

Sesay-St. Paul, M. (n.d.). Teacher tip: Teacher reflection questions: Five questions to help you evaluate your effectiveness in instruction. Retrieved from http://www.scholastic.com/teachers/article/teacher-reflection-questions

Stewart, K. E. (2010). *The role of reflection: Preschool teachers' use of reflective thinking to translate higher education learning into teaching practice*. Minneapolis, MN: Capella University.

Index

A

Abraham Maslow, 141

Abuse, 29, 39, 69, **71-74**, 125, 225, 227, 268, 323, 337, 343

Accident, 26, 29, 36, 256, 260

Administer, 35, 48-50, 71

Adolescence, 115, 138

Adolescent, 17

Advocacy, 275, **341-345**

Advocate, 71, 298, **340, 342**, 345

Age-appropriate, 14, 52, 118, 144, 163, 165, 168

Aggressive, 257, 266, 269, 298, 309, 310, 333

Airbags, 26

Alarm (s), 12, 13, 26, 27, 34

Allergies, 18, 21, 31, 41, 43, **44**, 50, 52, 54, 57, 283, 300

Alphabet, 164, 167, 169, 170, 172, 183, 188, **191**, 192, 247

Ambulances, 12, 13

Anecdotal records, 314

Animal, 31, 41, **43**, 61, 132, 137, 146, 148, 166, 188

Anti-bias, 89, 278, 329

Antibiotics, 47

Antiseptic, 15

Anti-time-out, 267

Anxiety, 122, 227, 270, 294-296

Appetite, 45, 261

Appliances, 79, 82, 83, 85, 93, 95

Applications, 170, 171, 300, 311

Appreciation, 289, 290, 329

Approaches to learning, **218-220, 222, 223**, 281

Approaching, 24

Arrival, 60, 98, 100, 103, 106, 107, 150

Arrive, 11, 44, 100, 103, 154, 156, 292, 295

Art (s), 23, 77-80, **82-84**, 87, **93**, 94, 96, 104, 105, 107, 110, 112, 132, 143, 145, 147, 151, 154, 155, 171, 172, 192, 198, 199, **201, 202, 204-207**, 210, 211, 220, 225, 227, 235, 249, 257, 262, 264, 287, 288, 298, 307, 308, 314

Art Center, 23, 28, 30, 73, 79, 84, 192, 201, 204, 257, 264, 308

Artist, 207, 235

Artistic, 194, 204-206, 309

Artwork, 96, 102, 150, 160, 164, 201, 203, 204, 207, 210, 220, 287, 315

Asbestos, 11

Asleep, 59, 101, 150, 175, 306

Aspirator, 62

Assess, 250, 301, 306, 316

Assessment, 51, 224, **306**, 311, 317, 335

Association, 3, 10, 52, 74, 78, 119, 127, 160, 168, 275, 291, 302, 321, 327, 332, 334, 340, 341, 343

Asthma, 40, 47-49

Attack, 48

Attendance, 100, 164, 194, 295

Attention, 44, 49, 55, 70, 72, 97, 98, 127, 145, 146, 151, 162, 182, 183, 185, 189, 191, 195, 197, 214, 219, 220, 222, 229, 243, 261, 263, 268, 269, 331, 333, 336, 344, 345

Attitude, 97, 150, 194, 221, 237, 311

Audio, 89, 170, 190, 209, 315

Authority, 29, 105, 227, 269

Authorization, 33

Authorized, 16, 28, 35, 70, 323

Autism, 43, 51, 241, 302, 321

B

Bacteria, 28, 43, 54, 64, 65

Bandage (s), 15, 32

Bath, 12

Bathing, 165, 186

Bathroom, 13, **21**, 28, 40, 45, 59, 67, 68, 81-83, 101, 102, 106, 227

Bathtub (s), 28, 172

Beat, 148, 208

Beating, 71, 73

Bed (s), 18, 20, 27, 59, 156, 241, 288

Bedding, 20, 41, 69

Bed-wetting, 72

Behavior, 22, 24, 36, 44, 45, 70, 72, 73, 85, 138-140, 144, 149, 150, 199, 216, 220, 221, 225, 239, 242, 244, 245, 251, 254, 255, **257-263, 265-269**, 271, 272, 278, 305, 307, 310, 311, 313, 335-337

Behavioral, 46, 71, 72, 230, 255, 265, 268

Bias, 171, 221, 231

Biological, 116, 276

Biology, 114

Bite, 32, 43, 58, 72, 144, 258

Biting, 22, 24, 36, 71, 216, 258

Blanket, 48, 59, 118, 145

Bleach, **39-42**, 58, 66

Bleeding, 31-33

Blindness, 51

Blinds, 12, 13, 17, 18

Blocks, 23, 24, 26, 77, 78, 81-87, 89, 92-95, 105, 112, 117,
    118, 120, 125, 128-133, 139, 146, 156, 158, 172,
    177, 178, 192, 200, 201, 211, 221, 232, 256, 257,
    280, 288, 289, 301, 307, 312

Blog, **293**, 345

Blueprint, 78, 79, 84, 86

Book Area, 168

Bookcase, 82, 83

Books, 26-28, 49, 57, 61, 64, 68, 77, 81, 84, **88-96**, 100, 103,
    118, 122, 125, 128-130, 132, 142, 147, 150, 152,
    153, 155, 156, 158, 160, **162-172**, 176, 178, 181, 182,
    185-192, 194-196, 200, 201, 208, 213, 214, 220, 226,
    227, 230, 233, 235, 237, 242, 243, 248, 249, 252,
    255, 260, 270, 272, 277, 282, 283, 288, 289, 300,
    301, 311, 314, 317, 321, 327, 339, 344

Bookshelf, 12, 13, 118

Bookstore, 172

Bottles, 18, 19, 53-55, 98, 129, 132, 147, 206

Bowel, 67

Braces, 17

Brain research, 133, 143

Brainstorm, 36, 71, 202, 210, 272, 287

Breakfast, 100, 182, 214

Breastfeed, 52

Breast milk, **53**

Breastfeeding, **52**

Breath, 32, 45

Breathe, 62

Breathing, 32, 33, 45, 49

Bruises, 15, 72

Building, 18, 24, 26, 27, 34, 35, 86, 87, 93, 94, 104, 107,
    112, 118, 130, 132, 133, 146, 151, 154, 157-159,
    172, 178, 187, 190, 201, 206, 219, 239, 242, 251,
    256-259, 263, 269, 278, 280, 289, 311, 312

Builds, 59, 100, 117, 127, 128, 146, 214, 256, 259, 262, 302

Bulletin, 103, 131, 282, 291, 292, 315, 318

Bullies, 239, **269**, **270**, 272

Bully, 89, **269**, **270**

Burn (s), 19, 26, 32, 72, 257

Burning, 27, 30, 71

Bus safety, **26**

Buses, 26, 36, 132, 283

C

Cancer, 21, 47

Candidate (s), 4, 5, 6, 9, 31, 38, 75, 113, 135, 161, 198, 217,
    238, 253, 274, 303, 325, 345

Car safety, 20, **26**

Career (s), 1, 4, 199, 326, 339

Cause-and-effect, 91, 149, 150

Causes, 20, 33, 227, 259, 261, 308

CDA, 2-6, 9, 31, 38, 75, 113, 135, 161, 198, 217, 238, 253,
    274, 296, 303, 325

CDA Exam, 5

CDA National Credentialing Program, 4

CDC, 43, 53

Census, 275

Center Time, 201

Challenging behavior, 254, **257**, **258**, 261, **268**, 269, 271,
    305

Chemical, 40, 56

Chickenpox, 46, 47

Child advocacy, 342-344

Child care resource and referral, 324, 340

Child development, 1-5, 278, 296, 298-301, 327, 328, 341

Child-directed, 96, 305, 338

Child-including, 263

Child-initiated, 99

Child-modeling, 112

Childproof, 50

Child-rearing, 294

Child-sized, 13, 19, 40, 58, 63, 85, 244

Choice, 88, 91, 100-102, 104-106, 146, 149, 181, 189, 245,
    246, 254, 262, 266, 285, 307, 312

Choice time, 100-102, **104-106**, 149, 181, 246, 254, 285, 312

Choking, 11, 12, 18, 19, 31, 32, 56

Cholesterol, 56, 59, 127

Chronic, 47-49, 52, 63

Circle Time, 82, 83, 100, 102, 105, 120, 262

Classes, 272, 300, 301

Classrooms, 180, 210

Classroom-websites, 294

Cleaners, 42, 130, 132

Cleanup, 102, 107, 208

Climate, 40, 62, 199

Clinic (s), 69, 234, 244, 324

Clinical, 20, 143

Coaching, 247, **229**

Code of Ethical Conduct, 10, 74, 334, 336

Cognitive, 6, 57, 67, 68, 76, 78, 88, 110-112, 130, 133, **135-138**, **143**, **146-149**, 150, 152, 154, 174, 183, 208, 222, 241, 273, 305, 317, 320

Cognitive development, 111, 133, **136-138**, **143**, 241, 273

Cognitively, 24

Colleague, 16, 34, 208, 209, 264, 293, 295, **322**, 332

Color-code, 164

Commercial materials, 24

Communication (s), 6, 42, 56, 111, 161-163, 173, 174, 181, 186, 187, 211, 240, 271, 278, 280, 287, **291**, 334

Community, 5, 69, 74, 89, 92, 107, 137, 140, 149, 158, 165, 185, 211, 218, 239-241, 245, 246, 251, 252, 254, 264, 265, 270, 287, 296, 299, 300, 304, **322-324**, 329, 334, 337-339, 341, 344, 345

Community-based, 344

Competency, 2-8, 110-112, 183, 216, 229, 273, 303, 325

Competency Standard, 5-8, 110-112, 216, 273, 303, 325

Competition, 204, 245, 273

Computers, 20, 79, 84, 160, 201

Conferences, 295, **296-299**, 339, 340

Conflict, **249-251**

Consultant (s), 122, 322, 323

Consulting, 70

Contagious, 44, 46, 70

Contaminate, 17, 18, 64, 65

Conversation (s), 23, 29, 55, 57, 58, 68, 94, 97, 101, 104, 111, 112, 136, 139, 149-152, 158, 167, **173-181**, 185, 187, 190, 191, 197, 225, 226, 229, 235, 271, 272, 292, 295, 297, 301, 315, 317, 318

Cooperation, 245, 246, 291, 334

Cooperative play, 216, 242-244

Coordination, 57, 114, 119, 127, 129, 130, 202, 227, 289

Cords, 11-13

Costumes, 82, 83, 209, 214

Cot, 179, 261

Couch, 81-84

Cough (s), 45, 62

Coughing, 50, 59, 60, **62**, 69

Counting, 85, 94, 100, 107, 147, 148, 150, **155**, **156**, 167, 172, 290, 314

Covers, 65, 145, 153, 166, 169, 171

Crawling, 34, 114-116, 118, 120, 121, 151

Crawls, 117, 144

Creative, 6, 77, 85, 96, 110, 112, **198-204**, 206-209, 212-214, 287, 309, 314, 343

Creativity, 20, 77, 79, 85, 91, 96, 112, 130, 199-204, 206, 208-210, 214, 223, 245, 278, 299, 312, 328, 337

Credentialing process, 3-5

Cry, 24, 73, 111, 125, 141, 144, 173, 222, 263, 309

Cubbies, 40, 80-83, 94, 102, 107, 150, 163, 164, 246

Cuddle, 92, 267, 280, 281, 285

Culture, 95, 140, 165, 209, 211, 225, 230, 231, **278**, 282, 286, 333

Curiosity, 6, 68, 97, 111, 135, 144, 146, 148, 152, 191, 199-201, 223

Curriculum, 6, 48, 68, 89, **95**, **96**, 125, 135, 210, 219, 241, 281, 286, 304-307, 316, 317, 321, 327, 328, 335, 337

Cycle of curriculum planning, 316

D

Daily schedule, 6, 75, 76, **97-106**, 164, 280, 287, 307, 323

Dance, 85, 87, 112, 119, 122, 148, 167, 179, 199, 202, **208-211**

Data, 44, 152, 157, 158, 202, 221, 302, 307, 310, 313, 317, 318, 342, 344, 345

Décor, 87, 94

Decorate, 202, 245

Decorations, 20

Dental care, **63**, 64

Dentist, 28, 64, 70

Departure, 97-99, 102, 106, 150

Depression, 235, 236, 270

Dermatitis, 64

Design, 76-78, 80, 84, 86, 128, 147, 200, 204, 205, 209, 241, 242, 245, 287, 312

Detergent, 66

Development, 1-6, 17, 43, 57, 58, 68, 76, 78, 87, 88, 94-97, 100, 103, 104, 110, 111, 113-116, 119-122, 127-134, 136-138, 140, 141, 143, 150, 152, 154, 162, 163, 173, 174, 178, **180, 181, 186, 191-194**, 196, 197, 200, 208, 216, 219, 220, 232, 239-242, 245, 247, 251, 252, 257, 273, 275, 278, 291, 296, 298-301, 303-307, 310, 313-315, 317, 318, 322, 326-328, 334, 337-343

Developmental Context, 5, 273

Developmental summaries, 319

Developmentally appropriate, 6, 12, 13, 24, 97, 100, 105, 113, 135, 137, 161, 170, 178, 198, 222, 254, 257, 261, 279, 299, 337, 345

Developmentally appropriate choices, 261

Diabetes, 47, 49, 127

Diaper-changing, 21, **64, 65**, 66

Diarrhea, 46, 47, 66

Diarrheal, 60

Diet, 220

Dietary, 55, 56, 318

Digestive, 54, 57

Disability, 51, 269, 298, 335

Disagreements, 250, 322

Disaster, 35

Discipline, 258, 264, 265, 267

Discriminate, 335

Disease (s), 17, 20, 43, 46, 53, 60, 63, 64, 117

Disinfect, 40-42, 62, 68

Display, 20, 44, 59, 62, 88, 91, 94, 95, 162-164, 166, 169, 185, 192, 201, 202, 207, 214, 220, 226, 227, 230, 257, 295, 315

Diverse, 90, 204, 231, 334

Diversity, 89, 90, 94, 96, 231, 232, 281, 300, 329, 336, 340, 345

Divorce (s), 225-227, 276, 300, 318

Doctor, 49, 95, 172, 202, 212, 244, 245, 289

Documentation (s), 6, 94, 164, 195, 207, 220, 280, 282, 310, 313, 315, 316, 318, 321

Documenting, 94, 293, 304, 309, **314-316**

Documents, 39, 173, 224, 311, 314

Doll, 48, 49, 59, 144, 166, 188, 241, 243, 262

Door, 94, 163, 280

Downtime, 106, 306

Dramatic play, 30, 48, 49, 57, 59, 64, 78-80, 82, 83, 93-95, 132, 149, 157, 172, 179, 181, 199, 201, 210, **212, 213**, 222, 227, 235, **243-245**, 257, 259, 262, 286-288, 304, 314, 315, 331

Drawing (s), 79, 84, 94, 95, 110, 130, 131, 142, 151, 152, 192, 201, **203-207**, 234, 237, 252, 255, 289, 297, 314

Dress, 21, 32, 66, 149, 230, 237, 244

Dress-up, 41, 93, 95, 130, 132, 202, 213, 221, 333, 335

Drink (s), 46, 54, 55, 58, 129

Drinking, 14, 18, 40, 56, 59

Drop-off, 225, 271, 291, 292

Drown, 21, 28, 31

Drug (s), 72, 268

Dual language learners, 88, 109, 160-162, 164, 171, 174, **183-185**, 197, 241, 329, 337

Dyspraxia, 122

E

Earned self-esteem, 228

Earthquakes, 35

Easel (s), 82-84, 93, 130, 131, 194, 257, 262

Educate, 4, 326, 342, 344

Educated, 1, 210

Egocentrism, 139

Electric, 107

Electrical, 11-13, 20, 79, 84, 85

Electricity, 35, 79

Electronically, 45

Emergencies, 27, 29, **31, 34**

Emotion, 191, **234**, 252

Encouragement, 67, 200, 204, 224, 227, 236, 259, 263

Engagement, 6, 75, 104, 125, 137, 170, 222, 223, 236, 244, 279, 298, 306, 341

Enroll (s), 226, 271, 279-281, 294, 321

Enrolled, 166, 281

Enrollment, 282, 300

EPA, 42

EPA-certi, 17

Epilepsy, 47, 48

Equipment, 6, 11-14, 17, 20, 23, 29, 50, 76, 78, 79, 84, 87, 101, 105, 113, 118-120, 122, 146, 168-170, 202, 247, 256

Eric Erikson, 141

Ethical decisions, 326, **332-336**

Ethnic, 90, 92, 211, 333, 336

Ethnicities, 232

Ethnicity, 89, 140, 165

Evacuate, 27, 34, 35

Evacuation (s), 12, 26, 27, 34-36

Evaluation, 3, 224, **316**, **317**

Exercise (s), 41, 49, 85, 110, 119, 120, 125, 138, 210, 235, 237

Expectations, 55, 69, 72, 116, 121, 216, 226, 230, 241, 255, 259, 272, 278, 328, 332

Experiment, 85, 94, 96, 131, 138, 159, 182, 192, 199, 204, 206, 207, 212, 221, 244, 255, 261

Extension, 16, 324

Extinguish, 34

Extinguisher (s), 12, 13, 26, 34

F

Faculty, 3

Failure, 72, 121, 199, 204, 223, 236, 257, 270

Families, 5, 6, 10, 35-37, 45, 52, 54, 56, 59, **69-71**, 74, 76, 89, 90, **94**, 96, 102, 107, 140, 144, 150, 162, 164-166, 181, 183, 184, 186, 187, **194-197**, 210, 211, 218-220, **224**, 226, **230-232**, 234, 240, 254, 268, **271-302**, 305, 313, 315, 317, 321, 323-326, 330, 334-338, 340-345

Family board, 81-83

Family circumstances, 219, 224-226, 268

Family composition, 225

Family participation, 275

Family-style, **57**, **58**, 70, 101, 149, 156, 247, 260

Fears, 29, 49, 212, 227, 245, 284

Feedback, 204, 223, 229, 323, 328, 331, 332

Feelings, 6, 29, 44, 71, 73, 85, 103, 139, 142, 145, 161, 166, 176, 187, 191, 201, 204, 210, 213, 216, 218, 228, 229, **232**, **233**, 235, 236, 238, 240, 245, 247, 250-252, 257, 258, 261, 267, 268, 270, 272, 285, 288-290, 296, 298, 311, 332

Field Trip, 21

Fine motor, 114, 115, **127-132**, 319

Fire, 12, 13, **26**, **27**, **34**, 300

First-aid, **15**, **32**, **33**

Floor, 340, 343

Flooring, 13, 80

Focus, 22, 121, 131, 182, 190, 203, 214, 222-224, 229, 236, 244, 248, 254, 262, 264, 268, 270, 281, 284, 293, 296, 297, 302, 318, 326, 331, 332, 341, 345

Food, **18**, **19**, 21, 40, 41, 44, 49, 50, 52, **55-60**, 63, 69, 70, 93-95, 101, 132, 141, 150, 159, 172, 206, 218, 220, 260, 283, 287, 323, 324

Formulaic speech, 184

Formulas, 21, **54**

Frequency, 311

Friends, 6, 23, 32, 49, 124, 140, 211, 220, 229, 238, 239, 247-249, 255, 268, 269, 279, 280, 283

Friendships, 239, **246-249**, 318

Functional Area, 6, 7, 31, 110-112, 216, 273

Furnishings, 11-13, **17**, 29, 78, 85, 86, 169, 244

G

Gender, 68, 89, 95, 167, 219, **221**, 335

Geometry, 85, **157**, 158, 288, 289

Global self-esteem, 228

Government, 277

Government-funded, 302, 338

Gross motor, 6, 81, 82, 95, **113-125**, 127, 130, 195, 306, 317, 319

Group meeting, 100, 105, 107, 156, 246

Groups, 58, 78, 80, 86, 90, 100, 101, 136, 140, 145, 152, 168, 183, 185, 187, 189, 190, 201, 211, 218, 219, 222, 225, 231, 233, 239-241, **245-248**, 254, 267, 300, 316, 321, 324, 328, 331, 338-343

Guidance, 6, 160, 195, 216, 237, 250, **253-272**, 278, 300, 332, 334, 335

H

Hand washing, 7, **60**, **61**

Handwriting, 194

Happy, 61, 73, 212, 232-234, 309, 312

Hazardous, 72

Hazards, 11, 12, 17, 72

Head Start, 1, 2, 77, 183, 281, 285, 317, 341

Headache, 33

Healthier, 39, 49, 235, 236, 341

Healthily, 62

Healthy, 6, 7, 21, **38-74**, 70, 100, 102, 127, 172, 202, 228, 234, 236, 267, 300, 322, 326, 331, 334, 342

Hearing, 17, 43, 51, 133, 136, 173, 176, 179, 182, 188, 192, 272, 279, 302

Heat (s), 19, 30, 40, 41, 53, 148

Heated, 290

Heaters, 12, 13

Helmet (s), 14, 25, 27

HEPA, 18

Heterosexual, 276

HIV, 47, 54

Hives, 32, 33

Home language, 6, 37, 69, 161, 165, 166, 175, 183-185, 209, 225, 257, 282, 295, 317, 319, 335

Home visits, 226, 240, **294-296**

Homophobia, 90

Homosexual, 276, 333, 335

Hospital (s), 12, 13, 33, 36, 70, 252

Housekeeping, 221

Howard Gardner, 142

Hurricane (s), 35, 235

Hygiene, 7, 57, 59, 64, 69, 71, 72

I

IDEA, 51, 224, 321, 337

IEP, 51, 179, 224, 264, 269, 284, 298, 318, 321, 323, 333

IFSP, 51, 224, 269, 284, 298, 318, 321, 323

Illness, 6, 17, 18, 38, 39, **45-49**, 62, 125, 225, 268

Immigrant, 226

Immigration, 284, 335, 344

Immune, 41

Immunization (s), 39, **43**, 69

Immunize, 41

Incidents, 35, 310

Inclement, 281

Individual planning form, 319, 320

Indoor, 10-14, 16, 22, 35, 39-41, 76-80, 86, 94, 95, 99-101, 104, 116, 120, 153, 181, 256, 307

Indoor-setting, 12, 13, **76-82**, 84, 86

Infection (s), 32, 52, 60, 62

Infectious, 64

Injured, 15, 29, 36, 283

Injury, 31, 36, 51, 71, 323

Intentionality, 144, 205, 326, 327, 329, 342

Internet, 20, 293, 324, 337, 338

Intervention, 51, 88, 111, 224, 244, 247, 263

Itching, 72

J

Jean Piaget, 137

Job chart, 172, 282

Journal (s), 100, 169, 194, 195, 235, 310, 331, 339, 345

Journaling, 301, 331

K

Kidnappings, 35

Kindness, 237, 248, 252, 258

Kitchen, 30, 34, 79, 85, 94

L

Label (s), 42, 50, 52, 62, 95, **163**, 164, 172, 229, 264, 266, 310

Labeled, 40, 41, 69, 203, 266

Labeling, 160, 163, 264

Landscaping, 87, 202, 301

Language-building, 175

Language-rich, 166

Language (s), 56, **162**, **174**, **178**, **184**

Lead-based, 17

Lead-free, 11, **17**, **18**

Learning center, 78, **84**, **85**, 109, 132, 172, 185, 244, 245, 260, 308

Learning disabilities, 302

Learning Environment, 7, 75-80, 84-89, 91-107, 109, 162-165, 192, 196, 200, 201, 219, 222, 230-232, 241-243, 249, 277, 285, 295, 304, 305, 308, 318, 322, 337

Learning story, 311, 312, 315

Learning styles, 142, 143, 223, 229, 329

Lesions, 47

Lesson plan, **108**, **109**

Letters, 84, 93, 94, 131, 132, 163, 166, 169, 172, 185, 188, 191-195, 205, 289, 290, 314, 345

Lev Vygotsky, 139

Lice, 46, 47, 71

Licensed, 50

Licensing, 322, 324

Lighting, 80

Limits, 49, 141, 216, 259, 273

Linens, 71

Lingual, 340

Linguistic, 142, 173, 307, 340

Listening Area, 169, 190

Listening Center, 83, 287

Literacy, 6, 70, 78-80, 82-85, 94, 100, 112, 132, 147, 154, **161-163**, **168-170**, **172-174**, **178-184**, 190-192, 194, 196, 197, 201, 208, 233, 266, 267, 287, 289, 301, 305, 317, 341

Literature, 89, 96, 168, 211, 339

Loft (s), 79, 80, 169

Lullabies, 101, 170, 175, 176, 208

Lunches, 149, 246

Lunchtime, 260, 261

M

Mail, 88, 172, 291

Mailboxes, 281

Maintenance, 23, 69

Malnourished, 142, 220

Maltreatment, 71, 72

Manager, 6, 303

Manipulative movement, 116, 126

Materials, 8, 10, 11, 20, 23, 24, 65, 75, 76, 78, 84, 86, **88-96**, 100, 103, 104, 106-109, 111, 112, 118-120, 127, 129-132, 137, 144, 146, 147, 155, 158, 159, 163, 168, 170, 172, 175, 176, 195, 196, **200-204**, 206, 207, 209, 210, 214, 216, 219, 221, 223, 232, 241-246, 255, 258, 260, 271, 277, 286, 287, 297-299, 305, 306, 317, 321, 328, 332, 335, 336

Math, 57, 70, 78, 83-85, 94, 100, 132, 146, 151, 154, 155, 157, 158, 160, 172, 192, 202, 235, 266, 290, 305, 317, 319

Mathematical, 8, 142, 158

Mathematically, 158

Mathematics, 6, 78, 154, 312

Mattresses, 12, 20

Meal, 19, 55, 94, 101, 106, 149, 241, 300, 315, 318

Measurement, 84, **157**, 290, 315

Medication (s), 15, 21, **47-50**, 60, 69, 261, 283

Medicines, 12, 13, 37

Mentor (s), 331, 332, 342

Mentoring, 332, 338

Menu, 56, 59, 172

Menus, 56, 57, 59, 70, 95, 292, 299

Minorities, 90

Model, 20, 29, 55, 58, 59, 62, 64, 103, 130, 131, 146, 157, 175, 177, 193, 194, 216, 222, 233, 235, 237, 245, 247, 249, 252, 254, 258, 270, 275, 276, 285

Mold, 40, 84

Motivation, 2, 214, 222, 234, 245, 246, 249, 261, 264, 312

Movement, 6, 7, 67, 78-80, 83, 85, 89, 110, 114-116, 119-121, 124-127, 132, 133, 145, 148, 172, 176, 198, 199, 201, 202, **208-211**, 287, 290

Multicultural, 89, 95, 340

Multiple intelligences, 142, 223

Music, 6, 77-80, 82, 83, 85, 87, 89, 95, 96, 112, 119, 120, 122, 132, 148, 157, 172, 175, 176, 179, 198, 199, 201, 202, **208-211**, 230, 246, 286, 287, 290, 296, 299

Music & movement, 6, 78, 80, 89, 132, 148, 198, 199, **208, 211**, 287

Musical instruments, 85, 94, 95, 131, 132, 202, **208-210**, 299, 301

Musicians, 172

N

Nap (s), 13, 41, 20, 58, 59, **68**, 69, 77, 81, 97, 98, 101, 120, 150, 179, 210, 255, 261, 268, 283, 306

Napping, 59, 76, 98, 106, 315, 332

National Association for the Education of Young Children, 1, 3, 10, 74, 78, 160, 275, 321, 327, 334

Nature, 25, 26, 28, 49, 96, 102, 142, 159, 160, 164, 172, 220, 221, 235, 290, 332

Neglect, 39, **71-74**, 323, 343

Neighborhood (s), 25, 28, 136, 140, 150, 192

Neighborhood walk, 28, 150, 192

Network, 302, 344

Neurological, 17

Newsletter, 171, 293

Nose blowing, **62**

Nutrients, 53, 56

Nutrition, 6, 7, 52, 57, 69, 101, 300, 324

Nutritional, **55 -58**, 70, 72

Nutritionist (s), 55, 57, 59, 299, 301

Nutritious, 7, 18, 39, 52, 55

O

Obesity, 127

Objective, 74, 265, 268, 293, 298, 308, 309, 313, 329, 333

Observation, 6, 88, 122, 130, 151, 179, 191, 219, 261, 302, **304-313**, 317, 329, 339

Observational data, 44

Online, 20, 185, 302, 339

Onlooker play, 242

Open-ended, 84, 91, 96, 101, 104, 105, 112, 121, 124, 130, 177, 178, 187, 190, 201-204, 207, 213, 282, 285, 286

Optimism, **234, 235**

Oral language, 162, **173**, 312

Organize (s), 21, 71, 75, 102, 216, 255, 297, 314, 318

Organized, 64, 86, 110, 144, 331

Organizer, 303

Orientation, 167, 271, 281, 291, 295, 335

Outdoor, **10-14**, 16, 21, 22, 34, 35, 40, 41, 78, 87, 89, 94, 95, 98-102, 104, 107, 116, 118, 119, 120, 123, 125, 159, 181, 202, 301, 304, 307, 332

Outdoor-setting, **87**

Outings, 50, 197

Ovens, 19, 53

P

Pace, 58, 114, 116, 143, 171, 174, 179, 195, 207, 243, 306

Pain, 33, 46, 72, 205, 269

Painful, 63, 265, 336

Paintbrush, 131, 172, 205, 206

Painted, 18, 171

Painting (s), 73, 84, 94, 95, 110, 131, 142, 199, 201, **203-207**, 228, 237, 242, 249, 288, 289, 297, 314

Paints, 18, 73, 93, 132, 171, 203, 206

Paints-including, 93

Parallel play, 77, 92, 93, 216, 242, 246

Parasites, 43

Parent meetings, 294, 299

Parent workshops, 37, 70, 226, 301

Parental, 44, 227, 278, 284, 286, 317, 318

Parenting, 272, 276, 280, 300, 324

Parents, 10, 15, 16, 20, 21, 29, 31-33, **35-37**, 43-46, 48, 50-52, 54-58, 62, 65, 67, **69-71**, 73, 74, 76, 88, 94, 99, 100, 102, 107, 120, 122, 130, 140, 141, 152, 170, 171, 179, 181, 184, 185, 196, 206, 209, 210, 221, 224-227, 234, 240, 249, 268, 271-273, 275-282, 284-289, **291-302**, 306, 311, 312, 316, 318, 321, 323, 329, 331, 333, 335, 338, 342, 345

Participation, 8, 50, 57, 125, 245, 246, 266, 275, 285

Pattern, 72, 128, 147, 150, 155, 157, 158, 167, 294

Pedestrian safety, **24**, 25

Pediatric, 29, 31, 35

Pediatrician (s), 45, 49, 54, 69, 71, 122, 130, 269, 301

Pediatrics, 15, 43, 52, 128

Perceptual motor development, 133, 134

Persistence, 144, 222, 234, 237, 312

Pet (s), 19, 24, 29, 41, 57, 61, 85, 132, 156, 159, 220, 233, 244, 245, 275, 283, 296, 315

Phenomena, 85, 139

Phones, 34

Phonological awareness, **181**, 188, 192

Physical, 6-8, 10, 17, 22, 43, 44, 56, 57, 67, 68, 71, 72, 74-76, 78, 88, 110, 111, **113-129**, 131-134, 138, 148, 150, 158-160, 200, 205, 208, 212, 219-222, 224, 232, 248, 269, 273, 297, 305, 317

Physical abuse, 71, 72

Physically, 45, 52, 127, 141, 221, 232, 245, 249, 269, 334

Physician (s), 43, 51, 283, 335

Physiological, 141, 218

Pills, 49

Planning, 55-57, 70, 76, 78, 95, 100-102, 104, **107**, 148, 178, 222, 229, 284, 286, 299-301, 303-305, 313, **316-321**, 324, 328, 330

Planning for groups of children, 316, 321

Planning for individual children, 317

Planning form, **318-320**

Plants, 10, 11, 13, 14, 16, 37, 87, 94, 153, 157, 158, 315

Play, 6, 8, 10, 11, 14, 18, 20, 23, 24, 26, 28, 30, 34, 40, 41, 48, 49, 57, 59, 61, 64, 73, 75-80, 82-85, 87, 89, 91-102, 104-107, 110-112, 119-122, 125, 127-129, 131-133, 136, 139-141, **145-150**, 154-159, 162, 163, 172, 175, 176, 178, 179, 181, 182, 184, 185, 192, 196, 197, 199, 201-203, 205-213, 216, 219, 221, 222, 227, 230, 235, 237, **239-249**, 254-257, 259-262, 266, 269, 280, 281, 284-289, 292, 299-301, 304-307, 311, 314, 315, 322, 331, 332, 335, 337

Playground, 14, 121, 148, 151, 159, 184, 314

Playhouse, 87

Playpen, 20

Poison, 12, 13, 37

Poisoning (s), 17, 31

Poisonous, 14, 15

Policy, 1, 3, 69, 74, 206, 271, 340, 341, 343-345

Portfolios, 5, 164, 169, 195, 207, 220, 225, 293, 314, 315, 333

Potty, 40, 60, 67

Practice, 8, 13, 22, 24-27, 34, 60-62, 64, 85, 93, 106, 116, 118, 119, 121, 122, 124, 129, 131, 154, 155, 157, 169, 170, 173, 178, 189, 191, 193-195, 204, 214, 219, 229, 234, 243, 255, 257-259, 271, 308, 327, 329, 330, 335, 338, 342-345

Praise, 61, 67, 204, 229, 230, 233, 255, 328

Prediction, 149

Prejudices, 311

Preschool, 13, 78, 80, 83, 84, 97, 99, 104, 112, 119, 126, 130, 146-148, 166, 168, 177, 179-181, 193, 201, 202, 216, 235, 243, 244, 247, 268, 269, 286, 289, 300, 338, 341

Prescription, 50

Pretend, 20, 61, 77, 79, 80, 85, 87, 91-94, 112, 121, 125, 139, 148, 150, 157, 163, 166, 172, 188, 197, 212, 213, 237, 241, 243, 245, 287, 335

Pretend play, 20, 80, 85, 87, 112, 139, 163, 197, 213, 237, 241, 287

Prevention, 43, 117, 258, 300, 342

Prevents, 6, 38, 46, 127

Problem solving, 6, 146, 199, 216, 223, 250, 258, 327

Professional development, 4, **326**, **338-340**, 342, 343

Professional Portfolio, 5

Professionalism, 5, 6, 281, 322, 325-345

Program Management, 5, **303-318**, 321, 322, 324

Project, 100-102, 107, 110, 160, 236, 249, 252, 286, 293, 315

Prop (s), 95, 114, 202, 213, **243**, 301

Prosocial, 239, 245, 248, **251**, 317

Psychiatry, 17

Psychological maltreatment, 72

Psychologist (s), 137, 139-142, 241, 247, 301

Psychology, 3

Psychosocial, 141

Publishing Area, **171**

Punishment, 52, 55, 258, 259, 265, 266, 270, 271

Puppet, 73, 94, 168, 169, 210, 235, 286, 287, 301, 314

Puzzle, 110, 128, 130, 131, 153, 172, 222, 247, 251, 261, 262, 285, 290

Q

Questions, 10, 34, 44, 45, 55, 68, 76, 96, 97, 101, 103-105, 139, 146-153, 155-157, 159, 160, 166, 167, 174, 177, 178, 185-190, 201-203, 207, 213, 214, 223, 243, 248, 255, 260, 281, 282, 284-293, 295-297, 299, 301, 305, 312, 313, 327, 328, 330, 331, 333, 342

R

Rabies, 43

Racial Identity, **231**, 232

Racism, 90, 232

Racist, 232, 336

Rating scales, 311, 313, 314, 317

Reading, 17, 28, 57, 68, 84, 88, 92-94, 98, 100, 101, 104, 133, 137, 148, 151, 152, 162, 163, 165, 167-169, 173, 174, 178, 180, 181, 183, **186-192**, 195-197, 211, 233, 248, 285, 286, 296, 300, 307, 311, 339

Reading aloud, 57, 162, 186, 189, **191**, **286**

Reasoning, 6, 23, 135, 258, 335

Recess, 270

Recording, 45, 190, 229, 263, 296, **307-311**, **313**, 332

Reflection, **329-333**

Refrigeration, 54

Refrigerator (s), 54, 85, 149

Reggio Emilia, 96, 210

Regulation, 148, 258

Report, 31, 32, 36, 48, 66, 71, 73, 74, 227, 267, 305, 323

Research, 59, 133, 136, 138, 143, 147, 160, 168, 181, 186, 188, 196, 236, 268, 269, 271, 275, 278, 279, 316, 326, 328, 335, 338, 340, 344

Resilience, 234, **236**, **237**

Resources, 20, 69, 72, 79, 88, 167, 171, 206, 209, 258, 272, 282, 294, 298, 300, 301, 304, 321, 324, 333, 338, 340-343

Respect, 6, 44, 52, 56, 67, 97, 112, 175, 204, 207, 216, 219, 230, 231, 238, 245, 248, 251, 252, 258, 265, 268, 270, 271, 278, 279, 282, 284, 291, 296, 332, 336, 340

Respiratory, 60

Reward (s), 52, 55, 199, 258, 267

Rewarding, 279, 285

Riding Toys, 25

Rodents, 19

Role-playing, 202

Room-including, 185

Room-temperature, 54

Rotate, 19, 98, 166, 200

Routine, 56, 62, 97, **104-106**, 122, 150, 307

Routines-including, 106, 315

Rule-making, 256

Rules, **22-25**, 28, 29, 35, 121, 141, 146, 148, 157, 173, 177, 195, 202, 216, 230, 241, 248, 254-257, 259, 264, 281, 323, 331, 335

Running records, 310, 314

S

Safe, **6-11**, **14-37**, 39, 41-74, 76-80, 84-89, 91-107, 109-111, 114-120, 122-129, 131-134, 136-160, 162-197, 199-202, 204-214, 218-237, 239-252, 254-273, 275-302, 304-318, 321-324, 326-345

Safeguarding, 10

Safeguards, 69

Safer, 29

Safety-approved, 20

Salmonella, 43

Sampling, 308, 311

Sand play, 49, 78, 202

Sandbox, 14, 61, 87, 121, 242, 247, 280

Sanitation, 71, 300

Sanitized, 39, 65

Sanitizer, 66

Sanitizing, 42, 61, 64

Scaffold (s), 146, 151, 152, 154, 179, 191, 203, 245, 256, 285, 326, 338

Scaffolding, 139, **151**, 154, 176, **178**, 337

Scalding, 13

Science, 6, 57, 70, 78, 80, 83, 85, 87, 94, 100, 106, 132, 135, 136, 148, 151, **154**, **158-160**, 172, 195, 202, 287, 290, 301, 312, 314, 319

Science center, 132, 151, 195

Science-related, 314

Scientists, 136, 237

Scribble (s), 92, 115, 128, 193, 204, 205

Scribbling, 192, 193, 203, 205, 314

Seatbelt, 29

Seating, 77, 170, 195, 260, 297, 299

Seats, 26, 84, 85, 155

Second language, 22, 183, 184, 241

Security, 7, 28, 48, 141, 218, 247, 259, 266, 344

Seizure, 33, 48, 267

Self, 6, 117, 142, **217-237**, 267, 273, 329

Self-abusive, 72

Self-actualization, 142, 218

Self-awareness, 291, 329

Self-conscious, 194

Self-control, 144, 145, 259, 264, 267, 288

Self-esteem, 71, 106, 141, 183, 188, 218, 228, 229, 234, 236, 246, 259, 266, 269

Self-evaluation, 329

Self-image, 90

Sexism, 90

Sexual, 72-74, 167, 227, 335

Sexual abuse, 72, 227

Shapes, 91, 128, 158, 167, 201, 205, 232, 288, 289

Sharing, 35, 69, 111, 216, 239, 244, 246, 247, 249, 255, 260, 278-280

Shelter (s), 27, 41, 141, 218, 252, 284, 323, 324

Shelves, 17, 19, 84, 95, 106, 163, 164, 282, 306

Shelving, 287

Sibling (s), 49, 103, 140, 141, 226, 227

Sick, 39, 44-47, 49, 60, 69, 70, 261, 281, 283

SIDS, 20

Sign-in, 81-83, 172, 282

Singing, 85, 98, 101, 107, 111, 112, 145, 176, 197, **208**, 209, 243, 286, 296

Single-parent, 276

Sleep, 20

Small group, 97-100, **103-105**, 107, 108, 124, 130, 181, 189, 246-248, 285, 318, 321

Snack, 55, **58**, **59**, 61, 87, 93, 94, 98, 101, 102, 104, 148, 155, 156, 172, 178, 243, 308, 318, 332

Sneezing, 59, 60, **62**, 69

Social, 6, 8, 55, 57, 67, 76, 78, 88, 94, 111, 127, 133, 135, 136, 140, 142, 145, 151, 154, 158-160, 173, 177, 191, 212, 216, 220-222, 231, 232, 234, **238-252**, 254, 257, 259, 265, 268-270, 273, 317, 319, 322, 323, 335

Social development, 111, 133

Social skills, 6, 57, 127, 212, 216, 238, 239, 242, 244, 246, 249, 269, 270, 317, 335

Social studies, 6, 78, 135, 151, 154, **158-160**, 319

Socioeconomic, 140, 269

Socio-economic, 181

Software, 20, 94, 160, 170, 171, 195, 209, 293, 321